Environmental Policy Analysis and Practice

Environmental Policy Analysis and Practice

MICHAEL R. GREENBERG

RUTGERS UNIVERSITY PRESS

NEW BRUNSWICK, NEW JERSEY, AND LONDON

LIBRARY OF CONGRESS CATALOGING-IN-PUBLICATION DATA

Greenberg, Michael R.
    Environmental policy analysis and practice/Michael R. Greenberg.
        p. cm.
    Includes bibliographical references and index.
    ISBN 978-0-8135-4275-1 (hardcover : alk. paper)
    ISBN 978-0-8135-4276-8 (pbk. : alk. paper)
    1.   Environmental policy — United States.   2.   Environmental protection — Political
aspects — United States.   3.   Environmental protection — United States — Public opinion.
4.   Environmental responsibility — United States.   5.   Policy sciences.   I.   Title.
    GE180.G7535   2007.
        363.700973 — dc22   2007022039

A British Cataloging-in-Publication record for this book is available
from the British Library.

Visit our Web site: http://rutgerspress.rutgers.edu

Manufactured in the United States of America

To Gwendolyn Barker Greenberg,
who has been patiently listening to me talk
about the subjects presented in this book
for more than 30 years. Without your support,
I would not have written this book.

CONTENTS

LIST OF TABLES

PREFACE

In 1966, I earned my first bumps and bruises trying to navigate the realities of environmental policy making. I was a graduate student at Columbia University during the worst drought on record in the northeastern United States. Across the region, the amount of available potable water was down by one-third, and in some locations there was less than half the normal supply. Some reservoirs looked more like mud flats than deep lakes, and water restrictions were in place. I went to my advisers, George Carey and Leonard Zobler, with an idea for a thesis that made sense to me because I believed that policy was based on science. Quite simply, we would rescue areas that were running out of potable water by transferring it from places that still had a surplus. Technically, we would determine the sources of potable water and the locations that needed water, the capacity of the pumps and pipes that link sources and sinks for potable water, and the costs of moving surplus water, and suggest specific transfers.

We spent months obtaining data, and then we ran a mathematical model that optimized the supply of water across the region. Everything worked on paper: We could move water through the network and reduce the impact of the drought. I was shocked when our recommendations were not embraced by many of the municipalities and private water purveyors. Some did not accept the premise that they should share their surplus. They were concerned primarily with their jurisdiction's needs and argued that they would run a deficit if they shared their surplus. Others were willing to provide water, but only if they could raise prices to levels that I thought were outrageous. Remarkably, some opposed our idea because they disliked their counterparts in neighboring jurisdictions for reasons that were both personal and organizational and apparently had originated even before I was born.

In New Jersey, which epitomized this resource problem, Governor Richard J. Hughes finally ordered some of the most recalcitrant municipalities to share their water. My first lesson in environmental policy, then, was that you need good science, but you had better learn who pays, who benefits, and who dislikes their neighbors. Morality—or at least my sense of it—did not count for much in the late 1960s where the distribution of public potable water was concerned. So much for my first bona fide effort to be a policy hero.

There have been many more bumps and bruises over the past 40 years, and once in a while I have even earned a gold star. I have worked on locally unwanted land uses such as nuclear power plants, incinerators, and dams; on cleaning up chemical or nuclear weapons facilities and Superfund and brownfield sites; on sprawl; on environmental asthma and cancer; and on a variety of other environmental policy subjects. These projects have replaced my fantasies about how policy is formed with the reality of how and why decisions are made. Now I can laugh at my naiveté, but then I was horrified at the idea that good science was not the dominant consideration. I learned that good science was necessary for good policy but did not guarantee it; that as much as I would like to, I could not start every policy analysis with ecological and human health as the first consideration; and that I must consider six criteria for each policy option:

1 The likely reaction of elected government officials and their staffs
2. The likely reactions from the public and special interests, including not-for-profit organizations, business, and the media
3. Human and ecological health
4. Short- and long-term economic costs and benefits
5. The moral imperative
6 Flexibility and time pressure

I have used these six factors as a policy framework to assist governors, senators, and other elected officials; to talk with reporters; to lecture in various countries; and to teach at Columbia and Rutgers Universities. Whatever the policy issue, I write down and assess every argument, pro and con, for every option. For example, suppose the issue involves reducing the risk from left-over chemical weapons: Options include destroying by incineration, destroying by hydrolysis or another similar method, packing and shipping to another location, and a few others. Each of these options has advantages and disadvantages. Knowing them and evaluating them allows me to compare what we already know with what we need to know and to be assured that I have not missed a key policy driver. That exercise has almost always led to a more informed decision for me and sometimes for decision makers and their staff.

I am not going to assert that using the six criteria as a framework will provide a comprehensive understanding of every policy option, although it will certainly lead to a more complete view of the advantages and disadvantages of those options. Nor will I claim that policy makers will be impressed by all this information. In fact, the amount of information I have provided about multiple options and multiple criteria has led some recipients to assert that I am confusing the decision-making process by obfuscating the key variables with a barrage of data. I disagree because I have too often observed that decision makers have a tendency to jump on one or two drivers before due diligence has been given to all the potential key factors. I am convinced that too often what decision makers consider to be the critical criteria are not; their perceptions are too short-sighted, and they ignore important effects that they should have considered. So I try to provide all the credible information possible, even if it is resisted.

When you have finished this book, I hope that you will have a better understanding of the factors that have driven some key environmental health decisions in the United States. However, it is important to remember that issues age. In a decade, some of these issues will no longer be considered important, although nuclear and chemical weapons, nuclear power, and environmental cancer will not age much. I would like you not to dwell too much on the policies themselves, but rather to recognize that adopting the framework and learning key theories and tools will place you in a good position to respond to the new policy issues that emerge. I would also like to share the excitement of this field by describing some of the most challenging environmental policy decisions we have faced. I have asked some very knowledgeable people to help me talk about these subjects.

I have been writing articles for my peers for decades, and I hope they will find some new insights in this book. But although it profiles the work of some great colleagues, I have not written this book for my peers. It is intended for upper-level college students and graduate students who are interested in the environmental policy process. I want this book to help attract ambitious and talented young people to environmental policy as a career. Bumps and bruises aside, working on environmental policy is challenging and rewarding.

ACKNOWLEDGMENTS

Many family members, friends, colleagues, and students have directly and indirectly contributed to this book. I was born the South Bronx, about a 10-minute walk north of Yankee Stadium; we lived a rich environment. Children everywhere, innumerable professional and other athletic events, parades, and constant excitement. My parents, Sydney and Mildred Greenberg, and my uncle Sol Saletra encouraged me to "use my head," which was shorthand for figuring out what was happening in the neighborhood and why. In school, Mr. Brown, Mr. Cohen, and Mrs. Smith, who were my teachers in the 8th, 9th, and 10th grades, respectively, steered me toward environmental science. Mr. Brown convinced me that roads, train lines, and other routes could be modeled with graph theory, which was immense fun. Abraham Cohen showed me that policy needs pushed scientists to work on specific projects; his favorite example was nuclear weapons. Matilda Smith arranged a National Science Foundation scholarship one summer, during which I learned how to take water quality samples. In college, history professor Lorman Ratner encouraged me to read environmental history, which I found much more interesting than political history. In graduate school at Columbia University, I was incredibly lucky to have George Carey, Leonard Zobler, Douglas McManis, Arthur Strahler, Abraham Jaffee, and William Vickrey as major professors. They threw so much information at me that for the first time in my life, I felt overwhelmed. After terrifying me, they convinced me that I should believe in myself.

I thank my colleagues at Rutgers University for providing an environment that has allowed me to explore a wide range of topics. Jim Hughes, Donald Krueckeberg, Richard Brail, Bob Burchell, Briavel Holcomb, Frank Popper, David Listokin, Joe Seneca, Jerome Rose, Susan Fainstein, Salah El-Shakhs, and Dona Schneider have been my colleagues for more than 20 years. There was never a time when they would not sit down and discuss an environmental-related topic with me. I am grateful to my colleagues who were willing to be interviewed for this book: Arthur Upton, Daniel Wartenberg, Bernard Goldstein, Henry Mayer, Charles Powers, and Connie Hughes. I hope you enjoy reading my interviews with them. They are truly role models for anyone who is thinking about a career in an environmental-related topic.

Four of my former graduate students played a direct role in developing the materials needed for the book. Karen Lowrie has worked on environmental management studies with me for more than a decade. Her efforts are particularly prominent in chapters 1 and 4. Josephine Faass helped me conduct the interviews of the three mayors in chapter 1 and got me thinking about natural resource damages (chapter 7). Justin Hollander worked with me on brownfield and Superfund-related issues reflected in chapters 1 and 5. Elizabeth Nash compiled much of the background material used in chapters 3 and 6. I thank the New Jersey League of Municipalities and, in particular, director Bill Dressel for allowing me to use portions of "Building Brownfield Coalitions: The Perspectives of Three New Jersey Mayors" (*New Jersey Municipalities*, January 2005, 28–32) in chapter 1. Similarly, I thank John Wiley and Sons, Inc. for permitting me to use part of a table in a paper I wrote that was published in *Remediation*, Winter 2005, pages 91–105 ("End state land uses, sustainable protective systems, and risk management: A challenge for remediation and multigenerational stewardship").

I'd like to thank former New Jersey governors Richard Hughes, Brendan Byrne, Thomas Kean, James Florio, Christine Todd Whitman, Donald DiFrancesco, and Jim McGreevey and Senator Bill Bradley for challenging me with some tough policy issues.

I end by acknowledging students who eventually provoked me into writing this book by insisting that I needed to make the time to spell out and illustrate the six criteria in writing, not just verbally.

Environmental Policy Analysis and Practice

Introduction

A Quick Walk through a Framework
of Six Environmental Policy Criteria

I usually begin my senior-level course on protecting public health and the environment with the following statement: "Think of an environmental policy problem that you are really worried about, that distracts you (maybe keeps you up at night), that you talk about with your family and friends, and that probably brought you to this course." After a minute, they tell me what these problems are, and I write them on the board. Then I ask, "Why haven't we fixed these problems?" Some students seem surprised by the question, and they aim quizzical looks at me. I can feel them asking themselves, "If he's the expert, why is he asking us?"

I start the course this way because even the youngest students have already learned a lot about why we have not fixed the environmental health problems that they fear the most. Most of them have learned from tales, but some have grounding in theories and tools too. This introduction describes the way themes, tales, theories, tools, and tasks (the five T's) are used in this book to illuminate the six policy criteria, the organization of the volume, and the objectives of each chapter, as well as some of the methods I have used to teach environmental policy.

Themes, Tales, Theories, Tools, and Tasks

These are my equivalent of the three R's. Themes are the policy subjects, such as indoor air quality, the use of pesticides on crops, children's exposure to lead, the stockpile of chemical warfare agents, and nuclear power. My teaching of these subjects has led me to use several out-of-the-ordinary teaching devices. First, I do not provide an absolute answer to policy questions. That is, I do not say that government should do this or that. Instead, I provide clues, and, more specifically, I steer students into weighing the advantages and disadvantages of different decisions. There are tables in chapters 1 through 6 that pull together these advantages and disadvantages. Then I organize tasks that require students to debate

1

policy options. I also quote and paraphrase the views of people with whom many scientists, myself included, disagree. I do this because elected officials and their staffs do not readily dismiss the odd, unconventional opinion; they may cling to it because it fits their predilections. Like it or not, the policy process makes room for the unconventional.

Tales are stories told about policies orally and in articles, books, newspapers, magazines, government documents, and the so-called gray literature. Like almost everyone else, I derived my first lessons about the environment from listening to tales. It is not by chance that a lot of my work is directly related to vivid memories. Although this book is not a walking tour of my life and feelings, a personal example will make the point about the importance of tales. When I was a child living in New York City, my father impressed me as a fastidious person. It seemed to me that he was always clean shaven and well dressed, and he smelled of cologne. So I was shocked when my father and my grandfather told me about a drought so severe that New York City had shaveless and bathless days. I could not imagine my father smelly and unshaven. I went to the library and found the actual *New York Times* stories of the drought, including photos of men who had not shaved. The point is that the tale my father and grandfather told me made such an impression that I was primed to try to do something about our poor policy response to drought when the opportunity arose. In class, I go through the exercise of asking my students to share vivid environmental health tales with me. Everyone, I'm certain, has some to share.

My students' interest wanes when I get stingy and do not tell enough tales to prime theme discussions. For example, I remember trying to describe the laws and treaties agreed to by the U.S. government on the destruction of its chemical weapons stockpile. The students were somewhat interested — but only somewhat. Their curiosity increased exponentially when I described how I was required to demonstrate that I could use a gas mask and then had to take the gas mask and three syringes with me before I was allowed to walk into a shed that held chemical weapons.

Using tales requires being personal, sometimes using colloquial language, or as one colleague said, being "folksy." This book contains a lot of personal stories told by my colleagues and me. Because I am from the Northeast, the tales are disproportionately from the Northeast. But the themes, such as brownfields, nuclear power, automobile additives, pesticides, genetically modified organisms, and others are national in scope, and all of them have international equivalents.

Tales prime students' interest and are great teaching tools. Moreover, they give rise to nuanced insights. But tales typically lack generalizability. Theories are formed when a person takes disconnected tales, readings, meetings, and conversations and ultimately shapes what he or she has learned from them into generalizable expectations. I cannot describe all of the fascinating theories I have read or heard about environmental policy, but chapters 1 to 6 include discussions of key theories. Each chapter focuses on one theory whose standing is assessed by me and also by one or more experts who have been involved with the theory in their work. There are many more than six important theories that have a bearing on environmental health policy, so the chapters briefly discuss some other key theories as well.

My own theory-building journey and view of environmental policy probably have more in common with historians or other social scientists who have looked at issues over time than with any other discipline. Some history books are directly relevant to today's — as well as yesterday's — environmental issues. Craig Colten's *An Unnatural Metropolis: Wresting New Orleans from Nature* (2005). Adam Rome's *The Bulldozer in the Countryside: Suburban Sprawl and the Rise of American Environmentalism* (2001), and Andrew Hurley's *Environmental Inequalities: Class, Race, and Industrial Pollution in Gary, Indiana, 1945–1980* (1995) speak directly to the impact of Hurricane Katrina, sprawl as a national concern, and environmental justice, respectively. Others, such as John Cumbler's *Northeast and Midwest United States: An Environmental History* (2005), Clay McShane's *Down the Asphalt Path: The Automobile and the American City* (1994), and David Stradling's *Smokestacks and Progressives: Environmentalists, Engineers, and Air Quality in America, 1881–1951* (1999), are more expansive in space or time.

All of these books are full of tales and theories about why policies emerged where and when they did. My favorites are Joel Tarr's *Devastation and Renewal: An Environmental History of Pittsburgh and Its Region* (2003) and Martin Melosi's *Effluent America: Cities, Industry, Energy, and the Environment* (2001). These books say a good deal about the struggle between public health/environmental perspectives and capital's relentless need to grow, and the inconsistent role of elected officials and their staffs in protecting public health and the environment. The literature also provides an idea of the complicated role of the media as an information gatekeeper, a discussion of ethical imperatives and how they sometimes influence policy, and an idea of how time and the desire to be flexible have periodically been important policy drivers. There are many lessons to be learned from these histories. Historians may not come out and state the importance of the six policy criteria, but they are embedded in these books.

The protocols, processes, and quantitative and qualitative methods used to test the generalizability of proposed theories are the tools that allow the evaluation of policy options. This book will present a set of tools, such as risk assessment, environmental impact analysis, interviewing, content analysis, regional economic impact modeling, optimization modeling, checklists, and cost/benefit analyses.

Lastly, I am a firm believer in doing. A deep understanding of an environmental policy requires a knowledge of the five T's. The best way to achieve a deep understanding is to engage in a task that causes you to interact with them. I could never grasp a theory or tool or recommend a policy unless I worked with it. I have always created tasks for myself and for my students. Hence, each chapter ends with some suggested tasks.

The Organization of the Book

The book is divided into two parts. Part I has six chapters; each is devoted to one of the six policy criteria that together constitute the framework. Every chapter in part I has four sections. The first section begins with a theme that illustrates the particular criterion. For example, chapter I uses brownfield redevelopment policy to illustrate the critical role of local elected officials and their staffs in the development and implementation of environmental policy. Each theme section has two features. One highlights how that particular theme is interconnected with other policy themes. So, for example, chapter I highlights the relationship between the brownfields program, smart growth, and Superfund. The theme sections conclude with synopses of key pro and con attributes organized according to the six policy criteria.

For instance, a positive human and ecological health attribute of the brownfields program is that remediation and redevelopment reduce the potential exposure to residual contaminants. A possible disadvantage is that the policy could engender a backlash from public health practitioners and the public itself if remediation is not done properly, or is not maintained, and people are exposed. In other words, these synopses represent my back-and-forth wrestling with all six sets of criteria that could substantially influence the policy. I have written complete — but tedious — policy analyses. Rather than presenting them in full, I display them in tables as bulleted points. Typically, these points are what decision makers read, and sometimes they then ask questions and demand more details. In other words, before focusing on one policy criterion (the reaction of elected officials and their staffs in chapter I), these synopses summarize all six key policy criteria operating on the theme.

The framework presented here and expressed most clearly by the tables of bulleted points in chapters I through 6 is summarized by table I. A policy issue is identified along with options for addressing it. The six policy criteria are used to evaluate the options. In turn, each of the six criteria is assessed using themes, theories, tales, tools, and tasks. These evaluations are captured as the advantages and disadvantages of each policy option for each criterion. Then an overall assessment is made and used to inform the policy decision. Sometimes it is possible to integrate across the six criteria and arrive at a ranking or general ordering of policies into excellent, good, fair, or poor options. However, the policy makers I have dealt with rarely want me to assign weights to each of the six policy criteria. Chapter 8 describes how we could aggregate and weigh different criteria.

The second part of each of the first six chapters describes a key theoretical question that links the theme of the chapter and the policy criterion. For instance, chapter I focuses on regime, regulation, and sustainability theories as frameworks to understand mayors' implementation of brownfield policies. In the third section of chapters I through 6, I use a tale to illustrate the application of the policy criteria. In chapter I, for example, three mayors who are considered national leaders in developing and implementing brownfield policies talk about conditions in their

TABLE 1

Framework for policy analysis and practice

Identifying the policy issue and plausible options

Step 1: Assess the options using the six criteria.

- The reaction of elected officials and their staff
- The reaction of nongovernment interests, such as not-for-profits, businesses, the media, and the public
- Health and ecological implications
- Economic considerations
- Moral imperatives
- Time and flexibility considerations

Step 2: Make sure that you bring the five T's to bear to examine each policy criterion for each option.

- Themes
- Theories
- Tales
- Tools
- Tasks

Step 3: Summarize the results of steps 1 and 2.

- Prepare a list of the key advantages and disadvantages and uncertainties of each option.
- Prepare a longer report providing support for the list.
- If appropriate and possible, prepare a summary integrating the assessment.

Step 4: Reconsider the policy issue and options in light of the analysis.

---

towns. The goal is to show how the specific policy criterion (the reaction of elected officials and staffs) was critical in the decision-making process. The last part of each chapter briefly points to tools in chapters 7 and 8 and describes a task that I have used to help understand the policy criterion and theme.

Part 2 of the book describes a set of over 20 tools that are widely used in policy analysis. The two tools chapters blend together protocols and processes and qualitative and quantitative tools. Each chapter describes the tools and then illustrates them with examples drawn from the themes, tales, and theories presented in chapters 1 through 6 as well as selected others.

The tools chapters are separated from the themes, tales, and theory chapters because some tools are used in many stages of policy analysis. For example, content analysis is widely used not only to study the actions of elected officials, but also to examine media reporting and the minutes of public meetings. Assigning content analysis to the elected official/staff chapter rather than the public/special interest or ethics chapter would have been arbitrary. Hence, it is described in a chapter that focuses on understanding individuals and groups. The intent is to introduce the tools so that readers will understand why they are used; it is not to provide advanced training. In other words, you will not become an expert after reading chapters 7 and 8, although I hope that they whet your appetite to learn more. References to papers and books with advanced examples are provided. Most of these tools are more quickly and effectively learned in the classroom context, however.

Many of the analyses presented in this book involved advanced multivariate statistics. Those analyses are summarized in words, not equations. I assume that readers are familiar with measures of central tendency dispersion and the ideas of association (correlation) among characteristics.

Chapter Contents

The first chapter is about the central role played by elected officials and their staffs. The illustration is the brownfield remediation program in the United States. Born out of the Superfund cleanup, the program has been a major priority for urban mayors and many other local elected officials. The theoretical focus of the chapter is on sharply different views of urban redevelopment. Historically, the economic needs of capital were emphasized, which meant that entire areas were bulldozed and rebuilt. More recently, theories of environmentally, economically, and socially sustainable development have challenged this perspective, adding the needs of public health, environmental protection, and community needs to pecuniary interests. J. Christian Bollwage, Douglas Palmer, and Joseph Vas, the mayors of three medium-sized cities, explain how political coalitions in support of brownfield redevelopment have come together during a period when the nation was hemorrhaging manufacturing jobs, when other federal programs to support urban areas were reduced, and when suburban mayors wanted to reduce the pressure to develop their green space.

Chapter 2 examines the role of nongovernment stakeholders, including businesses, not-for-profit organizations, the media, universities, the National Academies, labor, and the public. I use environmental cancer as a case study to illustrate how journalists use their sources to directly or indirectly influence environmental policy. I ask, What is cancer? Environmental cancer? A cancer cluster? How big is the environmental cancer problem? After answering these questions, I review the critical role of journalists as gatekeepers for information about cancer and every other health and ecological problem. The theory section examines what a newsworthy story is. Is it public health importance or is it something else?

I enlisted the help of two experts to help me tell tales and place environmental cancer in perspective. Dr. Daniel Wartenberg of New Jersey's Robert Wood Johnson Medical School is an authority on cancer clusters and is frequently interviewed by journalists. I interviewed him on November 6, 2006, and he describes the detection of cancer clusters from the perspective of a leading scientist. Dr. Arthur Upton, a physician who was director of the National Cancer Institute (NCI), was interviewed on February 9, 2006, and he talks about NCI's efforts to work with government agencies, not for-profits, the media, and other stakeholders during an exciting period in the institute's history. While the chapter focuses on the media as a stakeholder, cancer has other powerful stakeholder groups. These are reviewed as a force in policy development and as an influence on the media coverage of environmental cancer.

Focusing on human and ecological health criteria, chapter 3 examines a policy conundrum that the United States and other nations cannot seem to solve. What gasoline additives should be allowed in automobile engines? For three decades, there have been heated debates about lead, MTBE (methyl tertiary butyl ether), methanol, and others. Protecting public health should be a key driver of these policy changes. Yet every change or argument for change has come with new public health complications. Chapter 3 describes the long and complex history of this policy issue, from the human and ecological health concerns of each additive to the formidable economic, political, and ethical concerns. The theoretical focus is the principles we use to evaluate scientific evidence to protect people and the environment. I discuss the idea of safety and how evidence is obtained, weighed, and critiqued, as well as how scientists evaluate it. Then I compare the scientist's perspective with that of the general public and the courts. Helping me explain the complicated role of science is Dr. Bernard Goldstein, who has been involved in many risk-based policy issues in the United States and abroad. Dr. Goldstein was director of the Office of Research and Development at the U.S. Environmental Protection Agency when some of the automobile additive issues were debated and also spent many years at New York University, Robert Wood Johnson Medical School, and the University of Pittsburgh's School of Public Health, where he was dean. I interviewed him on December 26, 2006.

Chapter 4 uses the remediation of nuclear weapon wastes to illustrate cost and benefit criteria. Public health has surely been the key criterion for decision making, at least in the past. But an in-depth analysis of decisions shows the growing importance of costs and benefits. The cleanup and management program for nuclear weapon wastes is the single most expensive focused effort of its kind in the world. It will go on in perpetuity at some sites. The United States has already spent $70 billion. Will it spend another $150 to $400 billion in the future? The theoretical section focuses on stewardship. What does it mean to be responsible for the health, safety, costs, social justice, local economics, and other impacts of a legacy that will last many generations beyond the life of the steward and cost billions of dollars? How does a steward balance engineered, legal, and human controls to build a sustainable plan? What are the practical options?

An expert perspective is provided by Dr. Henry Mayer, who was vice president and treasurer of Merrill Lynch and CFO of American Anglican, a multinational company that purchased municipal water and sewage treatment companies. During the past five years, he has been working on the Department of Energy's (DOE's) infrastructure and weapons residuals programs. I interviewed Dr. Mayer on January 30, 2007, and he explained how DOE's stewardship role, including its responsibility for sound fiscal management, is challenged by projects with an unprecedented degree of complexity.

Ethical concerns often fall by the wayside when policy is formulated. That is not to say that decision makers are not aware of or do not care about ethics. The problem is that the first four policy criteria seem more immediate. Using the ban on pesticides in the United States and its suspension as an illustration of the complex interactions among laws, environmental justice, cultural norms, and concerns about subsequent generations, chapter 5 highlights how moral imperatives change. The theoretical framework is drawn from environmental ethics and environmental justice. The fundamental issue is the sale of banned pesticides in developing nations by U.S. companies and the development of genetically modified organisms. Vanderbilt University and former Yale ethics professor Charles Powers, interviewed on July 11, 2006, helps put this complex issue in context.

Chapter 6 is about the importance of timing and flexibility as policy considerations. The United States clearly has an energy problem that appears to be worsening and a greenhouse gas issue that is being widely discussed. Should the government advocate for nuclear power? If it does, it will need to solve the chronic problem of nuclear waste management, find locations, and confront the relationship between the proliferation of nuclear weapons and nuclear power. How much support should the federal government provide? I interviewed Connie Hughes on December 11, 2006. An expert in energy policy and a member of the New Jersey Board of Public Utilities, she describes the role of state government in choosing fuels, siting facilities, and protecting the state economy and the public interest with regard to energy and other infrastructure.

Chapter 7 describes the tools used to assess the risk to human and ecological systems, including risk assessment and environmental impact analysis. Embedded within these processes are such diverse methods as toxicology, epidemiology, and geospatial mapping and siting, among others. Chapter 7 describes tools for understanding individual and group actions, including the use of content analysis to study laws, media coverage, and the policy statements of elected officials. The chapter also reviews interviewing, polling, and innovation diffusion tools. The third part of chapter 7 focuses on economic tools such as discounting, life-cycle cost analysis, assessment of the damage to natural resources, and regional economic impact assessment. The objective is to describe how these approaches have been applied to a range of critical policy decisions.

Chapter 8 considers methods for aggregating the information from the six policy criteria, including written checklists, optimizing single-criterion models, cost-benefit, and multi-attribute interactive decision models. The chapter ends with a review of environmental laws, regulations, rules, executive decisions, changes in leadership, and budgets, which have been the ultimate policy tools in the United States, and the difficult challenge of communicating information on risk.

PART I

Six Policy Analysis Criteria

Themes, Theories, Tales, and Tasks

1

The Reaction of Elected Officials and Staff Criterion

The Brownfields Redevelopment Policy

Introduction

Brownfields are abandoned or underutilized factories, commercial structures, rail yards, gasoline stations, and other visible urban environmental scars left in the wake of over a century of industrialization and subsequent de-industrialization in the United States. Estimates of the number of brownfield sites in this country range from 500,000 to 1 million (National Governors Association, 2000; Simons, 1999). The U.S. government formally defines them as a "real property, the expansion, redevelopment, or reuse of which may be complicated by the presence or potential presence of a hazardous substance, pollutant, or contaminant" (U.S. Environmental Protection Agency [EPA], 2003). Most brownfields do not represent a serious threat to public health or the environment, but some are so repulsive that they act as neighborhood cancers, spreading blight (Greenberg et al., 2000). I visited scores of industrial neighborhoods during the 1980s and 1990s, and I would walk away shaking my head in disbelief and despair. It is essential that these eyesores be identified, controlled, remediated to a safe level, and brought back into productive use.

The effects of brownfield properties are, for the most part, confined to the immediate neighborhood in which they are located. Hence, most of the efforts aimed at returning them to safe and productive use are local. Although federal and state governments can catalyze brownfields redevelopment by providing information, funds, and technical assistance, mayors, local governing bodies, and their staffs pull the political strings. City hall must therefore direct the creation of a municipal plan that incorporates former brownfield sites into a vision for the future. The mayor (or a designee) must motivate the city bureaucracy to support the idea and persuade not-for-profit organizations to provide moral and/or financial support. The mayor has to inspire local people to support (or at least not oppose) redevelopment and persuade business and state and federal governments to provide funds for demolition, remediation, and new projects. In this chapter, I use mayors and brownfields environmental policy to illustrate the reaction of elected officials and staff policy criterion.

Theme: Brownfields Redevelopment and Interconnected Policy Themes

The brownfields policy intersects with policy options for controlling sprawl and managing the legacy of industrial hazardous waste. The first two sections of this chapter describe these two critical linkages.

Brownfields Redevelopment and Smart Growth Policies

Brownfields redevelopment is a separate policy activity that has been pursued for well over a century, especially in the United Kingdom and elsewhere, as an approach for rehabilitating declining neighborhoods and reclaiming land (Dennison, 1998; Towers, 1995). In the United States, brownfields redevelopment has been tethered to control of sprawl as a so-called smart-growth policy option. Briefly, sprawl is low-density development of housing, commercial, and industrial development in formerly undeveloped areas often referred to as "greenfields." Sprawled developments leapfrog developed areas with existing infrastructure and thus need new water and sewerage system connections; new or substantial additions to schools, police, and fire services; and road expansion to accommodate an automobile-oriented lifestyle. People think of low-density single-family homes on what were farms as prototypical sprawl. But large-box shopping malls, garden apartment units, and spread-out production facilities can also be considered sprawl if they leapfrog into open space; incur major infrastructure additions; destroy important ecosystems; cause massive traffic jams; and in other ways burden people, communities, and the environment.

In contrast to sprawl, smart growth clusters people and their activities in central places and along corridors. Efforts are focused on filling in skipped-over areas in cities and older suburbs, redeveloping already developed parcels such as brownfields, and concentrating new greenfield development in clusters adjacent to existing infrastructure.

In addition to urban redevelopment, there are five other major options for achieving or promoting smart growth. I will summarize them briefly because they are very different from brownfields redevelopment. Changing transportation policies is one option (Cervero, 1986). Government subsidies of highway construction and maintenance, low gasoline prices and taxes, differences between urban and rural car insurance, and many other government-sponsored or permitted actions have sustained sprawl. Reducing or revoking these subsidies would make it more difficult to continue to build in undeveloped areas. Government can provide incentives for high-density development in specific urban locations by building light rail lines, providing more bus service and bus lanes, and subsidizing mass transit. It can also build bridges, overpasses, and bicycle lanes to make it easier to walk and bicycle to work, schools, and recreation.

Another option is that government can directly purchase or facilitate the purchase of land in environmentally sensitive locations (Brenneman and Bates, 1984). The Trust for Public Lands, the Nature Conservancy, and other nonprofit organizations purchase land or receive lands gifted to them. State and local governments have also begun using tax and bonding powers to fund the purchase of land and to provide economic benefits to those who donate conservation easements, preserve farmlands, and protect coastal zone areas, barrier beaches, and other desirable open spaces. In some places, property owners can transfer their development rights in return for economic benefits. In essence, the idea is to take the land out of circulation and hold it for future generations.

A third option is to make it more difficult to develop farms, forests, and other greenfields by not providing water, sewerage, and other infrastructure for such developments; by requiring large impact fees that cover the actual long-term costs of leapfrog low-density development; and by requiring the regional review of proposed developments. Some states and local governments instituted these approaches long ago, but many more have begun talking about them during the past decade (Bosselman and Callies, 1972; Delafons, 1969; New Jersey Office of State Planning, 1999). I am not sanguine about these approaches because some developers and local governments are adamantly opposed, arguing that their home rule rights are being violated.

Regional government is the fourth option. The combination of fair-share housing agreements that cover entire regions, regional tax collection and sharing, and regional planning and review of development (Rusk, 1999) would make businesses and the public think twice about their ability to avoid taxes and the land uses and people they do not want near them.

Rewarding architects, builders, bankers, planners, and mayors who promote compact settlements is a fifth smart growth option. Sprawl has been directly promoted by zoning and building code requirements that do not allow more compact development forms. Building new communities and infrastructure around central areas that provide employment, shopping, recreation, and inexpensive and frequent mass transit would facilitate the creation of compact neighborhoods in greenfield areas analogous to those in cities and older suburbs.

Although a comprehensive analysis of this set of options is essential for those who really want to understand the relative strengths and weaknesses of each of them, it is beyond the scope of this chapter. However, a great deal has been written about the origins and implementation of some of these policies (see Burchell et al., 1998; Burchell, Listokin, and Galley, 1999; Dennison, 1998; English, Peretz, and Manderschied, 1999; Kreitner, 1998; National Resources Defense Council and Surface Transportation Policy Project, 1997; Urban Land Institute [ULI], 1998).

Making brownfields policy part of smart growth, I believe, has improved its political chances. With some exceptions, brownfields policies are supported by environmental and public health advocates, urban and suburban mayors, some governors, social justice advocates, a growing number of businesses that support sustainable development, government agencies like EPA, the Department of Housing and Urban Development (HUD), and the presidents and vice presidents of the United States (English, 1999; Janofsky, 1999; President's Council on Sustainable America, 1996). All of these individuals and interest groups generally view brownfields and related redevelopment policies as tools for preserving open space and farmland, keeping air and water clean, reducing development costs and fiscal burdens on local governments, and, in general, raising the quality of neighborhood and public life (Burchell et al., 1998; Downs, 1994; ULI, 1998).

The Legacy of Superfund and the Future of Pollution Prevention

Understanding the full strategic importance of brownfields policy as an environmental initiative requires taking a step back and summarizing the remediation programs that came before it. During the late 1970s and early 1980s, in response to media-amplified fears of toxic time bombs catching on fire and exploding in New York, New Jersey, Tennessee, California, Louisiana, and elsewhere (Brown, 1979), the public became agitated about hazardous waste. For example, in 1983, the Environmental Task Force asked 46,000 Americans to rank environmental problems. A total of 62 percent ranked hazardous and toxic waste as the most serious of them. Water pollution was a distant second at 38 percent.

The federal government passed a series of laws directed at these problems. One of them — the Comprehensive Environmental Response, Compensation, and Liability Act of 1980 (CERCLA or Superfund) — required EPA to develop a National Priority List (NPL) ranking contaminated properties according to the level of risk they presented. The object was to clean up the more dangerous sites first. The initial NPL list had 400 sites. EPA and the states also maintained a list of almost 38,000 potentially contaminated sites (the Comprehensive Environmental Response, Compensation, and Liability Information System or CERCLIS) that were possible Superfund sites (Gibbons, Attoh-Okine, and Laha, 1998; Meyer and VanLandingham, 2000). Overall, the Superfund legislation addressed public fears, cleaned up some sites, and controlled many others to reduce offsite seepage into the environment. The Superfund policy sensitized elected officials, businesses, and the public to the serious implications of out-of-sight, out-of-mind management of hazardous materials.

The federal government also passed legislation publicly declaring that emissions were the least desirable environmental management option. In 1984, the Hazardous and Solid Waste Amendments to the Resource Conservation and Recovery Act gave priority to management approaches that minimized the generation of waste. The Pollution Prevention Act of 1990 (P.L. 101–508) prioritized approaches. Source reduction; product reformulation; redesign, equipment, and procedural modifications; improved maintenance; worker training; inventory control; and other steps that reduce the use of resources had the highest priority.

The literature includes some amazing stories about how industry was able to reduce waste by thinking hard about production processes. In one case I worked on, for example, a company with an air pollution emissions problem went to the staff operating the control room, and these employees figured out how they could cut down emissions by altering the flow process. The company saved over $10 million that it was scheduled to spend on an incinerator.

Recycling was the second environmental management option, followed by waste treatment. Disposal, the standard practice for decades, was the least preferred option. Pollution prevention has become a major means for business to cut down on emissions, reduce the use of resources, and polish its tarnished image with the public and elected officials (Browner 1993; Dorfman, Muir, and Miller, 1992; EPA, 1995; Freeman, 1990). Like Superfund, the Pollution Prevention Act has sent a strong message to business and other generators of environmental emissions.

Despite their accomplishments, these policies, like all environmental decisions, have opponents. For the purposes of this chapter, I focus on how some mayors changed from praising to criticizing Superfund and how their views added pressure to create the national brownfields program. Initially, the largest outcry came from business, especially the chemical industry. Funding for the program came from a tax on oil and 42 specific compounds (Committee on Remedial Action Priorities for Hazardous Waste Sites, 1994; Superfund Fact Sheet, 1981). Only a relatively small amount was to come from general federal revenue. Not everyone in EPA agreed with this approach. For example, a former senior EPA official (now deceased) told me that the program should have been directly funded by the federal government. The funding mechanism that was chosen, he said, turned him into a tax collector instead of an engineer.

The original Superfund budget was $1.6 billion, and in 1986 the act was extended for another five years and another $8.5 billion was added to supposedly finish the job. However, both the time and monetary boundaries were exceeded. During the 1990s, $14 billion was spent by EPA and another $20 billion by responsible parties (U.S. General Accounting Office, 1999). The liability provisions set forth under the act were also a major area of contention. Because of strict liability, EPA did not need to prove negligence to force a business to pay. Via joint and several liability, CERCLA also allowed EPA to obtain funds from parties that were not necessarily the major polluters at a site. In one case that I was involved in, a major computer company was sued for millions of dollars after a few drums bearing its label were found in an NPL site. Lastly, to discourage litigation, defendants could be sued for triple damages in court (Landy, Roberts, and Thomas, 1990).

Business tried to collect some of the cleanup costs from their insurance companies, which led to lawsuits and countersuits ("America needs a new system," 1991). Industry also sued local governments and small business, arguing that part of the cost of remediating sites was due to municipal trash and other wastes that were deposited by local governments (Schneider, 1991; Tomsho, 1991). For example, I live in a small town of 13,000 people. That town was sued for $3 million as part of a $36 million cleanup of a local landfill. In my opinion, the amount of the suit was absurd. When the town settled in court for $85,000, the town attorney was highly praised for his "great work" (Leitich, 1998, B2). Municipal governments went to Congress, which granted relief from these lawsuits. Yet by involving insurance companies and local government, business astutely succeeded in getting small businesses and (notably) local governments to reconsider their strong support for Superfund.

Superfund-related actions also had an unfortunate and unintended chilling effect on urban redevelopment. Many developers were afraid to reuse any of the sites on the CERCLIS list for fear they would be brought into the Superfund legal tangle and held liable for cleanup and other penalties (Meyer and VanLandingham, 2000; Powers et al., 2000; Stroup, 1997). James Perron, the mayor of Elkhart, Indiana, decried the halting of redevelopment in his community, characterizing Superfund as "a smart bomb that lands on the deepest pocket it can find" (Zremski, 1995, B7). In the same article, Representative Martin Meehan, a Democrat from Massachusetts, charged that the Superfund program was functioning as "a new form of redlining," in essence forcing business and housing to the suburbs. These two labels are milder than some I have heard at meetings of urban mayors.

I believe that the Superfund program has become a political hot potato and a target for politically motivated policy actions. The past five years have been particularly difficult for the program. Using data from an EPA report, the Sierra Club (2005) declared that human exposure to hazardous chemicals is not under control at 149 Superfund sites and that groundwater pollution continues to be out of control at 226 sites. The Sierra Club (2005) charges that the Bush administration has abandoned the "polluter pays" principle for funding cleanups of Superfund sites. These charges have been echoed by the leadership of the Democratic Party, which asserts that while 82 percent of Superfund moneys in 1995 came from fees paid by polluters, none of the funding in 2005 came from the trust fund and that cleanup costs have been shifted primarily to the taxpayers (Pelosi, 2005). The data suggest that, in fact, there has been a reduction in the number of sites with completed cleanups and in the funding of the Superfund program. I recommend watching the funding of this program during the next decade. While not as expensive as the Department of Energy's nuclear weapons site cleanups (chapter 4), the management of Superfund sites is a good indicator of the federal government's interest in cleaning up the industrial legacy in the United States.

The EPA's Brownfields Pilot Program

The responses of local officials to Superfund were essential to launching the brownfields program. Also, two other circumstances intervened. From personal experience in working with congressional staff on brownfields legislation, I know that it was not a coincidence that the program changed from a concept to the object of strong federal government support during the early 1990s, when many major cities were literally hemorrhaging manufacturing jobs and dealing with abandoned factories. Nationally, the number of jobs rose from 90.4 to 117.2 million between 1980 and 1995, but the number of manufacturing production jobs fell from 8.4 to 7.3 million during the same period. The number of unemployed workers jumped from 7 to 9.6 million between 1990 and 1992 (U.S. Bureau of the Census, 1996).

Another precursor to the national brownfields program was the dramatic reduction in federal government support for the poor, including welfare, health care, and housing. Considerable angst was directed at the government by city officials and their supporters. The federal brownfields program, I believe, was an action on which the disputing parties could agree. It would help cities and business by turning eyesores into new jobs and tax-ratable industries.

In 1993 and 1994, EPA started cautiously by awarding 31 grants averaging $200,000 each to local governments to begin cleaning up brownfields. A decade later (by 2002), EPA had provided 436 grants totaling $87 million. The amount of money spent on this pilot is, of course, minuscule compared with most national government programs and is tiny even if programs that followed the initial pilot program are included. But the symbolism of the program was not lost on many local officials. For example, writing in the *Dallas Morning News*, Loftis characterized Superfund as having "paralyzed thousands of cleanups" and praised EPA for "launch[ing] a brownfields initiative to remove roadblocks to redeveloping polluted urban lands" (1995, A1). Writing in the *Washington Post*, Brachman characterized Superfund as a "horror story" and the brownfields program as capable of "produc[ing] a winner for everybody" (1995, C1).

The brownfields grant program drew high praise. For example, the commissioner of planning for Niagara County, New York, was quoted this way in the *Buffalo News:* "I can't tell you how excited I am for Niagara County. We're still celebrating" (Vogel, 1998, p. D1). Scott Allen, a reporter for the *Boston Globe,* summarized the sentiment of many participants when he quoted David Struhs, the commissioner of Environmental Protection for Massachusetts, as follows: "The whole notion of brownfield redevelopment is so commonsensical that people see it as something that is going to move" (1996, p. A1).

Also, and critically important, EPA removed most of the 38,000 sites listed from the CERCLIS list because of evidence that they were not a threat. Indeed, many of the sites that the three mayors talk about later in this chapter were once on the list. In short, the federal brownfields pilot program was designed to target a specific urban redevelopment/environmental management problem and to overcome existing environmentally based regulatory programs that some mayors argued were stifling urban redevelopment. Further, I believe that it was a message to urban mayors that they were not being abandoned by the federal government. Unlike welfare, public housing, and other policies that appear to have political litmus tests, the brownfields policy was a bipartisan political effort (see later comment by Mayor J. Christian Bollwage). Other efforts have expanded the initial program by providing additional funds and priority access to other federal government funds. In addition, states like Michigan, New Jersey, New York, and Pennsylvania have created their own brownfields programs.

The EPA brownfields initiative was the spark that led to the need for mayors to build political coalitions with federal and state governments, businesses, not-for-profits, and community groups. Among the recipients were municipalities whose mayors viewed the reuse of the abandoned or idled sites within their borders as key to the physical, fiscal, and social rehabilitation they envisioned for their cities and, indeed, for the state as whole (see later comment by Mayor Joseph Vas). They realized that the construction of new housing, as well as new commercial undertakings on these previously underused but often well-situated properties, could boost the local job and tax base and reduce the threat to public health. The perspectives of three urban mayors who have been at the forefront of these efforts are presented later in this chapter.

Six Policy Criteria: A Synopsis

This section summarizes the advantages and vulnerabilities of the brownfields policy as 48 points to be considered by policy makers (see table 2). I then use these points to identify key policy drivers.

TABLE 2

Six policy criteria for brownfields redevelopment

Criterion	Advantages	Vulnerabilities
Reaction of elected officials and staff	Mayors of urban and older suburban areas are strong supporters. Suburban mayors are supportive to protect their open space. Presidents and Congress are supportive. EPA, HUD, and other federal agencies are supportive. Selected state governors are strongly supportive.	They could get caught in the backlash against smart growth practices. It could threaten neighborhood groups and stir local opposition to the use of eminent domain. It could prove a challenge to government departments not used to working together. Local governments with limited resources will not be able to compete for funds.
Reaction of nongovernment stakeholders	City populations that do not want to relocate to the suburbs can stay in their neighborhoods in new housing on remediated brownfield sites.	Developers will want cheap land, tax relief, and other incentives.

TABLE 2

(Continued)

Criterion	Advantages	Vulnerabilities
	Developers are supportive. So far, the media have been strong supporters.	Objections to using government funds to benefit private investors could be raised. Knowledge of public preferences for living on remediated brownfield sites is lacking. The media could turn against the program if remediation fails to protect the public and graft is proven.
Human and ecological health	Health threats can be reduced by removing and containing contaminants. More people will walk, bike, and use mass transit. Compact development reduces energy use and auto travel time. Concentrating people reduces the distance to emergency care. There is less lawn watering, fewer problems with septic systems, and less contamination of potable water supplies. A larger customer base will support city water and sewerage system infrastructures. There is the opportunity to preserve more open space by developing brownfields instead of greenfields. Open space in urban centers is increased.	Construction workers are exposed to contaminants during remediation. Caps and other containments are vulnerable to failure. Deed restrictions are violated. Concentrating people puts more of them at risk from natural and human-caused hazard events. Urban and older suburban water systems are inadequate and need upgrading to meet demand. Air pollution hot spots could be created. There is a possible loss of open space to developers who need more parcels to redevelop.

(Continued)

TABLE 2

(Continued)

Criterion	Advantages	Vulnerabilities
Economic costs and benefits	Costs to society are lower when sprawl is controlled. Less use of gasoline contributes to a reduction in the balance of payments. Better use of existing infrastructure avoids sunken costs. High benefits for developers and municipalities are likely at the best sites. There will be sites for community facilities and open space.	There is a long wait for benefits at brownfield sites compared with others. There is more economic uncertainty compared with greenfield sites. The low benefit to developers at many sites means no redevelopment without large subsidies. Government investments are needed to prepare sites in some locations.
Moral imperatives	Space is saved for future generations. Investments are kept in cities instead of dispersing them. Poor residents get access to affordable housing and jobs in cities.	There is a possible loss of housing and open space to developers who want to increase market-rate housing and provide busin-opportunities. Failure to communicate to residents could lead to confrontations.
Time and flexibility	The loss of open space is arrested.	The economics of redevelopment are uncertain. A rapid pace increases the likelihood of errors.

Even with caveats about large information gaps, brownfields redevelopment appears to be the smartest smart growth policy around. More specifically, in terms of public health/ecology and moral imperatives, it has the benefit of reducing environmental stress on the metropolitan edge and improving inner-city and industrial suburban environments. None of the other options, with the possible exception of marked changes in transportation policy and regional government, has the potential to benefit the environment and public health at the metropolitan edge and in the core at the same time.

In terms of acceptability to government, interest groups, and the public, all of the options face an uphill climb. Brownfields redevelopment should face the least opposition because it does not clearly interfere with new development on greenfields. There is no obvious group to oppose it, unless environmental advocate groups and community residents become convinced that building on brownfields is a major public health threat. It will not offend powerful government and business interests that oppose restrictions on sprawl, and it will be supported by those who are invested in revitalization. By contrast, regional government will have little support from many elected officials and people. Deliberately making sprawled developments more costly faces vehement and unrelenting opposition. Building compact settlements in the suburbs is an idea that makes perfect sense if it is acceptable to banks, elected officials, and consumers, but it continues to draw resources away from the inner cities and older suburbs, so its geographical appeal as a smart growth policy is limited. Land acquisition is popular in the East and Midwest but not in the West, where many elected officials vehemently oppose having government take any more land.

If brownfields redevelopment has an Achilles heel, it lies in economic feasibility and perhaps time pressure. The problem is uncertainty. A major brownfields redevelopment program has existed only since 1995, and the economic data needed to make credible estimates of the costs and benefits of developing different types of sites is still lacking. By contrast, whatever the moral and political warts of the alternative policies, there are better data to estimate costs and benefits for those who would invest in them. Further, the pressure to redevelop brownfields is not as strong as the pressure to stop sprawl before it destroys more of the Florida Everglades, puts more people in the path of floods, and makes irrevocable changes in fragile ecosystems in other ways. While everyone wants the brownfields program to succeed, enthusiasm is greater than the knowledge of what it takes to make it succeed. A little less urgency and a bit more knowledge would help. Nevertheless, in conclusion, having noted the economic uncertainty, brownfields redevelopment has environmental, political, and moral advantages that the other options cannot match. It is politically the smartest smart growth option.

Is brownfields redevelopment better off being tethered to smart growth or as an independent policy? Doster (1999) suggests that the two should be kept apart. During Vice President Gore's presidential candidacy in 2000, control of sprawl was emphasized more than brownfields redevelopment. Many people do not understand the relationship, and so brownfields redevelopment has been moving ahead almost independently of efforts to control sprawl. If there is any connection, it is that city revitalization should occur to make sure that there is enough space for affordable housing (Danielsen, Lang, and Fulton, 1999). As noted earlier, there is a danger that brownfields redevelopment will be caught in an angry backlash against smart growth options. The danger seems low at this time, but it needs to be monitored carefully. Overall, integrating across all the advantages and disadvantages of smart growth policy options, I believe that brownfields redevelopment has easily been the best political option, as well as a strong option by itself.

Theory: Regime, Regulation, Sustainable Communities, and Coalition Building

Urban regime and regulation theories were the dominant urban political theories in the literature for over a decade. I will first review them and then add sustainability concepts as a more recent way of understanding urban redevelopment programs, including brownfields. Regime theory focuses primarily on local political practices, and regulation theory focuses on nonlocal political influences (Lauria, 1997). Both emphasize the alignment of capital, big labor, and political interests around economic development. Sustainability theories concentrate on rebuilding cities around natural and cultural attributes and emphasize residents' long-term quality of life. The literature on these theories is substantial, growing, and provocative. I cannot do justice to all of it in this chapter, but there are excellent reviews and individual studies (Chertow and Esty, 1997; Clark and Goetz, 1994; Davies 2002, 2003; Fainstein and Fainstein, 1983; Harrison, 2000; Imbroscio 1997, 1998a, 1998b; Jonas and Wilson, 1999; Lauria, 1997; Leo, 1998; Logan and Molotch, 1996; Mossberger and Stoker, 2001; Portney, 2003; Portz, Stein, and Jones, 2000; Savitch and Kantor, 2002; Stoker and Mossberger, 1994). I will summarize those elements of theory that are central to understanding the nexus of redeveloping brownfields and building a political coalition.

Regime Theory

Urban regime theory focuses on private business interests that have investments in cities and use their resources to pressure everyone else into a redevelopment plan that favors their pecuniary situation (Stoker, 1995; Stoker and Mossberger, 1994; Stone, 1989, 1993). With regard to brownfields, it follows from this theory that business would pick the best-located and largest brownfield sites and try to gain additional tax and other benefits from state and local governments. For example, in a survey of private developers, Meyer and Lyons (2000) found that developers favored deeply discounted and high-value locations, larger parcels, and high rates of return.

Regime theory's focus on the power of private capital is appropriate for brownfields redevelopment. Yet the role of business is increasingly constrained by local officials. For example, in late 2005, one mayor of a small older industrial suburb told me a story that captures the change occurring in some cities. A developer came to this mayor with a proposal to turn an abandoned site into five retail stores. His initial plan called for a pink stucco exterior and no energy-saving technologies. The mayor's response was that the town would not accept a proposal that seemed more suited for a warm climate like Fort Lauderdale, Florida, than it was to her area. She recommended that the developer redesign the building with this particular town in mind. The mayor got the redesign she wanted, as well as the new businesses. Her stance reflects a new vision of urban redevelopment, one not grounded in desperation and unwilling to sacrifice the needs of the public.

Private capital is rarely intransigent when it can compromise and still make a profit, nor is private capital interested in controlling the redevelopment of an entire inventory of brownfield sites, especially when they are contaminated or perceived to be so. Business wants specific sites with accompanying infrastructure and little risk of litigation. Many contaminated sites are poorly located with regard to transportation and infrastructure, are oddly shaped and near poor residential areas, and in general are not attractive to existing local private interests. All of these factors further lessen the likelihood that local business will dominate a citywide brownfields program (Davis and Margolis, 1997; Greenberg et al., 2000).

Regulation Theory

Regulation theory focuses on the links between urban regimes and external capital and political power (Imbroscio, 1997, 1998a, 1998b; Lauria, 1997). In essence, regulation theory posits that a set of institutional rules regulates activity so that capitalism is enhanced. These rules and behaviors tie together national, state, and local governments; businesses; unions; and national and community organizations to promote development: In other words, all the ducks are in a row (Gladstone and Fainstein, 2001). Regulation theory helps explain the various roles of federal and state government and community groups, including labor and environmental groups. For example, when a school, highway, or other public facility is constructed on a brownfield site in a state with prevailing wage requirements (usually union wages and benefits), the project is likely to get strong union support. Workers, like private capital, should be part of a coalition benefiting from brownfields redevelopment. But I believe that regulation theory, like regime theory, places too little emphasis on noneconomic values in policy decisions, especially those regarding brownfields.

Environmental justice is one of these noneconomic values. EPA constructed the brownfields program as an opportunity to help reverse the decline in jobs and tax ratables, but also because of the earlier commitment of President Clinton and the EPA to environmental justice (Clinton, 1998; see also chapters 5 and 8). The brownfields program included provisions that would appeal to cities with large minority populations and an interest in environmental justice. As part of a competitive application process, a local government had to provide a community-based plan, including elements relating to community involvement and environmental justice. It also had to prepare a needs assessment, an implementation plan, and evidence of long-term benefits and sustainability.

Research shows that brownfield sites are disproportionately found in economically distressed neighborhoods with many minority residents (Greenberg et al., 2000). This observation implies that mayors and their staffs had to make a convincing case, at least in writing, to EPA about how they would involve local communities in the programs. Solitaire and Greenberg (2002) found that the initial recipients of brownfield grants were local governments that had significantly higher proportions of minority and poor residents than later recipients and nonawardees did. This study is the best evidence that the federal government deliberately recognized the environmental justice issue, as well as the issue of jobs and tax ratables, in choosing recipients.

In much of the literature on urban redevelopment, community groups are often identified as losers or as only limited beneficiaries compared with business (Harvey, 2001; Jonas and Wilson, 1999; Logan and Molotch, 1996; Smith, 1991). Stone (1989) suggests that stakeholders with limited resources to commit to the enterprise will be relegated to "small opportunities." In addition to proving that funding has gone to cities that lost a lot of jobs and tax ratables and have a lot of poor people, the brownfields program has to demonstrate that the needs of communities have not been ignored.

Can a brownfields program contribute to a sustainable environment, not only for business and elected officials, but also for residents, even poor ones? Portney (2003) argues that he cannot distinguish between sustainable cities and what most people think of as livable cities that manage growth to accommodate the social, cultural, and other needs of residents and investors. In a study of 24 U.S. cities, he found that sustainable cities have elements of economic development, environmental protection, public involvement, and social justice. While noting that the last two typically fall short of what many would like to see, he notes that they do exist in the cities he has studied (Portney, 2003).

When the program began, I could not have made a case for sustainability through brownfields redevelopment because the objectives of federal and state environmental protection agencies sometimes seemed disconnected from their name. On multiple occasions, I heard their representatives state that their goals were to promote new industrial and commercial redevelopment and increase jobs and tax ratables and that the main mechanism for accomplishing these goals was to attract private investment. For example, I sat at a meeting in Perth Amboy, New Jersey, arguing with a representative of the state environmental protection agency about his views that it would not support parks, open space, or community facilities on a brownfield site. Yet EPA and its state progeny changed their position, recognizing that not all brownfield sites are going to attract private investment. This means that parks, schools, and other uses are now permitted (DeSousa, 2004; Harnik, 2000; U.S. Conference of Mayors, 2003). In other words, the goal has shifted from a narrow focus on jobs and taxes to making cities more livable and attractive to investors and people. The shift from focusing on the needs of business to neighborhood redevelopment is apparent in the three case studies in the next section.

Tales of Three New Jersey Mayors:
Building Coalitions in Support of Redevelopment

I picked three New Jersey cities that I knew from experience had strong mayors, contained many brownfield sites, and were small to medium in size (population 47,000 to 120,000). Table 3 shows that Elizabeth, Perth Amboy, and Trenton are densely populated and have a large and growing Hispanic population. By either New Jersey or national standards, all three cities are relatively poor and densely settled.

Unlike the leaders of very large cities, who may not be aware of the details of every project, I expected these mayors to be familiar not only with the individual brownfield projects, but with surrounding neighborhoods. I wanted to hear about the political thinking that went into building a citywide coalition to support redevelopment, and I wanted to hear it directly from the mayor, rather than from a subordinate.

Of course, selecting three mayors from a single state and from medium-sized cities has limitations. The mayors of New York, Chicago, Los Angeles, and other very large cities and the mayors of smaller cities as well have developed somewhat different protocols for their brownfields programs. But I have interviewed the leadership of smaller and larger cities across the United States and feel confident in asserting that the issues that these three New Jersey mayors have dealt with confront the mayors of every large and small city in the United States. These three mayors have been deeply involved in brownfields redevelopment, not only in their own cities, but also at the national level, where they have headed the brownfields group of the U.S. Conference of Mayors.

Context

J. Christian Bollwage, the mayor of Elizabeth, is of European origin. Joseph Vas, the mayor of Perth Amboy, is Hispanic. Douglas Palmer, the mayor of Trenton, is African American. The three of them have a lot in common. Each was born in the city that he now serves and spoke with great pride about his personal motivation to rebuild his city. All were elected in the early 1990s, replacing mayors who had been in office for a decade or more. Moreover, these three mayors have been in office long enough to be able to address my questions personally.

Each mayor was sent a list of questions that explored the types of proposals, the impact on the city, the role of national and state governments, community involvement, and the political implications for their governance, among others (see chapter 7). The interviews were open ended and averaged about an hour and a half; additional time was spent with their staff. Follow-up conversations were held to fine-tune initial observations. When a draft was completed, I sent it to each mayor so that any errors could be identified.

In addition to interviews with mayors and staff, I obtained background information about each city's brownfields program, city planning documents,

TABLE 3

Characteristics of the three case-study cities

Indicator	Elizabeth	Perth Amboy	Trenton	New Jersey
Mayor's first year	1992	1990	1990	NA
Population in 2000	120,568	47,303	85,403	8,414,350
Population change, 1990 to 2000 (%)	9.6	12.7	−3.7	8.8
African American population in 2000 (%)	21.6	11.4	53.6	14.4
African American population change, 1990 to 2000 (%)	19.3	9.4	4.7	16.9
Hispanic population in 2000 (%)	49.5	69.8	21.5	13.3
Hispanic population change, 1990 to 2000 (%)	38.5	41.7	46.7	50.9
Median family income, 1999	$38,370(59)[a]	$40,740(62)[a]	$36,681(56)[a]	$65,370
Renter-occupied housing units (%)	70.3	59.5	54.5	34.4
Area in square miles	13.66	5.95	8.15	7,419
Population per square mile in 2000	9,866	9,892	11,564	1,134
Per capita property tax base in 2002	$35,131(36)[b]	$35,539(38)[b]	$21,804(7)[b]	NA

Sources: Center for Government Services, 2003; and Bureau of Government Research, 1991; both from Edward J. Bloustein School of Planning and Public Policy, Rutgers University, New Brunswick, NJ.

Note: NA = not applicable.
[a] Percentage of New Jersey median family income in 1999.
[b] Number of New Jersey municipalities with lower values (out of 566).

and news stories about their urban redevelopment programs. Because the mayors are so instrumental in the organization of coalitions, I have emphasized their views rather than secondary sources or the viewpoints of others who were consulted.

Findings

The mayors' goals for their brownfields program were remarkably similar: (1) to protect health and safety and (2) to reclaim abandoned and contaminated sites in order to stabilize property taxes, replace thousands of industrial jobs, and provide opportunities for middle-class families and better housing and community facilities for the poor in their cities.

Each mayor had built a broad political coalition based on local conditions. Differences in political strategies seemed to be directly related to local attributes rather than to differences in philosophy or values. Briefly, important environmental attributes of Elizabeth are the location of Newark airport and Port Elizabeth within the city, two exits on the very heavily traveled New Jersey Turnpike, and close proximity to New York City and the massive northern New Jersey market. Elizabeth, in short, has a great deal to offer large-scale retailers and wholesalers.

Perth Amboy borders on Raritan Bay across from New York City and has a large marina. With a view of New York Bay and the promise of greatly expanded ferry service to New York City, it provides a niche for those who appreciate a view of the city and waterways.

Trenton hosts the state capital complex, including museums and galleries, and borders on an attractive stretch of the Delaware River. It has a stop on the Northeast Corridor rail lines, a nearby airport, and a small light rail system.

Because there were no obvious differences in the values and philosophy of the leadership of the three cities, I have reported key parts of their responses regarding coalitions rather than every response to every question.

MAJOR SOURCES OF CAPITAL: OUTSIDE BUSINESS AND NOT-FOR-PROFITS. When asked about the role of private enterprise in their plans, all three mayors noted that local business lacked the funds to build large projects. Mayor Vas of Perth Amboy summarized their collective view:

> We lost over 20,000 manufacturing jobs during the last 20 years. The sites were abandoned or left with phantom operations to avoid cleanup costs. Government cannot provide the level of investment needed for an ongoing transition from the old to the new. We needed a major investment of private capital that would, in turn, attract more reinvestment.

The mayors spoke about a signature project, hoping that it would bring additional projects, yet they wanted this and other undertakings to fit within their community-oriented vision of their cities. The mayors were aware of the risk they were taking. Mayor Bollwage illustrated this point in talking about the construction of the 1.7-million-square-foot Jersey Gardens Mall on a former 166-acre landfill (Morgan, 2000; Sinderman, 1999). The project has cost hundreds of millions of dollars, including a developer-financed $140 million exit from the New Jersey Turnpike.

Jersey Gardens Mall was a great coup. But it was a major risk for me and the city. Developers came to the city in 1993, after I was elected in November 1992, having defeated an incumbent who had been in office for 28 years. They told me that they would build this shopping mall on an old landfill. They were going to spend hundreds of millions of dollars and the state was going to help pay for the remediation of the site. The city should be responsible for building a road to the site. The estimated cost was $10 million. I said: "You want me to build a road to a dump? Then you want me to run for reelection? That's not a good political platform. What guarantees are you giving me that you will build the project?"

Satisfied that the proposal was legitimate, but without complete certainty that the project would be completed, the city chose to take the gamble because of the depressed economic climate. As Mayor Bollwage put it:

> I had just engaged in and won a political battle. My opponents were wait-
> ing for us to make a big mistake. They still are. We were just coming out
> of a recession in 1992, people in my city were not working, and there was
> a lot of uncertainty. Crime was high. I had to do something or be consid-
> ered a fluke. I had to address the crime issue and had to increase oppor-
> tunities through redevelopment. President Clinton's crime bill helped
> provide us with the money to reduce crime, and the brownfields idea let
> us try redevelopment.

Taking a big gamble, the city council agreed to sell $10 million in bonds to pay for the road. The developer took the risk that the project would be blocked by federal or state environment officials, cost more than anticipated, or be opposed by other interest groups. The Regional Plan Association of New York–New Jersey–Connecticut lent its support to the project by picking the site from among the various possible locations and helping with the more than 20 permits needed from EPA, the state Department of Environmental Protection, and the Corps of Engineers. RPA (Regional Plan Association), a not-for-profit organization, was a key member of this Elizabeth coalition. In 1996, when he ran for reelection, Mayor Bollwage was still not sure that the project would be completed. He noted, "Spending $10 million on a road to a dump was a problem." He was sued because of the project and was criticized during the campaign, but he won. He said: "We talked throughout the process with the community. My opponents did not have a better alternative than what we proposed, and the people realized it." The mall opened and seems to be successful. When I tried to do some holiday shopping there in December 2005, I had to drive around for 10 minutes to find a parking space.

The other two cities also had their signature projects. In Trenton, it was the minor league baseball stadium where the Trenton Thunder (a Yankees affiliate) now plays. It was built on the site of an old U.S. Steel mill site. After explaining the importance of the signature project, Mayor Palmer emphasized that this initial success has allowed the city to be much more demanding of new developers, noting that it went into negotiations with developers with particular emphasis on market-rate housing. Because the goal is to keep middle-class residents and attract new ones, Trenton takes control of the properties and cleans them up to its satisfaction. Only after the sites are ready does the city show them to developers.

Mayor Palmer emphasized that developers do not walk into Trenton and do whatever they want. Pointing to bad experiences in his city and elsewhere and connecting these to regime theory, he emphasized that city officials would no longer accept housing development proposals that were not of the highest quality:

> Developers are shown specific parcels and work with us to iron out any inconsistencies between what they want to do and what we and the neighbors want. All of these projects involved negotiations, which means that we must be thoroughly prepared and go back and forth between us, the developer, and the community.

Perth Amboy has attracted over a billion dollars of private capital and has, like Trenton, emphasized the building of quality housing. Mayor Vas put the city's efforts into perspective. About 1,000 acres out of 3,031 in Perth Amboy consist of old industrial sites that have been abandoned or are underdeveloped. The city is marketing its brownfield sites to private interests from the West Coast, as well as to Canada and New York City. Mayor Vas has appeared in a television advertisement in which a former brownfield site becomes a new housing development. He told us:

> If we are going to rejuvenate the economy of this and other industrial cities, this type of redevelopment can't happen by chance. There are a million acres of abandoned and underutilized former industrial sites in New Jersey. In my new role in the state assembly, I intend to push the position that the best way of revitalizing the state economy and controlling sprawl is to revitalize brownfields redevelopment by working with private interests, government, not-for-profits, and our residents.

In short, private capital, argued the mayors, was essential to turn contaminated eyesores that covered large areas of their cities and reduced the quality of life — and possibly threatened public health — into desirable land uses. The mayors recognized the risk that their cities and they personally were taking, and a decade after starting their programs they remain committed to attracting private investment. They see their cities as negotiating from a stronger position than they did a decade ago. A coalition with business was essential.

COALITION WITH FEDERAL AND STATE GOVERNMENTS. The mayors believe that the brownfields program represents an unusual instance of bipartisanship in the United States (Bush, 2001; Clinton, 1998). When testifying before Congress about the brownfields program, Mayor Bollwage noted that he labeled it a major bipartisan effort no less than 10 times. When questioned about this characterization, he said that both President Clinton and President Bush supported the idea and that both Ted Kennedy and the late Jesse Helms supported brownfields programs — a rare event in U.S. national politics during the later part of the 20th century.

Federal government support has been critical, initially as a clear signal that the Superfund era of conflict was going to be replaced by a federally led effort to foster cooperation between environmental protection and urban redevelopment. Each of the three cities received an EPA pilot grant of $200,000. This afforded an opportunity to hire a staff member charged with inventorying and prioritizing all potential sites. Trenton was 1 of the first 10 cities to receive such a grant. Mayor Palmer emphasized the city's commitment to working with federal and state bureaucracies, in part, by doing all the paperwork on time and in the required format. To avoid surprises, Trenton assumed that every site was contaminated and then determined the degree of contamination. But paperwork, Mayor Palmer emphasized, does not replace personal relationships with federal and state officials, with whom he has spoken repeatedly during his tenure. Mayors Bollwage and Vas repeated this sentiment.

Mayor Vas recognized that there have been setbacks in relationships with state and federal governments and hence that persistence and optimism were needed. He also emphasized that unlike the case with many other urban programs, it is critical to have a key staff member with a strong background in health and environmental sciences to facilitate discussions with environmental agency personnel. Notably, his chief brownfields program staffer has a degree in environmental science, which I believe sends a message about the importance of environmental issues in this city. The three mayors pointed to the importance of ongoing support from local government staff. Mayor Bollwage noted:

> The mayor just telling people to do something is not going to produce success. I don't know how some of the smaller towns can do this. They have part-time mayors and very little professional staff. I need to visit every site and talk to the residents and the property owners in the areas. I have a very professional staff that briefs me about every one of our projects. I must have them buy into what we are doing.

Not every branch of government has been a willing partner in brownfields programs. The most obvious source of intergovernment angst in New Jersey involved the New Jersey Department of Education. Elizabeth, Perth Amboy, and Trenton are all so-called Abbott School Districts, which means that the state is committed to spending $6 billion to build new schools or rehabilitate old ones in these cities and 27 others. In areas such as these, where available land is scarce, new school construction must compete with other land uses.

An article in a major New Jersey newspaper asserted that some cities had deliberately picked the most contaminated brownfields for future schools. The objective, asserted the reporter, quoting prominent officials of the New Jersey Schools Construction Corporation (the state group responsible for coordinating between school boards and the state government), was to save the best sites for business and housing and to get the state to pay for expensive cleanups. The article also implied that children were potentially placed at risk (Lane, 2003). Two of the three cities identified in the story were Elizabeth and Perth Amboy. I asked each mayor to comment on this story, which illustrates the difficulty of establishing and maintaining a coalition with every stakeholder. Mayor Bollwage stressed the difficult issue of finding suitable sites:

> The opposition had a lot of fun with that one. I was accused of putting children at risk by picking these sites, which is ridiculous. The reality is that it is not so easy to find large sites for schools in this city. We identified two sites that were rejected. But I already have developers who want to put housing and business on these sites, so I'm not trying to unload unwanted property. I'm not being an obstructionist, but I don't want to condemn viable businesses or tear down a block of good housing to build a school. I don't know what the answer is to the school siting question in this city. We don't have much land that does not pose some type of risk and will not require some cleanup. The state needs to work with us rather than taking shots at us in the newspapers.

Three years after this story broke, two new schools are under construction on old industrial brownfield sites in the area. But the story is not finished. The area badly needs a new health care facility, and there is no obvious site. So, as I was writing this chapter, I was helping the city with efforts to find and evaluate sites for such a facility.

Mayor Vas, who has emphasized the importance of schools in his city revitalization program, was clearly distressed by the accusation. He put forth a strong counterargument that showed the complexity of the issue and added an important philosophical point about cities versus suburbs that did not come across in media reports of the controversy:

> The Department of Education places tremendous requests on the school board and city about site location, size, and use. These requirements are not very realistic for a city. We cannot afford to build a $20 to $30 million building on prime property that is only going to be open from 7:30 AM to 3:30 PM, like they do in the suburbs. That building has to serve as a community center, library, and facility for needy families that lack health care. In a city like Perth Amboy, the school has to serve the people and their families for their entire lives, not just the 12 years they are in school.

Mayor Vas summarily dismissed the charges that the city would allow children to be exposed to toxins and added that Perth Amboy was holding a design competition funded by the Rockefeller Foundation to build a school that would meet the needs of a city, not a suburb. Mayor Palmer has not had a problem finding sites suitable for schools, but emphasized that it is a problem for almost every city and that he would not tear down good housing and businesses for a school. Decades after slum clearance and urban renewal programs caused considerable distress across the country, all three mayors made a point of wanting to avoid displacing people as part of their coalition-building efforts.

The collective sense of Mayors Vas, Bollwage, and Palmer is that the Department of Education is under pressure to build and rebuild a lot of schools and does not have the funds to build all of them if a great deal of the money must be used for decontamination. The mayors argue that the department has to negotiate with them and base decisions on the needs of the cities, rather than on a blueprint of how suburban school districts build and use their schools.

COALITION WITH COMMUNITY GROUPS. To provide a context for the questions about partnering with local residents, I examined the demographic characteristics of the areas with major brownfields projects in each of the cities. They have hundreds of brownfield sites ranging in size from multiple-acre landfills to gasoline stations and are located in virtually every neighborhood.

In Elizabeth, the 3 census tracts (out of 24) that so far have been the focus of brownfields redevelopment had a slightly lower income: Median family income was 87 percent of the average of the other 21 census tracts and 59 percent of the average for the state. African American and Hispanic residents comprised two-thirds of the residents of these tracts, almost exactly the same proportion as in the city as a whole.

In Perth Amboy, much of the work has been done in 3 of the 11 census tracts, and 5 tracts have projects planned to begin in a few years. The tracts with the brownfields projects were virtually identical to others with regard to race, ethnicity, and income. Median family income in the tracts with the projects was 89 percent of that found in the other tracts, and the proportion of African Americans or Hispanics was 87 percent, compared with 84 percent for the other tracts. As was the case in Elizabeth, these differences were not statistically significant.

In Trenton, 10 of the city's 24 census tracts have active projects. Median family income in these 10 tracts was two-thirds of that found in the other 14, and the proportion of these redevelopment tracts consisting of African American or Hispanic residents was 87 percent, compared with only 63 percent in the other 14. In short, poor and minority residents are clearly the majority in the areas chosen for redevelopment in all three cities.

Given this context, the mayors offered two observations about those who live near brownfields projects: (1) Every project had a unique community that included but was not limited to the immediate neighbors, and (2) while not every stakeholder was happy with every brownfields-related decision, it was essential to have overall support for the entire program. As the interviews progressed, I was impressed by the encyclopedic knowledge the mayors and staffers had about the projects and their neighbors. Mayor Palmer noted that the first thing residents wanted was to remove contaminants and then to demolish dilapidated structures. The small size of his city meant that he would be personally involved with community interests at each site.

> A lot of residents had lived next to sites for decades, and they did not understand why we didn't demolish them [and] what the contaminants were. We had to be aggressive at these sites. We didn't have a choice. Trenton's Magic Marker site [a former lead battery facility] is a poster child for public health and community involvement. People lived across the street for 40 years from a site that left lead contamination. Now a school is going on part of the site, and the site will be cleaned up to a safe standard. The community was opposed at first to the school. But we showed them how valuable a school could be on the site, and we compromised with them about the exact location of the school. The school location allows other entities that they want to locate in the neighborhood.

Next, he discussed the controversial issue of institutional controls for brownfield sites, including a variety of deed restrictions that preclude some uses of parts of the sites:

> In a city like Trenton, where there is so much turnover, I don't trust institutional controls, nor do the residents. I want all the sites cleaned up to a residential standard, even if it costs more money, in order to protect us and the public's investments. Maybe we'll cap the area where cars are parked, but not where housing goes or where children play.

Mayor Palmer emphasized the importance of building local community capacity via brownfields redevelopment. His goal is to keep the people in the city, draw some who have left back to the city, and build the capacity of local church-based community development groups to be a positive force in redevelopment.

> The churches are a powerful force in this city. By making them central to our housing redevelopment program, we keep parishioners in the neighborhoods and build the capacity of the churches to be a positive force for change in the city. The brownfield program has allowed us to build community capacity.

With regard to gentrification, Mayor Palmer pointed out that, rather than replacing existing affordable housing, all the new housing in Trenton was a net addition to the city's inventory because it was built where old industrial, commercial, or dilapidated commercial sites had stood. Like Mayors Bollwage and

Vas, he noted that cities cannot thrive on rental and lower-income housing. The city was deliberately increasing the number of market-rate homes to retain people who would otherwise move out to the suburbs and to improve the city's tax base.

Mayor Bollwage made similar remarks and gave an example of how he dealt with fear on the part of residents that they would be forced out of their neighborhoods:

> I told the public that they were not going to be forced out by gentrifica-
> tion when the city built its HOPE VI [Housing Opportunities for People
> Everywhere] project. The public was told that they would have back-
> yards, which they never had before, and that they would have first crack
> at the new housing. The local community group picked the developer
> from among three chosen by the city and asked the city to fire one devel-
> oper who was not performing [which is what happened]; the tenants
> picked the carpets, the colors, [and the] color of the bricks, and made
> just about all the other optional selections.

Not all interactions between the leadership and the neighbors involve major projects. For example, in Elizabeth, the city wanted to build a soccer field on a cleaned-up brownfield site. The community also wanted a basketball court, so the city condemned a dilapidated adjacent property and built a basketball court in addition to the planned soccer field. The basketball court, a neighborhood gro-cery, and others like it are what Stone (1989) called "small opportunities." But many of the projects were not small, and the cumulative impact of all these small projects on neighborhoods is not trivial.

Stakeholder groups include more than neighbors and local religious and sec-ular institutions. Mayor Bollwage noted that the Jersey Gardens Mall project did not draw much neighborhood interest because the site was a dump and not in a neighborhood. Yet the project was a big boost to the construction industry, which hires many local people, and so workers were part of the coalition that supported the project.

Since opening its doors, the mall has continued to be a major source of local jobs, employing some 5,500 workers, many of whom reside in the city (Morgan, 2000). Also, Mayor Bollwage added that the project was supported by environ-mental activist groups because locally dredged materials were used to cap the dump. The alternative had been to dump dredged materials along the New Jersey shore (Morgan, 2000).

Mayor Vas tied city and environmental planning directly to community involvement. Years before any projects were built, the city put together a FOCUS 2000 redevelopment plan that eventually designated 800 acres of Perth Amboy for redevelopment. That process included 23 hours of formal public hearings and numerous informal conversations with interest groups and individuals. Mayor

Vas was brought up half a block from a group of former brownfields where the new vocational school sits. He strongly believes that the cities must rehabilitate their schools and that the public wants schools to be community facilities and new housing to be placed near new schools.

The first Perth Amboy project we talked about was the construction of a vocational high school on two dilapidated former chemical plant sites. This project, he said, was an initial signal to residents and business that Perth Amboy was not going to continue losing people and jobs and was going to rebuild the city in ways consistent with community desires. Funds to clean up and demolish multiple buildings and to build the $28.6 million county vocational school were acquired from EPA, the state, and the federal government through Senator Frank Lautenberg. The school serves county residents, many of them from Perth Amboy, and the county community college uses it for evening courses. It is located in the midst of new housing developments that are under construction.

The mayor's assertion about community congruence with city plans is supported by a survey. At the invitation of several churches and secular groups, Greenberg and Lewis (2000) surveyed 204 residents of Perth Amboy about preferences for uses of remediated brownfield sites. Over 80 percent of respondents "preferred" or "strongly preferred" play areas and parks, community facilities, and health care facilities on cleaned-up brownfield sites. Over half favored child care centers and schools, and 40 to 50 percent supported houses, small businesses, and retail establishments. Less than a third wanted more warehousing and new factories.

The mayors classified existing local business as part of the community rather than as a distinct business entity. For example, Mayor Vas (like the other mayors) gave two examples of local service providers that were expanding their activity in the city. Yet by far the most interesting example of the way a city dealt with a community member was Perth Amboy's relationship with the Chevron Corporation, which has ranked among the top 20 on the Fortune 500 list. This massive petrochemical company is the largest landowner in the city, controlling 330 acres, or 10 percent of city land. It closed its refinery, and after many years of sometimes acrimonious debate with the city over its underutilized properties (some of which were contaminated), the company agreed to make 26 acres available for warehousing. The warehousing site is in an industrial, rather than a residential, area and replaces an eyesore. According to Mayor Vas:

> Our path with Chevron was difficult at first. Chevron now realizes that it is to their advantage to work with us. They are now partners with this community and clearly see the business advantages of that position.

Conflict with the businesses and people who are in the path of relocation is the most difficult problem the mayors face. They noted that since the vast majority of the land being redeveloped is abandoned or underdeveloped, there is not much relocation, especially compared with the days of urban renewal and high-way construction. However, there is some, and it poses a moral problem. Mayor Vas put it this way:

> It's hard to ask people to sacrifice their property. None of us want to do that. We try to find another location for them in the city. It almost always is possible for the few people who need to be relocated, but not for busi-ness — this has specific requirements. But we cannot allow the interest of one or a few property owners to stop what the larger community wants. These are the toughest decisions we have to make.

We discussed and visited some local commercial sites that are to be displaced by Perth Amboy's plans for new housing and community facilities. Both are indus-trial operations that have been part of the city for years. One is a marginally viable business occupying a site with a strategic view of the harbor, and the second is an underutilized brownfield. Their removal is consistent with public preferences.

EVALUATION OF SUCCESS. Coalition building is a worthy but insufficient outcome for cities that have staked a great deal on a brownfields redevelopment program. It is essential to show tangible benefits flowing across the city. Some context for the mayors' descriptions of what has been accomplished and what they hope to accomplish is appropriate at this point. All three cities have a median family income of about 60 percent of the income of the state as a whole, and over 90 percent of the 566 municipal governments have higher per capita property values than these three. Trenton is the most stressed and Elizabeth the least stressed of the case study cities (table 1.2).

Each mayor provided evidence to demonstrate the overall value of his city's brownfields program. As background for his remarks, Mayor Palmer said: "My vision for revitalization grew out of a desire to change the hopelessness and despair that had overtaken this city." Pointing to recent data, such as a rise of 30 to 40 percent in property values, leading to an increase of $32 million in the value of property in the city (a reversal of the past trend), the mayor is optimistic. He feels that it has taken a decade to get control of the brownfield properties and remediate them. Evidence of the turnabout that is occurring is the construction of 1,400 to 1,600 housing units, mostly affordable housing, to stop the decline of the middle-class residents. Further, he noted that 500 units are under construc-tion and another 500 are planned. This, he notes, illustrates Trenton's growing ability to attract market-rate housing as well as build affordable units. Commercial enterprise has been slower to come to Trenton, but the mayor cited the example of a major law firm that moved in from a suburb as a sign that the success the city is having in rebuilding its housing base will attract more business. The latest effort is the redevelopment of a 23-story abandoned telephone building into a mixed-use facility. Mayor Palmer says that it will be the largest project to use green building approaches in the United States.

Arguably, Elizabeth started earlier than the other two cities and has so far reaped the most financial benefit. Jersey Gardens Mall, which as a landfill paid $63,000 a year in taxes, now generates $5.7 million. Mayor Bollwage hopes that it will eventually generate $10 million a year in taxes out of a total city revenue stream of $57 million. The second more general benefit is that other developers now see Elizabeth as a good place to invest. Developers come to the city, they invest, and the growing tax base allows the city to turn other brownfield sites that private interests do not find desirable into Little League fields, retail stores, community facilities, and other things the community wants.

Mayor Vas added his perspective on how Perth Amboy's efforts connect to the international economy: "City government and local business are not the big bad wolf seeking to devour the local people, as I sometimes hear." The world economy, he noted, has created problems for former industrial cities, and it is up to city leaders and their supporters to gradually replace the old with the new. Between 1976 and 1990, he reported, the city lost over $600 million in tax ratables, along with over 20,000 jobs. His plans will add $800 million in ratables or the equivalent of $15 million in new taxes to a city budget of $45 million. The old industrial base is being replaced with market-rate and affordable housing, new commercial enterprises, new schools, and a small industrial base.

These projects are enhanced by a shoreline restoration project, a safety/youth facility, a high-speed ferry to lower Manhattan, and a new road connecting many of the redeveloped areas. A former chemical plant is being considered as a location for a minor league baseball stadium, an indoor arena, retail shopping, and restaurants. These additions, Mayor Vas believes, will allow growth to be sustained without raising local property taxes, the bane of many older fixed-income homeowners.

SUMMARY. The primary goal of this section was to describe mayors' efforts at building coalitions in support of revitalizing cities through brownfields redevelopment. I deliberately picked three cities led by mayors who were born in their cities and were first elected in the early 1990s, just before the national brownfields program started. I stipulate that not everyone I spoke with agreed with all of the mayors' ideas and decisions, although the criticism I heard was directed at specific sites. Notably, no one disagreed with the overall strategy of rebuilding the cities, including the downtown areas, by first concentrating on former brownfield sites. Further, no one disagreed with the need to build broad-based coalitions in support of these efforts in order to spread the risk and benefits among all of the collaborators.

An important insight from this work is that traditional urban redevelopment theories overemphasize market economy forces and understate ecological thinking about cities. With regard to the dominance of the market economy, I agree that there is money to be made by capitalists in these cities, and I further stipulate that a great deal of the money that is made will go to people who do not live in these cities. Yet the interviews show that the primary goal for brownfields redevelopment was not unbridled growth. The motivation and on-the-ground strategies I observed were more connected to the literature on sustainable cities than to regime or regulation theory. Even if many of the projects are small opportunities compared with the economic benefit obtained by the signature project, the cumulative impact of these small and incremental projects is not small.

All four elements of sustainable development certainly exist in the three case study cities. Each uses the words of economic boosterism; that is, the mayors openly seek investments. Yet words and, more important, deeds show that environmental protection, public involvement, and social justice are among the goals. The mayors pointed to instances where the brownfields programs reflect all four of these elements.

Contrary to market dominance, sustainable development implies perpetual analyses; adapting to new knowledge, values, and ethical concerns; and making choices and decisions informed by public and private decision makers rather than by a very small group of people with bottom-line pecuniary interests (Harrison, 2000). This is what appears to be happening in the three case study cities; their mayors, while politically strategic, are also analytical in their approach to data gathering, analysis, and planning. Each required that substantial analysis be done and aired before commitments were made. Rather than literally giving away tracts of land to the first source of private capital that arrived at city hall, they moved slowly, consulting with collaborators, and continue to hold back specific strategic parcels to have time to weigh the alternatives.

A second reason for suggesting that sustainable development and ecological thinking are core elements of what has occurred in these cities is the pivotal role of EPA and its state counterparts. At the national political level, President Clinton (1998) and President Bush (2001) supported brownfields redevelopment. In addition to the pilot program, EPA has deepened its involvement by instituting collaborative programs with other federal departments and agencies.

The brownfields program has been an opportunity for EPA to repair strained relationships with many urban mayors. The agency has played a role throughout the process. It pressed to initiate the program, it has adopted economic development into its portfolio of outcome measures, it helps coordinate among multiple federal agencies in support of the program, and, most important, its regional officials have been deeply involved with local officials in individual projects. Keating and Krumholz (1999) show that U.S. urban policy during the past half century has been disjointed and has tended toward extremes. Notwithstanding the fact that a change in leadership could change EPA's role, it would be irrational for the agency and its state equivalents to reduce their role in the brownfields program.

Given the important and continuing involvement of EPA and state departments of environmental protection in these efforts, I believe that the brownfields program and the urban redevelopment process will inevitably be guided in the direction of thinking about development ecologically rather than thinking about land solely as a marketable commodity (Chertow and Esty, 1997; Hula, 2001). EPA's signature urban redevelopment program has had strong support from the National Governors Association (2000). The U.S. Conference of Mayors (2000) has been no less enthusiastic, and not-for-profits have touted the job-creation, fiscal, environmental justice, and public involvement elements of the process (Powers et al., 2000; Simons, 1998; Van Horn et al., 1999).

An obvious reason why the national brownfields program has widespread support is that it does not start with antipathy toward interest groups that have too often been put in opposing positions in policy debates over health care, welfare, education, and many other issues. The program allows business to benefit at some locations, while poor and disadvantaged minorities appear to benefit at other sites in the same city. Environmental groups, although worried about exposing people to toxins, have been generally supportive.

Castells (1989) observed that the more the economy becomes globalized, the less individual cities can do to control their environment. Yet these three case study cities show that cooperation and coordination among governments, businesses, not-for-profits, and communities have merit as countervailing processes that will result in livable and sustainable cities. I recognize that some cities that have concentrations of brownfields and therefore need to follow similar processes will not do so. They will not be able to provide enough benefits to attract outside investments or to cope with the changing power of interest groups that follow from a major brownfields effort or with controlling the environmental and social externalities produced by large-scale remediation and reuse. Whether Elizabeth, Perth Amboy, and Trenton are the norm or the exception is an important question that cannot be answered at this time. I can, however, assert with confidence that the local political process must build a broad coalition to have a chance of succeeding in an entire city.

I expect federal and especially state and local governments to continue efforts to redevelop brownfield sites. More challenges are on the way, however. On June 23, 2005, the U.S. Supreme Court decided in favor of redevelopment over prior private property rights interests in *Kelo v. City of New London* (2005). The 5-to-4 decision asserted that local government had the authority to take private land for purposes of economic development. This has caused a backlash — frankly, an overreaction — in many states. Some are considering legislation that would restrict government's ability to take private property. This issue will take many years to resolve.

If local governments face substantial restrictions in taking property, the kinds of programs described by the three mayors would be much more difficult to plan and implement. Finally, we must not forget that the brownfields program started as an effort to reduce health risks. Nowhere have I seen definitive guidance on how clean a site has to be before it can be redeveloped. Given the stresses on local and state government budgets, I am concerned over who is going to make sure that developers do not take inappropriate shortcuts that later place public health and ecosystems at risk. (See chapters 3, 5, and 8 for discussion of Washington, D.C.–based legal controls of exposure to hazards and the use of risk assessment to gauge the danger.)

Tools and Tasks

Brownfields redevelopment is such a multidisciplinary endeavor that I cannot identify a single tool in part 2 that is irrelevant. In chapter 8, I use a checklist developed for local officials considering brownfields to illustrate that tool.

I developed a set of tasks for the undergraduate and graduate students in my Protecting Public Health and the Environment class. The best example for urban redevelopment is as follows. Students are asked to identify a contaminated or impaired site (poor location, dysfunctional shape, lack of infrastructure) in their town or in a nearby one. First, they must visit the site and prepare a map of the site and environs. (I do not require that the maps be high quality, but they must have a scale, a directional arrow, and a legend describing the surrounding land uses. Some students submit hand-drawn maps and others use their computers.)

Second, I ask them to visit the city planner or city engineer. Before this meeting, the class discusses the questions they will ask. I find this to be a more effective learning experience than just giving them questions myself. At the meeting with city officials, they ask about future plans for the site, discuss constraints in the redevelopment process, and ask about each of the six criteria. Time and access permitting, they examine written plans, talk with the mayor and the developer, and attend a city planning or zoning department meeting.

Third, they prepare a paper that discusses the city's plans in terms of the six criteria and presents their own evaluation of those plans. For many students, this is the first time they have ever visited a brownfield site or interviewed a city official. The final products are the paper and a class presentation.

A second task focuses on environmental justice. The student locates the impaired site on a map and then on the U.S. Bureau of the Census decennial census tract map and answers the following questions:

1. How does the population of the tract compare with the population of adjacent tracts, the city as a whole, and the county with regard to per capita or family income, educational achievement, race/ethnicity, and age?
2. How does the housing compare with regard to age, quality, and value?
3. Does the host census tract appear to be different from the adjacent tracts or from the city? Why do you think so?

Next, I help the class develop a short survey consisting of questions that probe residents' perceptions of the impaired site compared with other neighborhood problems. Using language borrowed from the American Housing Survey, students, with some guidance from me, ask 6 to 10 people whether the impaired site bothers them and whether it bothers them so much that they would like to leave the area. The same question is asked about other neighborhood character-istics, such as crime, physical decay of residential or commercial structures, traf-fic, factories, noise, recreational facilities, appearance, and so on. The student must also ask how the residents rate the quality of their neighborhood on a 10-point scale, where 1 is the worst neighborhood and 10 is the best. Finally, the sur-vey asks for relevant demographic characteristics, such as age, race/ethnicity, and education. The final product is a report that evaluates the environmental justice context of the site.

A third exercise is aimed at the media. Development and redevelopment are frequently covered in local newspapers, on television, and on the radio. Students are asked to find five newspaper stories about development or redevelopment in their community. Using content analysis (see chapter 7), they analyze the stories for tone, sources, use of enhancements, and other critical information. They report on the perspective presented by the media and compare it with the infor-mation they gathered from speaking to nearby residents. This means incorporat-ing nearly all the questions presented as part of the second exercise and in addition asking about residents' preferences and responses to the planned development.

In most universities, the second and third tasks will require the completion of Internal Review Board (IRB) forms. The survey should receive an expedited review because students will not record any identifiers and will tell respondents that they need not answer questions that make them uncomfortable. Tasks two and three, in short, are a way of introducing the IRB process to students (see also chapter 7).

2

The Reaction of Nongovernment Stakeholder Groups Criterion

Environmental Cancer and Cancer Clusters

Introduction

Cancer is a group of diseases caused by abnormal cells that compress, invade, and destroy normal cells. Cancer cells grow and migrate. In the United States, more than 550,000 people die of cancer every year; in 1935, that number was 138,000 (Centers for Disease Control and Prevention, National Center for Health Statistics, 2003; D. Levin, 1974). This increase is somewhat misleading because the population has grown as well, especially the elderly population, which accounts for more than half of all cancer-related deaths. Also, the influence of smoking on cancer was only beginning to be felt during the 1930s. Yet cancer preys on all age groups, on all racial and ethnic populations, on rich and poor, and on all regions, not just on older people who smoked for many years. Cancer cells are fearsome opponents. Cancer ranked eighth as a cause of death in the United States in 1900, but second in 2001, when it accounted for 23 percent of all deaths. Only heart disease (29 percent) caused more deaths than cancer.

When an unexpectedly high number of cancer cases are observed in a neighborhood or during a short period of time (a year or two), the terrifying label "cancer cluster" is applied. I have been involved in many cancer cluster investigations and have observed palpable levels of public fear; some people literally work themselves into a frenzy and develop psychosomatic symptoms. The policy issue tackled in this chapter is how state government should respond to reports of cancer clusters. The pressure that groups outside the government, especially the media, can exert on policy is examined in detail.

Public fear of cancer is not groundless. There is no disease more dreaded than cancer because of its capacity to disfigure and cause a slow, painful wasting away (Weitz, 2001). Financially, cancer costs, including diagnosis, treatment, care, rehabilitation, transportation, increased household expenditures, special diets, and counseling, are around $200 billion a year (American Cancer Society [ACS], 2005). In addition, patients and family members lose time from work, and their productivity may decrease because of stress. The psychological impact of cancer can be devastating.

Cancer clusters increase stress because they seem to be sudden, stealthy, and uncontrolled invasions of personal living or working space. One day a neighborhood is a wonderful place to live (85 percent of U.S. residents rate their neighborhood as excellent or good [Greenberg and Schneider, 1996]). A week or a month later, the same neighborhood appears to be devouring its residents.

Theme: Policy on Cancer Clusters and Interconnected Policy Themes

Cancer cluster investigations are deeply embedded in two intertwined and powerful themes in post–World War II U.S. history: the war on cancer and the war on pollution.

The War on Cancer

Probably everyone who reads this book has dealt with the consequences of cancer. In his January 1971 State of the Union address, President Nixon officially declared war on cancer and requested an additional $100 million to be added to the budget of the National Cancer Institute (NCI) for research. In October 1971, he made a strong symbolic statement by converting the Army's Fort Detrick, Maryland, biological warfare facility into a cancer research center (subsequently called the Frederick Cancer Research Center). On December 23, 1971, he signed into law the National Cancer Act (PL 92–218), which declared that "the incidence of cancer is increasing and cancer is the disease which is the major health concern of Americans today." President Nixon added, "I hope in the years ahead we will look back on this action today as the most significant action taken during my administration" (quoted in National Cancer Institute, 2006).

The federal government and scores of other public and private organizations directly or indirectly focus on cancer. I cannot examine all of the major players, from Action Now of California to the Women's Community Cancer Project in Boston, in this chapter. I choose to look primarily at the media. But to understand the media in the context of the war on cancer, especially cancer clusters, it is important to know about other key interest groups. Hence, I will summarize the role of three of the most important organizations: NCI, ACS, and the International Agency for Research on Cancer (IARC). I first describe these organizations and suggest how they influence policy. Then I review some of the criticisms of their activities, concentrating on the charge that they do not pay enough attention to pollution. It should be noted that that the criticisms leveled at NCI, ACS, and IARC have, to a much lesser extent, been aimed at the U.S. Environmental Protection Agency (EPA), the Food and Drug Administration, and the World Health Organization (WHO). Engaging in the war on cancer means that an organization or a person is going to be second-guessed, and some of the criticism will be newsworthy.

NATIONAL CANCER INSTITUTE (NCI). Paul Starr (1982) argues that the federal government's health research institutions figured out that the most effective way to obtain public support for medical research was to concentrate on one disease at a time. Cancer was the first choice. NCI is the lead federal agency in the war on cancer. The federal government took the first important policy step in 1937, when Congress unanimously voted to pass the National Cancer Institute Act (P.L. 244), which created NCI. The law directed NCI to conduct its own research, promote research in other institutions, and coordinate cancer-related actions across the nation. The act placed NCI within the Public Health Service, directed the surgeon general to promote research, and established the National Advisory Cancer Council. In 1974, the National Cancer Amendments (P.L. 93–352) added construction grants for new or remodeled research facilities and funds for information dissemination.

In 1978 (in P.L. 95–622), Congress mandated an expanded research program related to occupational and environmental exposures to carcinogens. Since 1980, more than 15 tasks have been added to NCI's agenda. These include increasing the dissemination of information; screening for breast, cervical, prostate, and colorectal cancer; regulating facilities that offer mammography; establishing a national cancer registry; reducing underage smoking; and providing coverage for consultations and minimum hospital stays for selected cancers.

NCI has been allocated more funds than have been given for the study of any other cause of death and morbidity. President Nixon authorized $400 million for fiscal year 1972, $500 million for fiscal year 1973, and $600 million for fiscal year 1974. In addition, other funds were set aside for cancer control (NCI, 2006). NCI's average budget for fiscal years 2004 through 2006 was $4.8 billion out of a National Institutes of Health (NIH) budget of $28 billion (U.S. Department of Health and Human Services [HHS], 2006).

One of NCI's stated objectives is to translate the results of its research into a reduced incidence of cancer and mortality (Kaiser, 2002). Wars tend to attract less attention when they are won. This one has not been won, however. Some of the most vociferous charges and countercharges have been about the cancer rate and NCI's failure to win the war. In 1900, the death rate from cancer was 64 per 100,000 of the population. In 1970, the date I have used to mark the official declaration of war, the rate was 162 per 100,000 (Bailer, King, and Mason, 1964; Greenberg, 1983; President's Science Advisory Committee Panel on Chemicals, 1973; U.S. Department of Health, Education, and Welfare [HEW], 1974). Some explanations for the increase in cancer rates are obvious, notably the substantial increase in the elderly population. Another explanation is that cancer is more accurately diagnosed than it was in 1900.

Assuming that no change in the human gene pool that might have led to these increases could possibly have occurred in such a short period of time, then some set of environmental factors is responsible. Clearly, the extraordinary increase in smoking has been a major factor, underscored by the 20-fold increase in male lung cancer rates between 1930 and 1970. Yet at the same time, the death rate for stomach cancer fell by two-thirds, suggesting that other environmental conditions have changed. It has been argued that the introduction of the cigarette and better food preservation largely explain these two changes.

During the 1970s, when the wars on cancer and pollution were declared, WHO was widely quoted as asserting that 60 to 90 percent of all cancer is related to environmental factors, including cigarette smoking but also including occupational contaminants and emissions into the air, water, and land. In short, the war on cancer has been directly linked to the war on pollution since at least the mid-1970s.

The increase in cancer and the link to the war on pollution have been a critical context for NCI, which like many large government agencies has been criticized for having a bloated bureaucracy and spending too much on salaries and non-cancer-related activities. But charges like these are leveled at every major organization. The important criticisms for this book are that NCI has focused too much on basic research to produce a cure for cancer and drugs that slow down or destroy cancer cells (Epstein 2003, 2005a; 2005b; Proctor, 1995). This emphasis on looking for the "magic bullet" for cancer, argue detractors, leads NCI to put insufficient stress on prevention (with the exception of smoking) and to mislead Congress and the public into believing that the cancer rate is decreasing when it is not.

With regard to the war on pollution, the argument continues that NCI policies deliberately blame people who have cancer by focusing too much on what we must do to protect ourselves and that NCI does not stop polluters that spread carcinogens into the environment. Notably, NCI is criticized for forming an alliance with corporate polluters that also produce cancer drugs and other treatments. In short, NCI is the biggest player and largest target for other interest groups.

AMERICAN CANCER SOCIETY (ACS). The largest not-for-profit organization focusing on a single set of diseases is ACS, which was founded by New York City physicians and business leaders in 1913 as the American Society for Control of Cancer (ASCC) (ACS, 2004). In 1936, with rates climbing quickly, Marjorie Illig, an ASCC field representative, proposed creating a women's field army to fight a war against cancer. Within a few years over 150,000 volunteers joined the cancer army and vaulted ASCC to the top of the volunteer organization hierarchy. ASCC became ACS in 1945. Starr (1982) notes that its chief architects, Mary Lasker and Florence Mahoney, brought modern advertising techniques to ACS, leading to the use of contributions for medical research.

Before 1950, the society began to build its research and public education programs. During the past half century, ACS has been in the middle of every major cancer-related policy issue, such as smoking as a cause of cancer, the utility of the Pap smear, mammography, and many others. In its public documents, ACS takes pride in having funded 38 Nobel prize winners, many before they won the award. ACS is equally proud of its community-based network of volunteers who organize cancer walks and staff phones to help people with cancer. According to its self-description, ACS is "the nationwide community-based voluntary health organization dedicated to eliminating cancer as a major health problem by preventing cancer, saving lives, and diminishing suffering from cancer through research, education, advocacy, and service" (2004).

Given that NCI is a government agency, one would expect it to be the target of criticism. But ACS is a not-for-profit with a humane mission and apparent accomplishments, so it is hard to imagine that it could also be the target of severe criticism. But it has been, and, in fact, a cynic would say that every major government organization and not-for-profit is a prime target for those who have their own mission and can promote it by criticizing major players. In the case of ACS, the most vitriolic words have come from Samuel Epstein (2003, 2005a, 2005b, 2006), who has charged that an inappropriate association with business has led ACS to focus on screening and cures that companies sell. This focus, he argues, keeps ACS at arm's length from prevention. Epstein (2005a, 2005b, 2006) labels the ACS the "world's wealthiest 'nonprofit' institution" and one that has, among other things, spent disproportionately on salaries, overhead, and travel. He accuses ACS of pressuring NCI to adopt its pro-business agenda and to overlook pollution as a cause of worker and general public exposure. While Epstein is clearly the most powerful spokesperson for this position, others (Organic Consumers Association, 2005; Proctor, 1995; Wargo, 1996) have articulated similar views. The war on cancer, argue these advocates, must focus more on the war on pollution. (See Bailar and Gornik, 1997, for a presentation with suggestions and much less invective.)

INTERNATIONAL AGENCY FOR RESEARCH ON CANCER (IARC). The major purpose of this organization is to identify the causes of cancer (IARC, 2004). It is not charged with patient care, and its cancer control functions are limited to science-based strategies. Moreover, it is not in the business of making policy. It emphasizes epidemiological and laboratory-based methods (see risk assessment, chapter 7), and the results of its scientific investigations are published as reports and presented at conferences and in courses. These clearly influence cancer policy. Organizationally, it is part of WHO. The combination of a scientific agenda and residence in a world body suggests that it would be buffered against outside influences and political criticism.

In 2003, an editorial in the influential journal *The Lancet* questioned IARC about conflict of interest, undue industry influence, and lack of transparency. The editorial called for transparency and audits: "It only needs the perception, let alone the reality, of financial conflicts and commercial pressures to destroy the credibility of important organizations such as IARC and its parent, WHO" ("Transparency at IARC," 2003, 189). Responding to these criticisms, an IARC advisory group noted that it is difficult to find experts who have no interest in the agents under review. The group concluded that "IARC succeeds in large measure in maintaining proper conduct with respect to these important principles" (Sixth

Advisory Group, 2003). Scientists with a financial conflict are not barred from IARC service.

In May 2004, the National Institute of Environmental Health Sciences (NIEHS) consulted 20 experts about IARC's monographs. Since 1992, NIEHS and the National Toxicology Program have contributed about $90,000 a year to IARC. The experts concluded that "IARC monographs are based on the best possible science, and high quality, and make a contribution to the ability of NIEHS to carry out its mission" (Toxicology Excellence for Risk Assessment, 2004, 3). They added that IARC was responding appropriately to criticism of undue influence but that NIEHS needed to appoint a direct liaison to IARC and monitor how NIEHS funds are being spent.

So even IARC is vulnerable to newsworthy criticisms. To reiterate, no major player in the war on cancer, including doctors, clinics and hospitals, drug companies, industries, health care payers, prestigious university-based cancer centers, and the three major institutions in the war on cancer (ACS, IARC, NCI), is immune to controversy. With regard to funding, every barb and dagger aimed at any of the big three organizations hurts the war on cancer if elected officials and the public decide to not increase NCI's budget, to withdraw funds from WHO, or to contribute less to ACS. The funds can go to HIV/AIDS, heart disease, stroke, or one of the many other groups competing with the war on cancer for public and private funds.

The War on Pollution and the War on Cancer

The war on pollution merged with the war on cancer during the Nixon presidency. After a decade of frustration from seeing visible signs of environmental degradation, Congress and the Nixon administration sent two clear messages by passing the Environmental Policy Act of 1969 and creating EPA (see also chapter 7 for a discussion of NEPA).

With regard to cancer and the war on pollution, some chemical and physical agents have been established as occupational carcinogens. For example, asbestos has caused thousands of deaths among miners and the textile mill, insulation, and shipyard employees who handled it. If these employees also smoked, their chances of developing lung cancer increase exponentially (Doll and Peto, 1981). Aromatic amines, arsenic, benzene, cadmium, chromium, ionizing radiation, nickel, mustard gas, and vinyl chloride are some of the other known carcinogens.

Moreover, air, water, land, and food contain hazardous substances, including carcinogens. The scientific issue boils down to these questions:

1. Will a single molecule of the substance cause cancer?
2. If not, are the concentrations high enough and are they present for long enough to cause cancer?

I will present the highlights of the ongoing debate about environmental cancer to underscore the uncertainty about it and the reality that the greater the scientific uncertainty, the more the media's role as a gatekeeper for information becomes critical to all of us. I look first at the proposed link to air pollution and then at water pollution. It should be noted, however, that a considerable amount of interest is now focused on the impact of pollutants on birth defects, the reduction of sperm counts, and other noncancerous outcomes. The war on pollution is no longer simply a war on cancer (see chapters 3 and 5). In 1932, in a book entitled *Cancer: What Everyone Should Know about It*, Tobey (1932, p. 190) asserted: "Endeavors have . . . been made to show that smoke may have some influence on cancer, but there is actually no reliable data to incriminate smoky atmospheres, undesirable as they may be from the standpoint of general hygiene."

This statement is not remarkably different from others made during the past century. For example, 50 years ago, Stocks and Campbell (1955) argued for a link between air pollution and cancer. They observed that urban cancer rates in England were twice as high rural rates and attributed 40 percent of the excess to air pollution. Within a few years, similar papers that directly or indirectly provided evidence that air pollution causes cancer were published in the United States and other Western countries (Dean, 1961; Haenszel, Loveland, and Sirken, 1962; Haenszel and Taeuber, 1964; Hammond and Horn, 1958; M. Levin, 1960; Manos and Fisher, 1959; Prindle, 1959; Schiffman and Landau, 1961).

Those claims were criticized by others who asserted that the urban excess of cancer was primarily due to smoking, occupational exposures, and better identification and reporting of cancer in the cities (Wynder and Hammond, 1962). The debate has gone back and forth for decades. Some authors have stepped across the border that separates science from policy to comment on the implications of the debate. For example, arguing for pollution as a cause of cancer, William Hueper, chief of NCI's Environmental Cancer Section, in a remarkable 1966 book based on a review of over 1,000 studies, observed:

> It should be obvious that any wide acceptance of such scientifically unsound and socially irresponsible claims concerning the principal role of cigarette smoking in the causation of cancers, especially respiratory cancers, would paralyze not only a legitimate and urgently needed pursuit into the various environmental factors inducing such cancers, particularly the many industry-related pollutants of the urban air, but has provided already effective legal arguments before civil courts and compensation boards for denying justified claims for compensation of occupational respiratory cancers to the victims of such hazards as well as to their widows and orphans. (1966, pp. 14–15)

The debate boils down to the dose people are exposed to and for how long and whether a single dose or cumulative doses can cause cancer over the typical latency period of 20 to 40 years. A National Academy of Sciences Conference on the Health Effects of Air Pollution summarized the evidence and the uncertainty: "There are substances present in polluted atmospheres which have been demonstrated in experiments on animals to be mutagenic or carcinogenic. The concentrations required in such experiments have been very much higher than those which might be encountered in polluted atmospheres. The atmospheric pollutants here considered may be among the factors contributing to the higher rate in urban areas, but definite evidence is lacking" (1973, p. 9).

The urban air pollution/lung cancer debate has been paralleled by a water pollution/urinary tract cancer debate. Drinking water has low concentrations of contaminants, including carcinogens. In 1974, Robert Harris of the Environmental Defense Fund observed that the rates of urinary and gastrointestinal tract cancer for white males were quite high in those areas of Louisiana, including New Orleans, where people drank water drawn from the Mississippi River. This river system drains much of the Midwest, and so it was not much of a leap to assert that the water was full of carcinogens from industrial, farm-related, and other sources. The argument was so powerful that I believe it was the major reason that the Safe Drinking Water Act was passed shortly thereafter (P. Rogers, 1978). The New Orleans results led to follow-up studies of cancer rates related to potable water supplies (Greenberg and Page, 1981; Hileman, 1982; National Research Council, 1978; Page, Harris, and Epstein, 1976; Schneiderman, 1978; Shacklelford and Keith, 1977; Wilkins, Reaches, and Kruse, 1979). These studies reported concentrations of toxins, including carcinogens, and some found elevated rates of cancer.

This link, like the link between air pollution and lung cancer, has been challenged. Various analysts regrouped the Louisiana data, studied other regions, and found no excess of cancer (DeRouen and Diem, 1975, 1977; Tarone and Gart, 1975). The studies are ongoing, and some find excess rates of urinary tract cancer and others do not. I would be remiss if I neglected to state that the link between pollution and cancer has been broadened to include breast cancer, leukemia, lymphomas, and various other forms of the disease. This will be the subject of debate as long as cancer exists.

Summarizing, the bulk of the evidence shows a relatively small excess of cancer or none at all. But the case for or against a link between pollution and cancer is not possible to prove or disprove conclusively.

1. First, the data on exposure to contaminants are typically imprecise (that is, we cannot pinpoint the duration of exposure; see risk assessment, chapter 7).
2. Confounding exposures such as smoking, occupation, and nutrition are not always available.
3. Cancer has a long latency period, which means that people who die from the disease today may have lived in another region for much of their life.

The fact that researchers find carcinogens in the environment has not convinced key analysts that pollution is a major cause of cancer. Doll and Peto (1981), Wynder and Gori (1977), and Higginson and Muir (1979) attributed one-third of cancer to tobacco and alcohol and another 35 to 40 percent to diet and nutrition. Occupational exposures were estimated to cause about 5 percent of cancers. Pollution was estimated at 2 percent, with a range of less than 1 percent to 5 percent. Although some strongly disagree with these estimates, the consensus is that only a small proportion of cancers are related to pollution and that nearly all of these are occupational exposures. Of course, just because a large percentage of cancer cases are not attributable to pollution does not mean that dangerous exposures are acceptable for some people. I for one am not ready to dismiss the need for a war on pollution. Nor, in fact, do I accept the idea that proportional allocation of cancers is a good way of understanding the factors that contribute to the disease (Rothman and Greenland, 2005).

This high degree of uncertainty about environmental cancer is a dilemma for everyone, but especially the media. Should they report the umpteenth study that finds an excess of cancer or the umpteenth study that denies the existence of a link? The answer depends on the newsworthiness of the particular new report compared with what else is happening at the time (newsworthiness will be discussed later in this chapter). When there are more cancer cases than expected in a particular market area, there will be media coverage.

Policies on State Cancer Clusters: What to Do?

Elaborating on the definition given earlier, a cancer cluster is a situation in which there are more cancer cases within a small period of time (one or two years), geographical area (neighborhood, workplace, school), or specific population than would be expected from comparative citywide, state, or national data. For example, suppose a neighborhood with 50 houses reported 10 cases of cancer during a two-year period when only 1 case would be anticipated. Are 10 cases, compared with only 1, evidence of a time-space cluster (excess of cancer in a specific time and place)?

The answer is that 10 cases are a lot in a small, low-density neighborhood, but a minuscule number in the larger context of over half a million cancer-related deaths in the nation. The policy dilemma that state officials face may be summarized as two opposite policy positions:

1. Clusters are the tip of the iceberg in terms of the impact of industrial pollution on public health. Every reported cluster should be thoroughly investigated, and when evidence shows a cause and effect, then those responsible should be prosecuted for criminal violations and civil actions.
2. Clusters are random events, and it is foolish to use limited health research funds on such unproductive efforts.

Clusters have been reported for many decades, but in the mid-1970s, the chance of their being reported by government officials became more likely because of data building and maps prepared by NCI. The institute calculated age- and gender-controlled cancer mortality rates by county in the United States and then mapped these rates, which showed clusters of counties and states with high death rates from cancer (Mason and McKay, 1974). Within a year of the publication of the cancer atlas, officials were being pressured to explain why their state, their county, or their city had high rates of cancer. The possible link to pollution was an obvious place to look for an explanation.

My home state of New Jersey was reported to be in the middle of a Northeast corridor (the so-called cancer alley) where cancer deaths were more than 10 percent higher than in the rest of the nation (Greenberg, 1983). I spent three years trying to understand New Jersey's high cancer mortality rates. What I found was that the higher rates in New Jersey and much of the Northeast were primarily due to higher rates of smoking, nutritional habits that were brought over from Europe, and industrial exposure to asbestos and other substances. By the time the NCI atlas was published, the difference between rates in New Jersey and the rest of the United States had decreased to almost nothing. But the firestorm created by front-page headlines, including an unflattering cartoon of the author talking about one of his studies, did not dissipate quickly.

In a state with a high cancer rate like New Jersey, it comes as no surprise that clusters are reported. Of these, I can discuss the Rutherford case because I played only a minor role in the analysis. Rutherford, a primarily residential community of 20,000 people that is located about 10 kilometers west of New York City, is known today as the home of the New York Giants stadium. But in the late 1970s, it became infamous for a large number of cases of childhood leukemia and non-Hodgkin's lymphoma. Residents of this middle-class community reported what seemed to them to be an unusually high number of children who had cancer and attended Pierrepont Elementary School. State scientists found 13 cases of leukemia between 1973 and 1978 compared with 14 expected by chance. But 10 of those 13 were among people 39 or younger, compared with the 2.9 expected by chance in that age group. With regard to non-Hodgkin's lymphoma, 9 cases were observed versus 4.1 expected. The state also calculated observed and expected cases of cancer for the surrounding municipalities. Epidemiological studies (see chapter 7) verified the public's fears that there was an excess of cancer (Halperin et al., 1980). This epidemiological investigation was followed by resident surveys and environmental monitoring for plausible causes and some highly unlikely ones. Nothing was found to explain this cluster (Burke et al., 1980).

The Rutherford cluster followed the norm: A cluster was found, but it could not be tied to any cause. This does not mean that there was no cause. There were more than 20 industrial sources in the immediate region, but none in the town itself. Every one of these was examined, although some had been closed for years. The available data were limited. The state took many environmental samples, but nothing was found, despite a large expenditure of money and the efforts of talented and unbiased researchers. There was no large multinational corporation that could be sued as there was in the case of the famous Woburn, Massachusetts, cancer cluster memorialized by the book *A Civil Action* (Harr, 1995) and the movie *Erin Brockovich* (2000).

Since the Rutherford cluster, I have been involved in other such investigations, with similar results. Because the results of cluster cases are so politically sensitive, I had to sign pledges that I would not speak publicly about them to anyone, including journalists, until the report was completed.

The political circus and legal charges that can result from reports of cancer clusters mean that there is nothing simple about such clusters from the perspective of someone who is responsible for deciding how much to spend on an investigation. One reality is that there will be an excess of cancer in some places and times. For example, the California Department of Health Services (1994) estimated the number of California towns or census tracts that would have a cluster. Focusing on 80 different kinds of cancer, the department concluded that 8 out of 100 towns or census tracts would have a cluster simply by chance. Since there were 5,440 localities in California, this means that the state could be investigating 44 clusters a year. California has about 13 percent of the U.S. population. If the same likelihood holds for the rest of the country, this means about 340 cluster investigations a year. Greenberg and Wartenberg (1991) did a survey to determine how many requests states receive for cluster investigations. The answer was 1,300 to 1,650 a year, number that has not changed much, according to other surveys.

What happens to requests varies considerably by location. About three-fourths are addressed by state or local health officials with a phone call. The remainder require some follow-up, which typically consists of finding out which kind of cancer is involved, who has contracted it, and what the ages, dates of diagnosis, and other pertinent information are. This information is then summarized and compared with what would be expected by chance. Studies suggest that about 5 to 15 percent are found to have an excess of cancer (Greenberg and Wartenberg, 1991). Some of these are followed up with thorough environmental investigations, such as was done in Rutherford. The Centers for Disease Control and Prevention (1990) prepared guidelines for these investigations. Also, the California Department of Health Services (1994) has prepared an excellent 11-chapter guidebook that includes science, math, and sections on developing partnerships with local physicians and the community. Numerous other studies offer suggestions. But all of these are merely guidelines, not requirements, and some states do not follow up on requests.

States vary widely in their policy responses. Some, like New Jersey (because of its history), do proactive surveillance in search of clusters. When a cluster is detected, the state systematically follows up. Other states frankly do nothing. Arguably, they do worse than nothing by not responding to reports initiated by the public. One official told me that he was not about to shake the trees looking for cancer. Are states like New Jersey following the right policy, and are other states callous in their disregard for public health by not searching for clusters? (See Wartenberg's recommendation later in the chapter.)

The essence of the debate among scientists and the quandary presented to decision makers was summarized in a special issue of the *American Journal of*

Epidemiology (1990). The first remarks were in an editorial that speaks directly to the dilemma for scientists: "Many real or suspected clusters are reported initially by members of the public or by astute clinicians. Calls for an investigation are thus often fueled by preliminary or partial data and are frequently lacking a scientific hypothesis to explain the cluster. The resultant reaction direction of the study, from data toward a hypothesis, is in stark contrast to the scientific method of developing a hypothesis first and then gathering data to confirm or deny it" ("Clustering of Health Events," 1990, p. S1).

The very next article in the issue, by epidemiologist Ken Rothman, asserted that "there is little scientific value in the study of disease clusters" (1990, S6). He continued: "We spend less time reacting to reports of disease clustering, less time trying to detect general patterns of disease clustering, and less time developing new methods to conduct these activities. Instead, we should focus more on exposure assessment and where indicated, cleanup" (Rothman, 1990, p. S6).

Warner and Aldrich (1988) concluded that cancer cluster investigations have not produced notable scientific discoveries, but that they have benefits in terms of allaying public fears and building goodwill toward government agencies. In the spirit of that observation, the media are critical players insofar as they are the gatekeepers for almost all the news we receive.

Once frightened residents call their mayor, doctors, other elected officials, health officers, or attorneys, the local media are almost certain to cover the story, at least initially. Aldrich and Sinks (2002) searched U.S. newspapers for stories that used the words "cancer cluster." They found 2,006 stories that appeared between January 5, 1990, and January 5, 2000, but did not report conducting a content analysis of these stories. Greenberg and Wartenberg (1990) conducted a content analysis of 176 newspaper articles about four cancer clusters (see chapter 7). The articles told readers timely facts about the types of cancer, noted how many cases there were, and explained that research was being conducted. Some 43 percent of the paragraphs dealt with risk, and most of them offered mixed opinions about risk. Follow-up discussions with newspaper journalists showed that they felt an obligation to cover the stories, but that the scientific jargon and lack of certainty were problems for them.

Very different observations were made about television coverage. We analyzed 421 stories about clustered health events (including cancer) shown by ABC, CBS, and NBC's 22-minute flagship evening news from 1978 to 1987 (Greenberg and Wartenberg, 1990). These stories represented about 14.4 hours of television time — less than one story a week or one story in every 26 nightly news broadcasts. Unlike the newspaper stories, the television versions focused on dramatic visual opportunities, controversial information on risk, parties that could be blamed, and political symbolism. There were 99 stories about Love Canal, the former major hazardous waste site near Niagara Falls, New York, where a cancer cluster was asserted to have appeared. Taken as a whole, the Love Canal television coverage leaves the impression of watching a soap opera with a focus on good people and bad people.

In contrast to cancer clusters as television entertainment, National Public Radio aired a "Talk of the Nation/Science" about cancer clusters on July 20, 2005. Ira Flatow, the reporter, interviewed three epidemiologists who were from California, Nevada, and Boston and had worked on cancer clusters (2005). For this broadcast, they talked about a reported cluster in Fallon, Nevada, but more generally they talked about the difficulty — with rare exceptions — of making definitive statements about the causes of clusters.

Journalists in areas with high rates of cancer have been drawn into the debate about environmental causes. For example, Michael Brown (1979) wrote a brilliant, award-wining book that tied the infamous Love Canal hazardous waste site to cancer, and he also tied cancer to toxic waste in a variety of other locations across the United States. But for most journalists, clusters are an environmental story that comes and goes. There may be little coverage for a year or more, and then a report that catches the media's attention is filed. When the media are attracted, they become intensely involved.

A final point of context regarding the media's concern over cancer clusters is that my colleagues and I wrote a book (now in its third edition) titled *The Environmental Reporter's Handbook* (Sachsman, Greenberg, and Sandman, 1988) to address the needs of journalists covering environmental stories. That book began with our asking reporters what topics they wanted us to cover. The answers led us to write more than 20 briefs about issues such as cancer clusters (treated in the first brief at the request of journalists), asbestos, and air pollution.

Six Policy Criteria: A Synopsis of a State Government's Dilemma

This section summarizes the advantages and vulnerabilities of a state decision to vigorously pursue cancer cluster reports. I note 36 points for policy makers to consider. Then, I use these to identify key policy drivers, including media pressure.

There is no simple go/no-go switch with regard to cancer cluster investigations. State officials must carefully weigh their options. Politically, if the governor, key members of Congress, or a state assembly presses for an investigation, then there will be one. If the commissioners of health and the department of the environment see the advantages to an investigation, then there will surely be one. If the commissioners do not, then there is likely to be some give-and-take among these leaders about a staged search that begins with verifying cases. Such a staged investigation allows the state to move carefully before committing hundreds of thousands to millions of dollars on environmental samples. At the local level, some mayors and members of Congress will press as hard as they can for an immediate and thorough investigation. Whatever the outcome, an elected official who presses for early resolution can portray himself or herself as decisive for the next political campaign. Local community groups can tip the balance in favor of an investigation if by putting pressure on the right people they can persuade

TABLE 4

Points state policy makers should consider
in pursuing reports of cancer clusters

Criteria	Advantages	Vulnerabilities
Reaction of elected officials and staff	There can be pressure from mayors who have a reported cluster and want to address community concerns. Members of Congress pressure federal agencies and state officials to examine the problem immediately. CDC is available to provide technical expertise. The staff of some state departments of health or environment may embrace the scientific challenge and moral imperative. Communicating the results to the public presents an opportunity to increase trust and government credibility.	Some mayors may bury their head in the sand to avoid the stigma. This situation presents a challenge to government departments not used to working together. Governments with limited resources will not be able to follow appropriate protocols or muster the resources, thereby creating an equity issue. The staff of some state departments of health or environment may actively or secretly oppose the use of funds for this purpose.
Reaction of nongovernment stakeholders	The local media will cover the issue and press the government for action. Local clinicians feel a need to resolve the issue on behalf of their patients. The local ACS chapter may be interested. Some local business will urge that the problem be investigated to avoid stigmatizing the area. Some local community and activist groups will put great pressure on elected officials and staff to perform analyses.	The local media will become bored with the topic if nothing important is found. Local clinicians are unlikely to know much about analyzing clusters. The local ACS chapter may not be willing to be involved. Some local business may be adamantly opposed, fearing that they will become caught in a cancer-pollution witch-hunt. It is likely that more affluent neighborhoods will get preference for studies, possibly leading to charges of environmental injustice. Activism may be misdirected, with other local environmental health issues ignored.

(Continued)

TABLE 4

(Continued)

Criteria	Advantages	Vulnerabilities
Human and ecological health	Health threats will be reduced by removing and containing any contaminants.	Public health will be hurt in the long run if no resolution is reached and the public believes that government cannot be trusted. Open space could be torn up in search of a pollution-type smoking gun that does not exist.
Economic costs and benefits	The sooner the stigma of cancer is removed, the sooner economic development will occur. Removing fear costs little in the short run.	The neighborhood will be hurt by the perceived stigma that is left. Investors will disengage from the area. Businesses that are falsely accused could leave or not make new investments. Limited monitoring and surveillance resources will be used with little chance of finding anything.
Moral imperatives	Government has the responsibility to investigate clusters to protect the community. Injured parties will be able to use the evidence in legal proceedings. Communicating the results to the public will provide reassurance that causes are being addressed.	Government has the responsibility not to investigate circumstances that will not lead to any resolution Pursuing clusters will create opportunities for unjustified lawsuits. Failure to adequately study and communicate results to residents could lead to loss of confidence in government, loss of economic value in the area, and serious psychological ramifications for people who are frightened.
Time and flexibility	A delayed response puts people and investments at risk.	Uncertain outcomes suggest that care must be taken before major resources are committed to investigations.

Note: ACS = American Cancer Society;
CDC = Centers for Disease Control and Prevention.

elected officials that a study is essential. The media, by relentlessly pursuing an investigation, can make it difficult for the state government not to pursue a study. Overall, from the perspective of state government, the major benefit of conducting an investigation is likely to be communication and the building of trust.

The major reasons for not conducting a study are primarily economic and scientific. Money for scientific investigations is scarce and is likely to come from funds that would have gone for other monitoring or surveillance programs. While hundreds of thousands of dollars are spent looking for the cause of a cluster in a tiny part of the state, cutting back on other monitoring programs to fund the search could inadvertently allow pollution to spread into a potable water supply or a disease to spread without being noticed.

A potentially distressing outcome is that a positive public health result can still mean a negative outcome for government officials. Negative information is much more salient than positive information (Slovic, 1993). If a cluster is reported, the fear is likely to penetrate deeply into the public mind. Even if that cluster is later found not to exist, the fear will linger. If the public does not like the process government uses to resolve the science, there will a loss of trust that will be hard to regain (McComas, 2003; G. Rogers, 1997).

Kasperson et al. (1988) show that once the science is presented, the risk is likely to be amplified or attenuated by social, institutional, cultural, and psychological processes, with the media playing a key role. Long, drawn-out scientific investigations of cancer clusters by state government may reassure some people, but most are likely to become distressed by continued coverage, even if the conclusion is that there is no threat.

Sociologist Alan Mazur (2004) argues that rather than provide true warnings, the media raise too many false alarms. While he did not include cancer clusters, in my experience these observations ring true for media reporting of cancer clusters insofar as there is a high probability of increasing fears in the process of making a story newsworthy.

Theories of Newsworthiness and Environmental Cancer Coverage

I have been interviewed by journalists hundreds of times. The results have been mixed, although I have gotten much better at being interviewed. Indeed, a colleague and I wrote an article suggesting how sources should interact with journalists (Greenberg and Chess, 1992) and have spoken more than two dozen times to scientists about the subject. After embarrassing myself many times, I began to understand that I nearly always inflicted the scars myself by making false assumptions about journalists and journalism. Journalists are not interviewing us to parrot whatever we tell them. They do not believe every word we say or every press release they read. They are skeptical. They want to verify what we say.

Journalism is a business, and journalists, not scientists, know what motivates people to read the newspaper, listen to the radio, or watch television. Public health importance is one of a set of key attributes that reporters take into consideration when they choose what to write about and where to place the story in the newspaper, magazine, or broadcast. But public health importance is newsworthy only if it is interesting and not boring.

Interesting almost always means that the emotions of the audience are stirred by the story, that it has personal significance for them and their loved ones. Reporters enhance interest by using sources, verbal symbols, photos, and other devices to engage the audience. Many excellent books and papers have been written about newsworthiness, the impact of the media on policy, and related topics. I suggest the following: Atkin and Wallack, 1990; Berridge and Loughlin, 2005; Dennis, 1990; Fortunato, 2005; Graber 2006; Hance et al., 1990; McCombs, 2004; National Research Council, 1989; Powell and Leiss, 1997; Protess, 1991; Sandman et al., 1987.

Controversy

My work on cancer has drawn more media coverage than anything else I have done because reporters find environmental cancer a remarkably newsworthy subject. Introducing controversy about facts and blame is a tried-and-true way of achieving instant newsworthiness. If there is a cancer cluster in a neighborhood or if a state has a high cancer rate, people, elected officials, scientists, and reporters want to know why. The scientist or government official who shoots from the hip and blames pollution from a nearby factory or at least hypothesizes that the factory could be implicated relieves the pressure from the public, at least temporarily. However, controversy arises because factory owners are unlikely to accept the blame or even the suggestion that they caused the problem. The accomplished reporter will bring together data about the factory, look for inside tips from a whistle-blower who remembers dumping something into the river or releasing something into the air at night, and interview parties on both sides. Stories that center on blame can become the media equivalent of a television soap opera. Watching a hundred Love Canal stories one after the other was like watching a soap opera. Every day a new episode was aired. After a while, even though the subject was deadly serious, we could not help but be distressed at what the media were doing — stringing out and amplifying the issue.

Anguish

If controversy is hard to find or cannot be sustained, then anguish is effective. There is nothing more riveting than seeing a forlorn parent whose child has died from cancer standing in front of a factory. Scientists deplore this kind of journalism because it implies a relationship that may be spurious. Journalists let the images speak for themselves. To use my favorite personal example of this technique, a major television network asked me to talk about a cancer study that I had recently completed. They wanted to do the filming in the field right across from the largest petroleum refinery in the Northeast. I knew what message the network had in mind, and it had little to do with my study, so I declined the invitation.

Novelty

Controversy and anguish are truly the best ways to enhance newsworthiness, but there are others. One is that stories that are new or bizarre are newsworthy. Dog does bite man, but if man bites dog, that is bizarre. With regard to cancer, everyone is familiar with the impact of smoking. But in 1986, former Surgeon General C. Everett Koop made national headlines when he focused on the cancer implications of chewing rather than smoking tobacco. Although this was not a new finding and smoking is much more likely to cause cancer than chewing, it was a new twist on an old theme and it was presented by a charismatic and energetic government official. The former surgeon general clearly was ahead of the curve in understanding the media.

Importance

This is another criterion of newsworthiness. But importance does not strictly mean public or environmental health significance as measured by deaths, morbidity, or prevention. Importance can be political, economic, or legal as well as environmental, and importance is local. An earthquake that kills 500 people in the United States will get a lot more media attention in this country than one that kills 500 people in Asia. Within the United States, hazardous waste sites that are claimed to cause cancer will get more coverage in the region where a particular site is located than across the country. For example, we studied nightly network news coverage of hazardous waste sites in the United States. The three networks were much more likely to cover sites that were near their main studios than those that were far away.

Proximity

In practical terms, this meant that New York, Los Angeles, and other major population centers were much more likely to have their hazardous waste sites on television than smaller sites in regions hours away from the nearest studio. In other words, spatial proximity makes a story more newsworthy. A common way to see this is as a main national story on a subject followed by a smaller story presenting the local version. For example, with regard to cancer, a new treatment, potential cause, or other important finding will merit a national story followed by another story that has a local perspective. Reporting a national story that involves a cancer cluster in the Midwest or West will be marketable to a New York audience if the reporters can refer to and recall a famous cancer cluster story in New York.

Timeliness

Journalists also recognize the competitive importance of timeliness. Not every important story is covered equally by all the media. One reason is that the media do not want the same story as their competitors. If someone has the information already, the story is unlikely to be on the front page. My favorite example is a press conference that had been scheduled so I could talk about a cancer study. Unfortunately, I had already talked to a reporter about the study the day before. He had a front-page story in the newspaper the next day. The press conference therefore drew 2 reporters to a room that could have held 300. I had allowed one newspaper to scoop its competitors, which I learned was inappropriate.

With regard to timeliness, coverage has a pattern. That is, newsworthiness changes over time. With regard to environmental stories, the initial coverage is the event itself — an accident that exposes someone, a reported cluster, or something else about which reporters will first focus on who, when, and where. The story will remain newsworthy if there is some controversy attached to it, if it is bizarre, or if it is geographically proximate. Stories that continue to be newsworthy after these attributes attenuate are rare and must have a long-term moral message. For example, the media like to remind people about Love Canal when they talk about new hazardous waste sites, and the same is true of cancer clusters. They introduce the new report and remind people about the previous one. Some stories are so memorable that they are worthy of anniversary stories.

The Role of the Spokesperson

The final way of commanding attention is to have the story delivered by a prominent speaker. The president of the United States can make a small story newsworthy and vice versa; a governor and a mayor can raise newsworthiness. A lower-level official is not going to receive as much media attention, unless he or she is known to be a fantastic speaker or is to present emotionally charged information, which the media have been told about.

Most stories do not feature prominent officials who dominate the story more than the information. When faced with an ordinary story with no star sources, the media try to balance sources. If there is only enough space for one source, then a reputable source, usually a government official, will be chosen. Notably, however, government officials have their own agendas, which include protecting the organization. In the case of a cancer cluster story, this is likely to translate into an assertion that the agency is taking the appropriate steps to address the possible cluster. If the reporter does not know what those appropriate steps might include, he or she may be misled. When there is space for multiple sources, journalists are likely to balance pro and con opinions. For example, if a cancer cluster is reported, a journalist may contrast a community representative who is convinced that the ABC Chemical Company is responsible with a company representative who denies the allegation. Depending on the newsworthiness of the story, different sources will be used to keep public interest alive.

The Role of News Pegs

A final point about the newsworthiness of environmental health stories is that the clear majority result from news pegs — releases to the media written by sources. My long-time colleague David Sachsman, whose doctoral dissertation was on environmental news coverage, tells me that 90 percent of environmental news in the San Francisco Bay Area came from sources, not from investigative work by reporters. News pegs give the source a distinct advantage in shaping the tone of a story. A good reporter will call someone else for an opinion, but unlike the original source, who had a great deal of time to think about and craft the news peg, the second source has little time to think before responding.

In the case of cancer clusters, reporters are frequently approached by residents and medical personnel who have a story to tell. Reporters are likely to contact the source of the pollution claimed by the residents or, if there is no obvious source of pollution to be blamed, the state government. All of these sources are likely to be blind-sided and respond hesitantly or not at all. Some media would not report the story before conducting their own investigation and checking with reputable sources. But others will simply write a story. Even if the cluster turns out not to exist or if no cause is found, the lasting impression is the cluster and the fear that it engendered. The media bear a large and difficult burden in determining how to report a cluster story.

A Salient Example

To summarize the factors that influence newsworthiness, I present my favorite example, which includes cancer but does not focus on it. On September 6, 1990, the U.S. Department of Health and Human Services (HHS) (1996) issued a press release, *Healthy People* 2000. Secretary Louis Sullivan lauded it as a key to setting the nation's health promotion and disease prevention goals for the next decade.

The 474-word press release was timely, yet there was relatively little coverage. The CBS nightly news had a 20-second story on September 6, but ABC and NBC had no coverage at all. We searched 38 daily newspapers for the period September 1 to December 31, 1990 (see chapter 7 for a longer discussion of content analysis). These newspapers had a daily circulation of 15.6 million, or 25 percent of the total circulation of all daily newspapers in the United States. Four of the newspapers (the *Wall Street Journal, USA Today*, the *Los Angeles Times*, and the *New York Times*) each had a circulation of over a million. Twenty of the 38 newspapers carried a story about the press release. Only 3 had more than one story. Thirteen of the stories were taken from the Associated Press story or from a wire service. Only one article made the front page.

Why was there so little coverage of a study that arguably was among the most important public and environmental health reports of the decade? Because the press release was devoid of any controversy. Because nothing about it was couched as a new issue or a new twist on an old issue. It talked about smoking, drug abuse, the need for exercise, and other behavioral changes. Reporters had covered these many times; the information was boring. It did not mention the fact that there had been substantial debate over including family planning and gun control in the report. These had been noted by the National Academy of

Science's Institute of Medicine Committee, which reviewed the report. The release had no data by region or state. There was no obvious opportunity for stories based on proximity. Moreover, it was presented by Louis Sullivan, not the first President Bush.

Marlene Cimons, the health and environment reporter for the *Los Angeles Times*, wrote the only first-day front-page story (page 4 in the *Los Angeles Times* and page A1 in the *San Francisco Chronicle*). She made this into a front-page story by introducing controversy. When I interviewed her about this story, she attributed her success with the story to years of casting a "jaundiced eye" at government health and environmental press releases. With four sources, her 780-word article reported Secretary Sullivan's theme that "we must assume more responsibility for our own good health and the health of others." She contrasted this theme with the views of Representative Henry Waxman (D-CA) and Senator Edward Kennedy (D-MA), who argued in favor of more funding for prevention and national health insurance.

Another plausible explanation was that there was too much competition for media coverage. It was during this time that Iraq invaded Kuwait (the first Gulf War), which certainly distracted the media. But, in fact, other health issues were covered in the mass media during this period. For example, during the week of September 6–12, 1990, when CBS had one 20-second story on *Healthy People 2000*, it had five stories (7 minutes and 50 seconds) on Kimberly Bengalis, a woman who allegedly got AIDs from a dentist; on steroid abuse; on murders in New York City; and on a new abortion law in Michigan. NBC had five stories (10 minutes and 10 seconds) on the war against drugs, AIDS, the marketing of cleaner automobile fuels, and misleading medical research. Each of these stories had a controversy or new scientific or legal information that was the basis for human interest.

I also interviewed someone who was involved in developing the story. He said that the federal government intended it to reach local and state health officials and did not consider it to be a public story. He also indicated that the government was probably pleased that there was so little coverage because the report could have been used to portray the administration in an unfavorable light.

In a Nutshell

Well-tested theories tell us that a newsworthy story gains and holds audience interest through conflict, unusual information, the consequence for the specific audience, the proximity to the event, the prominence of the person presenting the information, and the timeliness of the presentation. Cancer clusters are clearly newsworthy; there are few better environmental health stories. Cancer cluster stories are first about cancer. They involve conflict, despair, and other powerful emotions, and sometimes it can be alleged that a corporation was the cause. Clusters are unusual; that is, they rarely happen in a neighborhood. They can have major consequences for local residents (those living near the event), including physical and psychosomatic symptoms caused by stress and economic loss due to stigma. For television, a cluster can be made visual by showing distressed people or by featuring the alleged cause of the cluster on camera. The cause might be emissions from a smokestack or water discoloration, which is supposedly evidence of toxic emissions. The prominence of the presenter is a key variable in the newsworthiness equation. The media would prefer to have a governor, mayor, or health commissioner conduct media broadcasts. A lower-level scientist will not have as much newsworthiness. Overall, a cancer cluster is potentially a great media story.

Tales: Credible Science and Interacting with Key Interest Groups

This section summarizes my interviews with Arthur Upton and Daniel Wartenberg. Both are world-class scientists who, rather than work in a laboratory or behind a desk, chose career paths that have required continuous interaction with some of the most powerful government, for-profit, not-for-profit, and community interest groups in the country.

Upton and Wartenberg represent two important stages in the nation's efforts to understand the link between cancer and the environment. Upton helped establish the link through his research, and he played a prominent role in NCI's efforts to elevate the study of the environmental causes of cancer and establish a cancer prevention program. Wartenberg developed statistical methods for detecting cancer clusters and has been a bridge between concerned citizens and government officials. Both men represent the merging of scientific creativity with a deep sense of public responsibility.

Neither expected to play a prominent role in environmental cancer. Upton trained as a physician. But he became frustrated during his internship by how little he felt was being learned about the causes of disease. He said, "I was putting Band-Aids on people, and I really wanted to understand what caused them to become sick. I decided to go into pathology." After further training, he was invited to work at Oak Ridge National Laboratory, which is one of the U.S. Department of Energy's major sites for the study and production of nuclear weapons, energy technology, and environmental protection (see chapter 4). At Oak Ridge, he focused on the health effects of radiation. He notes: "The idea of being paid to do research at Oak Ridge was irresistible. We found that radiation caused cancer. We thought that some chemicals also caused cancer. We wanted to determine how radiation caused cancer compared to how chemicals might cause cancer. We didn't know enough about biology to determine the causes and point to credible solutions."

As part of his research at Oak Ridge, Upton served on NCI committees, for example, the Carcinogenesis Advisory Panel in 1972. He said, "I never expected to be director of NCI. But these things happen in life." Looking back at his nomination to be director in 1977, Upton notes that his work examined the environmental causes of cancer and that the nation had entered a period of focusing on problems caused by pollution: "I was unaware of it at the time, but the national concern about the environment and studies that suggested that pollution caused cancer was probably one of the reasons why they asked me to serve as director."

Environmental issues and prevention both became major issues during his tenure (July 1977 to December 1979). As Upton says: "John Bailar, the editor of the *Journal of the National Cancer Institute*, wrote an editorial that the cancer effort was not addressing the causes. He emphasized pollution. As a result, he [Bailar] concluded that the effort to win the war on cancer could not be successful."

Upon becoming director, Upton formed a task force to determine what was known and not known about environmental cancer and what NCI could do about it. As he puts it: "I wanted to be as inclusive as possible. The committee had members from NCI, ACS, NIH, and others. I regard that committee as the turning point of sorts within NCI. It led the institute from focusing primarily on cure to the study of causes and prevention."

As NCI and other parties delved deeper into environmental causes of cancer, it became clear to Upton that they needed to work together:

> I had no rigid ideas of who should do which tasks. For example, Dave Rall [director of NIEHS, 1971–1990] and I found that both of our organizations were duplicating analyses. They were studying a variety of chemical impacts, and we were studying cancer. We decided to turn over the entire job to NIEHS. We retained our epidemiological work, but they took over the toxicological analyses.
>
> When NIOSH [National Institute for Occupational Safety and Health] was formed, they had a limited budget. We worked with them to do tests that they could not. Given limited resources, we wanted to avoid duplication. It turned out reasonably well. There was a lot of collaborative work back then [and] not much in the way of turf wars.

I asked Upton how he became involved in NCI's antismoking programs. He remembers it this way: "[In 1978], I was summoned by Secretary Califano [Secretary of HEW under President Carter]. He wanted to be persuaded that money was being prudently spent." Upton and Don Frederickson, who was the head of NIH from 1975 to 1981, visited Califano: "During the briefing, I told the secretary about the recent paper by Richard Doll that showed a dose-response relationship between cigarette smoking and cancer. He was fascinated and wanted more."

Upton briefed Califano on several occasions and accompanied the secretary to Capitol Hill when Califano labeled tobacco "public health enemy number 1." The tobacco lobby tried to stop this effort. According to Upton: "They sent their henchmen, who told me that I had better cease and desist or they would take away my budget." Califano told Upton to continue these efforts: "The secretary took a powerful stance against cigarettes. I was telephoned by anonymous callers at night and told to back off. It was a powerful experience for me. The tobacco people played hardball. But the secretary was right; we were right to do what we did."

Upton strongly praised the former secretary. To provide some context, Joseph Califano was a Brooklyn-born attorney who first served under President Johnson. While secretary of HEW, Califano also advocated for childhood immunization and prevention of alcoholism, and he initiated the first surgeon general's report on health promotion and disease prevention.

Upton is a realist about NCI's spending priorities: "I'm not close enough to NCI any more to assess its priorities. When I got there, we focused on diagnosis and treatment. I helped change the focus. But you can't forget about those who have cancer. We want to rescue them. It is not a matter of this program is good and that program is bad. You try to make the best use of your resources, given your knowledge. When I got there, we spent only a tiny amount on diet and cancer. We've learned more, and now more is spent."

He noted that NCI's budget dwarfs that of ACS, EPA, IARC, and the various other organizations that have staked out an interest in cancer: "NCI has to make sure that the important areas are addressed in cooperation with these other organizations that have much smaller budgets for research."

Upton laughed when I raised the issue of the media. On the one hand, he praised the media, saying: "By and large, they were very helpful, knowledgeable, and supportive of our [NCI's] efforts to fight cancer." On the other hand, he recalled several instances where the media clearly sent a message to the public that contradicted what he [Upton] had indicated. For example, on March 28, 1979, one of the nuclear reactors at Three Mile Island near Harrisburg, Pennsylvania, suffered a partial meltdown of the core. The accident unfolded over the course of about five days. Upton was called in as an expert: "After studying the information, I told the public that there was very little fallout, less than they would get from background levels of radiation. I told them not to worry. If there were risks, they were small. I also told them, in response to a question, that there was no threshold for radiation and cancer risk. The next day a newspaper headline said 'Expert says no threshold.' This contradicted my message, which was intended to be reassuring. The local media also played to the public's fears. Good news doesn't sell."

Cancer clusters are never good news stories, except possibly for the reporters who write them. Daniel Wartenberg's status as one of the world's leading experts on cancer and other disease clusters evolved over the course of a decade and included several shifts in address and changes in academic focus. As Wartenberg puts it: "I love the outdoors, birds, plants, and animals. I wanted to study oceanography and ecology." After graduating from Cornell with a degree in ecology, he crossed the country to study oceanography at the University of Washington at Seattle. He found global warming to be a fascinating challenge and wanted to use mathematical models to study its implications. He then returned to the Northeast, where he worked with Robert Sokal of the State University of New York at Stony Brook in pursuit of his ecological interests. While at Stony Brook, he became involved in a local controversy over the spraying of Aldicarb (tradename Temik) on potato crops. This is an insecticide (nematicide) that is produced as granular powder, but also gets into groundwater. He said: "I was always interested in statistics, and I learned about spatial statistics in ecology. The more I studied public concerns about Aldicarb, the more I could see that we could use math and computers to address these concerns."

In 1984, he learned about the Woburn cancer cluster and moved to Boston to study at the Harvard School of Public Health. He became involved in the study of a cancer cluster in Randolph, Massachusetts, where 49 cancer cases were verified in one neighborhood, and with the challenge of cluster investigations: "Massachusetts had set up a [cancer] registry in 1982. We found some omissions in it. After correcting for errors, we found a cancer excess just where the community said it was. We obtained data from the environmental agencies. We looked at pesticides, gasoline leaks, and other possibilities. We couldn't explain the cluster."

During this period, Wartenberg became convinced that desktop computers should be used to study clusters: "At that time [1984], I started working on my home-grown GIS [geographic information system]. I did this because the community wanted and deserved answers. It took nine months from the time an analysis was requested from the state to get back the answers. I knew that we could be more responsive by putting the data into the computer on my desk. We have to be more responsive. I have been supported by CDC and others who see the value of this work."

I asked Wartenberg, as a leading scientist who works with the government and with communities, to describe the two or three key issues about cancer clusters that are most troublesome. He identified three. From the community perspective, the biggest issue is that what the community calls a cluster may not be one or is not likely to be demonstrated to be a cluster: "Most of the time, there are not enough cases to even justify a study. I try to explain to people that a statistical analysis will not reveal a significant cluster. Also, I try to explain response bias. By that I mean that people who are really worried will respond. Other people will not respond because they are worried about the impact on their property values. The results will not be valid. I explain these realities to community groups, and usually they understand that a study could actually hurt their case. But it's very frustrating for them."

With regard to state government, Wartenberg points to tension between the state and communities in that "the state is obligated to protect the confidentiality of people identified in the data. This causes a problem because the data are needed to respond to reported clusters." His solution is for the state to proactively conduct surveillance:

> We should monitor records and determine those areas that have clusters, instead of waiting for communities to do it. I don't buy the argument that we will not have enough money to investigate every cluster we identify. Depending upon the availability of resources, a priority list of the worst can be developed and investigated. If we do not conduct

proactive surveillance, there will be obvious inequities. Some states will not do any studies and will stonewall their populations. Other states will focus on those communities that have the strongest connections with state government. Either way, poor communities get ignored. Proactive surveillance and follow-up based on more objective criteria make it fairer to everyone. I would use birth outcomes, as well as cancer, for such investigations because births are more prevalent than cancer and the data are systematically collected.

From the scientist's perspective, he emphasized the challenge of maintaining objectivity: "People want us [scientists] to take sides. Even though the community has fewer resources than the state government and industry, I've been chosen as an expert by both because of my reputation. You cannot cross that line into advocacy and maintain credibility."

We concluded our conversation with a brief discussion of the media. According to Wartenberg, "It is a real challenge. They accurately report what you say but may put it into a context that contradicts your findings. You have to be careful with everything you say. Their agenda is to sell newspapers."

Tools and Tasks

Cancer cluster investigations use the tools of risk analysis (chapters 3 and 7). States that have performed cluster studies have a record of their research. Students with a scientific bent will benefit by reviewing these studies and answering questions about the study design and implementation. The CDC (1990) guidelines mentioned earlier can be used as the gold standard. Students should determine how many cases were reported, what kinds of diseases were involved, what efforts were made to verify the cases and to add others, and what methods were used to compare actual and expected numbers of cases. When environmental samples were taken (a rare occurrence), students can learn about exposure by reviewing what samples were taken and why.

Cancer cluster investigations are reported to the public. Students can learn about risk communication by studying what was reported. One task is to identify a health event that clustered in time, space, or time and space. These include cancer, HIV/AIDS, asthma, influenza, Lyme disease, and various others. The goal is to determine how the media covered the cluster. (See chapter 7 for a review of content analysis.) Students would also benefit from studying official reports by government agencies and seeing how these compare with the media coverage of the same reports. The emphasis should be on what the differences were and why they appeared.

3

Scientist Stakeholder Criterion

Gasoline Additives

Introduction

The first commercial automobile, a delivery wagon designed by Henry Ford, was shown to the public on January 12, 1900 (Brinkley, 2003). In 1950, the world had 53 million automobiles; 50 years later, it had 532 million, of which over 130 million were owned by U.S. residents — roughly one automobile for every two Americans (Brown, 2000; U.S. Bureau of the Census, 2006). The auto industry has a unique impact on the United States. A committee of the National Academy of Sciences (Committee on the Future of Personal Transport Vehicles in China, 2003) estimated that one out of every six U.S. workers makes, fixes, sells, finances, insures, licenses, drives, or maintains motor vehicles or their infrastructure.

Our awareness of cars is first based on style, comfort, and cost. Next, many of us sit in traffic jams and spend a good deal of time looking for a place to park, and so traffic congestion is a second issue. Indeed, for some people, the word "automobile" has become an oxymoron. Digging deeper into the issue makes it clear that Americans have become more aware of the relationship between oil imports and our national balance of payments problem and the impact of oil dependence on foreign policy (see also chapter 6).

The major purpose of this chapter is to identify a fourth automobile-related issue — the impact of gasoline additives on public health and the environment — and to use that issue to illustrate how scientists are stakeholders in policy. Most of us know little if anything about the additive problem and do not realize that there is a clear difference in how scientists, the public, and judges evaluate information on risk. We need to understand how science and scientists are involved (too often as pawns) in business-based policy debates.

Gasoline additives provide a good historical illustration of the use and abuse of science. The United States has been looking for an additive or additives to control engine knocking (the premature ignition of fuel) for almost a century and — more recently — to reduce detrimental emissions. The additives issue has become a source of major frustration during the past two decades. Briefly, the Clean Air Act (P.L. 91–604) passed in 1970, and subsequent amendments focused on outdoor air quality standards for particulates, sulfur oxides, carbon monoxide, nitrogen oxides, ozone, hydrocarbons, and lead (also see chapter 8). Emissions from motor vehicles have continued to contribute to unacceptable concentrations of ozone, nitrogen oxides, and hydrocarbons in urban areas, whereas emissions from factories have been substantially reduced.

Two decades after the passage of the Clean Air Act, as part of efforts to amend it, the U.S. Environmental Protection Agency (EPA) called for a new standard for motor vehicle fuels that would have required additives made from renewable resources, specifically ethanol, in order to control auto-related emissions. The National Corn Growers Association welcomed the proposal, but the petroleum industry objected, saying that ethanol and some of its by-products were hazards and that fuels such as methanol, propane, or compressed natural gas were superior alternatives (Gettinger and Hosansky, 1994). They offered to reformulate gasoline. After negotiations among EPA, state officials, oil and auto industry groups, gas retailers, suppliers of oxygenates, environmental organizations, and consumer groups, the federal government introduced the reformulated gas (RFG) program into the nation's most polluted cities in two phases.

The auto industry could meet this requirement through adding either 11 percent methyl tertiary butyl ether (MTBE) or 5.7 percent ethanol by volume. This change would reduce air pollution — summer smog, winter carbon monoxide, and year-round air toxins (Government Accountability Office, 2005; Nadim et al., 2000).

Bernard Goldstein (2001) believes that these changes in the Clean Air Act were implemented without a thorough evaluation of potential human health and environmental consequences and have, in general, burdened people who are sensitive to MTBE. I feel that his views, described in detail later in the chapter, are also true for many other decisions that have been made in this country. To name just a few, I can point to acid rain, alar, asbestos, and too many other cases where economic and political advocates have exploited science to bolster their preexisting positions. The public expects scientists to engage in unbiased fact-finding and draw conclusions based on these data. Unfortunately, too often the public does not get what it expects.

Theme: Gasoline Additives and Interconnected Policy Themes

Although gasoline additives have become a formidable public health and environmental challenge, the additive issue is deeply embedded in the more daunting problem of the nation's addiction to oil. I believe that the United States is going to be in and out of disruptive military, economic, and political crises associated with energy, especially oil, for the foreseeable future (see also chapter 6 on nuclear power). Hence, before focusing on gasoline additives, I will summarize two public policy themes that have led directly to the gasoline additive problem and other issues: (1) the building of suburban America and (2) national security and oil dependency.

After presenting these two themes, I will focus on gasoline additives, first presenting options and the role of science (much of which has been advocacy) and then examining two very different policy protocols for resolving the issue. The first is when government manages the issue and relies heavily on science, and the second is market-driven management and reliance on advocacy science.

The Building of Suburban America

Very few of us can remember a time when Americans were not in love with their automobiles. But in *Down the Asphalt Path: The Automobile and the American City,* historian Clay McShane (1994) points out that serious concerns about cars powered by the internal combustion engine existed in the early 20th century. Using the New York region as a case study, he concludes that the domination of personal travel by the automobile was both a political and a cultural triumph by the auto industry. The public at first wanted improvements in mass transit — that is, replacing horses with steam-powered vehicles and using fast trains on rail lines. But these options had problems, among them killing and injuring pedestrians, fear of boiler explosions, and strikes by operators. McShane (1994) concludes that the image of mobility promised by the automobile won out over safety and other concerns.

The growth of the automobile-based culture has been astonishing. Geographer Peter Muller (1981) calls the period since the end of World War II the "freeway era." The automobile, no longer a luxury, became essential for traveling to work, shopping, and socializing. Freeways were constructed to surround and connect metropolitan areas. Cities and towns without a freeway were bypassed and lost jobs and people.

Census data highlight the geographic impact of automobile-abetted suburbanization. In 1950, the U.S population was 151 million, and by 2000, it was 281.4 million. Demographia (2006) compared population growth in the core city and suburbs for 39 urbanized areas that had at least a million people in 2000. In 1950, 52 million (34 percent of 151 million) lived in these 39 areas, while in 2000, 120 million (43 percent of 281 million) lived in these large urbanized regions. The city-to-suburb shift within these 39 areas is striking. In 1950, 34.1 million (65 percent) lived in the core city and 18.1 million in the suburbs. In 2000, 81 million lived in the suburbs and 39.1 million (33 percent) in the core cities. In other words, the population in these cities increased 15 percent, while the population in their suburbs more than quadrupled.

In 1999, the Fannie Mae Foundation chose the top 10 influences on U.S. metropolises during the past 50 years and the 10 most likely influences during the next 50 as the theme for its annual housing conference. With regard to the period from 1950 to 2000, the most important factor was interstate highways and the dominance of the automobile. Most of the other 9 were directly or indirectly tied to the automobile. For example, de-industrialization of the central cities, urban renewal, racial segregation and job discrimination, and the urban riots of the 1960s all came about as the middle class gradually abandoned the central cities and moved to the suburbs. The loss of the middle class, in turn, reduced services and opportunities in the central cities, which along with the globalization of manufacturing led to widespread abandonment of job sites, unrest, and the creation of brownfields (see chapter 1). Mass production of suburban tract housing and enclosed shopping malls were also among the top 10. Finally, sprawl has occurred across the suburbs, especially in the South and West. Sprawl is directly dependent on highways.

Only 2 of the 10 arguably would have happened without Americans' love for the automobile. One of the two was U.S. government-financed mortgages to help soldiers returning after World War II. The second was the spread of air conditioning, which greatly helped expand the population in the South and West.

With regard to the next 50 years, respondents to the Fannie Mae survey and conference attendees emphasized growing disparities in wealth among Americans, most notably between the affluent suburbs that now control both federal and state legislatures and the central cities and older suburbs that have lost political power and financial resources. While new auto-dependent suburbs grow in numbers and wealth, the cities and older suburbs are scrambling to redevelop and provide basic public services (see chapter 1).

Much more has been written about the implications of the dominance of the automobile. For readers of this book, the relationship between driving, physical activity, and diseases that appear to be associated with a lack of exercise is a particularly important one. Brownson, Boehmer, and Luke (2005) summarized a good deal of the research, showing that miles traveled have increased but that physical activity has decreased. Notably, those who own two or more cars make about 7 percent of their trips on foot or bicycle. Those who own one car make about 12 percent of their trips on foot or bicycle, versus 37 percent among those with no car.

Less than half of the U.S. population meets the minimum national standard for physical activity developed by the Centers for Disease Control and Prevention. While the automobile is not the only cause of a lack of physical activity (Giles-Corti and Donovan, 2002; Lavizzo-Mourey and McGinnis, 2003), the fact that few people walk to work, to school, to shopping, or even to social events leaves them at a higher risk of diabetes, heart disease, arthritis, and other ailments.

The relationship between the automobile culture and obesity underscores the need to realign the fields of design, planning, and public health (Coburn, 2004; Greenberg et al., 1994). Readers interested in this topic should examine the August 2003 issue of the *American Journal of Public Health* and the September/October 2003 issue of the *American Journal of Health Promotion*, which contain more than 40 articles on this subject. The books by Frumkin, Frank, and Jackson

(2004) and Frank, Engelke, and Schmid (2003) provide excellent summaries and commentaries.

National Security and Oil Dependency

During the mid-1950s, elementary school children like me read the *Weekly Reader*, a newspaper that informed children about current events. I can still remember an issue that described the finding of massive new oil reserves in Texas, Louisiana, and the Middle East. These supplies, the *Weekly Reader* assured us, meant a growing and wealthy U.S. economy.

Half a century later, oil wealth has proven to be both a blessing and a curse. Indeed, recent issues of the *Weekly Reader* discuss the impact of oil drilling on wildlife preserves and the issue of global warming. The United States has only 4 percent of the world's population, yet it produces 25 percent of the world's wealth. With some exceptions, Americans are remarkably affluent compared with most of the rest of the world's population and are more affluent than previous generations of Americans. Cheap oil has played a prominent role in accumulating wealth. The downside is a growing dependence on cheap imported oil, which makes us as a nation vulnerable to economic shocks from rising oil prices and real or artificial shortages (e.g., 1973) and imposes uncomfortable long-term political, moral, and military challenges.

The United States is not the first country to become dependent on external energy resources. Former Secretary of Defense James Schlesinger (2005) points to Germany's seizure of Alsace-Lorraine after the Franco-Prussian War, Britain's early-20th-century efforts to secure Persian Gulf energy, and Japan's seizure of Southeast Asian energy supplies as examples of the military and political conflicts associated with energy dependency. U.S. dependency on foreign oil began during the 1970s. In 1950, U.S. oil consumption was 2.31 billion barrels annually, of which about 2 billion came from domestic producers. Consumption today is over 7 billion barrels a year, and the additional 5 billion barrels are imported (Puplava, 2005).

The challenge of ensuring an inexpensive supply increases as the economies of China, India, and other nations grow even as the world's supply of inexpensive oil resources declines. The United States is so dependent that we will be forced to pay whatever the market demands. Higher oil prices mean higher costs to grow food, to manufacture products, and to ship them, and therefore higher costs for consumers. People will have less money to consume durable products or to save for their children's college education. Buying fuel-efficient cars, adding solar panels, insulating homes, and other steps can help (see the interview with Connie Hughes in chapter 6).

But 50 years of investing in a way of life that depends on cheap gasoline means that trillions of dollars have been committed to a lifestyle that cannot be changed in the short run. Because of this dependency, the United States has made political decisions that are unpopular and not consistent with American political principles and committed the military to difficult and costly challenges. Moreover, the nation has been forced to swallow the fact that some of its oil payments are diverted to terrorists. Overall, we have become dependent on volatile politics in the Middle East, South America, Africa, and other locations with energy resources. Our economy can be pushed into a recession by events in other nations and by natural disasters like Hurricanes Katrina and Rita. About half of our large and rapidly growing balance of payments is oil related. In a nutshell, U.S. international policies are compromised by oil dependency in ways that are becoming abundantly clear.

We can drill in the Arctic, build nuclear power plants, add windmills in some locations, use solar panels, develop substitutes such as ethanol, and increase our oil-refining capacity. We can build more fuel-efficient cars, increase public transit, consider a gasoline tax, and try to convince people to insulate their dwellings and drive less. But our underlying problem is that for more than three decades, domestic production has not grown and our demand has. There is no quick fix. The United States, in the words of Schlesinger, is going to have to "live with various degrees of insecurity" (2005, p. 2).

Gasoline Additive Policies: A Past and Future History

Compared with the implications of cheap oil for the suburbanization of the U.S. population and the impact of oil on our foreign policy, the problem of gasoline additives seems at first glance like it would be easy enough to solve. But the country has been trying to solve parts of it, with limited success, for almost a century. The automobile engine derives its power from the explosive burning of gasoline mixed with air. The explosions drive a piston that turns a shaft. The rotation of the shaft is transferred through a series of gears and linkages to an axle and, ultimately, to the vehicle's wheels. Automobile engines produce pollutants and make a knocking sound when the gas ignites prematurely and does not fully combust.

This section begins with a discussion of lead, moves to MTBE and ethanol, and briefly examines other additives. In each case, I present some of the key scientific arguments and other information used to support and oppose the use of the particular additive.

TETRAETHYL LEAD (TEL). About a century ago, Thomas Midgely discovered that adding iodine to gasoline reduced engine knocking. In December 1921, however, he discovered the antiknock properties of TEL, which began to be manufactured in 1923 at a small operation in Dayton, Ohio. Notably, in 1925, Charles Kettering announced a new fuel called Synthol, a mixture of alcohol and gasoline that doubled gas mileage. However, oil companies preferred TEL because ethanol reduced vehicle dependence on gasoline by 20 to 30 percent. Public health experts from Harvard and Yale wrote to Midgely and others and contacted the

U.S. Public Health Service, expressing grave concern over the poisonous nature of TEL (Nadim et al., 2000; Rosner and Markowitz, 1985; Silbergeld, 1995).

General Motors Corporation (GM) adopted TEL as part of its upgrade of the Ford Model T. TEL was key to this marketing strategy since it permitted the use of high-compression internal combustion engines and a dramatic improvement in performance and fuel efficiency (Ozonoff, 1985). The auto industry rapidly became the corporate backbone of U.S. economic growth, and so the acceptance or rejection of leaded gasoline had profound implications for these industries.

GM contracted with DuPont and Standard Oil of New Jersey to produce TEL and easily overrode complaints about its toxicity, in part by characterizing opponents as hysterical and antiprogress (Silbergeld, 1995). Opponents argued that lead compounds were already known to be a slow, cumulative poison that should not be introduced into the environment. They argued that that even at low levels lead was dangerous to children (Silbergeld, 1995) and also said that because of industry's reckless disregard for the health of workers and the public, the federal government needed to step in to protect the nation's health. TEL opponents added that workers were not responsible for their own poisoning, an assertion that had been made by some pro-TEL experts. Opponents also asserted that the burden of proof should be on companies to prove that TEL was safe rather than on opponents to prove that it was dangerous (see the later discussion of the precautionary principle).

These scientific arguments were countered by people who seemed equally credible. For example, Dr. Emery Hayhurst, who was an industrial hygienist with the Ohio Department of Health and was funded by TEL producers, wrote in an unsigned editorial that appeared in the *American Journal of Public Health:* "Observational evidence and reports to various health officials all over the country . . . so far as we have been able to find out, corroborated the statement of 'complete safety' so far as the public health has been concerned" (Rosner and Markowitz, 1985, p. 347).

This gave readers the impression that public health professionals had determined that leaded gasoline posed no threat to public health (Rosner and Markowitz, 1985, p. 344). Frank Howard of the Ethyl Corporation invoked "industrial progress" as a response to opponents. He said that since at least a decade of research had gone into the effort to identify TEL, he called its discovery an "apparent act of God." He put the opponents on the defensive by casting them as reactionaries whose limited vision of the country's future could retard progress and harm future generations. Thomas Midgely, called the "Father of Ethyl Gas," explained that careless workers were responsible for any problems (Rosner and Markowitz, 1985, p. 348). He later applied pure TEL to his hands in front of a crowd to demonstrate its safety.

As is so often the case in risk-based disputes, a committee was formed to investigate further. The Ethyl Corporation announced that it was suspending the production and distribution of leaded gasoline until the scientific and public health issues were resolved. So the surgeon general of the United States was called on to organize a blue ribbon committee of the nation's foremost public health scientists to investigate leaded gasoline. These included David Edsall of Harvard University, Julius Steiglitz of the University of Chicago, C.E.A. Winslow of Yale University, and the American Public Health Association. Seven months later, the committee concluded that "in its opinion there are at present no good grounds for prohibiting the use of ethyl gasoline . . . provided that its distribution and use are controlled by proper regulations" (Rosner and Markowitz, 1985, p. 350). Robert Kehoe, who carried out the studies for the Ethyl Corporation, wrote: "As it appeared from their investigation that there was no evidence of immediate danger to the public health, it was thought that these necessarily extensive studies should not be repeated at present, at public expense, but that they should be continued at the expense of the industry most concerned, subject, however, to the supervision of the Public Health Service" (Rosner and Markowitz, 1985, p. 351). He concluded that his study failed to show any evidence of hazards.

But by 1970, evidence against TEL was accumulating. In the early 1970s, ethylene dibromide (EDB) was added to leaded gas to reduce the damage on car engines from lead. EPA banned the use of EDB in 1974 because it is a carcinogen and a mutagen. Catalytic converters were introduced in July 1974, and unleaded gasoline was required to be sold nationwide because lead fouls catalytic converters (Menkes and Fawcett, 1997). I believe that the fouling of catalytic converters was the last straw for TEL.

The phase-out of leaded gasoline began in 1973 as a result of the Clean Air Act, which was signed into law in December 1970 (Marshall, 1984; Nadim et al., 2000). This phase-out of leaded gasoline was accelerated during the Reagan administration, despite its initial efforts to hold up the rules and to remove controls on lead (Marshall, 1984). On March 4, 1985, EPA announced new restrictions on TEL in gasoline by mandating that refiners remove 90 percent of the TEL by the end of 1985. Prompted by two studies showing a strong statistical correlation between low amounts of lead and high blood pressure in adults, particularly white males, the total ban on TEL was moved up seven years from 1995 to 1988. According to EPA, previous studies reported that about half the lead in the blood of people surveyed came from gasoline. EPA estimated that the cutback would reduce cardiovascular disease among white males and probably black males as well. The agency reported that a 90 percent reduction in the use of TEL could prevent 1.8 million cases of high blood pressure and reduce the number of heart attacks in 1986 by 5,000 and the number of strokes by 1,000 (Sun, 1985).

Scientists and regulators realized that TEL from auto exhaust was getting into the brains of American children and causing neurodevelopmental impairment. This impairment was shown to increase the number of children with mental retardation, to reduce the number of truly gifted children, and to increase the number of adolescents with a propensity for violence and criminal behavior. As a consequence of the phase-out of TEL, the level of lead in Americans' blood rapidly declined by over 90 percent, a remarkable public health achievement.

A U.S. Senate Environment subcommittee proposed to ban the sale of leaded gasoline in urban areas on April 17, 1991, along with prohibiting the use of lead in many other products. Lead in gasoline was completely banned in 1995. But it had taken two decades, and every step presenting evidence along the way was challenged, sometimes with personal attacks on scientists.

METHYL TERTIARY BUTYL ETHER, OR MTBE. This compound is produced from natural gas or as a by-product of the petroleum refining process (Bohm and Hirschhorn, 1999; U.S. EPA, 1995, 2004; Menkes and Fawcett, 1997). At room temperature, MTBE is a volatile, flammable, colorless, water-soluble liquid. It blends easily with gasoline and has been used since the late 1970s as a substitute for TEL and to increase the octane rating in order to reduce carbon monoxide (Nadim et al., 2000). MTBE helped reduce ground levels of ozone by 18 percent during 1996, reduced the use of benzene, and reduced the levels of carbon monoxide in some large U.S. cities by 10 percent (Nadim et al., 2000).

Unfortunately, MTBE causes a strong reaction in some people and can seriously pollute water. MTBE leaks from underground gasoline storage tanks have been implicated in repeated incidents of groundwater contamination. MTBE creates taste and odor problems in water at very low concentrations, and it may be a carcinogen (McCarthy, 2005). Moreover, it has been detected in groundwater at low levels in thousands of locations across the country. MTBE is more soluble in water, has a lower taste and odor threshold and a higher transportation rate, requires more time to be remediated, and must be treated by more complicated and expensive technologies (McCarthy and Tiemann, 2005; Nadim et al., 2000).

Evidence to the contrary has been introduced by MTBE proponents. A study published in 1999 found that naturally occurring microbes can digest MTBE and convert it into less toxic by-products. There is evidence that this decay process is more effective in nature than it is in the laboratory ("Scientists Find MTBE Degrades Naturally," 1999; see also Medlin, 2000; and Tenenbaum, 2000). It may also be that MTBE is less of a health hazard when mixed with gasoline (Fiedler et al., 2000). Further, MTBE is arguably an improvement over TEL, but do two wrongs make a right? Yacobucci (2004) reports that replacing the energy lost from the production of MTBE would require about 2.7 billion gallons of gasoline or about 4.1 billion gallons of ethanol each year. California banned MTBE at the end of 2003, and there has been pressure to ban it everywhere except where states explicitly authorize it (McCarthy and Tiemann, 2005).

ETHANOL: THE HEIR? Henry Ford proposed to run his Model T on ethanol. Ethanol is produced from biomass (mostly corn) and is mixed with gasoline to produce a cleaner-burning fuel called "gasohol" or "E10" (gasoline blends with up to 10 percent ethanol). Ethanol serves as an oxygenate (to prevent air pollution from carbon monoxide and ozone), as an octane booster (to prevent early ignition or engine knocking), and as a gasoline extender (Yacobucci and Womach, 2002). RFG (reformulated gas) used in the Midwest contains ethanol. Most areas use ethanol to meet the oxygen requirements (Yacobucci, 2004). Now it is being considered for broader use as a replacement for MTBE.

Ethanol politics have been debated for decades. An EPA rule handed down on June 30, 1994, required that 15 percent of RFG use a renewable energy source such as ethanol. Oil interests were concerned (Gettinger and Hosansky, 1994), and ethanol has been hotly debated in Congress. For example, Archer-Daniels-Midland Co., a Decatur, Illinois–based agricultural company that makes 75 percent of U.S. ethanol, contributed to Democratic congressional campaigns, presumably to obtain congressional support, whereas congressmen from oil states, such J. Bennet Johnston, a Democrat from Louisiana (an oil state), said that requiring ethanol was a giveaway to special interests who produce ethanol from corn and that it would not provide cleaner air (Gettinger and Hosansky, 1994). Tom Harkin (D-IA) said that an ethanol mandate means that ethanol can compete with the oil industry, which benefits from its own heavy federal subsidies (Gettinger and Hosansky, 1994).

With regard to public health and the environment, ethanol does not persist in the environment as long as MTBE, but it appears to enhance the diffusion of benzene when ethanol-enriched gas leaks from tanks, and some of its by-products are hazardous (McCarthy and Tiemann, 2005). If the scale of usage were expanded, it might present groundwater contamination threats similar to those from MTBE (Harder, 2003). The main environmental advantages of ethanol are that it is a renewable, fully sustainable resource that is less polluting than gasoline. However, energy is required to produce corn and ethanol. The greenhouse gas from ethanol makes no net contribution to global warming. As a fuel, ethanol produces less carbon monoxide, oxides of nitrogen, and photochemical pollutants than gasoline. Gas pollutants are reduced both by replacing gas with ethanol and by the use of ethanol as an additive (Wheals et al., 1999). In January 2000, the California Air Resources Board, the State Water Resources Control Board, and the Office of Environmental Health Hazard Assessment found that an ethanol substitute for MTBE would have benefits in terms of water contamination and that there are no significant adverse impacts to public health or the environment from switching to ethanol (Nadim et al., 2000).

Will ethanol replace MTBE? Will science play a serious role in deciding the issue? The *National Journal* reported a decade ago that MTBE versus ethanol is a fight for market share, not a battle over science ("MTBE: 'Stealth' Lobby Stokes Fuel Additive Debate," 1997; Katz, 1994). In 1999, 87 percent of RFG contained MTBE. After state bans on MTBE were implemented, 46 percent of RFG nationally contained MTBE in 2004 (McCarthy and Tiemann, 2005).

OTHER CONTENDERS. Methyl cyclopentadienyl manganese tricarbonyl (MMT) is an antiknock agent added to gasoline ("Is Airborne Manganese a Hazard?" 1998; Joselow et al., 1978). MMT was developed by the Ethyl Corporation in the 1950s as a substitute for TEL. Now that corporation markets MMT as an alternative to MTBE, saying that MMT is cheaper and reduces tailpipe emissions of nitrogen oxides, which include precursors to smog. EPA estimated that if MMT were used in all gasoline, 5 to 10 percent of the population could be exposed to manganese, and in 1994, EPA denied Ethyl Corporation's request to introduce MMT into unleaded gasoline. EPA says that there are not enough studies on the potential effects of low-level, long-term exposure to manganese (Kaiser, 2003). However, in October 1994, a federal appeals court in Washington, D.C., ruled that MMT could be sold and that the Ethyl Corporation could test the additive while selling it and set no deadline for the completion of such testing (Landrigan, 2001). Joselow et al. (1978) wondered earlier why another substance whose safety has not been adequately assessed would be marketed, especially when occupational data show risk to workers.

Dimethyl carbonate (DMC) is a possible MTBE replacement that helps gasoline burn cleanly. A cheaper approach to making DMC was presented in 2002. The starting materials and by-products are nontoxic, and the process could be designed to tap the carbon dioxide present in oil fields instead of releasing it to the atmosphere, thereby helping to prevent the buildup of greenhouse gases (Service, 2002).

The U.S. auto industry began developing cars to run on methanol in the 1992 model year because of concern about meeting air pollution standards. Methanol burns more cleanly and has an octane rating of 100, compared with 93 to 97 for gasoline (Moffat, 1991). Methanol appears to be one of the most feasible substitutes for widespread use and for improving air quality. Because of its low atmospheric chemical reactivity, it could be effective in reducing the formation of photochemical smog and ozone (Russell, St. Pierre, and Milford, 1990).

The first President Bush included methanol in his clean air plan unveiled on June 12, 1989. Opponents criticized this plan as the "methanol mandate" and claimed that it was written by "methanol enthusiasts" who were wildly optimistic about the price and availability of natural gas as a feedstock for methanol production. The plan was also criticized because methanol may be more toxic to humans than gasoline. But EPA said that the toxicity risk was slight compared with methanol's clean air benefits. Another criticism is that cars using methanol will emit more formaldehyde (formed by the incomplete combustion of alcohol). Formaldehyde is a carcinogen and an irritant, and it forms ozone at five times the rate of gasoline. However, methanol is praised because toxic compounds from gasoline, such as benzene, should diminish with its use.

Oil companies argued that the formula proposed in the Clean Act Air Amendments (CAAA) was tilted toward ethanol and against other potential competitors, primarily methanol. The oil industry seems inclined toward methanol because it could enter and control the market since methanol is made primarily from natural gas, which the oil industry also produces. In 1990, President Bush dropped the aggressive alternative fuels program that would have mandated the production of about 1 million methanol-fueled cars (Pytte, 1990).

UNCONVENTIONAL OPTIONS. Two other obvious alternatives are to develop an alternative power source for the automobile, such as electricity, and to make the internal combustion engine as clean and as green as possible. The Federal Clean Car Incentive Program (FCCIP), which came out of the Clean Air Act of 1970, mandated that cars built beginning with model year 1976 have emissions that were 5 percent of pre-1968 levels. The auto industry argued against compliance. In 1976 Congress passed the Electric and Hybrid Vehicle Research, Development, and Demonstration Act to make and market clean cars. The auto industry lobbied against that as well. The FCCIP went forward, and such cars were designed and tested, but the auto industry did not accept them. In 1993, the Clinton administration announced the Partnership for a New Generation of Vehicles, in which the government worked with the auto industry to develop a car that would get up to 80 miles per gallon of gasoline and emit few pollutants (Marshall, 1993).

Clean air will continue to be on the national radar (McCarthy, 2004, 2005). Because of MTBE, clean water has been added to the fuel additive balance sheet. Whether the replacement is ethanol or another additive, will decision making be more informed by credible science than the debates about TEL and MTBE have been?

Six Policy Criteria: A Synopsis of Policy Options

Earlier I stated that the issue of gasoline additives illustrates two decision-making paths: (1) one that would be part of a federal-government-led effort, which I label "centralized," or (2) another managed by world "market" forces. The first would depend on strong science and economic analyses, preferably evaluated by the National Research Council (NRC) of the National Academy of Sciences. The second would have a less comprehensive scientific program, and advocacy science would play a major and continuing role in formulating policy.

The centralized option involves having a government-led body of scientists consider the realistic options for dealing with the issue. That body of scientists would include participation from EPA, the Department of Energy (DOE), and state and local officials who have worked on the issue, but most of the participants would be credible university-based scientists. Business and other advocacy interests would provide testimony to the centralized group, but otherwise would play a relatively small role in the deliberations and the formulation of recommendations to the federal government. The body would have the resources to commission comparative risk analyses, economic impact studies, and others as required. The objective would be to provide Congress and the Executive Branch with information that they can trust, including detailed descriptions of uncertainty.

The market-based alternative involves further subdividing the additives problem into stovepipes for EPA, DOE, and other stakeholders. Some of the information presented to decision makers would be based on objective science, but other parts would be driven by stakeholder interests.

The next section summarizes the advantages and vulnerabilities of the centralized process of vigorously pursuing a solution to the fuel additives issue that is flexible enough to accommodate national energy policy decisions. In table 5, I note 30 points that policy makers should consider.

TABLE 5

Thirty points that policy makers should consider in deciding on a centralized or market-based approach

Criteria	Advantages	Vulnerabilities
Reaction of elected officials and staff	It could garner support from members of Congress who want a solution that will not fail a few years later and that appears not to bow down to vested interests. Support could come from EPA, CDC, and DOE staffs who favor a comprehensive solution that includes all their input. Support could come from state legislators and urban mayors who want a solution that will reduce air and water quality problems and keep the price of gasoline down.	There could be opposition from members of Congress and state governors who feel that a thorough analysis will undermine their regional or industry-based market. Some state officials could worry that they will lose local control of the issue. Opposition could come from members of government who oppose centralized government efforts to solve any problem that they consider solvable by market forces with a minimum of government interference. The staff of some government organizations may feel threatened by working as part of an interdisciplinary team that would weaken their control over the issue.

TABLE 5
(Continued)

Criteria	Advantages	Vulnerabilities
Reaction of non-government stakeholders	National business interests would support the concept as a way of fixing the confusing current situation in which business must be prepared to use a variety of motor vehicles and fuels. Strong support from eminent scientists is likely. Strong support from environmental advocacy groups and from proponents of environmental justice is likely if they are persuaded that their issues will be part of the analysis.	There would be strong opposition from business interests that feel their control of the issue would be lost. It is unlikely to be much of a media story unless a link to vested interests or specific cities can be made part of the story. There could be opposition from businesses fearing that centralized government management would stifle innovative technology-based solutions. Some activist and local community groups fear that a centralized analysis and solution will favor powerful business interests.
Human and ecological health	Solving the problem will reduce air quality health threats. Potential water quality problems could be reduced by considering them before a decision is reached. There could be an opportunity to integrate energy balance, ecological, and human health issues in a comprehensive way. There could be strong support from scientists who feel that new solutions such as ethanol will not be carefully scrutinized unless a centralized panel is involved.	Public health efforts will be hurt in the long run if no resolution is reached and the public believes that government cannot be trusted. A centralized process could produce a bad solution that harms selected populations and places.
Economic costs and benefits	The integration of scientific and economic impact analyses will produce solutions that decision	Opposition could come from those who believe that a centralized solution will justify

(Continued)

TABLE 5
(Continued)

Criteria	Advantages	Vulnerabilities
	makers can use to balance the costs and benefits of proposed options.	increasing fuel taxes to support the solution and protect businesses that adopt the government's solution from legal action. There will be fear that a government-based process will lock in a costly solution and not be open to innovative improvements. Midwest corn growers and oil companies have a lot to gain and lose and may feel threatened.
Moral imperatives	Government has the responsibility to comprehensively address this issue, which has been a problem for more than half a century. Government has the responsibility to protect the urban poor, who are disproportionately impacted by high amounts of air pollution and high gasoline prices.	Government has the responsibility not to take charge of an investigation, especially if its motivation is to merely delay the need to take action. Government should not engage if it believes that the marketplace and state government can resolve the issue.
Time and flexibility	A centralized, science-based solution has a better chance of surviving and being designed to accommodate technological innovations.	Science-driven efforts often take time, which leaves investments at risk.

Note: CDC = Centers for Disease Control and Prevention; DOE = U.S. Department of Energy; EPA = U.S. Environmental Protection Agency.

I believe that many actions that precipitate unintended negative consequences can be anticipated. I also believe that advocacy science is not trustworthy, even if the science is sound, because it is not interdisciplinary: That is, it is focused on promoting an outcome and so excludes possible weak points in an argument. My preference is for the centralized analysis of the gasoline additive problem and for that analysis to be part of a broader analysis of energy policy.

Frankly, too many avoidable bad decisions have been made in formulating and implementing gasoline additive policies. The burden of responsibility should be on the federal government, not the states, some of which cannot formulate policy on this problem even though other states appear more able and motivated to do so than the federal government. However, the federal government is clearly in the best position to set the agenda and organize groups of qualified scientists to examine the health, ecological, economic, and social consequences of this issue. Having stated my preference for a centralized, science-driven process, I do not expect it to happen for many of the reasons noted in table 5. Hence, I will settle for a systematic and thoughtful effort to weigh the public health and eco-logical implications of additives.

Later in the chapter, I will present the views of Bernard Goldstein on gasoline additives in the larger context of the scientific analysis of risk. In preparation for that presentation, the next section compares how scientists, the public, and the courts consider and weigh evidence.

Theories of Weighing Evidence

Policies to protect public health and the environment sometimes fail and even exacerbate the problem they were intended to solve and create new ones. Basing policy on evidence derived from good science should lead to better policies. Yet because scientific uncertainty is common, politics, economics, public percep-tion, ethics, and other factors described and illustrated in this book normally drive decisions. Gasoline additives illustrate how uncertainty has several times probably led to less than the best choice. Here, I show how scientists weigh evi-dence, how the public weighs risks, and how judges try to mete out justice when the scientific information is uncertain and disputed.

The Scientists' Perspective

In 2001, under the auspices of the Society of Toxicology and the College of Chemical Pharmacology (Gray, Baskin, et al., 2001), a group of scientists devel-oped a list of seven principles to guide the interpretation of scientific informa-tion. These scientists were all toxicologists, and they focused on data developed from laboratory studies that used animals (see chapter 7). I use these seven prin-ciples to characterize a scientist's perspective on weighing evidence.

RIGOR. A good study has clear and answerable research questions, and it describes data and methods in detail. Scientists pride themselves on keeping abreast of the best data-gathering and analysis methods. Hence, a rigorous study includes these best practices or explains why they were not used. Any limitations should be described, and their implications noted. Laboratory studies should follow the codes of good laboratory practices, and a good epidemiological study follows accepted protocols for retrospective and prospective studies (see chapter 7 for descriptions of these tools). Overall, a scientist will trust a study that appears to be rigorous more that one that does not appear to be. Sometimes a sound study appears to be less rigorous than it really is because the authors have not provided enough detail about data and methods; this is unfortunate but true for some science-based evaluation.

POWER. If everything else about a study is equal, more samples are better than only a few. In chapter 7, I describe why we have more confidence in public surveys of 1,000 people than in surveys of 500 or 250. When I read a human or laboratory study, I try to determine whether it was based on so few cases that it could not possibly detect the effect for which it was designed to look. For example, a laboratory study with only 25 to 50 animals can rarely find a significant risk of 10 percent or less.

CORROBORATION. Scientists feel more confident when a result has been confirmed by multiple researchers.

UNIVERSALITY. If the same effect or a similar one is observed in multiple species, if a similar dose produces the same response or a similar one, and if the result is observed across different routes of exposure (skin, inhalation, digestion), then scientists have more confidence in the result.

PROXIMITY. When similar effects are found in a species taxonomically similar to humans, at similar doses, and through similar routes of exposure, then the results will be considered more credible.

RELEVANCE. If scientists can attribute the effects to metabolic, damage and repair, or other specific biological mechanisms, the evidence will be more convincing.

COHESION. In the strongest case, all the evidence points to a biologically plausible explanation.

A Recent Illustration of the Use of the Seven Principles

Overall, these seven somewhat overlapping principles would guide unbiased scientists to give more or less credence to evidence. The Harvard Center for Risk Analysis (Gray, Cohen, et al., 2004) applied these criteria to bisphenol A (BPA), which is a plastic monomer. A monomer is a single molecule that can combine with identical or similar molecules in a process known as polymerization. BPA is used in baby bottles and many other food containers. If it is a hazard, it could pose a substantial risk because its use is so widespread. But some argue that BPA is also an artificial estrogen and that even at very low concentrations, it can cause toxicity in the form of adverse reproductive development.

The Harvard panel reviewed 19 laboratory studies of rats dosed with BPA, examining differences in the type of animal, the number of animals, the method of applying the dose and testing for effects, and confounding influences such as body weight. The panel concluded that BPA is not a significant estrogenic agent with impacts on the male reproductive tract. One persuasive piece of evidence was that BPA did not demonstrate the expected effects of estrogens, such as causing cancer at high doses. Second, the two strongest multigenerational studies did not show effects.

The purpose of summarizing the BPA example was not to agree or disagree with the evaluation, but rather to underscore the principles that these well-known scientists applied. Implicit in these seven principles and their use in the BPA study is the culture of science, so-called scientific rational thinking, which is notably different from the thinking of the public, the mass media (see chapter 2), and business (see chapter 4) and the legal processes of government (see the subsequent discussion in this chapter and in chapter 8).

I highlight these differences by comparing what scientists and the American people rely on when they weigh evidence (Krimsky and Plough, 1987). Scientists trust authority and expertise and weigh accumulated evidence and scientific theories. By contrast, the public trusts process, notably widespread public participation, peer groups, and traditions. Hence, I am speculating that a public response to the BPA expert panel would be that it was not representative of the public and that the evaluation criteria were too narrow. I think most people would rely more on people they already trust to advise them than they would a panel of unknown experts.

A second difference between scientists and the general public lies in what they think constitutes evidence. Scientists try to narrow the focus of evaluations, to reduce the scope of the analysis, in this case to the reproductive impact of BPA. The general public would likely look for any evidence that this substance or any relatively similar substance had proven to be or could prove to be a reproductive or any other kind of hazard. If some other plastic monomer had proven to be a problem, that evidence would be introduced.

Scientists normally do not seriously consider anecdotal information. The public, however, looks for and embraces it. While scientists look for consistent and universal findings, the public looks for the rare problem that could hurt someone. In this case, several studies did show that BPA introduced risk. For some people, that is enough evidence to suspect and even ban a product.

A third difference between scientists and the public is the universality of findings. Scientists typically review research findings and summarize the results as the probability that the general population will suffer an illness or injury or will die. The members of the public are not interested in the probability that someone in the general population will contract a disease or die. They want to know their risk and the risk to their family and friends. Bridging this difference is not only incredibly difficult, it is sometimes not possible.

A fourth point of difference between scientists and the public deals with uncertainty. Scientists tend to focus on what is known, not on what is not known. The public trusts negative information more than positive, and it will typically not be satisfied with findings that do not give a great deal of weight to what is not known. In other words, uncertainty is bad and increases the perception of risk.

Finally, facts about the BPA study not considered germane by scientists would raise public concern. The study was funded by the American Plastics Council, and some panelists were employed by business. Funding by business and the presence of business representatives on the panel were enough to convince some people that the study was unduly influenced by business and that the results were biased.

In short, the American public is not enamored of linear, reductionist, and expert-based decision-making processes funded by those it considers to have a vested interested in the outcome. It wants the opportunity to participate and not have the scope limited to discussions of quantitative, scientific results.

Outrage Factors and the Public

Peter Sandman (1989, 1993), a former colleague at Rutgers, has argued that people's evaluation of risk has much to do with what he calls "outrage" and relatively little to do with scientists' evaluations of evidence. He has described more than 20 factors that cause people to evaluate some hazards as high risk and others as low risk. (See also Lowrance, 1976.) I will briefly describe nine of them because they show the remarkably different ways experts and the public evaluate risk.

IMPOSITION/COERCION. A risk that is freely undertaken is considered less risky than one that is coerced and imposed. I, for example, played football, really enjoyed it, and did not worry about the consequences until I hurt my knee and needed surgery. Yet I refused to ski, which always seemed very dangerous to me. Skateboarding seems incredibly dangerous to me as well. However, I have friends who think football is brutal and skiing is art on snow. Some of my students love skateboarding and tell me that it is a lot safer than being tackled. One person's fun is another's coerced or imposed hazard.

LACK OF CONTROL. Controlling a hazard makes it seem less dangerous. I worked as a carpenter when I was in college, and that required climbing up and down ladders. I spent a lot of time setting up the ladders and never trusted anyone else to help me or even to support the ladder when I was on it.

INEQUITY. People take a severe view of hazards that disproportionately affect a limited number of people or places, especially if those places do not receive much benefit, did not volunteer to host the hazard, or have little control over it. The ongoing controversy over the storage of high-level nuclear wastes produced for

military uses is a good example. The state of Nevada has argued that it is dangerous to store nuclear waste in Yucca Mountain and that it is fundamentally unfair
for Nevada to bear the burden of this legacy (Committee on Technical Bases for
Yucca Mountain Standards, 1995; see also chapters 4 and 6).

LACK OF FAMILIARITY. Things that are familiar are considered less risky than
those that are not. A new facility that will manufacture an unheard-of chemical
product, a multisyllabic pesticide, or a genetically modified organism will likely
frighten people, leading to imagined horrors. By comparison, an existing but
poorly run facility that has already caused ecological damage and polluted the
local river is familiar and hence less likely to scare people.

MEMORABILITY. Some hazards leave indelible negative images. The mushroom
cloud is the classic case. Arguably, the history of nuclear power in the United
States might have been different if people mentally connected it with lighting
homes or powering businesses and holiday decorations rather than a mushroom
cloud from a bomb that wiped out five miles of Hiroshima and killed tens of thousands of people (see also chapter 6).

CONCENTRATION. Fear increases when many people die or are injured in a confined space or over a short period of time. The events of September 11, 2001, air-
plane crashes, and other major concentrated hazard events generate much more
public outrage than automobile accidents, drug overdoses, and other routine
hazard events spread out across time and space. The concentrated event is likely
to be called a catastrophe and be on the front page of the newspaper. The diffused
event is ignored as not newsworthy.

IMMORALITY. Child abuse, terrorist attacks on civilians, and deliberately polluting a potable water supply are considered evil actions, irrespective of the actual
risk associated with them. It almost does not matter that other hazards might be
far riskier or that the costs of controlling these immoral hazards may be very
high. For example, those who oppose the use of animals for laboratory testing
consider the practice immoral, irrespective of any benefits that arise in the form
of new drugs or surgical practices.

LACK OF CANDOR. People intensely dislike being lied to or deceived. If the mes-
senger cannot be trusted, then the message is not believable. DOE has had a serious credibility problem, which is the legacy of a secretive mission that did not
allow it to reveal its activities (see chapter 4).

HUMAN-MADE RISKS. Survey research shows that the public considers hazards
created by people more risky than natural hazards that scientists consider lesser
risks. A hurricane, an ice storm, an earthquake, or a flood is rated as less

distressing than an oil spill, a hazardous waste site, or a nuclear power plant. Somehow, natural hazards are perceived as uncontrollable, perhaps acts of God.

A DIFFERENT REALITY. Arguably, these nine outrage factors are a distraction from scientific reality — that is, some would argue that they lead people to make bad, irrational choices. However, I do not think that they are a distraction. They are, in fact, a different reality observed in hundreds of studies in scores of countries around the world and across ethnic, racial, age, and religious groups; men and women; and educated and uneducated people. These outrage factors are psychologically driven mental guides that people use consciously and subconsciously to weigh evidence and cope with stress.

For the policy maker, it is political suicide to ignore major public outrage. Both scientific-based studies of risk and perceptions are valid data; both have to be respected.

The Legal System

Scientific risk analysis also lives uncomfortably alongside and within the legal system. This reality frequently surfaces. For example, Robert Fri (1995), who chaired the National Research Council committee that examined the scientific basis for controlling high-level nuclear waste, noted that science could not resolve the regulatory questions DOE faced. He asserted that science could provide a framework and a starting point for debate. Sometimes, he added, scientists should note that they have nothing to say. Fri (1995) ended by saying that science cannot shield elected officials from making controversial decisions. Yet, in fact, scientific uncertainty is exploited by elected officials who do not want to make unpopular decisions. Do we not know enough about global warming, acid rain, and many other hazards? Or by continuing to study them, are elected officials delaying a decision until they are out of office?

AGENT ORANGE. The courts cannot duck the issue. For example, during the Vietnam War, a herbicide called Agent Orange was sprayed on the Vietnamese jungle to strip vegetation from areas where the Vietcong and North Vietnamese troops could hide. A decade later, American troops brought a class-action law suit charging that the herbicide caused them and their progeny to develop cancer, birth defects, and other health problems.

This complex case had numerous rulings. Here, I point to one part of the trial. Judge Jack Weinstein, a senior federal judge in the Eastern District of New York, dismissed all of the evidence derived from laboratory animal studies and industrial accidents (Schuck, 1986; see also Weinstein, 1995). In essence, he dismissed standard scientific practice — the methods used to calculate the impact of low-dose exposures when there are no data on such exposures. The judge did not dismiss scientists; that is, he did not toss out science because he did not trust scientists. This actually had become a major issue during that period because of widely publicized scientific misconduct (Jaroff, 1991). Rather he accepted only human data that reflected exposure at doses that the troops had been exposed to, which constituted very little information indeed. Whether the judge was right or wrong in this famous case is surely debatable. But judges, in general, struggle with the role of scientific evidence. Decades ago, I worked with colleagues from the American Arbitration Association to create a science court. It did not materialize, but courts have become more sensitive to scientific evidence or at least to expert qualifications.

BENDECTIN. The most famous modern case is *Daubert v. Merrell Dow Pharmaceuticals* (1135 Ct. 2786, 1993). The case dealt with Bendectin, a pill used to control morning sickness, and the issue was whether it caused birth defects in humans as well. The case reached the U.S. Supreme Court, which created guidelines for federal judges to use in deciding whether expert evidence was "relevant" and "reliable." The four major guidelines were as follows:

1. The theory or method has been tested or could be tested.
2. The theory or method has been peer reviewed or published.
3. The likely error associated with the method or theory is known.
4. The theory or method is generally accepted.

These guidelines seem like perfectly reasonable standards by which to rate a study from strongest to weakest: On a scale of 1 to 10, a good study might get a 9, and a weak study, a 2. However, the courts were instructed to act as gatekeepers; that is, studies that flunked the test could be ruled inadmissible and denied to juries. Scientists clearly do not work that way. Peer review is an imperfect process (Patton and Olin, 2006), but scientists read studies and assign whatever value they think is appropriate. I might not seriously consider every study I read, but I at least read it before I reach that decision. The courts mete out justice, and perhaps judges and juries therefore require a different level of proof than scientists. But should judges exclude evidence, especially when they are not necessarily familiar with all the methods scientists use?

A special issue of the *American Journal of Public Health* (American Public Health Association, 2005) included more than 20 articles that primarily criticized the Supreme Court for the *Daubert* decision and its progeny. The net effect, assert the authors, is to erode the ability of federal agencies to weigh all the evidence by excluding studies that they do not like and hence to allow private interests to exclude research.

At the heart of this controversy is the question of what we know, how we know it, and how much confidence we can have in this knowledge. On paper, the *Daubert* criteria are a simple road map; but if they are used by inexperienced gatekeepers, there is no doubt that both unbiased scientists interested in advancing knowledge and the public's interest in protecting public health and the environment will be compromised. Personally, I think *Daubert* frightens both business and environmentalists (see the comments by Dr. Goldstein later in this chapter).

In concluding this section, it is fitting that I quote the opinion of the D.C. Circuit Court with regard to EPA's phase-out of TEL:

> Contrary to the apparent suggestion of some of the petitioners, we need not seek a single dispositive study that fully supports the Administrator's determination. Science does not work that way; nor, for that matter, does adjudicatory fact finding. Rather the Administrator's decision may be fully supportable if it is based, as it is, on the inconclusive but suggestive results of numerous studies. By its nature, scientific evidence is cumulative: the more supporting, albeit inconclusive, evidence available, the more likely the accuracy of the conclusion. Thus, after considering the inferences that can be drawn from the studies supporting the Administrator, and those opposing him, we must decide whether the cumulative effect of all this evidence, and not the effect of any single bit of it, presents a rational basis for the . . . regulations. (*Ethyl Corporation v. EPA*, 541 F2d, p. 1, 37–38 [1976])

Tales: Credible Science and Interacting with Key Interest Groups

This section summarizes my interview with Bernard Goldstein, former head of EPA's Office of Research and Development and most recently dean of the Pittsburgh School of Public Health. According to Goldstein, "MTBE should never have been marketed before extensive analysis. It became such a big environmental risk and policy issue because MTBE became one of the largest products in commerce. It was 10 to 15 percent of winter-time gasoline in much of the country. The number of exposed people went from almost no one to over 100 million."

Goldstein described the evolution of the problem in this way:

> The goal was to reduce carbon monoxide emissions by adding oxygen to gasoline. High levels of carbon monoxide can cause problems for people with angina, which is a narrowing of blood vessels. A few locations, such as the tunnel entrances from New Jersey to New York City, violated the carbon monoxide standard during rush hour during the winter months. But few people walk or run at these high carbon monoxide locations. In contrast, many people are sensitive to MTBE. They are bothered by the odor and develop headaches, nausea, and other symptoms. EPA neglected to take these facts into account. In contrast, I am much more comfortable with ethanol because we have been exposed to it for centuries.

He then further elaborated on his frustration with the superficiality of the research: "All they had to do was wait. The carbon monoxide standard would have been met by the new automobile fleet. EPA did a classic animal study on MTBE. It showed some evidence of cancer risk. But it was ignored, despite the fact that almost everyone in the country was exposed. U.S. businesses spent hundreds of millions of dollars to adjust to MTBE in the fuel. The water pollution problem was only part of this mess. MTBE should never have been marketed without a thorough analysis."

Using Alaska as an example, Goldstein pointed to some exceptions to the use of MTBE: "Alaska got a waiver. Anchorage [and its environs] has a population of about 250,000. Nineteen thousand signed a petition saying that they were made sick by MTBE. The standard would have been exceeded once or twice a year in downtown Anchorage. Few would have been exposed. After much debate, Alaska was granted a waiver. Alaska was an exception to act first, think later."

Was MTBE an aberration, or can we expect more MTBE snafus? Goldstein views MTBE as part of the evolution of policy, which he hopes and strongly believes should be more strongly grounded in science.

> The specific failure was that MTBE was not caught by TOSCA [the Toxic Substances Control Act]. TOSCA was written to control new chemicals. TOSCA does not work well for pre-existing chemicals. MTBE was known for decades. Also, TOSCA did not adequately consider the amount of exposure. This brings up the "precautionary principle." As you know, I have said that we need to be cautionary about the precautionary principle. The principle is that we should err on the side of protecting public health. What this means [is] that laws, rules, regulations, and orders should place the burden of proof to prove safety, not to prove harm. For the precautionary principle to function requires openness, transparency, and public involvement.

Goldstein used the revisions to the Clean Air Act to illustrate these principles:

> Before 1990, EPA had to list hazardous air pollutants. So it listed benzene, mercury, and the rest of the small usual list. The provisions for listing were too cumbersome for EPA. So the agency changed from a risk-based to a technology-based approach. Congress told EPA to list 186 chemicals. To remove a chemical from the list, EPA had to prove that these were not harmful. Then they applied this technology-based standard. We were supposed to apply cost-benefit analysis, but there was too little [in the way of] benefit data, except for substances such as benzene. To avoid the cost, industry can switch to chemicals that were not on the list. But we knew little about many of these, which is very troubling. I worry about wide use of chemicals that we do not know much about. There is nothing easy about getting this right. We need to spend more time thinking through consequences, trying to anticipate unintended ones.

We briefly discussed the *Daubert* decision. Goldstein, like me, believes that "the courts are all over the place on this. Everyone is threatened by what it can do to their positions."

We ended our conversation by talking about his interest in environmental public health. Goldstein was born in the Bronx and spent much of his distinguished career in New York and New Jersey, where he chaired departments, built a graduate program, and started a school of public heath before moving to Pittsburgh to become dean of the School of Public Health. He noted:

> I was trained as a physician at NYU [New York University]. I joined the
> U.S Public Health Service and was assigned to work on air pollution in
> Los Angeles. Later I returned to NYU. I was interested in the health
> effects of air pollution. Norton Nelson was at NYU, but I did not meet
> him until I returned to NYU. I began to work with him on environmen-
> tal health problems. I learned toxicology and epidemiology. I came to
> New Jersey to start an environmental and community medicine depart-
> ment. I learned that the medical model would not solve these complex
> environmental issues. I became heavily involved in risk analysis. We
> need interdisciplinary teams to work on these complex policy issues and
> people who are comfortable with colleagues from different and comple-
> mentary backgrounds.

Tools and Tasks

Risk assessment is the key tool scientists use to draw conclusions about potential hazards (chapter 7). Sample risk and exposure assessments are available on the Web sites of EPA and other federal agencies and departments. But they are a challenge for the nonscientist. Journals such as *Environmental Health Perspectives, Risk Analysis,* and the *Journal of Human and Ecological Risk Assessment* often summarize key assessments. Newspapers — and less often other mass media — report some findings of risk assessments, but more likely deal with the political and economic implications rather than the science.

For science-based policy questions like MTBE, I strongly recommend a class policy memo project, which was introduced and demonstrated to me by my colleague William Rodgers. This project focuses on an issue, such as gasoline additives, pesticides, genetically modified organisms in food, or cholesterol-lowering drugs. Rather than try to have every student become a scientist, I divide the class into stakeholders. In the case of fuel additives, these would be the oil industry, producers of fuel additives, producers of ethanol, EPA, a state department of the environment, a national environmental organization like the Sierra Club, and a major national newspaper. Each group of students (3 or 4 in each group) is charged with investigating the subject from the perspective of its particular interest group. Each group must produce a 4- to 6-page memo for the U.S. Congress (or an equivalent decision-making body). That memo should contain four parts:

1. The mission of the organization
2. The position of the organization on the issue (e.g., pro-methanol, calling for more objective science, focusing on the economic impact on fuel for the poor, etc.)
3. The bases for that position (e.g., economic considerations, scientific evidence, concerns over environmental justice, national security, states' rights, etc.)
4. Any recommendations to Congress or another body (e.g., ban MTBE, not use ethanol, communicate to the public, ask the National Academy of Sciences to study the issue)

Each group submits a written report; also, a spokesperson for each group presents a 5- to 7-minute synopsis of its report to the class. Following these presentations, each group meets separately for about 20 minutes to reconsider its positions. Each is then offered 3 minutes to add to the presentation. Finally, I lead an open discussion to try to establish points of agreement and disagreement among the groups. The entire process takes about 80 to 90 minutes.

4

Economic Criterion

Costs of Environmental Management

Introduction

During the 1970s — the halcyon days of the environmental movement in the United States — many activists, elected officials, and agency staff behaved as if the costs of environmental management were not important (see the discussion of the Clean Air Act in chapter 8). But cost was always there and was considered. The case study in this chapter focuses on the balancing of economic and other considerations by the people who manage the U.S. nuclear weapons legacy. These stewards face an unprecedented responsibility.

Nuclear weapons development, testing, and manufacturing contaminated over 130 locations in 34 states. Most of these sites were small, and nuclear and chemical wastes have been removed. But at three massive sites — Hanford (Washington), Idaho National Laboratory (Idaho), and Savannah River (South Carolina) — large quantities of hazardous nuclear and nonnuclear toxic chemicals are stored in tanks above and below ground, in pits, in ponds, and in lagoons. These materials have leaked into the ground. They have sometimes even leaked into underground water supplies and nearby rivers. Some of these hazards will be dangerous for centuries, and they must be managed in perpetuity. It is not an exaggeration to assert that these three sites represent the most difficult environmental management problem in the United States — and one of the most difficult in the world. The economic challenge at these sites is unprecedented. How can we balance costs against the need for environmental management over many generations?

From 1989 to 2000, environmental management budgets at the three sites averaged almost $3 billion a year (Greenberg, Miller, et al., 2003; U.S. Department of Energy [DOE], 1997; DOE, Office of Environmental Management, 1995a, 1995b). This represented 47 percent of DOE's total environmental management budget. To my knowledge, environmental management costs at these three sites are the largest focused by a single organization on a single location in the world.

During the past two decades, I have visited some of most hazardous Superfund waste sites in the United States (see chapter 1). The cost of cleaning up and controlling Superfund sites typically runs a few million dollars, reached $30 million for some, and in the worst cases exceeded $100 million.

By comparison, the estimated cost of cleaning up and controlling these three nuclear weapons legacy sites will be tens of billions of dollars (DOE, Office of Environmental Management, 1995a, 1995b). One reason for these off-the-chart costs is the presence of high-level nuclear waste that has been mixed with other materials. Methods to neutralize and manage these wastes have not been proven. A second reason is that these three sites contain multiple hazardous waste sites — literally thousands of them. I will use the vitrification facility at Savannah River to illustrate DOE's cost containment problems.

Vitrification mixes nuclear materials with molten glass to immobilize the waste. The facility at the Savannah River site, the largest in the world, cost $2.4 billion to construct. Vitrification facilities being constructed at Hanford for a slightly different kind of waste could cost five to eight times as much (well over $10 billion) ("Hanford Cleanup to Take Four Years Longer Than Planned," 2005).

While a $10 billion dollar project may not raise many eyebrows when it buys a major expansion of the national highway system or sewage treatment plant upgrades across the nation, there is no overlooking this level of cost for a single environmental management project in a few locations. These massive invest-ments have created a large population that depends on continuing DOE expendi-tures (Greenberg, Lewis, et al., 2002; Greenberg, Miller, et al., 2003).

Local economic dependency creates tension for a site manager who knows that if he or she cuts the scope of a project and closes a site, there will be a seri-ous economic recession in the area. These stewards also face pressure to spend on risk management because of legal agreements between DOE and the states, tribal nations, and the U.S. Environmental Agency (EPA) that stipulate environ-mental management accomplishments by specific dates. Failure to meet these obligations, which assumed technological advances that often have not material-ized, brings additional pressure to bear on DOE from local groups, the courts, the affected states, tribal nations, congressional representatives, and local media. Failure to meet agreements, whatever the reason, implies to some that DOE is sacrificing the area and/or is incompetent.

Yet as stewards of taxpayer dollars, DOE managers are supposed to use envi-ronmental dollars prudently. Should they forge ahead with massive construction projects, recognizing that costs may be two to five times initial estimates and that they may not entirely solve the environmental problem? Or should they acknowl-edge that what was promised is not yet achievable, postpone unrealistic projects, and try to renegotiate agreements? Do we need a moratorium on some projects until scientists and engineers can more effectively use economic resources, or are we then merely postponing the inevitable in the form of high costs for managing this legacy?

DOE site managers and their headquarters counterparts are engaged in a delicate balancing act. On the one hand, they are balancing environmental needs and regional dependency; on the other, they face the strong congressional sentiment that these are large, inefficient public works projects. The costs are so high and so obvious in these three areas that whatever the stewards do will produce winners and losers and will lead to second-guessing locally and nationally.

Theme: The Legacy of Nuclear Weapons Waste and Interconnected Policy Themes

This main DOE theme intersects with two other themes that have emerged over the past 30 years, especially the past decade. One of these is, How clean is clean enough? This theme derives from the Superfund program, the Clean Air Act, and clean water legislation; it is also directly relevant to the more recent brownfields program (see also chapters 1 to 3 and 8). The second cross-cutting theme is the federal government's evolving land-use policies. The three DOE sites represent prominent examples of how the federal government annexed large tracts of land over 50 years ago, sometimes removing the occupants, and how it is now under pressure to restore the land to its original environmental "purity," return some of it, or use it to support local needs and national security.

Federal Land Ownership: The Ongoing Controversy

I cannot think of an intergovernmental and government–private interest dispute that goes back farther than land ownership (Gorte and Baldwin, 1999; Mollison and Eddy, 1982; Public Land Law Review Commission, 1970). It began when the original 13 colonies ceded, or, as some say, were coerced by the Continental Congress into ceding, their lands between the Appalachian Mountains and the Mississippi River to the federal government. These federal government takeovers occurred between 1781 and 1802. The issue expanded as the United States acquired vast amounts of land through the Louisiana Purchase (1803), treaties with Great Britain (1818) and Spain (1819), war with Mexico (1848), and the purchase of Alaska from Russia (1867). Overall, the federal government obtained 1.8 billion acres in North America.

The U.S. Constitution has two provisions that guide the federal government's land ownership. Article 1 (Legislative Branch), section 8, provides federal jurisdiction over federal enclaves. This has been interpreted to mean that state or local laws do not apply to these locations unless Congress stipulates that they do. In other words, state law can be preempted in these locations. Article 4 (the states), section 3, declares that Congress has the power to dispose of and make rules and regulations for U.S. land.

During most of the 19th and early 20th centuries, national policy was to transfer land to private and state ownership. About 1.1 billion of the 1.8 billion square miles were disposed of to finance government operations and debts and then to encourage the settlement and development of infrastructure. For example, the Homestead Act of 1862 (signed into law by President Lincoln), the General Mining Law of 1872, and land transfers to the railroads helped open up the West. States (notably Alaska) and the tribal nations were granted lands.

As prime agricultural lands disappeared, the federal government started withdrawing land. For example, in 1817, Congress authorized the selection of lands to supply lumber for the U.S. Navy. In 1872, President Grant signed the law creating Yellowstone National Park, leading to the establishment and designation of other national parks, including recreational areas, historical monuments, battlefields, culturally important sites, and various other designations. In 1891, the federal government started setting aside forest reserves, leading to the creation of the National Forest system. In 1903, President Theodore Roosevelt withdrew federal lands to protect wildlife habitats, leading to the National Wildlife Refuge system.

Debate over federal ownership of land continued well into the 20th century, at which point the federal government made it clear that it was going to retain much of the remaining land. The Public Land Law Review Commission examined the policies and practices of the federal government with regard to the ownership and administration of federal lands and offered 137 recommendations. Notably, number 104 stated, "No additional grants should be made to any of the 50 states" (Public Land Law Review Commission, 1970; "Summary of Public Land Law," 1970, p. 473). The Classification and Multiple Use Act of 1964 directed the Bureau of Land Management (BLM) to classify federal lands for disposal or retention and to manage the lands for multiple purposes. When this work was completed, BLM had classified more than 90 percent of the land for retention. Congress followed these deliberations with multiple debates. The Federal Land Policy and Management Act of 1976 (FLPMA, Public Law 94-579) ended the policy of disposal: "The Congress declares that it is the policy of the United States that (1) The public land be retained in Federal ownership, unless as a result of the land use planning procedure provided for in this Act, it is determined that disposal of the particular parcel will serve the national interest" (Section 102, p. 1; see Loomis, 2006, for an excellent discussion).

The National Park Service, the U.S. Forest Service, and the U.S. Fish and Wildlife Service manage over 350 million acres or more than half of all of federal lands. Withdrawals of land have also been made for purposes of national security. The DOE had a small fraction of the total, 2.4 million acres.

The remaining federally owned lands are heavily concentrated in a dozen Western states, especially Alaska, Nevada, Utah, and Idaho. There is less federal ownership east of the Mississippi River than there is in the West, but these lands are relevant to this chapter because they involve Department of Defense (DOD) and DOE lands, for example, the nuclear weapons sites at Savannah River (South Carolina) and Oak Ridge (Tennessee).

State governments have unsuccessfully challenged federal ownership. The most recent effort was the "Sagebrush Rebellion" (Graf, 1990). In 1979, Nevada passed a law asserting that it had title, management, and disposal authority over BLM lands within the state. Similar legislation was passed in Wyoming, New Mexico, Arizona, and Utah. In 1993, Nye County, Nevada (location of the Yucca Mountain DOE site and the Nevada test site), argued that it had title to lands and began bulldozing roads on federal lands without permits. The federal government sued and won. President Reagan, who was believed to support the Sagebrush Rebellion, issued an executive order establishing the Property Review Board to assess federal land for potential disposal (1982). Also, he chose James Watt as secretary of the Department of the Interior, which sent a signal that the Sagebrush Rebellion would be supported by the federal government. But Secretary Watt resigned, and the effort to turn BLM lands over to the states petered out.

Nevertheless, the issue has not disappeared. For example, in 1994, when the Republican Party had a majority in the Senate and the House, its "Contract with America" presented a vision of more state control and less federal control (Killian, 1998). Major changes in federal land-use policy did not occur, however. Bills continue to be introduced in Congress, and sometimes they are debated, but nothing major has occurred. Instead, there have been gradual changes that appear to be consistent with local circumstances or specific needs.

The focal point of the past decade has been differences between the policies of the Bill Clinton and George W. Bush administrations. The Clinton administration removed large tracts of federally owned land, declaring them wilderness and hence not open to development, road building, and, in some cases, use of snowmobiles and other vehicles. For example, 2.6 million acres of land in Utah were declared wilderness. The state of Utah sued, asserting that only Congress could make such decisions. In 2003, with the administration and Congress more supportive of states' rights, the federal government agreed that these decisions belonged to Congress (Janofsky, 2003).

Part of the context for that decision is the fact that the George W. Bush administration has focused on opening up more federal lands to oil and other forms of mineral exploration and to the logging of older forests, which were being preserved by the Clinton administration. In 2003, President Bush chose Michael Leavitt, three-term governor of Utah, as EPA administrator to replace former New Jersey governor Christine Whitman. This decision was praised by businesses, but got mixed reviews from environmental groups, which praised Leavitt for his efforts to protect air quality in the Grand Canyon and criticized him for opening public lands in Utah to industry and road building. Leavitt stated that his philosophy represented an attempt to balance conflicting needs (Seelye, 2003; see also chapter 8 for a discussion of changing leaders as a way to change policy).

The National Governors Association (NGA) has had an interesting perspective on land policy. Many governors want federal land. However, they face pressure from mayors and local businesses that want access not only to federal land, but also to state land. And the governors recognize the danger of becoming economically dependent on federal dollars (Seastone, 1970). NGA's (1996) state-ment on federal land policy calls for carefully balancing federal, state, and local needs — that is, determining what is best on a case-by-case basis.

Business generally opposed President Clinton's policies. For example, the American Association of Petroleum Geologists (2001) called for the reinstitution of multiple uses and the discontinuation of the policy of setting aside large areas as wilderness. The association argued that the country needs access to minerals and recreational sites.

I will conclude this synopsis of federal land policy by offering two additional tidbits of information to support my belief that this is a slowly evolving environ-mental policy area. The FLPMA, as noted earlier, has been controversial. The Clean Air Act, clean water legislation, and many other national federal laws affecting the environment have been controversial. A major difference between land policy and the others is that interest groups have been able to make small changes in the federal land use policy legislation. FLPMA was passed in 1976 and amended in 1978, 1984, 1986, 1988, 1990–1992, 1994, 1996, and so on. Congress appears to be willing to tinker with, but not fundamentally alter, land-use policy, unlike other major pieces of environmental legislation. I quote a statement made over 25 years ago by Congressman Morris Udall (1979) in response to the Sagebrush Rebellion: "I think the Congress has usually moved responsibly, and aggressively, to meet both these problems [federal versus state need for land]. I don't know if I'm ready to enlist in a rebellion — but I will settle for the same sort of quiet and orderly land transition that we've always had — and will have."

With regard to the economic stewardship of defense-related rural land and properties, the administration of George W. Bush has pressed federal depart-ments and agencies to more efficiently manage their land, noting in Executive Order 13327 (2004) that "it is the policy of the United States to promote the effi-cient and economical use of America's real property assets and to assure man-agement accountability." There appear to be three economic motivations for this order: (1) eliminating sites with inefficient technologies, (2) improving opera-tional efficiency, and (3) reducing economic liability.

DOD is the most obvious illustration. Beginning in 1988, 115 military bases have been closed and over half a million acres were turned over (General Accounting Office, 2002; Hansen, 2004; Montgomery, 2003; Sorenson, 1998). While the U.S. Army and Air Force are most commonly associated with closures, the U.S. Coast Guard and other federal units initiated analyses of their facility performance with the intent of increasing efficiency and shrinking the footprint (Dembeck, 2002; Fahrenthold, 2004). The process appears to be accelerating, at least for the DOD and for the smaller DOE sites. However, the three massive sites that are the focus of this chapter demand much more complex policy responses because of their high-level waste, multiple waste sites, and challenging legal his-tory, as well as the reality that they represent potentially important national secu-rity properties that the federal government may need. In 1998, Brown suggested that DOE's lands could represent a "land rush." I disagree, at least with regard to the three key sites that are the focus of this chapter.

How Clean Is Clean Enough?

The United States has a long history of buyer beware (caveat emptor). With regard to selling land and property, I would be surprised to find many transactions or leases today that involve a deliberate or negligent transfer of contaminated property. The evolving policy issue for the past three decades has been determining how clean is clean enough. This question must be answered whenever a contaminated site is proposed for reuse. Hundreds of thousands of former factories, railroad yards, gasoline stations, landfills, stores, schools, and even houses have some contamination or at least are perceived to have some. The overwhelming majority will have to clean up a heating oil leak, perhaps some lead-based paint residuals or asbestos, or even pesticides. Contamination is typically minimal, requiring the removal of soil or asbestos at the cost of some thousands of dollars. Of the hundreds of thousands of contaminated sites, a few thousand brownfield and Superfund sites (chapter 1) require extensive site investigations, cleanups, engineered barriers, deed restrictions, and other institutional controls (Gaspar and Van Burik, 1998). Costs at these sites can run into millions of dollars. A handful of sites, epitomized by the three described in this chapter, require billions of dollars and long-term stewardship.

Whatever the site, all share the need to answer the question, How clean is clean enough? The parties must determine whether there are substances on the site that are flammable, explosive, poisonous, carcinogenic, teratogenic, or mutagenic or that in other ways pose a hazard. Then, they must decide whether the land uses they propose are beneficial enough to offset the costs of cleaning up the site to the required level. Federal and state governments set required cleanup and management levels. With respect to Superfund sites, the federal government and sometimes state governments set the standards (see chapter 1).

Here, I will focus on brownfields. Cleanup requirements typically have been either very specific or very vague. One common approach is to require that the site be cleaned to "background levels," that is, the levels that existed before industrial uses. Such cleanups require the removal of all waste material, which can be extraordinarily expensive, essentially making the site unattractive to private developers. Other states have had no cleanup standard, basing their requirements instead on generalities such as clean enough to protect public health and the environment. Vague standards confused developers, who were not sure what level of cleanup was expected and therefore tended to ignore the property. Moreover, there is no guarantee that the state would not come back and demand further cleanup at a later stage. Another complication was the imposition of strict liability on the current owner (see chapter 1). Someone who purchased a site could be held liable for the entire cost of cleanup (this is characteristic of Superfund sites).

These policies stifled economic redevelopment (see chapter 1). Aware of these shortcomings, some states developed flexible risk-based standards that are less stringent than cleaning to background. These states also provided a degree of liability protection by stating that new owners will not be held accountable for the contamination caused by previous owners. Developers must therefore diligently assess the site before they purchase it, and sellers must disclose the existence of contamination. Also, some states provide assurance that they will require no further cleanup once the agreed-upon levels are reached.

The Mediation and Redevelopment Division of the state of Michigan's Department of Environmental Quality (State of Michigan, 2006) publishes a guide to the ownership and purchase of contaminated property that exemplifies the actions of a state that wants contaminated sites redeveloped. After explaining the liability issue (emphasizing the importance of adequate site assessment and the need to take care not to disturb contamination), the guide explains how Michigan links cleanup to future use. Three major choices are stated: residential, commercial, and industrial. The residential standard is the most stringent because of concern over children's exposure. For example, for an infant, the residential cleanup standard for noncarcinogens assumes 24 hours of exposure a day for 350 days a year for 30 years. The commercial and industrial equivalents are less demanding. Instead of 24 hours of potential exposure, they assume 8 to 10 hours; instead of 350 days a year, they assume 245 days; and rather than 30 years of exposure for an infant, they assume 21 years for an adult.

The Michigan law also requires consistency with environmental ecological and zoning requirements. In some cases, restrictions and engineering barriers are required to make sure that subsequent users do not violate exposure requirements. There are also requirements about using the sites for public potable water consumption.

These modified requirements have helped cities and developers better understand what is expected of them. This has made economic redevelopment easier. However, there has been a pushback from some environmental groups over the application of these approaches to large contaminated industrial sites. For example, environmental advocate groups from Michigan have petitioned the state not to sign an agreement that would allow the Dow Chemical Company to clean up land areas and adjacent streams contaminated with dioxin in the Midland, Michigan, area to levels that the petitioners argue will pose a long-term health threat (Bzdok, 2007; Ecology Center, 2002). The economic stakes are high for companies and for the surrounding regions. According to Smith, Sciortino, Goeden, and Wright (1996), cleanup standards that are too stringent have cost too much and not delivered a meaningful reduction in exposure.

This how-safe-is-safe issue is underscored at the three sites that are the focus of this chapter. They are not residential, nor are they likely to be in the foreseeable future. But there are no guarantees that they would never be residential — hundreds or thousands of years from now someone could attempt to occupy the sites. In the process, these pioneers of the future could punch a hole into the ground and attempt to extract water, which theoretically could expose them to unsafe levels of radiation and chemicals. As unlikely as this scenario may seem (to some, it seems like the introduction to a science fiction novel), the reality is that DOE has been challenged to remediate some of the most heavily contaminated sites to a residential level or even to a background level. If residential or background plans are required, DOE would have to dig down and remove many feet of contaminated soil and relocate it elsewhere on the sites. In the process of digging down and removing this soil, DOE would destroy and compromise ecological systems. Such removals and cleanup would likely cost three or four times as much as cleanup to a commercial/industrial use standard.

Should the federal government spend tens of billions of dollars at these sites to try to return them to a level of use that cannot reasonably be anticipated? Or should it take the position that the contaminated sections of the sites will always be held by the federal government and that, consequently, expenditures of $10 billion or $20+ billion are wasteful? It is an uncomfortable position for a steward, who can be accused of squandering taxpayer funds or of creating permanent "sacrifice zones" (scarred places that have been left with a bad environmental legacy by government).

The DOE Stewardship Dilemma: Local and National Perspectives

The United States has a history of providing assistance to war-ravaged areas. The Marshall Plan, aimed at post–World War II Europe, is the most visible postwar aid initiative (Hogan, 1987). More recent efforts were targeted at rebuilding Japan, Korea, and now Afghanistan and Iraq. But what about places in the United States where weapons of mass destruction, in this case nuclear weapons, were developed, assembled, and tested? As a visitor to many of these sites, I can attest that one does not see burned-out or devastated buildings and neighborhoods, such as the world saw in Dresden and Nagasaki after World War II.

But places where weapons of mass destruction and their waste products reside in the United States bear an undeniable legacy of contamination and stigma that may be far more difficult to overcome than it was in places such as Berlin, Dresden, Hiroshima, and Nagasaki or will be in Baghdad. The stigma of having a weapons site with its associated economic dependency makes it difficult to attract private investors and retain key people in the region. What is the responsibility of federal government stewards to these locations? I view these three DOE site-regions as victims of the peace that began when the cold war between the United States and the Soviet Union ended.

Viewed from this perspective, they could be called sacrifice zones. Keying these words into a search engine yields tens of thousands of books, papers, and reports describing alleged instances of sacrifice zones. The typical report accuses a mining or oil/gas company, DOD, or DOE of refusing to clean up a contaminated site (Kamps, 2001; Marshall, 1996; Walker, 2004). Environmental justice problems are mentioned in many of these assertions (see chapter 5), meaning that the area supposedly being sacrificed has a disproportionate share of disadvantaged minority populations. Because the literature connects environmental justice to sacrifice zones, we should find evidence of a disproportionate number of black, American Indian, and Hispanic minorities in these three site-regions.

A second potential ethical justification for aggressive government economic support is provided by Kai Erikson (1994). Working as a consultant in areas that had been devastated by floods, mercury contamination, leaking gasoline, and fraud, Erikson labeled some places as a "new species of trouble" (1994). The trouble started with a traumatic event, such as a flood, earthquake, or toxic spill. But in this scenario, the problem is not adequately addressed and the impact becomes chronic and deepens. He describes it as "a chronic disaster, one that gathers force more slowly and insidiously, creeping around one's defenses rather than smashing through them" (Erikson, 1994, p. 21). The residents, he suggests, are subject to rage, anxiety, and despair. They feel that nobody cares about them, that they have been abandoned. Notably, he identifies the Yucca Mountain nuclear waste repository as an example of the new species. Yet this site so far has no nuclear materials in it, whereas the sites described in this book have nuclear weapons and their waste products. If there is collective, as well as individual, trauma in these places, we should find evidence in the form of higher morbidity and mortality rates from stress-related diseases, injuries, and illnesses.

A third potential ethical argument is grounded in economic stigma. The assumption is that these locations are so stigmatized by the image of the mushroom cloud and by the fear of being gassed by chemicals that they have no possibility of competing for private capital (Mitchell, Payne, and Dunlap, 1989). It is not far-fetched to assert that the economic history of these locations has been unalterably changed for the worse. Brauer (1995) found that locations that were considered as nuclear weapons sites but were not chosen had performed better economically than those that were selected. Research shows that rural regions with major nuclear weapons sites have experienced roller-coaster fluctuations in their economies that are directly due to fluctuations in defense spending (Greenberg, Lewis, et al., 2002; Greenberg, Miller, et al., 2003).

In short, these three sites should have some of the most pronounced characteristics of sacrifice zones. Some 95 percent of spent military nuclear fuel and waste products are stored at Hanford, the Idaho National Laboratory, and Savannah River. In addition, because they were deliberately located in isolated places, we assumed that they would not easily benefit from the spillover of jobs and economic growth from urban-suburban development. Moreover, they are massive. The Idaho, Hanford, and Savannah River sites are 890, 580, and 310 square miles, respectively. By contrast, other locations where nuclear weapons of mass destruction were developed — for example, Rocky Flats (Denver), Brookhaven (New York), Argonne (Chicago), and others — can overcome their

TABLE 6

Three-sites study area

Site	Counties (number)	2000 population (in thousands)
Hanford, WA	Benton, Franklin, Grant, Yakima (4)	391
Idaho National Laboratory, ID	Bingham, Bonneville, Butte, Clark, Jefferson (5)	130
Savannah River, SC	Aiken, Barnwell, Edgefield (SC); Columbia, Richmond (GA) (5)	384
Total	14	905

legacy because they are located in thriving metropolitan regions (Greenberg, Lewis, et al., 2002; Greenberg, Miller, et al., 2003).

We chose the counties that surrounded the three sites, those that were completely or largely within 50 miles, to look for signs of distress. In 2000, these 14 counties in four states had an aggregate population of just over 900,000 (see table 6).

The population density of the counties adjacent to the three sites varies from less than 1 per square mile to over 600 in Richmond County, Georgia. But aggregate density is misleading in terms of risk and urbanization. All of the sites are located 20 to 70 miles from a large city, so they are relatively remote from major metropolitan areas. With regard to the three nuclear weapons sites, we are not focusing on the bombs themselves, but rather on the waste products. Whether it involves waste or part of a bomb, an element is radioactive when it has an unstable nucleus that releases energy (decays; see chapter 6 for a discussion of nuclear materials). High-level nuclear waste contains over 99 percent of the total radioactivity of the wastes, and these three sites contain nearly all of it (DOE, Office of Environmental Management, 1995a, 1995b). It does not follow that these three sites have nearly all the risk because if the waste is controlled, the risk is negligible. This means that wastes that are not so radioactive and chemical agents such as mercury discharged at the sites can constitute a higher human health risk than the high-level waste itself (DOE, Office of Environmental Management, 1995a, 1995b).

The Hanford site focused on fuel fabrication, irradiation, chemical separation, and component fabrication; and the Idaho site, on chemical separation. Savannah River focused on fuel and target fabrication, irradiation, chemical separation, and tritium production. Hanford was home to nine production reactors and four chemical separation facilities. Idaho, among its various functions, was a place where spent nuclear fuel from the U.S. Navy and from research reactors was processed. Savannah River had five production reactors and two chemical separation plants. Each of these sites has the two forms of nuclear waste that typically are of greatest concern: spent fuel and high-level waste. Spent fuel consists of fuel elements and irradiated targets from reactors, and high-level waste is material resulting from the reprocessing of spent fuel and irradiated targets (see chapter 6). Nearly all of this high-level waste is stored in underground tanks, but some of it is stored in bins. The risk of a nuclear explosion is negligible, although there is concern about leaking tanks. In the worst case, waste would expose workers, become airborne, and pollute surface and underground water systems.

The former head of DOE, Hazel O'Leary, spoke about the building of nuclear weapons as a "story of extraordinary challenges brilliantly met," then shifted to the cleanup of the environmental legacy: "We have a moral obligation to do no less, and we are committed to producing meaningful results" (DOE, Office of Environmental Management, 1995b, p. vii). Overall, these three nuclear sites are clearly hazardous. The tank risk is contained because the government spends billion of dollars a year trying to make sure that the risk is no more than negligible. But no immediate relief is in sight; some of the waste will be at these sites for a long time, in essence, in perpetuity. As long as there are tanks with liquid waste, the argument that these areas are sacrifice zones cannot be dismissed as irrational fear or unsubstantiated rhetoric.

With regard to disadvantaged minority populations, table 7 shows some evidence of a concentration of black and Hispanic residents in the study areas. Hanford, Idaho National Laboratory, and Savannah River had a higher proportion of Hispanic or black Americans than their states as a whole. At the Hanford site, there has been consistent tension between the Nez Perce, Umatilla, Yakima, and Wanapum Indians and DOE over the current and especially the future use of the site (Sussex, 1997).

If Erikson's (1994) new species of trouble applies to the three site-regions, then we should be able to find some signals in aggregate health, economic, and demographic data and in interviews. With regard to health, ideally we would like data that measure rage, distress, depression, efficacy, optimism-pessimism, and other stress-related outcomes over the entire population. Such data do not exist. No one has done population-based psychological studies of people who live near these sites and compared them with people elsewhere. What does exist is several cause-of-death measures that have historically been associated with people under stress. If these are psychologically distressed areas, we should find relatively high rates of suicide and homicide, and we should also find higher rates of death from chronic liver disease and cirrhosis. High rates of the first two would suggest distress leading to extreme hostility toward the self and others. The second is typically associated with alcoholism, and, indeed, about 45 percent of the causes in this death code are directly attributable on the death certificate to alcoholism.

TABLE 7

Key characteristics of the population living near the three sites

Site name (surrounding counties), state, and state rank	Death rate from suicide and homicide, 1979 to 1998[a]	Death rate from chronic liver disease and cirrhosis,[b] 1979 to 1998	Percentage of the population 25+ years old that graduated from college, 2000	Mean household income, 1999 (in thousands of dollars)	Percent population change 1990 to 2000	Percentage of the largest nonwhite racial/ethnic group, 2000
Hanford (4)	20.0	10.7	22.8	43.8	28.0	Hispanic
Washington	19.1	10.4	28.6	45.8	21.1	26.7
State rank	21	27	21	23	10	
Idaho National Laboratory (5)	24.9	8.8	15.5	34.9	21.3	Hispanic
Idaho	20.6	7.8	21.7	37.6	28.5	13.9
State rank	24	4	44	25	5	
Savannah River (5)	26.4	11.9	18.7	30.8	9.7	Black
South Carolina	22.4	11.0	19.0	37.1	15.1	48.0
State rank	31	35	47	42	15	

Source: Centers for Disease Control and Prevention, Wonder, 2/17/05. Deaths for 1979 to 1998 are classified using the 9th revision (ICD-9). Available at: http://wonder.cdc.gov/wonder/help/cmf.html.

Note: ICD = International Classification of Diseases.

[a] Age-adjusted homicide and suicide rates, all races and both sexes, age-adjusted to a year 2000 standard.
[b] Age-adjusted death rate from chronic liver disease and cirrhosis, ICD 571. Nationally, 45 percent of these deaths are directly attributable to alcohol abuse.

The first two columns of table 7 are age-adjusted (direct method, U.S. population, 2000 standard) death rates. Where 1 was the age-adjusted lowest rate and 50 the highest, Washington and Idaho ranked 21st and 24th, pectively, in death from suicide and homicide from 1979 to 1998. South Carolina ranked 31st. In other words, the host states are in the middle in death rates from suicide and homicide. Within the three states, the average death rate for the three study areas was higher than their respective state rates — in the upper one-third for combined age-adjusted homicide and suicide rates in their states. What is equally notable and not shown in the table is that the host county or counties (where the actual facility is centered) had one of the 10 highest combined homicide and suicide rates in all three states.

With regard to liver disease, Idaho had one of the lowest rates, and the other two had moderately high rates. The study areas have relatively high rates compared with other counties and their states as a whole. In short, these death rate results are consistent with higher stress in the study areas. They do not jump off the page as the highest rates in their host states, yet they are among the highest.

With regard to economic indicators, the regions hosting the three nuclear weapons sites have been dependent on federal dollars. DOE data indicate that the department's expenditures since 1992 accounted for 17 percent of the gross regional product for the Hanford and Savannah River regions and 20 percent for the Idaho region (Greenberg, Lewis, et al., 2002; Greenberg, Miller, et al., 2003).

Whatever the degree of dependency, we should and did find signs that the three areas are not growing in socioeconomic terms as rapidly as their host states. All three had lower rates of college graduates than their respective states. Further, the divergence between the state and study area rates increased during the 1990–2000 period. The educational achievement results were supported by income results. The areas had lower family incomes than their respective states. Two of the three also had less population growth during the decade than their states as a whole.

The three sites — especially Savannah River — present relatively strong mortality and socioeconomic cases for ongoing government economic support. Each site-region has relatively high suicide and homicide mortality rates, along with relatively low college graduation rates and income levels. Clearly, however, these are geographic, not individual, data, and we have no proof that the higher suicide-homicide and liver death rates in the host counties are directly related to living near the sites. Only psychological testing and detailed analysis of local health data that control for confounding by family and other local factors can make a definitive finding in that regard.

Recent surveys help us understand public concerns and perceptions about the sites. I highlight the results here (see Greenberg, Lowrie, et al., 2007a and 2007b for more details). While it is true that nuclear and chemical sites are known to evoke images of mushroom clouds, terrorists, and feelings of dread among the general population (Slovic, 2000), the reality is that most people living near these sites are no more concerned about site-related natural hazards than they are about other environmental issues in the area. About 20 percent of respondents "worry a great deal" that cleaning up nuclear waste will contaminate the environment, and a somewhat similar proportion feel that way about new nuclear-related initiatives at their nearby site (see table 8). Yet a larger proportion at each site are not "worried at all" about these activities. Similar proportions worried about contamination caused by non-DOE-related manufacturing, agriculture, and mining, and, although this is not shown in the table, loss of open space to urban development and sprawl. Also, over a quarter of all respondents worried a great deal about loss of jobs from a cutback in cleanup efforts at the three sites. But table 8 also shows that respondents want DOE to carefully monitor potential health and environmental effects and maintain control of the site. Not shown in the table, the overwhelming majority of respondents were not against new nuclear-related activities. At Idaho, a majority were opposed to a policy of no new nuclear-related activities. The majority of Savannah River and Hanford respondents wanted such a policy, but 46 percent and 39 percent, respectively, were opposed to one.

Why are relatively few people concerned? Weapons and hazardous by-products have been at these sites for decades; some of the people have worked there, and familiarity offers psychological protection against dread. Indeed, those who worked at the site or who had family members and/or close friends who did were hardly worried about site activities. In support of survey data, Lowrie and Greenberg (2001) found that articles about nuclear sites in local newspapers place a low emphasis on risk and that the economic impacts of site decisions are mentioned more than environmental or human health issues.

To summarize then, surveys at the sites suggest that many of the local people are not terrified of the waste and weapons and do not view DOE as an antagonist, but do expect the department to fulfill its stewardship role — to manage the site so that the chance of exposure to radioactive hazards is minimal. With regard to economic support, our data suggest that a large minority of the population would probably be willing to have officials negotiate with the federal government on the siting of new nuclear-related facilities. Implicit is the assumption that government would also continue major environmental management and other nuclear-related expenditures in these areas.

The case against a major increase in DOE expenditures at these three sites is in the performance record. In 1997, then Secretary of Energy Federico Peña stated that "we cannot continue to operate this program the same way as in the past" (DOE, 1997, p. 1). Secretary Peña and more recent secretaries have discovered that the department has a difficult time demonstrating a substantial decrease in risk, despite spending an average of about $6 billion a year on its waste management programs, much of it at these three sites (Top-to-Bottom Review Team, 2002). When she took over as assistant secretary for Environmental Management, Jessie Roberson commissioned a special team to review DOE's environmental management programs. I quote from the team's report: "During the past 12 years, the . . . EM

TABLE 8

Selected public perception data from the Hanford, Idaho, and Savannah River sites, 2005 (in percents)

Indicator	Hanford (WA)	Idaho National Laboratory (ID)	Savannah River (SC)
Rate county as an excellent or good place to live	83	90	83
How worried are you about environmental problems in your county in general?			
Very	8	9	9
Not at all	24	15	15
How worried are you that cleanup of nuclear-related waste would lead to environmental contamination in your area?			
Very	25	17	26
Not at all	24	28	28
How worried are you about new activities that involve the use of nuclear materials?			
Very	21	13	26
Not at all	28	31	21
How worried are you that the disposal of toxic wastes from mining and manufacturing in your area (non-DOE) will affect the environment of your area?			
Very	17	15	25
Not at all	29	24	27
How worried are you that area residents will lose jobs if the site reduces its cleanup efforts and activities?			
Very	24	24	32
Not at all	19	13	15

(Continued)

TABLE 8

(Continued)

Indicator	Hanford (WA)	Idaho National Laboratory (ID)	Savannah River (SC)
Want DOE to make this activity a highest priority (where "highest" priority equals a score of 10 on a scale of 1 to 10):			
Continuously sample the quality of the air and water at the site	68	57	76
Monitor the health of site workers	64	58	70
Create a trust fund to make sure the cleanup activities continue	42	39	55
Make sure the federal government owns the site until all hazards are removed	62	52	72
Do not allow any new-nuclear-related activity on the site	35	18	37

Source: Greenberg, M., Lowrie, K., Burger, J., Powers, C., Gochfeld, M., and Mayer, H. (2007a), Nuclear waste and public worries: Public perceptions of the United States major nuclear weapons legacy sites, *Human Ecology Review*, 14 (1), 1–12; and Greenberg, M., Lowrie, K., Burger, J., Powers, C., Gochfeld, M., and Mayer, H. (2007b), Preferences for alternative risk management policies at the United States major nuclear weapons legacy sites, *Journal of Environmental Planning and Management*, 50 (2), 187–209.

Note: DOE = U.S. Department of Energy.

[environmental management] program has expended tens of billions of dollars without a corresponding reduction in actual risk. In fact, in some cases the waste inventory awaiting treatment and disposal has increased, and a number of high-risk facilities continued to deteriorate without firm plans for decontamination and decommissioning" (Top-to-Bottom Review Team, 2002, p. 1).

One of the three core principles that the DOE team focused on was running the environmental management program "like a business" (Top-to-Bottom Review Team, 2002, p. 1). The U.S. House of Representatives' Committee on Commerce (2000) used a graphic title — *Incinerating Cash: The Department of Energy's Failure to*

Develop and Utilize Innovative Technologies to Clean Up the Nuclear Weapons Legacy — to summarize its views about DOE's investments in technology. It charged the department with squandering hundreds of millions of dollars on technologies that have not proven useful and for failing to effectively use technologies that have been developed.

Former senior EPA official and economist Milton Russell urged DOE to separate its role as the economic backbone of these regions from its need to have the flexibility to conduct environmental management programs (1998, 2000); he called his proposal a "productive divorce." Probst and Lowe described the DOE environmental management program as a costly, intractable legacy that was "so large in scope, [and] so technologically complex" that it "almost defies comprehension" (2000, p. vii). Robert Nelson of the Competitive Enterprise Institute suggested that the "federal government should abandon current nuclear-cleanup programs as economically wasteful and environmentally counterproductive" (2001, p. 1). His suggestions were based on four principles: minimizing the risk to human populations, recognizing that cleanup requires technological advances, realizing the high ecological value of DOE's former nuclear weapons sites, and enabling stewards to conserve the ecological value of the sites while protecting public health.

A good way of understanding the steward's job is to examine the key cost elements involved an aggressive expansion of site programs. Chapter 7 discusses life-cycle cost models that we designed for DOE because standard models rely on off-the-shelf existing technologies that DOE does not have and a life span that is much shorter than anticipated for DOE's sites (Greenberg, Mayer, and Lewis, 2004). I will briefly discuss these key economic elements, which we divided into endogenous and exogenous. Endogenous costs can be controlled by DOE. The first element is present cost, which consists of designing, pilot testing, constructing, systemizing, operating, maintaining, and eventually closing the facilities. Each of these elements is a forecasting project in itself, requiring considerable expertise. Estimating is difficult for a DOE project at these sites because it involves unique wastes and expensive technologies, many of which do not exist and must be developed and tested in stages before scaling them to full operational size. Some projects have not followed standard scale-up protocols from laboratory, to pilot size, and then to full scale. They have failed, costing DOE hundreds of millions of dollars (Top-to-Bottom Review Team, 2002). To me, more aggressive cleanup and development programs mean a higher probability of failure because scientists and engineers cannot be expected to anticipate all of the problems that can occur with these unique waste streams. A less aggressive program would recognize this complexity and not commit billions of dollars to projects that might not work.

Long-term stewardship consisting of legal, institutional, and engineering mechanisms to make sure that human and ecological health is protected is the second endogenous cost element. It includes monitoring and surveillance of surface and groundwater, land, birds, raccoons and other indicator species, and air. It requires monitoring infrastructure such as pipes, energy and computer technologies, detection systems, and leachate collection. Long-term stewardship also includes expenses for buildings, staff to make sure that controls are being maintained, and security fences and associated devices.

Long-term stewardship costs are not as complicated to estimate as project costs. However, studies done for DOE provided little detailed information about the basis for these costs (DOE, Office of Environmental Management, 2001). If DOE spends aggressively on new projects and these projects are successful, then long-term stewardship costs should be lower because fewer residuals will be left in dangerous configurations. But if enormous expenditures are made and the projects are not successful, there will be a bigger, more expensive cleanup and more stewardship costs.

Engineered systems sometimes fail and represent a third endogenous cost element. The problem could be a break in a fuel line and require soil cleanup and minor repairs. But it also could be a far more dangerous problem involving substantial expenditures to control and manage. In more serious cases, there could be severe human exposure and ecological damage. The failure component of endogenous costs will be reduced if DOE neutralizes and/or immobilizes liquid and gas wastes. If they delay these steps, the potential for high failure costs is likely to increase: for example, the failure of a tank holding dangerous nuclear and chemical wastes.

The second category of costs is exogenous, that is, costs that DOE has limited control or no control over, but that can substantially affect a project's life-cycle costs. One possibility is that environmental regulations could change and not necessarily in favor of lower DOE costs. Chapter 8 offers an example of a court ruling that for a short time had serious implications for the treatment of a waste stream. The difference between storing waste in insecure facilities versus requiring waste to be mixed with glass will be billions of dollars.

National and international events can have a major cost impact as well, as illustrated by changes in the value and availability of money. DOE and other departments currently discount future project costs at a rate that approximates the federal government's cost of borrowing. But when the project life extends for more than 50 years, the current weight may not reflect future values. Not only can the value of money change in half a century in ways that we cannot anticipate today, but the availability of money for environmental management can also change. Some experts believe that China and India will be the dominant economies in 30 to 50 years. Will the United States, already a debtor nation, be able to control the value of money as much as it does today? The answer to this question implies a more aggressive cleanup program at this time, rather than postponing decisions, because acting now means more control for DOE.

Terrorism is another exogenous issue. Since September 11, 2001, DOE has increased security. Assuming that nuclear waste is a terrorist target implies that rapid conversion from gas and liquid to solid waste is desirable. But as noted earlier, this is costly.

With regard to the economics of local assistance, will the federal government support a program based on a long-term environmental stigma targeted at a few relatively isolated locations during a period characterized by a huge budget deficit and major commitments to wars, antiterrorism, restoration of areas destroyed by hurricanes, rising costs of health care, and many other issues? If there is to be an economic assistance program, it is likely to be incremental and based on what Rescher (2000) calls "realistic pragmatism," emphasizing continued progress and strategic planning rather than a massive influx of funds and roles for the public and private sectors. What does a Marshall-like plan mean in the context of these locations? For example, in one series of simulations, these three regions lost 20,000 to 25,000 jobs. By increasing the size of the severance package, extending the length of health coverage, and providing educational and training opportunities, job losses during the next five years dropped to 3,000 to 4,000 (Lewis, Frisch, and Greenberg, 2004). These kinds of benefits, while less than local officials might hope for, can help the areas stabilize and arguably are warranted by the stigma of the legacy. They are also consistent with Milton Russell's (1998, 2000) call to separate economic assistance from cleanup activities. We expect that local governments will support these kinds of benefits, but local people may have other preferences, and these need to be understood.

I believe that long-term stewardship costs are influenced by the public's perception of the responsible party, in this case, DOE. In this regard, DOE has some problems to overcome. Lowrie and Greenberg (2001) interviewed local officials about DOE and another federal agency in the same region, such as DOD, BLM, and the Department of Agriculture. Five of the 15 sets of compared interviews were at the three sites. There and at almost every other site as well, DOE was considered to be less willing to involve local government in decisions that affect the region. Local officials said that DOE has a long history of secrecy, focuses almost exclusively on its mission, and lacks training and/or a mandate to work with local officials. When local officials feel comfortable with their federal government neighbor, they are likely to demand less costly engineered systems. Table 8 reinforces the perspective of local officials. A large percentage of local residents consider surveillance — the monitoring of people, land, and ecological systems — as the highest priority, and the vast majority want emergency systems installed, outright federal ownership of land (at least until the sites are cleaned up, which means in perpetuity for many of them), and other restrictions.

Six Policy Criteria: A Synopsis of the Implications of Aggressive Economic Spending in the Regions

This section summarizes the advantages and vulnerabilities of an aggressive federal government decision to clean up hazardous waste at the three sites and to provide economic assistance. In table 9, I indicate 39 points to be considered by policy makers. I then summarize the pros and cons for the U.S. government.

TABLE 9

Advantages and vulnerabilities of aggressive environmental management

Criteria	Advantages	Vulnerabilities
Reaction of elected officials and staff	Strong support will come from key local members of Congress. The governors of the three states are likely to support additional cleanup funds, but not necessarily new nuclear-related missions. Mayors of nearby areas need funds to support dependent local economies. EPA regions that were signatories to tri-party agreements are likely to support more aggressive cleanup, consistent with those agreements.	The Executive Office and Congress are already questioning the size and effectiveness of DOE's environmental management programs. Opposition will likely come from the governors of surrounding states through which shipments will pass. Local governments along the transportation routes are likely to be vocal opponents of additional shipments.
Reaction of nongovernment stakeholders	Strong support will come from the nuclear industry and its key supporters, as well as from other energy-dependent industries. Local businesses that depend on DOE sites will be strong supporters. Those familiar with the site are likely to be supportive. National public preferences for nuclear power have been increasing. The local media are likely to be supportive, especially of economic benefits.	Opponents of expanding nuclear power will oppose funds. Local businesses along the route may raise opposition. Most local people are against the expansion of new nuclear-related missions, but not opposed to economic benefits. The national media are unlikely to care unless a management or environmental problem occurs.

TABLE 9
(Continued)

Criteria	Advantages	Vulnerabilities
Human and ecological health	Local health threats can be reduced by removing and containing contaminants. Concentrating new activity at these sites allows the national risk to be located in a few places with a history and staff capable of managing these risks. Local ecology will benefit if large ecological areas are set aside and not disturbed as part of this program and other areas of the nation are not disturbed.	Local health risks could be increased by concentrating more nuclear-related activities. Local ecology could be disrupted if the existing cleanup is too aggressive and major areas are developed for new nuclear-related missions.
Economic costs and benefits	There will be lower costs and greater benefits to society if new nuclear-related activities are successful and applied as quickly as possible. The efficient use of existing infrastructure and expertise is prudent and avoids sunken costs at the sites. Economic benefits will accrue to local areas from large investments.	There will be a long wait for national benefits from new nuclear-related activities at the sites. The local long-term stigma is exacerbated by concentrating nuclear activities at the sites. More economic uncertainty for these regions and the country as a whole potentially results from putting too many eggs in the new nuclear-related technology basket. The economic dependency of these locations on the federal government will increase.

(*Continued*)

TABLE 9
(Continued)

Criteria	Advantages	Vulnerabilities
Moral imperatives	Aggressive implementation is needed to meet tri-party agreements. Investments prevent these areas from becoming sacrifice zones. The set-aside of large areas for ecological parks would preserve unique ecosystems for local populations, research, and future generations.	Opponents of nuclear expansion will label these investments as a moral mistake. Investments increase dependency on the federal government; this is morally wrong for a capitalist country. Large, indiscriminate, and rapid expansion at these sites could destroy valuable natural and cultural systems. Credibility problems for DOE could increase substantially, leading to confrontations with state and local governments and the local public, unless it establishes a strong community involvement program.
Time and flexibility	The decision to clean up aggressively will reduce the burden on future generations. Investment in new technologies is essential to get the nation to the next generation of technologies.	The decision to clean up aggressively is contrary to logic, which suggests waiting for better technology before making making major investments. Relying on new technologies has proven to be a mistake in the nuclear field.

Note: DOE = U.S. Department of Energy;
EPA = U.S. Environmental Protection Agency

The table underscores the high level of uncertainty with regard to a decision to invest aggressively in nuclear-related cleanup, storage, and new technologies and in the people living in the surrounding area. What is likely to happen will fall somewhere between committing immediately to investing tens of billions of dollars on projects that might fail or putting an iron fence around the three sites and allowing nature to take its course. I suggest the following as a likely decision.

With regard to land use, DOE and the nation are likely to need land for expansion of nuclear-related activities such as power plants, technologies, and waste management facilities. Because I do not expect the Yucca Mountain "permanent" storage site to open anytime soon, one or two of these three sites could serve as interim storage for nuclear waste. Interim storage would necessitate a large economic investment.

Nuclear-related uses constitute only a small portion of these three sites. About 80 percent of the land has been undisturbed for more than half a century. Burger and others (Burger, Leschine, et al., 2003; Burger, Greenberg, et al., 2004; see also Greenberg, Lowrie, et al., 1997) suggest enhancing the ecological value of the National Environmental Research Parks at these three locations and assert that these sites will become national ecological treasures, invaluable to the nation and to the local areas for research, sightseeing, and other uses.

With regard to the costs of cleanup, tri-party agreements were negotiated between DOE, EPA, and the states in the 1980s. At that time, DOE was overly optimistic about what could be accomplished. We do not yet know how to destroy radioactive wastes. We know only how to convert them from liquids to gases to solids. The cleanup and removal levels promised by DOE seem unrealistic, especially the idea of returning the sites to an uncontaminated background state and/or meeting a residential standard. Furthermore, Burger and others (Burger, Leschine, et al., 2003; Burger, Greenberg, et al., 2004) point out that digging up the largest tracts of land will destroy these ecosystems. In other words, political pressures notwithstanding, it makes no sense for an economic steward to try to reach unrealistic and problematic environmental goals.

With regard to economic assistance, there will be no precipitous decline in waste management at the sites anytime in the near future. Managing high-level waste in tanks is expensive and must be done. The question is how much to spend on massive facilities at Hanford. As noted earlier, recent estimates for this project exceed $10 billion.

Theories of Stewardship

Every responsible adult is a steward/manager of his or her own household affairs. Also, it is a common worldview that humans need to be stewards of the planet Earth. The term "steward" has taken on a host of meanings in different religious and cultural contexts, which I will summarize next.

Judeo-Christian Roots of Stewardship

The United States is a Judeo-Christian nation and has a European-American-oriented culture. Hence, I will focus on these roots of stewardship. Most Americans believe that all things are created by God, that humanity holds stewardship over God's creation and is ultimately accountable to God's will. In other words, people are not the owners, but merely the trustees of Earth's resources and must not plunder or waste them (Gill, 1996; Hall, 1990; Wilkinson, 1991). Stewardship is an orientation toward the goal of caring, a way of life rather than any specific set of required deeds (L. Russell, 1985). Christian scholars emphasize that we are all part of a divine plan that obligates Christians to address economic, social, and political issues and to care for the less fortunate (DeSouza, 1985; Reumann, 1992).

Proper and efficient administration of resources is a central tenet. The Greek word that has been translated to mean stewardship in the New Testament is *oikonomia,* which means administration of a household. As the root of our English word "economics," the word implies prudent management of resources. A steward is an economist who manages the household for the sake of contemporaries and beneficiaries (Winn, 1985). The monetary aspects of stewardship in the Christian church are found in the principle of tithing. Church members are expected to return a portion of their wealth to their church or other charitable endeavors.

Christian scholars have focused on the meaning of the parable of the "unjust steward" found in Luke 16:1–13. In this parable, a steward is scolded for squandering most of his master's money. He goes to his master's debtors and offers them favors in return for partial repayment of their debts, so he can take responsibility for rebuilding the wealth of the estate and regain his master's favor. The most common interpretation of the parable is that it is a warning to the disciples that they will be held accountable to God and must not misuse the trust placed in them by engaging in self-indulgent behaviors. Rather, as stewards they must use their possessions appropriately and efficiently. "And he called him and said to him, 'What is this I hear about you? Give an account of your stewardship, for you can no longer be steward'" (Luke 16:2). An alternative view is that the steward is to be praised for exercising wisdom in "understanding the seriousness of the situation, finding the only possible way out and proceeding resolutely along that way" (Ireland, 1992, p. 15). In finding a way to be charitable to his debtors and also fulfill his obligations to his master, he has been resourceful and decisive in "using the present to prepare for the future" (Ireland, 1992). Obviously, the religious context of stewardship covers much more than being economical. According to Mormon beliefs, if a good steward uses resources wisely and is accountable, then a utopian society will follow (Launius, 1995). Brigham Young emphasized stewardship of the environment as he instructed Mormons to live in harmony with one another because each was a part of God's domain (Alexander, 1994). Alexander (1994) noted that the European American entrepreneurial tradition clashes with this Christian teaching. He points out that during the Western expansion of the Mormons, Utah settlers ignored environmental stewardship in favor of resource use. Another piece of stewardship for Mormons is that science is important so that we can know how best to preserve and improve the Earth and improve the quality of life for our descendents. Wilkinson (1991), in discussing the "stewardship of creation," also notes that technology is important to stewardship because it helps us use our skills to heal environmental damage and minimize future damage.

A steward's view of the land is rooted in the ancient Hebrew tradition. According to the Old Testament, God is the giver who shares the land with his people. God forms a covenant with the people, but if they mismanage the land, they break the covenant and lose the land (Van Seters, 1985).

Other Cultural Perspectives

Stewardship plays a prominent place in the beliefs of American Indian cultures. Many of these hold that the land must be treated with respect. It is both provider and protector, and its resources are sacred. Stories passed orally from generation to generation tell of terrible consequences for violating the natural environment. For example, the "Ptarmigan Story" from the Inupiaq Eskimo culture tells of two young boys who abused a ptarmigan for fun and subsequently suffered a painful death (Smelcer, 1996).

There is an ethic in agriculture that farmers are stewards of the land and that they have a responsibility to look after it for future generations (Lawrence, Vanclay, and Furze, 1992). Thompson, Matthews, and Van Ravenswaay (1994) disagree with this assertion, calling it an agrarian myth, and declare that, in fact, the demand for increased crops is clearly at odds with prudent, sustainable long-term management.

With regard to corporations, the primary aim is to earn money for stockholders. However, top managers of some companies have interpreted stewardship as the need to care about more than just the bottom line. For example, DuPont and Dow Chemical, after many years of being heavily criticized for pollution, referred to stewardship as an attempt to encompass the interests of customers, employees, and other stakeholders (Reisch, 1999). Robert Purcell Jr., a manager for General Motors, noted that stewardship is a key business value because every business is entrusted with resources that must be managed with care and with appropriate regard for the rights of others (1998). He observed that proper values guide a company and add to its legacy.

Directly linking the business and religious realms, some Christian businesspeople have started "stewardship banks." Guiding these banks is the philosophy of returning to God what he has given by tithing profits for charitable contributions and also by practicing good management.

Not-for-profit organizations can play a critical role in stewardship. For example, the Marine Stewardship Council equates stewardship with promoting sustainable fishing standards and rewarding companies that do not compromise long-term fish populations (Constance and Bonanno, 1999). The Forest Stewardship Council plays a similar role with regard to virgin forests ("Science and Technology: From Poachers to Gamekeepers," 1998). With regard to historic sites, the Archaeological Conservancy purchases sites in order to maintain a legacy for the public (Fagan, 1995).

Historically, the concept of stewardship has always been connected with the idea that humans are responsible for caring for the land and preserving it for future generations. Modern environmental ethicists have expanded the idea, proposing so-called pluralistic stewardship, which means that humans should promote sustainable policies that consider the human, environmental, and economic environments (Barrett and Grizzle, 1999; see also chapter 5 for a discussion of the environmental ethic).

Federal Agencies

Federal government departments and agencies have articulated management principles, including stewardship. EPA's Advisory Group for Federal Facilities (EPA, Office of Solid Waste and Emergency Response, Federal Facilities Restoration and Reuse Office, Federal Facilities Environmental Restoration Dialogue Committee, 1996) outlined 14 principles to guide cleanup decisions. The first one identified a stewardship responsibility to protect lands on behalf of the nation. The report notes that because these lands are held in trust, it would be unethical to pass problems on to future generations. The Federal Facilities division considers stewardship a guiding principle of environmental restoration: "the federal government's ongoing, affirmative obligation to the public, including acceptance of responsibility and willingness to ensure continued protection of human health and the environment" (Woolford, 1999, p. 1). BLM and the Forest Service have included the concept of stewardship in their land management missions (Bengston and Fan, 1999). A key component of their effort is to bring interest groups together to listen to each other and find common ground so that local concerns are integrated into federal management policies. The process attempts to build trust and a sense of partnership and to prevent problems, rather than simply react to crises (Baker, 1999).

This background provides an excellent context for DOE's stewardship efforts. The department's stewardship policies and economic stewardship concepts are anything but clear. DOE announced an official stewardship policy in 1994. In a document entitled *Stewards of a National Resource* (1994), former Secretary Hazel O'Leary pledged the department to care responsibly for the lands and facilities entrusted to the DOE, make use of these resources wisely, and when possible share the DOE's land and facilities with the citizens of the United States. The former secretary's statement acknowledged a broad stewardship responsibility utilizing the principles of ecosystem management and sustainable development (DOE, 1994).

After O'Leary's departure in the mid-1990s, the term "stewardship" became primarily identified with long-term postcleanup responsibilities. That is, it went from a broad principle of environmental management to a specific set of activities at a stage of operations. The definition in a 1999 DOE document is "all activities required to protect human health and the environment from hazards remaining at DOE sites after cleanup is complete" (DOE, Grand Junction Office, 1999a, p. 1). In remarks to Congress, Assistant Secretary Huntoon referred to stewardship as the "final stage in the cleanup process" (2000, p. 1). Although DOE headquarters has focused on long-term protection of human and ecological health, some sites and other programs within the department have different and broader definitions. For example, a strategic plan for the Savannah River site is subtitled "Stewards of the Nation." Site managers defined stewardship as the "responsibility for careful use of money, time, talents and other resources, especially with respect to the principles and/or needs of a community" (DOE, Savannah River Operations Office, 2000, p. 21).

The economic responsibility of stewards is also found in the notes of DOE's Grand Junction Office, which is responsible for long-term surveillance and monitoring. Its report speaks of having provided cost-effective and efficient stewardship for more than a decade (DOE, Grand Junction Office, 1999a, 1999b).

In 2001, DOE's Office of Environmental Management published a report to Congress on long-term stewardship, which is defined as all activities required to protect human health after cleanup, disposal, or stabilization at a site or portion of a site. The long list of items that this implies includes engineered and institutional controls necessary to contain or prevent exposure, surveillance, record keeping, inspections, monitoring of groundwater, ongoing pumping to treat contaminated water, and repair of linings and caps, in addition to maintaining and closing facilities, maintaining barriers and containments, controlling access, and posting signs. All of these have cost implications. Overall, DOE has an official focus on long-term stewardship; but, in fact, it operates or tries to operate in a way that uses its resources economically and protects its human and ecological resources.

Tales of an Economic Steward

Dr. Henry Mayer brings a special perspective to the subject of economic stewardship and environmental policy. He was a senior executive for large international companies and has spent major parts of the past decade reviewing DOE's use of resources. He grew up in Cleveland, where he learned early the importance of carefully using resources. He graduated from Purdue University and Rutgers University with degrees in engineering, finance and business, environmental science, and planning. His primary focus has always been on economic stewardship. Dr. Mayer said: "I started out in banking with Chase. They emphasized the importance of openness and honesty as the way of building a strong business. Then I moved to Merrill Lynch, where I focused on short-term borrowing."

Mayer was assistant treasurer at Merrill Lynch, and his group changed the way securities firms borrow money. His group was able to secure short-term (1- or 2-day) loans from large Japanese banks, pay less for those loans than their competitors, and not be required to pledge securities. According to Mayer, "We borrowed $700 to $800 million overnight, used that money, and paid the banks back. We borrowed huge amounts. The foreign banks trusted Merrill Lynch; we were able to enhance the reputation of the company as honest, open, [and] innovative, and we also granted less expensive loans. The American banks initially scoffed at our approach. Later, they adopted similar approaches."

I asked Mayer, as a steward of the company, how he weighed the advantages and disadvantages of this new borrowing/loan policy. He replied: "My goal was to try to improve the value and reputation of our business. We had an innovative idea, and we were determined to capitalize on it. The only disadvantage was if we had failed, the big U.S. banks would have said, 'We told you so.'"

Next, Mayer became executive director and treasurer of Merrill Lynch's international banks and in that position focused on how the firm was using money. He said: "My goal was to connect Merrill Lynch to the rest of the world so that we could be as flexible as possible in how we used our money — trading securities, dollars, francs, yen, gold, silver, oil futures, etc."

Merrill Lynch built a computerized system for its offshore clients that connected financial markets and traders across the world. Clearly, there was risk, which Mayer described in this way:

> We were approving loans against collateral, for example, against the value of petrobonds in Mexican pesos for Mexican government officials. The bonds were converted into oil at a specific price. One risk was the price of oil. Also, I had to personally go to Mexico to ensure the repaid loan proceeds were repatriated to London. This part of the transaction was risky, but the overall goal I had as a senior steward of the company was to cultivate long-term profitable clients. The CFO of Merrill Lynch had to sign off on this project. If it had failed, I would've lost my job. The benefit was increasing the number of transactions from affluent customers who would consistently do business with us. The entire company stood to benefit from the risk that my group took.

He summarized his priorities for Merrill Lynch as follows: "My first priority was to the board of directors, because they made our policy decisions. Second, we wanted the best customers, that is, customers with a high net worth, who were stable, and who did frequent transactions with us. We had to provide innovative services. Third, I kept an eye on upper management (it was important to keep track of how your boss viewed your performance). Fourth, the stockholders are important, but in my position, they looked to the board to protect their interests." In short, as a senior executive for a major international finance company, Mayer knew that his role as economic steward was to build the company's reputation as creative, transparent, and accessible. This meant taking carefully measured risks that created large economic benefits.

We next discussed his role as treasurer of American Anglian, an international company that operated utilities for local governments, such as those in Scranton (Pennsylvania) and Buffalo (New York). Mayer explained:

This was a much more conservative and regulated business than Merrill Lynch. My job was to determine the cost to us of operating these water and sewerage systems, and then determine how much we should ask to operate the systems for 5- to 20-year periods. Our annual fee could not increase by more than the standard cost of living. We had the responsibility for labor, capital, maintenance, fines, and everything else. We were bidding against 8 to 10 other companies from around the world, and I knew that we had to be willing to take a loss for the first 3 years in order to make money over the length of the contract. The company was concerned about potentially losing money over the contract life. In one case, after I did the research, I recommended that we not compete for a contract because the local infrastructure was so run down. The bosses backed me. The company that got the bid walked into a real financial mess.

He summarized his strategy this way: "We would make money by reducing the workforce and by adding technology. We invested heavily for 3 years and amortized the investment over a decade. After 3 to 4 years, we broke even. Technology reduced labor, fuel, chemicals, and other costs. But there was risk, specifically, that we could not reduce the local workforce because of local politics and union contracts. Part of my job was to try to find other jobs for workers who would lose their jobs."

While Merrill Lynch and American Anglian were markedly different kinds of businesses, he noted two similarities that he believes are critical for any economic steward. "In both, we knew what the risks were and we spent hours and hours thinking about what could go wrong and developing strategies that could be used in response."

I asked Mayer to try to translate these experiences to DOE. Having spent years studying the department, he emphasized the problems a DOE economic steward faces: "There is an imbalance between the DOE's circumstances and those I encountered in private business. In private business, both sides had access to similar information and had experts to advise them. Maybe the public believes that local governments lack expertise, but when I negotiated with them, they really knew their systems. We were dealing with peers or near peers. In contrast, the DOE has a major competitive disadvantage. The contractors have operated these facilities for years, they have much more expertise and resources to put into a proposal than the DOE has to evaluate the proposal."

Further, he noted that DOE's history of secrecy and year-to-year funding means that few contractors will bid on DOE projects and still fewer have an intimate knowledge of the sites. In short, there is a lack of competition. As he puts it, "In the infrastructure business, the companies studied each other's bids and the municipalities talked with each other. The proposals submitted to the DOE are full of 'confidential' information, lessons learned are limited, and competition is very limited. The few contractors have enormous advantages."

He provided the following examples: "I don't understand why the Hanford vitrification facility project has learned so little from the projects at West Valley and Savannah River. The contractors claim that this is a one-of-a-kind project. Why? How can a steward be expected to do the job when the peer review is so limited and contractors can influence who can serve as peer reviewers?"

Our final point discussed the unusual role of environmental management stewards. Mayer noted:

> They are there to put themselves out of business. They have no long-term investment in these sites. The private companies always worried about their legacy. DOE EM [environmental management] is spending a lot of money at these sites and containing risks by and large. There is no board of directors pressuring them to more effectively use their resources, especially because of the tri-party agreements and pressure to continue to spend money at the large sites for regional economic support. These sites are like fiefdoms. In other words, there is pressure not to shift EM funds between sites. My advice would be to spend a lot more money on R&D [research and development] at the large sites and to set more realistic goals for their major waste streams. I would spend more money on the small sites, with the goal of eliminating their risks and closing the sites.

In other words, having been an economic steward for decades, he opposes spending vast sums at the large sites at this time.

Tools and Tasks

Four key economic environmental policy tools are described and illustrated in chapters 7 and 8. They are life-cycle cost, regional economic impact, cost-benefit, and natural resource damage analyses. All have been applied to the case study presented in this chapter.

The number of policies that are strongly influenced by economics and that a class can study is almost inexhaustible. These range from neighborhood/municipal to international, and from current to long term. As I wrote this chapter, my class was beginning to work on a hot economic policy topic: the distribution of federal antiterrorism funds.

Question: How should the federal government distribute antiterrorism funds to states and local governments?

Expected outcome: Major role-playing exercise and group paper (4 to 6 pages for each subgroup). See whether the class can arrive at a consensus. Students become active participants in policy formation.

Method: The class is divided into two sections. Then each section forms the following groups: (1) Federal Homeland Security, (2) New Jersey Department of Justice, (3) New Jersey League of Municipalities, (4) Port Authority of New York and New Jersey, (5) New Jersey Health Officers Association, (6) New Jersey Fire and Police Associations, (7) *Star Ledger* (most newspaper sales in New Jersey), and (8) citizen activist group.

Student roles: Students take on the role of organizations and participate in debate, using Web sites to develop background material for the group they represent. The memo and presentation should contain the following sections:

1. The mission of the organization
2. The position of the organization on the issue (e.g., distribute on the basis of the location of the population, jobs, or electricity-generating capacity; give more to local health departments; give more to fire/police departments; call for more objective analyses; have legislative committees allocate; or set priorities after major statewide debate
3. The basis for that position (e.g., jurisdictional equity, protection of key infrastructure, protection of the poor and other vulnerable members of society, states' rights)

An analogous neighborhood/municipal task is to investigate the economic advantages and disadvantages of revising cleaned-up brownfield sites for park space versus housing or retailing. An international issue is the economic ramifications of having the United States add further inspection requirements for foreign cargo or add more steps or restrictions for foreign students who want to study here.

An entirely different task is to examine the media coverage of environmental policy issues, but focus on the coverage of the economic components. For this exercise, I pick a topic, such as acid rain, global warming, loss of endangered species, or the impact of international trade on the environment. Then I have the students compare coverage by the *Wall Street Journal* and the *Economist* with more standard newspapers and magazines, such as the *New York Times*, the *Washington Post*, a local newspaper, *Newsweek*, and *Time*. How are the issues covered in these sources with respect to the location of the economic content and the importance of the economic perspective? If possible, it is useful to invite a local print, television, or radio journalists to provide a perspective on the content and method of coverage (see chapter 2 for a discussion of newsworthiness).

A third option for an economics-based task to invite a representative of local government, business, or a not-for-profit organization. This involves selecting a specific environmental policy that is relevant to the organization and also trying to determine the importance it ascribes to economics versus the other five criteria.

Before inviting the expert, the class should do some homework and develop some questions to send in advance. After the presentation, the class should use it as a point of departure to discuss the policy in depth. It may even be possible to take a small class to a facility, which was quite common when I began teaching but is much more difficult today because of security. The days of taking a class to a nuclear or fossil fuel plant, to a steel mill or chemical plant, or to an automobile plant have all but disappeared and may not return.

5

Ethics Criterion

International Trade in Pesticides and Genetically Modified Crops

Introduction

The first four chapters of this book examined environmental policy issues through the prism of elected officials, nongovernment stakeholders, environmental scientists, and economists. These interest groups are involved in every policy judgment, and it is not necessary to dig too deeply into an issue to find them. This chapter examines policy from the viewpoint of those who see issues as ethical and moral tests of our society. Ethical behavior seems like an oxymoron to people who distrust government and business because of highly publicized cases of bribery and fraud, fabrication of data by scientists, and other acts of misconduct.

This chapter is not about misconduct. Rather, it is about the morality and ethics of selling pesticides and promoting genetically modified (GM) crops in developing nations. "Pesticide" is a generic term for a substance used to destroy, repel, regulate, defoliate, or desiccate pests, including insects, rodents, molds, and weeds. The two general ethical questions I will examine require simple yes or no answers: Should the United States market pesticides that are banned here in other countries? Should we promote GM crops in other places if we are not certain of their impact? Embedded in these two simple queries are tough ethical questions. Specifically, should we sell these products if

1. The countries request them?
2. The countries argue that they need them to protect public health?
3. The countries argue that they need them to feed and clothe their population?
4. Their leaders do not want these products to be sold in their country?
5. We know that workers who apply these products are not adequately protected?
6. We know that these products might compromise native crop species?

There are no simple answers to these questions.

International sales of pesticides and GM crops are intertwined with other issues. The overarching one is the increasing worldwide demand for agricultural products. Included in this issue are world population growth, consumerism in Western nations, pressure on the food supply, crop management practices, large-scale mechanization and the increasing scale of production, and, of course, pest control. After I discuss these issues, I shift the focus of the chapter to the moral dilemma that the United States faces when it permits the sale of products that are banned in this country in developing nations and promotes genetically altered crops. Charles Powers, who has a PhD in ethics, was a professor of ethics at Yale and Vanderbilt Universities, and has decades of experience dealing with real-world environmental management challenges, will help me unravel some of this complexity.

Theme: Pesticides, GM Organisms, and Interconnected Policy Themes

A century ago, the world's population was about one-fourth of what it is today. Then, the vast majority of crops grown in the United States came from relatively small family-owned farms. Now, we have global just-on-time trade of almost every commodity, including agricultural products. As the largest international trader in the world, the United States is pressured by its private enterprises not to hinder competition. Yet the U.S. government faces increasing international scrutiny of its trade policies and is undeniably judged by the behavior and mis-behavior of its private enterprises. Our pesticide sales and GM crop policies exemplify the dilemma facing the U.S. government. Before focusing on pesticides and genetically modified organisms (GMOs), I will introduce two issues that have provided the context for this moral conundrum: (1) world population growth and the demand for crops and (2) crop management practices.

World Population Growth and the Demand for Crops
The population increase that took place during the 20th century was nothing short of astonishing. We started the century with about 1.6 billion people and ended it with 6.1 billion. Plotting population growth on a graph, with the x-axis marking time and the y-axis marking population, results in a line that looks like the letter J. This is geometrical growth (1, 2, 4, 8, 16, 32, 64 . . .) rather than arith-metical growth (1, 2, 3, 4, 5, 6, 7 . . .).

In 1798, before the world's population had reached even a billion people, Thomas Malthus, who was observing the rapid population growth associated with the Industrial Revolution in Europe, argued that such an increase was not sustainable because food production could not keep pace with growth.

Two hundred years after these predictions, birth rates in Europe have dropped, some to below replacement levels. Europe's proportion of the world's population decreased from almost 25 percent in 1900 to about 12 percent in 2000. The United Nations (U.N.) (2005) expects it to fall to 7 percent by 2050.

In contrast to Europe, population growth in Latin America, Africa, and parts of Asia has been explosive. Latin America's and Africa's share of the world's population increased from 12.6 percent in 1900 to 21.5 percent in 2000. According to the U.N. (2005; see also U.S. Bureau of the Census, 1999), the J-shaped curve for population will gradually change to an S-shaped curve; that is, the rate of population increase will slow down, reaching more than 9 billion by 2050. The world growth rate has dropped from over 2 percent during the late 1960s to 1.3 percent today.

The U.N.'s (2005) estimate of around 9 billion people by 2050 is reasonable, but no one can be certain. In the short run, some countries in Africa and Asia have been devastated by the HIV/AIDS pandemic. War could further reduce the rate of population growth. At the upper end, several papers have reported that the Earth could manage 40 billion, or even 150 billion people, although these estimates have been criticized as based on unrealistic assumptions ("Agriculture could feed 40 billion," 1988; Daily, Ehrlich, and Ehrlich, 1994; Ehrlich and Ehrlich, 1991; Livi-Bacci, 1997; Simon, 1990). In the coming decades, diseases, world conflicts, catastrophic events, the availability of family planning services, education, and the reduction of poverty will determine how rapidly the birth rate slows down in developing nations and how many people live. No one really knows whether the population will be 8 billion or 14 billion.

The impact of population growth in developing nations in Latin America, Africa, and Asia is one part of the pressure on world resources. The second component is increasing consumption in North America, Western Europe, Japan, and several other nations. Consumerism has had profound impacts on resource use, the environment, and global policies. In his best-selling book *The Population Bomb*, Paul Ehrlich (1968), like Malthus (1798), predicted dire consequences for humanity. He created an impact factor that was the result of the multiplication of population, affluence, and technology. In other words, high consumption by affluent populations could trigger a catastrophic shortage of resources. Population growth in developing nations is not the only threat (see also Commoner, 1971; Dooge et al., 1992; and Meadows et al., 1972).

Chapter 3 pointed to the economic, social, environmental, and political challenges facing the United States because of its consumption of and reliance on oil. This chapter points to the moral challenge facing this country because of its sale of pesticides and GM crops to developing countries. However, the greater challenge is to the developing nations that must balance their need to feed their population and provide clothing, shelter, education, and health services against the risks of applying pesticides and using GM crops.

The disasters predicted by Malthus (1798) and Ehrlich (1968) did not happen, but the frightening image of widespread starvation lingers. In a 1999 keynote address to the 10th World Congress of Food Science and Technology, John Lupien, director of the Food and Nutrition Division of the U.N. Food and Agriculture Organization (FAO), provided both sobering and optimistic perspectives. Hundreds of millions, nearly all of them living in Asia, Africa, and Latin America, are chronically undernourished. Food emergencies were observed in 37 countries as a result of war, bad weather, and transportation problems. Further, the increase in agricultural production had slowed, and meeting the increasing demand for milk, fruits and vegetables, processed foods, and especially beef (since affluent people generally want more beef) had become a challenge.

Yet Lupien (1999) added that the world's food supply had kept pace with population growth and that, in fact, the number of chronically undernourished people had decreased. He concluded by noting that the world could produce enough food to feed everyone and that the keys to feeding people were improvements in education, employment, immunization, infrastructure, and other elements of development. His optimistic message that the world has the capacity to keep pace with increasing demand has been echoed by others (FAO, 2000; Nelson and Chassy, 2000).

Crop Management Practices

The fact that overall world food production kept pace with population growth is remarkable. There have been two green revolutions. The first occurred where major investments were made in science, where land and other resources were available to develop and test products, and where transportation and other infrastructure were in place and could be expanded to store and move crops to market. For example, between 1930 and 1994, Illinois corn yields grew from about 30 to almost 140 bushels per acre (Nelson and Chassy, 2000). The second green revolution took place in developing nations, especially in Asia. For example, irrigated rice yield in the Philippines increased 50 percent between 1970 and 1984 (Nelson and Chassy, 2000).

However, these two green miracles have had some less desirable impacts as well. Both required the expanded use of fertilizer, irrigation, farm machinery, fossil fuel, and pesticides (Conway, 1997; Stark, 2001). More land was used for agriculture, but some of it was marginal and failed to produce higher yields (University of Michigan, 2006). Agriculture depends heavily on fresh water, and some areas had to make a choice between irrigating crops and providing potable drinking water. Technology has also tended to reduce the genetic diversity of plants (that is, a move toward monoculture), increase vulnerability to pests, and hence require large amounts of pest control agents. While about three-fourths of pesticides are applied in developed countries, about a quarter of the use is in developing nations. Finally, the green revolution should also be called the large corporate farm takeover revolution because it has required so much capital investment and planning that small farms have been hard-pressed to survive.

Will there be a third green revolution? FAO (2000) notes that much of the increase will come from intensifying land use (e.g., high cropping and multicropping) and increasing plant yields. GM crops are one way of increasing yields. Traditional breeding practices that selectively identify key traits and breed those without altering genes are another option (Union of Concerned Scientists, 2006). Nelson and Chassy (2000) think that GM crops could increase yields 30 to 50 percent; reduce the use of petroleum, fertilizer, water, pesticides, and herbicides; and allow crops to be grown in locations that are not currently arable. The products themselves would be bred to have fewer toxic compounds or none at all; be resistant to cold, heat, drought, and salt; and produce more nutrients. Ingo Potrykus, the Swiss-born inventor of golden rice, became a modern-day Johnny Appleseed on July 31, 2000, when the cover story of *Time* (Nash-Zurich, 2000) said that his genetically altered rice could save a million children a year. Others dispute these claims and point to potential dangers.

Can a third green revolution occur without GM crops or without large agricultural subsides? During 1987, for example, pesticides were supplied nearly free of charge to most Nicaraguan farmers through favorable exchange rates and negative real interest rates. As a result of subsidies, Nicaraguan farmers increased the number of pesticide applications in maize, and there was a serious epidemic of pesticide poisonings (see McConnell and Hruska, 1993; and later discussion in this chapter). McConnell and Hruska (1993) add that the subsidies induced farmers to overuse their lands, requiring more support and subsidies for continued supply (see DaMotta, 2001).

In short, the green revolutions have allowed food production to keep up with population growth in developing nations and to provide specialty foods to affluent people. In the process, agriculture has been dramatically altered in the United States and in other areas where the tools of the revolution were applied.

Pesticides, Crop Breeding, and the Moral Dilemma of Pesticides and GM Crops

In this section, I briefly describe the major types of pesticides, their impacts, their legal controls, and the international political issues they have engendered. Chlorinated hydrocarbon insecticides were commonly used in the past but were removed from much of the market due to health and environmental effects and persistence. Prominent examples of such pesticides are DDT (dichlorodiphenyltrichloroethane) (see the later discussion in this chapter) and chlordane. Organophosphate pesticides, a second type, affect the nervous system by disrupting the enzyme that regulates acetylcholine, a neurotransmitter. These pesticides were developed during the early 19th century, but their effects on insects and humans were discovered in 1932. Variations of these and other chemical pesticides have been used as weapons of mass destruction. Carbamate pesticides, a third type, also affect the nervous system. Pyrethroid pesticides were developed as a synthetic version of the naturally occurring pesticide pyrethrin.

Many other forms of pesticides exist, but no one is likely to think of them as pesticides. For instance, biopesticides are derived from natural materials including animals, plants, bacteria, and minerals. Examples include commonly used products such as canola oil and baking soda. Substances produced by plants from genetic materials that are added to them are pest control agents as well. Biochemical pesticides are naturally occurring substances that control pests by nontoxic mechanisms. Included among these are substances such as insect sex pheromones that interfere with mating and scented plant extracts that attract pests to traps, which often hang from trees.

The use of pesticides has grown exponentially since 1945. Profits from synthetic pesticides soared after World War II (Toxic Trail, 2006; Wargo, 1996). Over $30 billion is spent on pesticides annually, about a third of it in the United States (Kiely, Donaldson, and Grube, 2004). The global pesticide market is dominated by 10 companies. The leading pesticide companies have merged with or have been taken over by agrochemical companies, and they have expanded into the seed industry and genetic engineering. The fact that pesticide manufacturers are in the genetic crop engineering business is enough to make some people distrust safety claims about GM crops.

HEALTH EFFECTS AND BENEFITS OF PESTICIDES. The World Health Organization (WHO) estimates that each year there are 25 million cases of pesticide poisoning and as many as 20,000 deaths, primarily in developing countries. Regular exposure to pesticides often causes chronic illnesses, including, some argue, cancer and reproductive and neurological effects (Wargo, 1996). Most poisonings and 99 percent of deaths are in developing countries, although the Third World accounts for only 25 percent of the total worldwide consumption of pesticides.

For example, a mass pesticide poisoning was reported in Nicaragua in June/July 1987. More than half of these poisonings involved a carbamate insecticide, and the rest involved an organophosphate (McConnell and Hruska, 1993; see also Recena, Pires, and Caldras, 2006, for a Brazilian example). Most occupational pesticide poisonings in the Nicaraguan epidemic occurred because of backpack application (rather than the farm equipment used in developed nations), the absence of agricultural extension services (available in developed countries), and the fact that protective rubber gloves and respirators were either not available or not used. Also, Nicaragua (like most other Third World countries) does not require that imported pesticides be registered in their country of origin, and pesticides banned or restricted in their country of origin are widely used. These events imply an ethical burden for those who sell the products and the governments that sanction these sales.

DDT, DDE, and DDD (all are chemical cousins of DDT, the most famous chlorinated pesticide) have had a major impact on the environment (Carson, 1962) and have been found in humans, for example, in breast milk. Breast-feeding mothers eliminate DDT, DDE, and DDD much faster through milk production than through any other mechanism in the general population. Application of DDT results in an increase in exposure and, thus, a rise in DDT in breast milk (Bouman et al., 1992).

Some insecticides have exacerbated pest outbreaks because the chemicals kill beneficial insect predators as well as pests (see the vivid descriptions in Carson, 1962). The chemicals do not always kill eggs of the pests, so they emerge and reproduce without hindrance from predators, wreaking more damage than was the case before the insecticide was applied. Use of insecticides may increase crop losses over time because insects may develop resistance to specific pesticides and require more concentrated applications or a switch to a different compound. Pest resistance occurs when the hardy insects that survive breed and transfer resistance genes to their offspring so that eventually the entire species becomes resistant to the pesticide, thus eradicating its efficacy (Schmidt, 1998).

Despite these problems, pesticides have been a major public health asset. DDT has been applied to control the mosquitoes that cause malaria. My neighbor, a retired chemistry professor, swears by DDT. He fought in World War II and believes that the only reason that he did not get malaria is that he sprayed himself with it. DDT was discovered by Swiss-born scientist Paul Hermann Müller, who received the 1948 Nobel prize in medicine for the discovery. DDT is a contact poison that acts on the nervous system of insects, causing overstimulation of neurons and rapid death. Hailed as a major achievement because it provided an affordable way to manage the major public health risks carried by mosquitoes, lice, and other vectors, DDT became a key component of worldwide antimalaria efforts.

Malaria has been a serious public health threat. In 1995, WHO estimated that 40 percent of the world's population or over 2 billion people in a hundred different nations are exposed to malaria. Over 120 million clinical cases of malaria were reported, but this is a very low count; some believe that there are 360 million cases (Wargo, 1996; WHO, 2006). Africa Fighting Malaria (2006) advocates for increased access to DDT and argues that its limited use in homes and hospitals is a powerful and necessary tool in fighting malaria. Estimates indicate that DDT and other chlorinated hydrocarbons have prevented the exposure of over a billion people to malaria and prevented 7 million deaths (Wargo, 1996; WHO, 2006).

DDT's value is illustrated by KwaZulu-Natal, a South African province where DDT was sprayed until 1996. Because of pressure from other nations, the use of DDT was stopped and it was replaced by another insecticide. However, mosquitoes were resistant to the new product and malaria cases soared. DDT was applied again in 2000, and malaria was once more brought under control (Rosenberg, 2004). South Africa and 5 other countries use DDT for routine malaria control, and 10 additional countries use it for emergencies (Rosenberg, 2004). WHO (and FAO, which are both part of the U.N.) focused on pesticides as a way to help control malaria. In 1960, WHO called insecticide resistance the greatest threat to the future of malaria eradication (Wargo, 1996). According to a U.S. Agency for International Development (USAID) fact sheet, limited spraying of DDT inside houses is unlikely to have a major negative environmental impact (Rosenberg, 2004). In short, pesticides like DDT have undeniably protected the food supply, at least in the short run, and protected people. They are also relatively inexpensive to use and have a long shelf life.

MANAGING PESTICIDES. Substances with such potential to help and harm require management. The regulation of pesticides began early in the 20th century with the Insecticide Act of 1910 (Wargo, 1996). The Federal Food, Drug, and Cosmetic Act of 1938, which was the basic food law, stated that pesticide residues in food must not endanger public health. The Federal Insecticide, Fungicide, and Rodenticide Act (FIFRA) of 1947 required all pesticides sold or distributed in the United States (including imported pesticides) to be registered. EPA, which now has jurisdiction, can authorize the limited use of unregistered pesticides or pesticides registered for other uses to address emergencies and special local needs. The law required that so-called economic poisons be licensed, and it also required the prominent display of warning labels and instructions for use, so labeling was the real strategy. The early legislation contained no discussion of limitations or restrictions on the use of pesticides.

In 1954, the Miller Pesticide Amendment set limits on the amount of residues allowed in food. It required that the Food and Drug Administration (FDA) set tolerances to protect human health, but it did not give FDA the authority to demand that industry test additives before using them. Registration was permitted only if the manufacturer presented data demonstrating that residue levels on food crops posed no danger to public health (Wargo, 1996). Also, FDA had to recognize the need for "an adequate, wholesome and economical food supply," thereby creating a dual standard. This meant that two approvals were required from the government before a compound could be sold and used: a registration from the U.S. Department of Agriculture (USDA) and a tolerance from FDA (Wargo, 1996). It required that residue limits be established for raw agricultural products such as fresh fruits, vegetables, or milk (Wargo, 1996).

Next, the Delaney Clause of 1958 prohibited the use of synthetic carcinogens, including pesticides, in processed food. Although it prohibited residues, it also required that economic concerns be balanced against public health (Wargo, 1996).

FIFRA administration moved to EPA in 1970, reflecting the shift in policy toward a greater emphasis on minimizing the risks of pesticides to human health and the environment and away from economic-based policy. In 1972, EPA stopped registering DDT because of concerns over environmental threats and public health risks. EPA reported (1972) that the decline in the use of DDT was due to insect resistance, development of more effective alternative pesticides, growing public and user concern over adverse environmental side effects, and government restrictions on DDT. The DDT ban laid the foundation for the first reform of FIFRA since 1947. By 1972, FIFRA required that registration be contingent on EPA's finding no "unreasonable adverse effects on the environment, taking into account the economic, social and environmental costs and benefits of any pesticide" (U.S. Code, 2007). This means that even if EPA found that the health risks of a particular pesticide were significant, it could issue or continue a registration if it concluded that the benefits were substantial (Wargo, 1996).

The Federal Environmental Pesticides Control Act (FEPCA) of 1972 moved the mission of the government from accuracy in product labeling to protection of public health and the environment. The act created two categories of use: general and restricted. This was also reflected in FEPCA by specifying methods and standards of control in greater detail (Burros, 1993; Oleskey et al., 2004).

The Food Quality Protection Act of 1996 (FQPA) mandated that EPA better assess and prevent exposure to pesticides. For example, it directed EPA to apply a 10-fold margin of safety for infants and children, except where reliable data indicate that such a margin is not required. FQPA required EPA to find that a pesticide poses a "reasonable certainty of no harm" before the pesticide can be registered for use on food or feed (EPA, 2006a, 2006b, 2006c, 2006d). This meant that EPA was required to make the protection of human health the primary goal of pesticide regulation. It also required EPA to consider the cumulative effects on human health that may result from multiple exposures to many pesticides. In fact, this requirement created an incentive for the pesticide industry to conduct human testing to justify the relaxation of EPA's pesticide tolerance thresholds (Oleskey et al., 2004). However, under FIFRA, pesticide production data are considered confidential business information and are therefore not accessible to researchers even through the Freedom of Information Act. Because the pesticide industry does not accept federal funding, it is not required to establish institutional review boards to oversee research on human subjects (Oleskey et al., 2004).

EPA must judge the potential for every pesticide to cause health problems including cancer, neurological damage, reproductive failure, birth defects, mutagenic effects, and fetotoxic effects. Since the passage of FQPA, chemical manufacturers have done tests on human volunteers to establish the safe or threshold limits for human exposure, termed "no observable effect levels" or NOELs. Because these tests are done by private companies, the methods used and the prior informed consent for study subjects may be arguably less stringent than those required by the Common Rule (Oleskey et al., 2004).

Registration of a pesticide means that EPA has determined that its use does not pose unreasonable adverse effects on health or the environment. Pesticides that are not registered cannot be sold or used in the United States, but they can be manufactured and exported (Foundation for Advancements in Science and Education (FASE), 1998). Once a pesticide is registered, the way of controlling human exposure from food residues is by setting tolerances, which establish a legal limit on the amount of residue that can remain on food.

In 1999, the Clinton administration directed EPA to stop accepting information from pesticide manufacturer studies conducted on human subjects. In 2001, the Bush administration reversed this decision. Later that year, EPA announced a moratorium on human tests, but in 2004, the National Academy of Sciences recommended that EPA be allowed to receive test data from chemical companies as long as certain standards are met (Oleskey et al., 2004).

Overall, this summary shows that multiple agencies (EPA, FDA, USDA) manage pesticides and that Congress and the Executive Branch have evolved policies that have gradually tightened control over pesticides in the United States, albeit with periodic wavering.

EXPORTING POTENTIAL HAZARDS TO DEVELOPING NATIONS. The key international issues have been labeling and consent. The Federal Insecticide, Fungicide, and Rodenticide Act (FIFRA) of 1978 required minimum labeling requirements for all exported pesticides. Labels were required to include an ingredient statement and warning and caution statements, and if the product was highly toxic, a skull and crossbones and a statement providing proven treatment in the case of poisoning. All unregistered pesticides to be exported also had to carry the statement, "Not Registered for Use in the United States." All critical information, including precautionary statements, had to appear in both English and the language of the importing country (FASE, 1998).

A bill introduced in 1980 sought to place export licensing controls on banned products, saying that existing export notice provisions did not go far enough. Despite lobbying by industry representatives, President Carter signed Executive Order 12264 — "On Federal Policy regarding the Export of Banned or Significantly Restricted Substances" — in 1981. It sought to improve the export notices that were already required, called for annual publication of a summary of government actions banning or severely restricting substances for domestic use, directed the State Department and other federal agencies to participate in international hazard alert systems, and established procedures requiring formal export licensing controls on a limited number of extremely hazardous substances that may threaten U.S. foreign policy interests. These licenses would be granted only in "exceptional cases." Thirty-four days later, this order was rescinded by President Reagan, with the justification that imposition of export controls would result in a costly regulatory program to both the public and private sectors (Pearson, 1987).

EPA has some outreach programs for alerting international users of pesticides to their options. The Office of Prevention, Pesticides, and Toxic Substances has developed Web-based tools for chemical management specialists (EPA, 2006a, 2006b, 2006c, 2006d; see also FAO, 2006a, 2006b) and works with FAO to develop global strategies to address the risk of obsolete pesticides. EPA has developed an international training course called "Pesticide Disposal in Developing Countries." In Central America, EPA works with USAID to provide training courses in the disposal of obsolete pesticides and the strengthening of the analytical capacity of laboratories to monitor pesticide residues on food. EPA works with USAID and the U.N. Environment Programme (UNEP) to help regulatory officials in developing countries gain access to the Internet. They have developed a training program called "Using the Internet to Research Chemicals Management Questions." Under

FIFRA, all registered pesticides exported to other countries must bear a product label approved by EPA. For unregistered pesticides, exporters must meet the FIFRA requirements related to foreign purchaser acknowledgment statements, export notification, and labeling.

Many of these U.S. efforts are channeled through the United Nations and other international conventions. In 1985, FAO adopted an international code with voluntary guidelines for the export, testing, advertising, and management of pesticides. This code was created because of concerns over supplying banned and other hazardous pesticides to countries lacking the resources to ensure safe and effective use (FASE, 1998).

Two international conferences have placed the U.S. government at a point where it has cooperated with developing nations. The Rotterdam Convention on Prior Informed Consent (PIC) Procedure for Certain Hazardous Chemicals and Pesticides in International Trade, enacted into law in 2004, led to an early warning system about all bans and severe restrictions on pesticides. Pesticides banned by two countries in two regions are entered onto the PIC list, and importing countries must indicate whether they allow or prohibit import (Pesticide Action Network UK, 2005a). The Stockholm Convention on Persistent Organic Pollutants, enacted into law in May 2004, covers 12 chemicals that governments will take measures to eliminate or to reduce releases into the environment, including the pesticides DDT, aldrin, dieldrin, endrin, chlordane, heptachlor, hexachlorobenzene, mirex, and toxaphene. The Bush administration agreed to the treaty, with the exception of DDT for controlling malaria (Bate, 2003).

In addition to EPA's role with other organizations, there are more than two dozen international organizations concerned over the export of pesticides. Among them are the International Organization of Consumers Unions (concerned with the dumping of pesticides and consumer goods), Health Action International, Pesticide Action Network International, the Rainforest Alliance and Sustainable Agriculture Network, WHO, and the International Agency for Research on Cancer (see chapter 2).

The PIC Procedure for Certain Hazardous Chemicals and Pesticides in International Trade aimed to provide developing countries with information on bans or severe restrictions imposed by governments on a pesticide or chemical because of health or environmental concerns. Once a chemical is on the PIC list, governments will be able to prohibit its import. The Rotterdam Convention also requires labeling to follow the same standard required in the exporting country and stipulates that countries can request additional documentation such as the names of exporters and safety data sheets. The Rotterdam Convention contains no specific provision for technical and financial assistance (Pesticide Action Network UK, 1998a, 1998b).

The Reagan administration accepted PIC, although it was criticized by conservatives as an effort to hamper capitalism. Some have seen the export of pesticides as a moral issue. For example, Representative Sam Gibbons (D-FL) was quoted as saying in 1980: "The exportation of any product considered unsafe for Americans should be condemned. . . . It would be unconscionable on our part to stand back and allow this traffic in hazardous products to continue. . . . I urge the Administration to forge an export policy that protects the health and safety of consumers wherever they may be and preserve the integrity of the label 'Made in U.S.A.'" (Pearson, 1987, 144–145).

Anne Peterson, assistant administrator for Global Health at USAID, put it this way: "For us to be using in another country something we don't allow in our own country raises the specter of preferential treatment. We certainly have to think about 'What would the American people think and want?' and 'What would Africans think if we're going to do to them what we wouldn't do to our own people?'" (Rosenberg, 2004, 38).

There is a hidden double standard not included in these two statements. The United States and Europe used DDT to wipe out malaria, but once Western countries discovered that it was harming the ecosystem, it was no longer considered safe and is not permitted in far poorer and sicker nations. DDT's toxic image in the United States and U.S. influence over international policies make it unavailable to many nations that might want and need it to fight malaria (Rosenberg, 2004).

The idea of consent was introduced in the early 1980s when FAO promoted the International Code of Conduct on the Distribution and Use of Pesticides. It was amended in the Code of 1989 (Pesticide Action Network UK, 1998a, 1998b). The aim of this code was to promote and assist in the development of acceptable pesticide management practices within the framework of Integrated Pest Management principles. Also, UNEP (U.N. Environment Programme) addressed PIC in the 1989 London Guidelines on Exchange of Information on Chemicals in International Trade. PIC has operated through FAO for pesticides and UNEP for chemicals. A revised International Code of Conduct on the Distribution and Use of Pesticides was adopted by the FAO Council in November 2002.

U.S. businesses can sidestep existing U.S. government efforts to regulate and label pesticides, evaluate users, and obtain consent by relocating their facilities to countries with more relaxed environmental standards, thereby creating a so-called pollution haven (Pearson, 1987). Another interesting reality is that if EPA bans a product, manufacturers can ship remaining stocks overseas and continue production there, as allowed by U.S. law. The banned pesticides may then show up on food imported into this country (called the "circle of poison" by U.S. environmental and consumer interest groups) (Wargo, 1996). U.S. firms can legally produce and export a pesticide banned for use here. For example, U.S. manufacturers exported more than 465 million pounds of pesticides in 1990, 52 million of which were banned, restricted, or unregistered for use in this country. In 1993, U.S. firms exported 27 unregistered pesticides. Since 1998, FIFRA has required that U.S. firms notify foreign governments of shipments of banned, canceled, suspended, or restricted-use pesticides. Arguably, however, the process has been less than successful.

In the mid-1970s, developing countries began to express concern about industrial countries' export of products, particularly drugs and pesticides that were banned or unapproved for domestic use (Pearson, 1987). In a statement on the sale of banned or restricted products, the UNEP Governing Council said that "there have been unethical practices concerning the distribution of chemicals, drugs, cosmetics and food unfit for human consumption" and that "there is a need for harmonious cooperation . . . between exporting and importing countries" (Pearson, 1987, 140). The council urged that "governments . . . take steps to ensure that potentially harmful chemicals, in whatever form or commodity, which are unacceptable for domestic purposes in the exporting country, are not permitted to be exported without the knowledge and consent of appropriate authorities in the importing country" (Pearson, 1987, 140).

In 1984, the Organization for Economic Cooperation and Development (OECD) Council adopted a recommendation titled "Intermediate Exchange Related to Export of Banned or Severely Restricted Chemicals," which called on nations to provide information to permit the importing country to make "timely and informed decisions" about chemical exports (Pearson, 1987, 140). In 1984, UNEP adopted a provisional plan of export notification that is nearly identical to that of OECD.

In 1982, the U.N. General Assembly adopted Resolution 37/137, called "Protection against Products Harmful to Health and the Environment," with the United States casting the only dissenting vote. It called for an end to the export of "products that have been banned from domestic consumption and/or sale" in the exporting country unless permitted by the importing country (Pearson 1987, 141–142). Part of the resolution involved assembling an annual list of harmful products. The list is very controversial, and the United States continued to oppose it when it reemerged in 1984 (Pearson, 1987).

In a nutshell, the U.S. food supply — arguably the most plentiful, inexpensive, and varied in the world — would not be possible without pesticides. The pesticide industry argues that its products are safe and provide an inexpensive way to protect crops if used appropriately. Indeed, on the basis of data gathered over more than a quarter of a century, FDA has rarely found levels of residues that it regards as above-tolerance in foods. Yet that "if used appropriately" phrase is a problem for developing nations, and U.S. business and by extension the U.S. government are on shaky moral ground because of poor practices in developing countries:

1. There is evidence that information about prohibitions or use restrictions placed on the product in the country of origin has been withheld from the importing government.
2. The U.S. government has facilitated or at least not stopped the exportation of a product banned or severely restricted in this country into another country without the knowledge and consent of the authorities there.

3. Product labels that include warnings about safety precautions have not always been included or have not been in the language of the country of destination.
4. Home government regulations are avoided by shipping through subsidiaries in third countries or by changing the product name or formula.
5. The U.S. government has not acted on the reality that pesticide workers in developing countries are at high risk of poisoning because of a lack of education and understanding of the products, lack of health facilities, and the tendency of farmers to use what is available rather than what is appropriate.

Despite the positive applications of pesticides, the track record of applying and monitoring their impact makes many people uncomfortable.

GM CROPS: ANOTHER ETHICAL CHALLENGE. Crops genetically engineered for resistance to pests offer an option for farmers seeking chemical-free alternatives to pesticides. But there are some uncomfortable and distressing historical precedents that make me nervous. One familiar concern is that GM crops will be overused and will speed the rate at which insects become resistant to the altered gene (Schmidt, 1998). A second is that GM crops will drift and that genetic drift will compromise native plants. Third, I am not persuaded that the three-headed federal agency stewardship model can work for a technology as dynamic as that of GMOs. Last, and most important, the ethical performance of the pesticide industry that now controls many of the GM products has at times been less than honorable. I am not sure whether to be reassured or dismayed by the fact that the U.S. government and business want to treat GMOs as they have treated pesticides.

The preceding historical summary of pesticide management may seem obtuse, but the management of pesticides *is* obtuse. A National Academy of Sciences Committee (National Research Council, 1987) labeled the laws and regulations a "crazy quilt," which I think is a charitable description. Writing about legal reform in the People's Republic of China, Alford (2000) suggests that more legal codes do not mean more effective law. In the case of pesticide management, it appears that more policy means more opportunities for vested interests to bend environmental management to business, environmentalist, labor, anti-globalization, and other agendas.

Richard Stewart of New York University has written extensively about legal management (2001, 2002). He divided the legal control of risks into four levels that present a handy way of examining U.S. pesticide policies. The strongest control is to prohibit use. That has happened in this country with DDT, lindane, and other chlorinated pesticides, but only after strong evidence was produced and gradually accepted over the course of bitter and acrimonious debate (see also the discussion of tetraethyl lead in chapter 3). Emergency use of DDT is still permitted.

A major complication with regard to GM crops is the adamant opposition of the European Union (EU) (examined in more detail shortly). Also, some activist groups would like to ban GMOs and GM crops. Their arguments convey the image that GMOs are a Faustian bargain that will ravage the world. This same tactic, I believe, has contributed to the failed expansion of the nuclear power industry in the United States (see chapter 6). I already see some companies responding to consumer fear about GM crops by agreeing to use "organic" (i.e., supposedly safe) crops.

Stewart's (2001, 2002) second level of control is to insist on the use of the best technology and science. This would mean carefully monitoring and examining GM crop development, testing, and use, and then reporting and acting on the findings. We can expect GM applications in the United States to apply the best science. I am much less sanguine about the implementation of the same practices in developing nations.

Stewart describes requiring a margin of safety as a third level of control. That is, if there is a noticeable effect level, then a safety factor of 10 to 1,000 times is applied to field applications because some people, usually children and infirm and elderly people, are more vulnerable. The application of this approach to chemicals that are sprayed on plants is clear for pesticides in the FQPA (Food Quality Protection Act). How a similar approach would work for GM crops escapes me. Would the mixing of GM and nonaltered genes work? What about the mixing of GM and non-GM crops?

The weakest form of control, according to Stewart (2001, 2002), is labeling. Yet this is where most of the battle lines have been drawn. The GMO industry does not want to see GM foods singled out as a potential hazard. The U.S.-based industry is particularly distressed by opposition from the European Union, which argues that GM crops could be hazardous and that the public is frightened. Compared with pesticide-treated crops, the risks associated with GM crops seem less hazardous in the short run. The assertion of public fear has been studied by researchers who have found that the European public, rather than being adamantly opposed to GM foods, is mostly ambivalent about GM crops. Gaskell et al. (2004) suggest that the public's ambivalence is explained by the lack of information about the benefits of these crops. Given the history of the mad cow disease scare in the United Kingdom in 1996 and government reassurances, it is not surprising that the public does not trust authority and focuses on negative information (see the discussion of outrage factors and trust in chapter 3; and Pardo, Midden and Miller, 2002; and Pidgeon et al., 2005).

U.S. business and elements of the U.S. government believe that Europe is opposing GM crops to protect its agriculture. Paarlberg (2000) noted that new technologies provoke resistance and that opposition to GM crops is therefore not surprising. He challenges the ethical positions of both the United States and the European Union, asserting cynically that U.S. agro-food interests did not invest heavily in GM crop science until U.S. courts extended patent protection to these inventions. Rather than focus on what he calls the "food fight" between the United States and the European Union, he notes that public support for agricultural development has collapsed and that the largely U.S.-based companies will not invest in tropical markets that have so little purchasing power without the kinds of subsidies that were available during the first two green revolutions. Arguing that this technology is needed by poor farmers and poor consumers in tropical countries, Paarlberg (2000) criticized business, government, and nongovernmental organizations for frightening people and potential investors away from GM crops (see also Bernauer, 2003; and Hall and Moffitt, 2002).

Runge and Senauer (2000) added that GM crops are being opposed as a cause célèbre of the evils of globalization by a coalition that includes labor, environmentalists, and both left- and right-wing political activists who are anxious to protect national sovereignty. These authors call for a global agreement that connects agriculture, the environment, food security, and trade and for opponents to stop using environmental protection as a moral justification for restricting trade. In February 2006, the World Trade Organization struck down Europe's moratorium on GMOs. The European Union responded by tightening its GMO evaluation process. The U.S.-EU food fight will continue, at least over the short term.

Six Policy Criteria: A Synopsis of a Moral Dilemma

This section summarizes the advantages and vulnerabilities of a decision by the federal government to strongly support the development and export of GMOs and crops. In table 10, I indicate 32 points to be considered by policy makers and summarize the pros and cons for the U.S. government, which has a lot at stake in the future of GMOs and crops. Success will have a positive impact on U.S. business and the government during a period when U.S. prestige has declined. Failure of GM technologies could further undermine the government's credibility. So should the U.S. government promote or oppose GMOs and crops? I summarize the payoffs to the U.S. government in table 11.

If the optimists are right, that is, if GM crops trigger the third green revolution, and the U.S. government has been a clear advocate, then the political reward would be great. The federal government would be viewed as a strong supporter of U.S. business, international trade, and science and of the world's poor. If the U.S. government is less supportive, but not restrictive, there is still benefit. Government agencies can assert that they were appropriately cautious and have monitored the industry. If the results in the end are as successful as they were in the first two green revolutions, the U.S. government will benefit indirectly by association even if it opposed some aspects of the GM crop program. It would be a major loss to the U.S. government if the industry moved offshore to get around what it considers unnecessary government-imposed restrictions.

If the GM crop program fails to meet its ambitious goals to increase crops, reduce the use of pesticides, and increase tolerance to drought and other environmental constraints, then the government will be guilty by association. If it has strongly supported and advocated for GMO business against the European Union, for example, then the loss of credibility will be greater than if it has been more cautious in its support.

TABLE 10

Pros and cons for the U.S. government to support GM crops

Criteria	Advantages	Vulnerabilities
Reaction of elected officials and staff	There will be pressure from some members of Congress and the Executive Branch who want the United States to dominate this global economic activity.	Some members of Congress may fear the risk and negative implications.
	Governors of agricultural states will strongly support the policy.	It will be a challenge for FDA, EPA, and USDA to work together and to present a consistent view.
		There will be strong opposition from EU leaders, especially over the short term.
Reaction of non-government stakeholders	The media will cover the issue when scientific breakthroughs are made (the new green revolution) and will tend to make heroes of scientists.	The local media will become bored with the topic if nothing of importance is found and will amplify major mishaps.
	Strong support will come from agribusiness interests.	Opposition will come from organic food interests.
	There will also be strong support from large farm companies.	There will be strong opposition from some environmental activist groups.
	Support will come from the agricultural scientist community.	
Human and ecological health	Hunger and starvation will decrease.	Public health will be hurt in the long run if GM crops fail to increase yields.
	Health threats will be reduced by providing better, more resistant crops.	There will be a serious problem if valuable native crops are lost.
	The use of pesticides will drop.	There will also be a serious problem if some GM crops cause allergies and other health effects.

(Continued)

TABLE 10

(Continued)

Criteria	Advantages	Vulnerabilities
Economic costs and benefits	GM crops will potentially provide a strong benefit to the U.S. economy.	Relying on GM crops will create an economic dependence on increasing levels of technology.
	New products will help keep food costs down.	Small farmers will be undermined.
	These products will also help increase the food supply.	Organic farming will be undermined.
	They will increase international trade as well.	The U.S. economy will be hurt if GM crops fail.
Moral imperatives	Government has the responsibility to support a better and cheaper food supply for the United States and the rest of the world.	Government has the responsibility not to promote potentially dangerous organisms.
		Failure to seek consent from other governments could lead to a loss of credibility as well as legal issues.
Time and flexibility	Improved crop production will help keep pace with the growing demand for crops.	A monitoring program will need to be in place to track any environmental or health problems.
		A commitment to GM crops will reduce the resources available for other options.

Note: EPA = U.S. Environmental Protection Agency; EU = European Union; GM = genetically modified; USDA = U.S. Department of Agriculture.

I do not have a crystal ball, but I expect that the United States will be a strong advocate for the GMO industry. This could change with a less pro-business and more environmentally friendly Congress and president. It could also change if U.S. business decides that GMOs are too much of a threat to its markets — that retailers and the public will not buy GM foods. I think we should anticipate an escalation of the GMO debate.

TABLE 11

Potential results for the U.S. government

Policy action by the U.S. government	Success of GM crops	Failure of GM crops
Strongly support GMO development	The credibility of U.S. government and business will get a strong boost.	The U.S. government will suffer a major loss of credibility.
Constrain or oppose GMO development	The U.S. government will enjoy moderate gains in credibility.	The U.S. government will suffer a tolerable loss of credibility.

Note: GM = genetically modified; GMO = genetically modified organism.

Ethical Theories

Ethics is the part of philosophy concerned with defining what is right and wrong. Cheating, lying, stealing, and committing murder are universally unethical, and charity and honesty are ethical. Morality is defined as culturally specific ethics. For example, as noted in chapter 3, some believe that pollution is wrong. Others do not. Some countries will not put a murderer to death, but others will. Some adamantly oppose abortion and gay marriage, while others do not. Morality changes. When I was in the fifth grade, my teacher routinely hit students, including me, with her yardstick. Today, her behavior would be considered morally unacceptable. This section describes two of the key ethical cornerstones that have a bearing on the U.S. dilemma over pesticides and GM crops in developing nations.

The Environmental Ethic

The environmental ethic asserts, in essence, that actions preserving the beauty, integrity, and stability of biological systems are right and that actions that do not are wrong (Leopold, 1949). The ethic calls for more humane treatment of the Earth, that is, less consumption and more recognition of the Earth as a finite resource that humans share with other species. The need for an environmental ethic arises from the reality that humans are increasingly usurping the planet's resources. All species have a built-in imperative to survive and perpetuate. Humans, without the physical gifts of many other species, have relied on their mental capacity to develop technologies that have allowed them to expand across and use the globe.

Associated with our global expansion is a common belief that nature exists for humans to exploit. Individually, this has come to mean that success is measured by accumulating visible forms of wealth (Ayres, 1998; Becker, 2000). The most successful people are self-made individuals who pursue their own ambitions without deliberately harming anyone else. This viewpoint implies that resources are always available if we apply our superior intellect to harnessing them. Economic growth, then, can and should continue. Government's role is to help people and businesses continue economic expansion.

Proponents of the environmental ethic disagree with much of the preceding paragraph. They believe that our biological imperative to survive does not mean that humans should jeopardize all of the species on the planet. They support technology, but not all technologies because some are notably too destructive.

Advocates call on people to distinguish between wants and needs, to experience nature more and reshape it less, to use fewer resources, to recycle rather than discard, to think about how many children they really want to have in a world that has quadrupled its population since 1900, and to protect the Earth for future generations. They challenge business to consider its responsibility not only to stockholders but also to the population as a whole and to the yet unborn. Government has the responsibility, they assert, to protect the environment for everyone, including future generations, not just to foster economic growth.

Consent is part of the environmental ethic. Government, proponents argue, has the important responsibility to seek consent before subjecting any person or persons to a hazard (Crocker, 2004; Hugo, 1971). Charles Powers (see the discussion later in the chapter) disputed this last point, arguing that the environmental ethic is fundamentally about giving species the opportunity to control their own destiny. The environment, he asserted, is competitive. Species and individuals are always competing. There is, he says, no guarantee of consent.

The United States is by far the largest target of the environmental ethic because it consumes so much of the world's resources and because consent is often deliberately not obtained or not feasible to obtain, and some would argue that consent is coerced by economic necessity. Proponents want the U.S. government and population to accept the following three principles:

1. All living things are interrelated.
2. Humans cannot conquer nature, so they should work to minimize the damage to it.
3. Humans should preserve ecological systems, including their diversity, integrity, and sustainability.

In short, the message is that the human impact on the Earth is too pervasive and destructive and needs to be substantially controlled. For further reading on this subject see the following: Blackstone, 1972; McKibben, 1989; Nash, 1989; Partridge, 1981; and issues of the journal *Environmental Ethics*. The environmental ethic has been slow to be adopted in the United States.

Environmental Justice

The environmental justice movement, not the environmental ethic, is the most visible ethical challenge to the market-oriented business ethos. The movement was started by civil rights activists who identified some blatant cases of inequity in hazardous waste sites and used statistical methods to establish a general pattern that hazardous waste sites were disproportionately found in areas inhabited by economically disadvantaged minorities (Commission for Racial Justice, 1987; Greenberg 1993). Activists launched vigorous protests that led to what has been, I believe, the major environmental policy change in the United States since 1990.

On February 11, 1994, President Clinton issued Executive Order 12898 ("Federal Actions to Address Environmental Justice in Minority Populations and Low Income Populations" — see also chapter 8). The order required federal agencies to be in compliance with Title VI of the Civil Rights Act of 1964. EPA established an Office of Environmental Justice, as did other federal departments and agencies, and defined environmental justice as fair treatment of people of all races, cultures, and incomes with respect to the creation, implementation, and enforcement of environmental regulations, laws, and policies. Fair, in essence, meant that no group should disproportionately bear the negative consequences of risky industrial, personal, and government activities.

The intellectual foundation for focusing on fair and equitable treatment is found in three different philosophical views of how common resources should be used (Rawls, 1971; Shrader-Frechette, 1981, 1991). One view is that resources should be assigned so as to maximize the utility for all members of society. In other words, society as a whole should benefit from activities. In strong contrast, a second view is that resources should be used disproportionately to support an elite that will drive society's economic and intellectual engines. Without an elite, society as a whole and its poor will suffer. A third option is that resources should disproportionately be assigned to those who because of poverty, disability, or other conditions need help.

This third view is the basis for being concerned about social justice in general and environmental justice in particular. It asserts that we have an ethical obligation to give a large share of our tax revenues and other resources to relieve hunger and provide health care, education, and other services to the poor (Singer, 1972). This means that if the poor contribute — for the sake of discussion — 10 percent of the tax revenue, they should get back far more than 10 percent in the way of grants, services, and other benefits. The counterargument is that such policies make us feel better in the short run, but in the long run, helping a poor person in the present leads to many more poor persons in the future and serves only to exacerbate the inevitability of mass starvation (Hardin, 1974).

Critique

Like every major ethical assertion, environmental ethics and environmental justice can be challenged, especially as they pertain to the international sale of pesticides and GM crops. Both principles may be viewed as ethnocentric imperialism. That is, placing restrictions on the application of pesticides and GMOs in developing nations is a case of Westerners once again forcing cultural norms on other populations. After all, the United States has used DDT and various other forms of pesticides and is developing and marketing GM crops in this country. Now that we have found that pesticides can kill nontarget species and humans, do we have the right to stop others from applying these technologies or micromanaging their use? Behind our moral stance, some would argue, is an invidious comparison between "advanced" and "backward" countries. The people of developing countries cope with different political, social, and environmental circumstances. They want to develop their countries as they see fit, and those goals are likely stymied by the lack of a predictable food supply.

Justice, in other words, can be rigid, preventing other considerations from being factored into policy. In the pesticide and GMO cases, not allowing people to use pesticides and GM crops may conflict with the aspirations of leaders who may choose to take the associated risks instead of accepting the predictable toll of diseases and starvation in their country. In short, absolute justice about one issue can worsen other problems.

Hazardous Waste: The Typical Example

The issue of exported pesticides and GM crops is part of the larger ethical challenge involving exporting potential hazards, including some pharmaceuticals, contraceptive devices, toxic chemicals, food products, and consumer products that have been banned, severely restricted, or unregistered for use in their country of origin — and hazardous waste.

The most persistent domestic and international environmental justice dilemma has been about the disposal and management of hazardous waste. Within the United States, the argument is that hazardous waste sites for chemical, nuclear, and other wastes are disproportionately found in areas occupied by the poor and by racial/ethnic minorities. As someone involved in this morally grounded issue, I cannot wholly separate myself from my view. Nevertheless, I can summarize two opposing positions. One is that the largest and most noxious hazardous waste sites are disproportionately found in poor, African American, Hispanic, and American Indian areas (see chapter 4). Some charge that businesses and government deliberately sought out areas inhabited by relatively poor people (so-called procedural inequity). The counterargument is that there is no consistent excess of waste management facilities in poor and minority areas and that when there is a case, it is the result of historical patterns of industrial and population location rather than a deliberate choice to target poor areas (so-called outcome inequity). Much has been written about this subject (Anderton et al., 1994; Bryant and Mohai, 1992; Bullard and Chavis, 1993; Commission for Racial Justice, 1987; Greenberg, 1993). Whatever the merits of the evidence, government and business have become sensitive to the issue, and only the most foolhardy would seek to locate a noxious facility without investigating the environmental justice ramifications. In short, the ethical principle of environmental justice has been accepted as law and is active in practice in the United States, although I am sure that it is not always consistently applied.

The export of hazardous waste to developing nations has received much less attention. Waste management companies in the United States and Europe, facing increasingly tight restrictions on disposing of hazardous waste domestically, have attempted to dispose of it in Latin America and Africa (Bryant and Mohai, 1992; Bullard and Chavis, 1993; Uva and Bloom, 1989). Some of the sites chosen for disposal could not have been much worse; that is, they were on top of major sources of water and near populated areas. The practice has diminished but has not been completely eliminated. In fact, the relocation of hazardous industries to developing nations has reduced the need to export the waste. The entire production system, including the waste, is exported and is handed off to the government of that nation.

Proponents of the environmental ethic would begin their critique of hazardous waste management practices by asserting that we should use less of the products that create hazardous waste. Second, we should endeavor to follow the principles of pollution prevention (see chapter 1) so that little waste is created. Next, they would argue that waste management sites should be kept as far away from people and critical environmental resources as possible. Environmental justice advocates would point to the record of affluent Western nations that ship hazardous wastes and dangerous industries to developing nations.

I am certain that many more of these ethical dilemmas will present themselves. My certainty is based on more than three decades of following environmental issues. I conducted a nonrandom test of this belief by opening the June 2006 issue of *Environmental Health Perspectives*, which is published by the National Institute of Environmental Health Sciences. That issue contained two ethically laden subjects. One pointed out that we have been unable to produce a sufficient amount of vaccine to protect the public against anthrax, a possible terrorist weapon. However, tobacco plants are apparently excellent hosts for the production of anthrax vaccine and can be genetically transformed to fulfill that important task. I daresay that the federal government as a whole and FDA specifically face an interesting moral dilemma on how to treat a plant regarded by many as public enemy number 1 as a beneficial host (Stemp-Morlock, 2006).

Another interesting example in the same issue was about soy, which contains genistein. Some researchers are worried that genistein, a bioactive molecule, may have toxic reproductive effects later in life for children who consume it from birth. Yet soy in general is assumed to have positive health benefits because it has no cholesterol, is high in unsaturated fats, and is a good source of carbohydrates and fibers, as well being free of lactose (Barrett, 2006; Setchell, 2006). The topics in this particular issue are not atypical. Policy debates about good and bad substances are never fully closed. Environment-centered ethical challenges are always present.

Tales: Finding an Ethical Path through Complex Environmental Issues

This section summarizes my interviews with Charles Powers, whose interest in ethical policies dates back to his childhood or, more specifically, to his relationship with his father. Powers describes his father as a "moralist who believed that the world would respond positively if only you took the right moral positions." These beliefs notwithstanding, Powers observed that his father "got clobbered when he made moral decisions." His father balked at corruption, was a whistle-blower, and resigned from jobs when he saw morally questionable behavior. "My father almost always had the right ideas, but he could not make his moral decisions work for him and us. Our family suffered because of his morally-based actions."

These early experiences influenced Powers greatly. He went to Haverford College, where he studied religious philosophy, most notably Søren Kierkegaard, the 19th-century Danish philosopher and theologian who is considered the founder of existentialism. (The philosophy of existentialism emphasizes freedom, action, and personal decisions in human existence.) After he received his undergraduate degree, Powers enrolled in a seminary, where he became involved in trying to relate Christian and Jewish views of morality. During his second year of study, he went to Oxford University, where he again engaged in vigorous debates about morally appropriate policies and practices.

When he returned to the United States, Powers focused on policies toward Apartheid (extreme racial segregation) in South Africa. He wrote papers urging religious institutions to take moral positions on Apartheid. He wrote documents defining social investment policies for several religious institutions, such as the United Church of Christ, and the institutions adopted them. This engagement led him to switch from studying religion to studying ethics at Yale University. Ultimately, he received his PhD and later became a professor at Yale.

While still a graduate student and teaching at Princeton, he was asked by President Robert Goheen (who held that office from 1957 to 1972) to help the university address a serious controversy about the university's position on its investments. Powers notes: "The university had always invested only for economic return. There was a serious, potentially quite violent, confrontation brewing between the university administration and Princeton's African American students. The African American students wanted the university's investment policies, especially in relation to the operations of companies operating in South Africa, to take account of moral principles. I developed recommendations acceptable to both the students and the administration, and after an intellectual tussle finally won the support of the Princeton faculty for them."

Powers was instrumental in helping Princeton resolve this dilemma, and this experience was pivotal in persuading him that he could succeed where his father had failed. He could develop and explain ethical positions that he believed in and persuade diverse groups and colleagues to adopt them.

Upon returning to Yale, he started teaching a course and writing a book called *The Ethical Investor* (Simon, Powers, and Gunnemann, 1972), which presents the processes a university can use to evaluate and respond to requests from its communities to consider factors other than economic return when making investment decisions. The Yale Corporation, in fact, adopted the guidelines suggested in this book and, according to the *New York Times*, Yale was the first major university to adopt a social investment policy for its endowment. Subsequently, many other universities used these guidelines as a blueprint for their investment decisions. Powers states:

> I loved sorting out the role of moral issues in policy formation. But after five years at the university, I decided that the key question of our era would be how international corporations could deal ethically in the world; that is, could they develop principled ways of operating while also being responsive to different circumstances and cultures. At the time, there seemed to be two options: do as locals do, or adopt uniform ethical policies and practice in every country. IBM is an example of a company that tried to have the same policy in every country, whereas Cummins Engineering tried to find ethical uniformity that was also culturally sensitive.

During the late 1970s, Powers left a tenured position at Yale to join Cummins Engine Company, where he became chief environmental officer and vice president for public policy. He helped design ethically grounded public policy positions for this U.S.-based international diesel-engine-manufacturing company. For example, Cummins declined an invitation to build an engine manufacturing plant in South Africa after concluding that the facility would build engines for tanks that would be used against the local population. In India, Cummins had proven it could design a new manufacturing plant that used fewer robotics to help the country employ more workers. He believes that cultural responsiveness should not put the public at risk. He was involved in a case where Cummins was asked to support the building of a facility that would have caused serious air pollution risks. After Powers's analysis, the company chose not to build the plant, despite the urging of its local partner. The partner was distressed and argued that a U.S. company should not impose its values on public exposure to contaminants on another country. Powers said: "Sorting out what respect for persons really means is never easy and changes as circumstances change. To build an engine plant in South Africa today would be presumptively be a good—an ethical no brainer — except one would still have to weigh its emission impacts."

Powers, in short, has the ideal credentials to comment on the morality of U.S. companies' selling products in other countries when those same products cannot be sold or used in the United States. He offered strong recommendations regarding business and government policies. His first was that companies and countries have the right and obligation to change their minds as their principles interact with changed environments. According to Powers, "If new public health needs emerge and new science suggests a policy conclusion should be changed, then there is no reason not to change it just because earlier circumstances had led to a different moral conclusion. For instance, it was generally right to ban DDT, but the public health benefits of using DDT can still outweigh in very particular situations the legacy it leaves." He repeatedly emphasized the need to consult the best available science before taking ethical positions.

His second recommendation is that companies should insist on training workers and providing protective equipment, even if local government resists that policy. He cited an example in Mexico in which Cummins was trying to add noise control devices to engines Cummins was licensing to the Mexican government. The government did not see the need for such additions because they would make maintenance more difficult even though Cummins was offering the noise technology for free. Powers said, "I was in the country, and one night the sound of these engines woke me up. The noise was so intrusive that we decided we had to take a stronger position in favor of public auditory health, and eventually won the government's agreement."

We had a lengthy discussion on responsibility even when a company's contribution to a serious problem is highly uncertain. He stated emphatically: "If you're near it and can do something about it, whether you caused it or not, you should act, particularly if you are the last resort, that is, no one else is addressing the injury. To claim after a grave injury has occurred that you were not actually required to take action is not a position you want to be in."

Regarding GMOs, Powers believes that the potential good appears in many cases to outweigh the potential risk. He urged the U.S. government to embark on a major research program to develop the needed regulatory science and to assure that the responsibility for monitoring the health benefits and potential risk associated with GMOs can be met. Companies have responsibilities but need to be watched. The U.S. government, he believes, cannot simply rely on corporations to control the development, testing, and application of new technologies. Powers noted, "Human beings and their institutions often are not much better than are foxes when it comes to guarding their own hen houses."

Powers has advice for U.S. business and for the federal government. With regard to environmental policy issues, he believes that moral evaluation and science must be involved in a continuous feedback loop; that is, each informs the other about what is right and what is possible and what is at risk in developing policy options.

Tools and Tasks

Every policy includes explicit or implicit moral and ethical aspects. A decision to promote brownfields, reduce sprawl, reduce the use of methyl tertiary butyl ether, increase the use of ethanol, allow pesticides to be sold when they are banned locally, promote GM crops, or resurrect and build the nuclear power industry in the United States has ethical implications. A good exercise is to ask students to find and articulate the ethical principles in current policies. For sources, students can turn to media stories, public meetings, articles, and books.

I pick an issue and divide the class into pro and con policy groups: one group that supports an ethical principle and another that does not. Each must produce a 4- to 6-page memo for Congress (or an equivalent decision-making body). That memo should contain four parts:

1. The issue under consideration
2. The background of the issue (science, economics, politics, legality, management)
3. The ethical principle (environmental ethics, environmental justice, consent, state's rights)
4. Recommendations to Congress or another body on the choice of ethical principles

As in chapter 3, each group submits a written report; also, a spokesperson for each group presents a 5- to 7-minute synopsis of its report to the class. Following these presentations, each group meets separately for about 20 minutes to reconsider its positions. Each is then offered 3 minutes to add to the presentation. Finally, I lead an open discussion to try to establish points of agreement and disagreement among the groups. The entire process takes about 80 to 90 minutes.

6

Time and Flexibility Criterion

Nuclear Power Revisited

Introduction

Nuclear power is shorthand for using a uranium-fuel-based technology to generate electrical power. More than 440 licensed nuclear power reactors located in 31 nations produce about 17 percent of the world's electricity (World Nuclear Association, 2006). Some nations rely on nuclear power; others have rejected it. For example, in 2006, France had 59 operating nuclear power plants that supplied almost 80 percent of its electricity. In strong contrast, some of France's neighbors, Belgium, Germany, Switzerland, as well as Sweden, are planning to phase out nuclear power reactors. For example, Austria built a nuclear power reactor during the 1970s, but strong public opposition prevented it from opening. In short, nations that concur on many policies disagree about nuclear-generated electricity.

The United States generated the first nuclear-fueled electric power at an experimental reactor near Arco, Idaho. (This reactor is now housed in a small museum at the Idaho nuclear weapons facility.) The United States has more operating nuclear reactors by far than any other nation: 103 reactors that provide about 19 percent of the country's electricity (U.S. Nuclear Regulatory Commission [NRC], 2006). During the 1960s and 1970s, many utilities built nuclear power plants with federal government support. In 1973, the United States had 42 operating nuclear power plants. That number increased to 57 in 1975 and to 71 in 1980. However, new orders began to decline during the mid-1970s, and the Three Mile Island nuclear power plant accident in 1979 stopped the expansion altogether.

Some additional facilities that already had permits were completed, so that the total number of operating units reached 112 in 1990. But some have been closed and decommissioned, and so there were 103 at 65 locations in 2006 (Energy Information Administration, 2006). In essence, the U.S. nuclear power industry has been idling for a quarter of a century.

During that period, the country has become heavily dependent on expensive and greenhouse-gas-producing fossil fuels. Nuclear power technology is back on the political policy agenda, however. The next decade will witness passionate, scientific debates about mining uranium; locating nuclear power plants; safeguarding the facilities from human error, technological failure, and terrorist attacks; and storing the waste on-site or moving it to temporary or permanent storage sites, as well as reviewing current and long-term costs.

Second only to war/terrorism, nuclear power is the most difficult political hot potato for the U.S. government. By comparison, brownfields (see chapter 1) are for the most part a problem for neighborhoods and their local governments. Cancer clusters (see chapter 2) involve specific neighborhoods and normally become the responsibility of state governments. Although the choice of automobile additives (see chapter 3) affects every American, it is an issue that national and state governments and the automobile industry ought to be able to solve. Stewardship of our nuclear weapons sites (see chapter 4) has left a legacy that we will be living with in perpetuity, but it primarily affects those who live near the Hanford (Washington), Savannah River (South Carolina), and Idaho sites, and they have been dealing with the issue for over half a century. Pesticides and genetically modified organisms (see chapter 5) have a controversial past and doubtless an equally controversial future, but the controversy has more political resonance for the international image of the United States than it does at home.

By contrast, nuclear power rests, I believe, squarely in the hands of the federal government. If the federal government decides that it wants to promote nuclear power, then it can send political and economic signals to private enterprise. I am not saying that energy companies, states, scientists, and not-for-profits have no say or responsibility. They do. Yet the federal government ultimately will decide whether existing nuclear plants should be relicensed or closed; whether new plants should be encouraged and where they should be located; how much of a subsidy should be provided to utility industries; how this national nuclear factory will be protected; and, finally, how we will manage the waste that these plants have already produced and will continue to produce, if their numbers are increased.

If the federal government invests its prestige and dollars in complex nuclear technologies that fail, then distrust of government and big science will increase. Second-guessing will focus on lost opportunities to invest in less daunting technologies and in conservation. Depending on the extent and type of failure (a serious public health exposure would be the worst), we could view the investment as the technological equivalent of the Vietnam War. If, however, nuclear power revisited reduces the greenhouse gases that are generated by fossil fuels and helps bridge the energy supply gap for two or three decades, then American technological optimism will grow. In this chapter, we illustrate the time and flexibility criterion with nuclear power revisited.

Theme: Nuclear Power and Interconnected Policy Themes

The expansion of nuclear power is intertwined with efforts to control the proliferation of nuclear weapons and to find places where hazardous materials can be produced and wastes managed. The nuclear fuel cycle is the nexus of the three. Nuclear fuel used in power reactors consists of uranium oxide pellets, each of which can be held in a small tweezers. These pellets are stacked in long tubes, called cladding, that are made from a zirconium alloy and are bundled together to form fuel assemblies. Hundreds of these assemblies are then inserted into the reactor core, where they can be activated.

U.S. nuclear power plant fuel consists of 97 percent uranium-238 and 3 percent uranium-235. The latter is enriched so that it is reactive (fissionable) and can sustain a nuclear reaction. Nearly all the uranium-235 splits (fissions), producing heat and steam, which turns massive turbines. The power is converted to electricity that is put into the grid system and transmitted in response to the demand for electrical power.

Fission produces neutrons (subatomic particles) that sustain the reaction and lighter elements called fission products. Some of these products absorb neutrons, but they are too light to fission in the reaction. Neutrons produced during fission are also absorbed by uranium-238, resulting in heavy elements (americium, cerium, plutonium, and neptunium). These are called transmuted elements or TRU. As fission proceeds, fissile materials are consumed and fission products accumulate. Eventually, fission can no longer be sustained. When it ends, the leftover materials are called spent nuclear fuel (or sometimes SNF).

Spent nuclear fuel has been a major issue for over half a century. About 1 percent consists of TRU, mostly plutonium, which can be used in nuclear weapons. Also, spent nuclear fuel is extremely hot and radioactive, and some elements will be radioactive for thousands of years. The amount of spent commercial nuclear fuel is currently estimated at 53,000 metric tons (U.S. Department of Energy [DOE], 2006), and nearly all of it is stored in wet or dry forms in special facilities at power reactors. In addition, spent nuclear fuel has been produced by the military and is stored primarily in Hanford (Washington), Savannah River (South Carolina), and Idaho (see chapter 4).

Spent nuclear fuel can be separated to remove extremely hazardous elements, which can then be managed to reduce risk. If nuclear power expands using current U.S. technologies, there will be more spent nuclear fuel to potentially divert to the manufacture of nuclear weapons. Moreover, if nuclear power expands, the country will need places where plants can be located; where waste products can be managed; and where the technologies can be designed, tested, and operated, in addition to paths over which materials can be transported between locations.

Nuclear Power: A Timeline and Key Assumptions

This section presents a timeline of nuclear power in the United States and focuses on key issues, such as economics, antiproliferation efforts, and the equally difficult task of finding locations for nuclear-related technologies, power plants, and waste management.

THE ROLLER COASTER HISTORY OF NUCLEAR POWER IN THE UNITED STATES. The initial research that led to nuclear power was done in Europe and the United States. In 1939, Niels Bohr came to this country and suggested the idea of a self-sustaining chain reaction. In 1942, Enrico Fermi built facilities at the University of Chicago, thus ushering in the nuclear age. Three years later, in July 1945, the so-called Manhattan Project tested the first atomic bomb in Alamogordo, New Mexico. On August 6 and 9, 1945, the United States dropped atomic bombs on Hiroshima and Nagasaki, Japan. Overall, the initial public image of nuclear power was a bomb.

Business and the public resisted using nuclear fuel to generate electricity for over two decades. Yet even in 1946, the federal government was trying to create another image for nuclear materials. The Atomic Energy Act of 1946 (P.L. 585) created the Atomic Energy Commission (AEC) to manage nuclear research and regulate safety. The AEC was composed of five members appointed by the president with the advice of the Senate. The federal government initially asserted its ownership of all fissionable material, a decision that was later reversed by the Atomic Energy Act of 1954 (P.L. 83–703) (Hewlett and Holl, 1980).

In 1948, the AEC issued a report on the peaceful uses of atomic energy; in 1949, it identified a location at the Idaho nuclear facility for a national reactor test station; and in 1951, it authorized research on an experimental breeder reactor in Idaho. On December 3, 1953, President Eisenhower, who had commanded Allied military forces in Europe during World War II, presented his famous "Atoms for Peace" speech, in which he advocated the peaceful uses of atomic energy. Eisenhower proposed that nations with nuclear weapons allocate some of their uranium and fissionable material and create an international atomic agency to help manage the peaceful uses of nuclear materials (Hewlett and Holl, 1980; Neal, 1998).

This forceful speech attempted both to counter the negative image of nuclear weapons and to offer nuclear technology as a means of producing a clean, safe, and efficient source of energy. The speech was broadcast worldwide by the Voice of America. Notably, it never mentioned banning nuclear weapons, nor did it make it clear that plutonium would be a by-product of nuclear power.

In 1955, the United Nations held an international conference on the peaceful uses of atomic energy, and in 1957, it created the International Atomic Energy Agency (IAEA), first proposed by President Eisenhower. While U.S. government efforts to encourage nuclear power were growing, American businesses were very reluctant to engage because of the financial uncertainty and potential environmental and health effects.

A major step in attracting business investment was the 1957 Price-Anderson Act, which protects licensees in case of an accident at a nuclear power plant. This legislation limited private liability for reactor accidents to $560 million. The 1960s and 1970s were a period of growth for the nuclear power industry. In 1965, the first nuclear reactor was launched into space, demonstrating the peaceful use of nuclear power. Beginning in the late 1960s and lasting well into the 1970s, reactor safety was publicly debated and addressed by the AEC, the U.S. Congress, the nuclear industry, and the media. While the dangers of proliferation of nuclear weapons-grade materials and possible meltdowns of nuclear reactors were widely aired, these debates led to international treaties to limit the proliferation of nuclear materials and to the construction of dozens of nuclear power plants.

In October 1973, the nations constituting the Organization of Petroleum Exporting Countries (OPEC) embargoed oil shipments. Not coincidentally, many new nuclear reactors were ordered. In 1974, the Energy Reorganization Act broke the AEC into two distinct entities: the Energy Research and Development Administration (ERDA) and the Nuclear Regulatory Commission (NRC). ERDA later became DOE. This action was important because it separated health and safety from efforts to promote the technology. In 1982/1983, the Nuclear Waste Policy Act (P.L. 97–425) mandated that DOE manage spent nuclear fuel. This was an important step because previously there had been no policy for managing these fuels.

However, the positive steps ended on March 28, 1979, when the Three Mile Island accident occurred. Half of the core of one reactor melted (a description of public response appears later in the chapter). This accident had a chilling effect on the nuclear power industry.

On April 26, 1986, there was a meltdown at the Chernobyl nuclear reactors in Ukraine. Emergency workers were killed, thousands of cases of radiation sickness resulted, and clouds of radiation dispersed over Western Europe. By 2002, more than 4,000 cases of childhood thyroid cancer were reported (Medvedev, 1993; Neal, 1998). There is an exclusion zone around the site. Also, people living in the surrounding area experienced severe psychological effects, which were exacerbated by a lack of information from the state-controlled government media. No statement was made by then President Mikhail Gorbachev until May 14, nearly three weeks after the disaster. When he appeared on television, he denounced what he called the "mountain of lies" in the Western press (Medvedev, 1993; see also Neal, 1998). Over 300,000 people have relocated, and the regional economy has been severely damaged. People who heard the noise and felt the earth shake knew that something had happened, but since there was no report, they went about their activities. Children went to school, and there were soccer games, a wedding, and even fishing trips to the reactor's cooling pond. This interval lasted for nearly 40 hours (Medvedev, 1993; Neal, 1998). The Chernobyl disaster was a low point for nuclear power.

In 1988, New York State opposed the opening of the completed Shoreman nuclear power plant on Long Island. Having just witnessed the events in Ukraine, the fear was that the area could not be safely evacuated in case of an emergency. Problems for the industry continued into the 1990s, when it was discovered that some of existing nuclear power facilities were less reliable and that key parts were corroding.

Nevertheless, the roller coaster started going back up in the mid-1990s. In 1997, more than 150 nations signed the Kyoto protocol, agreeing to timetables for cutting greenhouse gas emissions by industrialized nations in order to slow climate change. Even though the United States was not a signatory, as part of the discussion, nuclear power plants were offered as a solution to the greenhouse gas problem. Business then became interested in nuclear power again. Large power companies and conglomerates of utilities, vendors, and large architectural engineering firms (Entergy, Exelon, Dominion Energy, NuStart) purchased more than a dozen existing nuclear power plants and began to work closely with the federal government in planning others. In 2005, the Energy Policy Act allocated $2 billion as insurance to protect companies against construction delays at six proposed reactors; also, the government granted tax credits for four new electricity-generating facilities. Moreover, loan guarantees were made available for technologies to reduce air pollution and greenhouse gas emissions, and the federal government extended liability on nuclear plants through 2025. These steps have clearly created incentives for private investment and nuclear power.

In addition, $1.25 billion was set aside for the design and construction of a nuclear-hydrogen cogeneration plant at the Idaho facility. In 2006, President George W. Bush called for greater reliance on nuclear power to break the nation's addiction to oil. Congress approved funds for DOE to reprocess spent nuclear fuel and recycled plutonium and invested in a new program to create a reliable and proliferation-proof nuclear fuel cycle (described in the discussion on proliferation later in the chapter). The fiscal year 2007 federal budget set aside funds for nuclear power research, and the government is planning to work more closely with utilities to obtain expedited licenses for new nuclear plants.

Summarizing, the nuclear power industry has clearly been on a roller coaster for five decades. The first decade demonstrated that nuclear materials could be used for bombs. All of us retain the indelible impression of a mushroom cloud (Weart, 1992). Yet soon after the end of World War II, the federal government began to take deliberate steps to encourage a nuclear power industry, a process that was helped by the oil embargo of 1973. Those events encouraged energy utilities to invest in nuclear power plants. Yet events at Three Mile Island and Chernobyl, long delays in construction, public fears, and inexpensive fossil fuels dampened growth and sent the industry down the roller coaster for the second time. But during the mid-1990s, with energy costs rising, with greenhouse gases becoming a major political issue for the United States, and with increasing U.S. dependence on fossil fuels from potentially hostile countries, the federal government has started the roller coaster on the upswing again.

SUMMARY OF KEY ASSUMPTIONS. Given the history of nuclear power in the United States, should the federal government advocate for nuclear power, and, if so, how much? A positive answer requires accepting some critical assumptions.

In terms of health and safety, proponents must assume that there will be no major or even notable nuclear accidents. If there are, public opinion will likely drop instantly to the levels observed during the Three Mile Island accident in 1979. A successful terrorist attack that causes even minor damage to a nuclear power facility would also have a chilling effect on efforts to reinvigorate nuclear power. Indeed, so-called dirty bombs that use radioactive material and are detonated with conventional explosives could also, at least for a short time, trigger considerable public fear about nuclear materials.

Another part of health and safety discussed later in greater detail is the need to protect against the theft of weapons-grade plutonium. In essence, the public expects — indeed, demands — strong regulatory oversight of the nuclear power industry. If the public comes to distrust the energy industry, and especially if it loses confidence in the federal government's ability to protect health and safety, then the billions of dollars and prestige invested in nuclear power will amount to a colossal policy blunder.

The historical performance of nuclear power with regard to health and safety has been mixed. In 1961, there was a partial meltdown of a prototype reactor at the Idaho facility; in 1966, there was a partial meltdown at an experimental breeder reactor in the Detroit area; and in 1971, the Union of Concerned Scientists claimed that the AEC's monitoring of the nuclear power industry was inadequate. Moreover, although the public health effects have been minimal, no one alive in 1979 will forget what happened at Three Mile Island; nor can we forget the Chernobyl meltdown, although the engineered safety conditions in Ukraine would not be acceptable in the United States. In 2002, the Ohio Davis-Besse nuclear plant was found to have corrosion and other safety problems, which pointed to a new safety threat at every facility. The 2005 Energy Policy Act requires "designed threat basis" exercises at facilities in preparation for a possible breach. If the government cannot guarantee that these facilities are safe and that it is prepared to deal with any problems, then these facilities will suffer the same fate as the completed but never operated Shoreham nuclear reactor.

Credible and successful environmental management of nuclear waste is the second essential assumption required to support a substantial expansion of nuclear power. DOE and the NRC must develop a system that will manage high-level nuclear waste in perpetuity. Whereas the current policy is to separate military and power plant nuclear waste, neither policy seems satisfactory to me. The current accumulation of spent fuel will increase as old plants are phased out and replaced by newer ones. The amount of spent nuclear fuel could increase substantially, and proponents of nuclear power must therefore assume that a high-level waste management problem can be addressed. The 1982/1983 Nuclear Waste Policy Act required DOE to manage spent fuel by 1998 and to identify two underground waste repositories.

The 1987 Nuclear Waste Policy Act amended the 1982 legislation and mandated Yucca Mountain as a single depository for the most dangerous nuclear waste.

Delays, complaints, lawsuits, and protests over this decision have dented DOE's credibility. Frankly, I do not believe that this politically charged and complicated waste management problem can be addressed by assuming that all of the most dangerous nuclear waste will reside at Yucca Mountain. The federal government has to forthrightly address the high-level nuclear waste management problem (see the discussion of the Global Nuclear Energy Partnership later in the chapter).

A third important assumption driving the current reexamination of nuclear power is the growing consensus that the use of fossil fuels is producing greenhouse gases that are polluting the environment and that could have catastrophic long-term implications for everyone. The stronger the evidence against greenhouse gases, the stronger the case for nuclear power. Indeed, a remarkable change is that nuclear power technology now has a pro-environment tinge (Gertner, 2006; Spurgeon, 2006).

The economics of nuclear power have gone up and down the roller coaster (Gertner, 2006). The fourth assumption that proponents of nuclear power must make is that there will be an economic payoff for three to five decades (Paine, 1996; Uranium Institute, 1999). The federal government has offered financial incentives in the form of risk insurance (at least through 2025), tax credits, and loan guarantees and has extended the cap on private liability for accidents. One of the key steps in the economics of nuclear power is the federal government's agreement to help utilities with the design of nuclear reactors. The 1992 Energy Policy Act states that only one license is required to begin the operation of a nuclear power plant. This means much more rapid approval of reactor designs than in the past.

Nevertheless, compared with coal and gas facilities, it is relatively expensive to build, operate, guard, and protect a nuclear power plant. To justify the high capital costs and risks associated with these plants, we must assume that oil and natural gas prices will increase and that current reliance on imported fossil fuels is too politically risky for the United States. If the world becomes a more stable place and if fuel prices then drop, the case for the economic benefits of nuclear power will be weakened.

The Atomic Energy Act of 1946 states that Congress is uncertain about the future of nuclear energy: "Until Congress declares by joint resolution that effective and enforceable international safeguards against the use of atomic energy for destructive purposes have been established, there shall be no exchange of information with other nations with respect to the use of atomic energy for industrial purposes" (chapter 724, P.L. 585, p. 13).

Sixty years ago, Congress was worried about proliferation. It is still worried about proliferation, in addition to cost, waste management, terrorism, public perception, and many other facets of nuclear power technology.

Proliferation of Nuclear Weapons Materials and Technology

The link between proliferation of nuclear weapons and nuclear power became part of public discourse as a result of President Eisenhower's advocacy. When the

United States attempted to reach agreements with the Soviet Union and other countries, the Soviet Union raised the issue of proliferation. It was again highlighted when J. Robert Oppenheimer, chairman of the AEC and director of the Los Alamos Laboratory during World War II, was accused of being a member of the Communist Party (widely debated). The federal government held hearings on Oppenheimer's proper role, which underscored the link between mega-watts and mega-tons (Bernstein, 2004; Cassidy, 2005).

Despite the efforts of President Eisenhower and others who have followed his lead to promote the peaceful uses of nuclear materials, the discussion of nuclear power is still linked to nuclear bombs. Indeed, the task has become more difficult. While the United States and Russia have about 97 percent of the nuclear weapons, during the past half century, China, France, the United Kingdom, Pakistan, India, Israel (undeclared), and North Korea (recently) have developed nuclear weapons, and Iran is probably trying (International Physicians for the Prevention of Nuclear War, 2006; Norris and Kristensen, 2006). Not only do more nations have nuclear weapons, but the weapons developed by the United States and Russia are markedly more destructive than those used during World War II. There is some small consolation in the fact that the number of operational nuclear weapons has dropped from about 70,000 in 1986 at the height of the cold war to about 27,000 in 2006. Nevertheless, there are enough functioning nuclear weapons to kill and injure countless millions. Moreover, few of the nonfunctional weapons have actually been destroyed.

Trying to prevent further proliferation of nuclear weapons has been a major objective of the United States, its allies, and the United Nations. In 1968, the Nuclear Non-Proliferation Treaty was signed, and it now has 189 signatories. Antiproliferation methods are both institutional and scientific. The major institutional responsibility is held by the IAEA, which attempts to account for nuclear materials, tightly control the spread of nuclear technology and materials, and make sure that announced uses of nuclear materials are verified by inspections. These efforts have been only partially successful, as evidenced by the development of nuclear weapons in India, Pakistan, North Korea, Iran, and Libya (which was secretly trying to develop nuclear weapons).

If nuclear power is going to play a larger international role, nonproliferation programs must succeed. Theft and diversion must be prevented, and the production of nuclear weapons materials in secret locations curtailed. Realistically, the past decade has taught us that institutional approaches will not be totally successful.

Innovative technology is a second approach for managing spent nuclear fuels. One approach, described in chapter 4, consists of preventing such fuels from being diverted by mixing them in a glass matrix, converting the matrix into solids, and storing the massive nuclear logs in perpetually managed depositories.

A more technologically ambitious approach is to redesign the nuclear power cycle so that weapons-grade material is rapidly consumed. Specifically, the

United States, Russia, and other nations have embarked on a cooperative effort to develop, test, build, and operate a new technology system. The Global Nuclear Energy Partnership (GNEP) seeks to demonstrate that spent nuclear fuels can be separated and consumed in so-called fast reactors and that residuals can be safely stored (DOE, 2006; Spurgeon, 2006; also, typing GNEP into a search engine will lead to DOE's GNEP site). Fast reactors would consume the legacy of spent nuclear fuels and reduce the threat of plutonium diversion. The goal is to have GNEP technologies in place in 20 to 25 years: that is, by 2030. If GNEP is successful, a substantial increase in nuclear power generation could be accommodated while at the same time reducing the chances for proliferation. Of course, there is no certainty that the technology can be made to work.

DOE is a planning the first environmental impact statement for mid-year 2007 (see chapter 7 for a description of environmental impact statements). It will present the arguments for the idea and compare it with other options, and if the government moves ahead to build the facilities, DOE will use the environmental impact statement process to consider alternative forms of the technology and select sites for the facilities. The primary objectives of GNEP are therefore to create a fuel source that reduces the dependence on potentially hostile foreign countries and the probability of proliferation of nuclear weapons-grade materials.

The U.S. government is also involved in international negotiations to support this effort. For example, O'Driscoll (2006) notes that the United States and Russia have begun to negotiate a bilateral effort to develop commercial nuclear power as the Group of Eight major industrial nations, comprising Canada, France, Germany, Italy, Japan, the United Kingdom, Russia, and the United States. Together, they account for about two-thirds of the world's economic output. Their goal is to produce a steady and stable price for nuclear fuel and to reduce greenhouse gases. As part of the agreement leading to GNEP, Russia will store spent U.S. nuclear fuel. The United States has also attempted to bring India into the program by helping it develop nuclear power technology rather than depending on coal-fueled electricity. However, the GNEP program is more theory than reality at this point. It might not survive Washington, D.C., or international politics.

Siting of Nuclear Power Plants and Associated Facilities

When I was a graduate student, my regional economics professor, Herman Otte, taught us how sites were selected for steel mills, chemical plants, electricity-generating facilities, and other industrial land uses. He focused on cheap, accessible, and suitable land; an abundant water supply; inexpensive labor; and distance from raw materials. I do not recall his mentioning public health, environmental protection, or social impacts as criteria. Three years after I took his course, the process of siting facilities changed with the passage of the National Environmental Policy Act of 1970 (NEPA, see chapter 7), which required federal agencies to assess the impact of their decisions, many of which involved large new facilities such as dams, roads, and power plants. States and local governments developed their own versions of NEPA, which covered private actions. Consequently, major energy-producing facilities have become subject to complex and often lengthy assessments. Environmental consultants, industrial hygienists, structural engineers, geologists, real estate loan officers, environmental lawyers, and many other experts are now involved in finding potential sites that can meet physical and legal requirements (Hess, 1998).

FINDING SITES. DOE's search for a repository for highly radioactive waste is, I believe, the most complex siting process ever undertaken (Bella, Mosher, and Calvo, 1988; Carter, 1987; Clary and Kraft, 1988; Lemons and Malone, 1989; Kunreuther et al., 1990; Macfarlane and Ewing, 2006). Under the Nuclear Waste Policy Act of 1982, the federal government's effort began with the objective of identifying at least two sites where hot and highly radioactive waste could be stored permanently. After that legislation was amended in 1987 (P.L. 100–203), DOE chose Yucca Mountain (in the mountains north of Las Vegas, Nevada). The Yucca Mountain decision has involved billions of dollars spent over several decades and has produced a tunnel, scientific uncertainty, and controversy. It dominates media coverage of nuclear waste management issues (Macfarlane and Ewing, 2006). The original plan of identifying two sites and exploring their physical advantages and disadvantages was short-circuited by the amended Nuclear Waste Policy Act. What was left was a single location in Nevada as the only possible site, leaving local residents feeling that they had been betrayed by the federal government and unwilling to accept reduced taxes in exchange for the repository (Kunreuther et al., 1990).

Sites for nuclear power plants, low-level nuclear waste facilities, fossil-fueled electricity-generating stations, wind farms, chemical and other manufacturing plants, airports, and other large facilities are never easy to find. But none is quite so hard as finding a single national nuclear waste depository that many consider to be a permanent sacrifice zone (see chapter 4).

The federal government has already demonstrated its willingness to try a variety of different locations to accommodate new nuclear power plants. For example, I worked on one project that proposed to locate such a plant in the Atlantic Ocean. The plant was to be built in the South and then brought up to New Jersey, where it would be placed on an artificial island. The major advantage of this proposal was that there was no nearby population to the north, east, and south. A second project, which colleagues worked on, was to build more than 10 nuclear reactors at one location. This effort proved to be a resounding failure, and the land once proposed for multiple nuclear power facilities is now occupied by middle-income suburban housing. The idea of clustering the facilities had the obvious advantage of raising political opposition in only one area instead of many. If we do build more nuclear reactors, I believe that they will be located in areas that already have nuclear-associated facilities (see chapter 4).

PUBLIC PERCEPTION OF SITES. The acronyms LULUs (locally unwanted land use) and NIMBY (not in my backyard) symbolize public sensitivity to locating factories, electricity-generating stations, highways, commercial or public facilities, and other land uses in particular neighborhoods or even in particular states (Boholm, 2005; Lake, 1987; O'Hare, Bacow, and Sanderson, 1983; Popper, 1985; Portney, 1991). In my experience, finding a physically acceptable, economically viable site for large production and distribution facilities is difficult and necessary but no longer sufficient. Public support is essential. The public does not actually have a veto, but public opposition comes very close to acting as one.

Chapter 4 summarized studies on the public perception of nuclear weapons, technology, and waste in the context of potentially siting facilities at the major former U.S. nuclear weapons sites in Idaho, South Carolina, Tennessee, and Washington. Briefly reiterating, these surveys found that a clear majority opposed new nuclear technology facilities, and about 40 percent adamantly opposed them. The respondents who were most opposed were unfamiliar with the technology, did not trust those who would operate it or the government to monitor the operators, and were worried about the local environment. But about 40 percent of the respondents who lived within 50 miles of one of the six former nuclear weapons sites were not adamantly opposed to hosting new nuclear technology facilities in their region. These respondents were familiar with the sites (many worked at them or had close friends or relatives who did), and they trusted DOE.

With regard to nuclear power plants, but not waste management facilities, those who take these surveys have asked tens of thousands of people all over the world about their perceptions of nuclear power, war, waste, and science. Some of these studies used sophisticated research designs, and others used less desirable convenience samples (see the chapter 7 discussion of surveys). When data are gathered in different countries, when different languages are used, or when the questions vary and are embedded in a larger survey that contains different issues, external validity — the degree to which relationships hold over variations in persons, treatments, and settings — is a concern. Among the more than 100 studies that have been done, only one set is directly responsive to the nuclear power revisited question and appears to be based on appropriate sampling (see the chapter 7 discussion of surveys).

Time series data provide trends in public support for nuclear power from 1983 through 2005. Using random-digit dialing (see chapter 7) and funded by the Nuclear Energy Institute, Bisconti Research (formerly RoperASW), asked 1,000 U.S. adults aged 18 and older a set of questions about nuclear-generated energy. Some of the questions have been asked every year, and others are relatively new. But there is an unmistakable trend in the data since 1996 toward more public support for nuclear energy.

The surveys asked people whether they strongly favor, somewhat favor, somewhat oppose, or strongly oppose the use of nuclear energy as one of the ways to provide electricity in the United States. In 1983, 49 percent were in favor of nuclear power. This increased to 52 percent in 1985 and ranged from 49 percent to 55 percent until 1994. Given that the margin of error for the survey is plus or minus 3 percentage points, there was no trend during these years. But there were some surprises. For example, crude oil prices plunged more than 50 percent between 1981 and 1986. The Chernobyl reactor meltdown occurred in April 1986. The first Gulf War started in 1991 and was marked by a slight increase in oil prices (WTRG Economics, 2006). If U.S. public opinion about nuclear energy responded to these events, people should have become more interested in nuclear power when fossil fuel prices increased, but there was no evidence of that in the data. Rosa and Dunlap's (1994) study of poll trends and nuclear power agrees with the conclusion that nuclear power was not well received by the public through the early 1990s.

According to these surveys, the obvious change in public perception occurred between 1995 and 1998. In 1995, 46 percent of the population favored using nuclear fuel to produce electricity. One year later, it was 49 percent, and it jumped to 61 percent in 1998 and to 62 percent in 1999. There was a slight increase in the price of oil between 1998 and 1999, but nothing commensurate with the change in public opinion. Beginning with the millennium, the proportion favoring nuclear energy has steadily climbed to more than 70 percent in the May 2005 Bisconti survey. These increases correspond to the terrorist attacks in the United States in 2001 and a substantial increase in fuel prices.

According to these surveys, not only is the public more supportive of using nuclear energy, but the difference between strong support and strong opposition has widened markedly. In 1990, about 22 percent were strongly in favor and an equal number were strongly opposed. But in May 2005, 32 percent strongly favored using nuclear fuel to generate electricity and only 10 percent strongly opposed it.

The surveys contain other data that support the trend toward a more positive public perception of nuclear power. For example, the 2005 survey reported that 85 percent of respondents agreed with renewing the license of nuclear power plants that continue to meet federal safety standards. Seventy-seven percent agreed that electric utilities should prepare now so that new plants could be built if needed, and 58 percent agreed that the United States should definitely build more nuclear power plants. These proportions have increased at least since 2003, when the Bisconti group started asking these questions. The answers imply that the American public does not want to apply the NIMBY policy to nuclear power plants.

The Bisconti (2005) data also show that the public is interested in clustering nuclear power plants. Specifically, respondents were asked whether it was acceptable to build a nuclear power plant next to the nearest operational nuclear power plant. In 2005, 69 percent said it was acceptable, compared with 57 percent in 2003. The data show a slight difference by major region, with 64 percent agreeing in the Northeast compared with 71 percent in the Midwest. But this is not a notable difference. Since 64 percent of the respondents said that there was a nuclear power plant in the state where they live, we can infer from these data that there is not an overwhelming NIMBY response.

I do not have the raw survey data, so I cannot model the factors associated with this major shift in support during the past decade. However the survey does provide some hints. People were asked what they associated with nuclear energy. More specifically, they were asked to comment on affordability, clean air, efficiency, energy security, reliability, and sustainability. The strongest associations were with clean air, followed by efficiency and reliability. Over half of the population associated nuclear energy with these three "a lot." Between 40 and 42 percent of respondents associated nuclear energy with affordability, energy security, and sustainability. Other parts of the survey suggest that the public is beginning to recognize global warming and realizes that nuclear power plants do not produce greenhouse gases. Also, the public perception that nuclear power plants are safe has increased to an all-time high. On a seven-point scale, less than 40 percent gave nuclear power plants a safety rating of between five and seven during the 1980s, corresponding to the events at both Three Mile Island and Chernobyl. But gradually the proportion rose to more than 50 percent, and in 2005 it was 66 percent.

The 2005 Bisconti report offers several other interesting tidbits. For example, 64 percent of the respondents agreed that the federal government should (1) provide limited investment incentives such as tax credits and loan guarantees to help construct the first set of advanced nuclear power plants and (2) partner with utility companies to develop new nuclear reactor designs. Finally, the report shows more support for nuclear power among men, so-called influential people, and Republicans than among women, less influential people, and Democrats.

The Bisconti time series and surveys that I conducted and that are described in chapter 4 show some consistency. First, they show that a large proportion of the population is willing to consider new nuclear generating facilities, even within their own state and region. There is evidence of NIMBY in these surveys, but there is also evidence of a willingness to consider new nuclear-related activities. Notably, those who know most about existing sites, who trust government, and who have a relatively high socioeconomic status are the most supportive. Since these people are relatively influential, the federal government has a good base of support. The challenge is how to broaden that support. Frankly, this will be very difficult unless the federal government tries hard to get meaningful public input. In fact, the government could try very hard to get public input and still fail to gain a majority of public support for siting new facilities. But I believe that if it does not try and tries instead to site new activities without making a bona fide effort to reach out to communities, then people who are not already strongly opposed or strongly in favor of siting will swing from the middle toward strong opposition, as I believe has happened in Nevada with the Yucca Mountain site.

Whenever I think about public reaction to nuclear power, I mentally return to the days immediately after the Three Mile Island accident in 1979. Those experiences, which unfortunately have been duplicated in other environmental health events during my lifetime, lead me to assert that a single problem at a nuclear power plant could undermine — indeed, totally end — efforts by the federal government to revisit and promote nuclear power. The only way to explain why I feel that way is to share some of the statements made by people after the Three Mile Island events. I will focus particularly on evacuation, reproducing some personal tales of people who lived through those events. First, I quote from Gazit's (1999) video recording entitled *Meltdown at Three Mile Island*.

1. "I was just upset with the way things were handled and that we were lied to" (Robert Reid, mayor of Middletown, Pennsylvania, which is upriver from Three Mile Island).
2. "People were calling from around the country saying 'get out of there'" (Robin Neenan Stuart, resident).
3. "My neighbors told me that I was to come down to their house. They have guns and they had a chainsaw and a big truck, and they would get up on the highway, cut down any barriers that were there and fight their way through, and we would leave any way we pleased. So the idea that there was going to be any kind of an orderly evacuation was pure fantasy" (Marsha McHenry, resident).
4. "We left so quickly on Friday that we basically took ourselves. The moment that's so crystal clear in my mind is driving on the highway trying to imagine what would happen to this area. All of this beautiful countryside would be destroyed, would be so contaminated that nobody could be there for hundreds of years. I looked as hard as I could at everything and tried to burn it into my mind what everything looked like because I wasn't going to see it again" (Marsha McHenry, resident).
5. "My father wouldn't leave. Dad was thinking of his neighborhood and he was going to stand guard. . . . It was probably a few of the most horrible moments of my life. I had to drive away. It was horrible" (Robin Neenan Stuart, resident).

Although evacuation orders affected only 12,000 people (pregnant women and preschool children), more than 140,000 people within 15 miles of Three Mile Island left their homes.

One percent of those living within 40 miles of the reactor evacuated, but 66 percent of households within 5 miles had at least one person evacuate. Most people left on Friday, three days after the accident, and half stayed away for at least five days. The NRC estimated that 50,000 households or 144,000 individuals evacuated. About 70 to 85 percent of those who left stayed with friends or relatives, and 50 percent of the evacuees traveled more than 90 miles (Houts, Cleary, and Hu, 1988). Many evacuated to the Hershey, Pennsylvania, sports arena, where the company provided tours of its zoo, amusement park, and Chocolate World museum and confectionary. Paraphrasing, former Governor Thornburgh recalled seeing bewildered mothers carrying babies, seeking reassurance that the situation was under control (Walker, 2004). There was a great deal of ambivalence about leaving. One woman woke up on Saturday morning and vomited from nerves. Her husband left to play golf, and while he was gone, she took their two children and left for Philadelphia (Walker, 2004).

Most left because of perceived danger. Eighty percent left because of confusing information (disagreement among experts) and because they wanted to avoid forced evacuation. More than half left to protect children (Houts, Cleary, and Hu, 1988). Reasons for staying included waiting for an evacuation and a belief that the situation was in God's hands. Some saw no danger, and 10 percent stayed because they had nowhere else to go. About 5 percent stayed because they lacked transportation (Houts, Cleary, and Hu, 1988); there is a striking parallel with Hurricane Katrina, when many could not evacuate because they had no transportation. Some people did not want to leave their jobs and were concerned about looting, although there was very little of that. Forty percent of the workers at Three Mile Island wanted to leave but could not because of work obligations.

While people were deciding whether to evacuate or not, one of the bars near Three Mile Island threw an "end-of-the-world" party (Neal, 1998). Many people spent time on the phone with friends in other areas. They heard that rumors were spreading across the country about evacuations by helicopter and about the obliteration of entire cities. The NRC's Victor Stello attended Mass in Middletown (Pennsylvania), where the priest offered general absolution to the congregation (this is offered only when large-scale loss of life is imminent). It was a very emotional moment for the parishioners.

Once the meltdown was under control, Neal (1998) found that 60 percent of the residents within five miles of Three Mile Island were against restarting it. For 6.5 years, there were protests and lawsuits over restarting the undamaged reactor. More than 1,000 people were involved in legal disputes claiming harm from the accident.

There were psychological impacts, including a 10 percent increase in intense distress among those living close to the site and increased clinical anxiety and depression reported by mothers of young children. Those living within five miles showed greater stress on psychological, physical, and behavioral measures than control subjects, even 17 months after the accident. Increases in purchases of alcohol, tobacco, sleeping pills, and tranquilizers were reported (Houts, Cleary, and Hu, 1988).

Reactions were not limited to local people. Public demonstrations took place, and a rally held in Washington, D.C., drew a crowd of 100,000 people (Walsh, 1988). The concern was that nuclear power technology would become uncontrollable. Protesters carried signs that said, "I Survived TMI — But What about My Baby?" "Every Dose Is an Overdose," and "TMI — Rotten to the Core." Joni Mitchell, Graham Nash, Jackson Browne, Ralph Nader, Jane Fonda, and California Governor Jerry Brown all spoke and/or entertained. Surveys showed that in 1977, 69 percent approved of building more nuclear power plants and 21 percent disapproved, but after Three Mile Island 46 percent approved and 41 percent disapproved. Disapproval went up, but the public did not want to abandon nuclear power altogether (Walker, 2004).

News media coverage was consistent with the expectations described in chapter 2. During the crisis, the media focused on the immediate danger and the possibility that radioactivity would spread along the eastern seaboard. Three months later, the media concentrated on who was to blame. In January 1980, the coverage was about how cleanup was going and how dangerous the situation was. By October 1980, the story had shifted to cleanup and accomplishments. Many felt that information was withheld or blown out of proportion. Sixty percent felt that information from Metropolitan Edison (the utility purveyor) was useless (Houts, Cleary, and Hu, 1988).

But some felt positive about government officials and the other agencies involved. Anne and Edward Trunk, residents, commented that the news media had invaded the area and were focusing on people who displayed emotion or fear (Walker, 2004). Harold Denton, director of Nuclear Reactor Regulation at the NRC and President Carter's personal emissary, helped calm people's nerves. Reporter Steve Liddick of WCMB radio explained to writer Mark Stephens that Harold Denton looked and behaved like a regular, down-to-earth kind of guy and was trusted by the people. Stopping short of granting Denton sainthood, Denton was perceived as a father figure to many traumatized people (Walker, 2004).

Unfortunately, the public cannot be reassured that another accident, or an even worse accident or event, will not happen. And if it does, I am certain that public reaction will be at least as strong as was observed after Three Mile Island.

Six Policy Criteria: A Synopsis

Table 12 summarizes the advantages and vulnerabilities of a proactive nuclear power policy as 41 points to be considered by policy makers. I will then use these to juxtapose opposing positions.

TABLE 12

**Advantages and vulnerabilities of a proactive
nuclear power policy**

Criteria	Advantages	Vulnerabilities
Reaction of elected officials and staff	Strong support can be expected from the current administration and key leaders of Congress. DOE will take the lead and will need to hire additional staff and upgrade expertise to meet ambitious goals. Some state governors will strongly support the policy.	The next administration may be less supportive of nuclear power. If the technology fails, there could be a major backlash against elected officials. The NRC and the U.S. Environmental Protection Agency could serve as roadblocks if they identify problems.

TABLE 12

(Continued)

Criteria	Advantages	Vulnerabilities
	Some mayors and local officials will support the policy, especially if local economic benefits are involved.	Some states will oppose the use of nuclear power and attempt to block shipments of nuclear fuel and wastes. Local governments that do not benefit will argue against shipping fuels and waste through their jurisdictions.
Reaction of nongovernment stakeholders	There will be strong business support, especially from high-tech industries and industries requiring large quantities of cheap electricity This could lead to a rebirth of nuclear science and engineering industries in the United States. The media will report new projects and new science in the business and science sections of newspapers. Public support has increased.	Objections will be raised to using government funds to support private utilities and high-tech business and research. There will be opposition from powerful and well-connected not-for-profits that oppose high-tech industry. The media will focus on the negative implications, especially any health or environmental problems. The public could quickly turn against nuclear power and is likely to be unforgiving.
Human and ecological health	Nuclear power could reduce the health effects from fossil fuel emissions. Using nuclear power will reduce the ecological damage associated with the extraction and use of fossil fuel. It might be possible to preserve open space that otherwise would be consumed by fossil fuel extraction.	Workers could be exposed to radiation during the start-up, operation, and closure of facilities. New sites will require building on open space and have the potential to devastate local ecosystems. Water resources could be diverted to cool reactors, depending upon the type. There is a potential terrorist threat. The public could be exposed to radiation through on-site releases or during the transportation of nuclear materials.

(Continued)

TABLE 12

(Continued)

Criteria	Advantages	Vulnerabilities
Economic costs and benefits	Costs will be lower when a stable source of electricity is available. Using nuclear power will reduce the balance of payments problem. Dependence on unpredictable and potentially hostile sources of fossil fuels will be reduced. Nuclear power will take the pressure off the need for a tax on fossil fuels (the so-called carbon tax). The use of nuclear power will create jobs and regional economic products at locations where facilities are built.	Turning to nuclear power increases economic dependence on an industry with a mixed record. Large capital investments, including substantial economic support from the federal government, will be required. Substantial legal and administrative support from the federal and state governments will be required.
Moral imperatives	As the steward of the nation, the federal government should not sit by and allow the U.S. economy and international position to be compromised by fossil fuel blackmail. The federal government has the moral imperative to protect large tracts of land from the effects of fossil fuel mining, water pollution, and air pollution.	The federal government has the moral obligation not to invest in a technology that could leave a massive public health and economic legacy for future generations to deal with. The federal government should not consider clustering nuclear power plants, technology development, and waste management facilities because they will create regional sacrifice zones.
Time and flexibility	Having the United States invest in nuclear power buys time to develop fusion or other technologies. Investments in nuclear power may provide enough time for the next generation to learn about and adapt to conservation.	The uncertain economics of nuclear power require the federal government to slow down its efforts to promote nuclear power. Concern about nuclear waste management needs to be addressed before large investments and political commitments are made.

Note: DOE = U.S. Department of Energy; NRC = Nuclear Regulatory Commission.

So should the federal government lead the charge toward more nuclear power? Technology optimists (see the discussion in next section) would say yes: They would say that the technology will work and that even if GNEP is not completely successful, there is enough uranium available to the United States to fuel a new set of nuclear power plants. Leaders, they would argue, are supposed to lead events, not react to them. The United States did not become a world power by allowing other countries to hold us hostage and drain our economic resources. Supporters of nuclear power assert that energy is part of national security and that nuclear power is the only viable bridge between fossil fuels and fusion, the technology they expect to follow nuclear power. Also, it is essential, they would argue, that we use nuclear power to slow down global warming, which could ruin the world economy.

Opponents view nuclear technology as a Faustian bargain. (Faust, according to legend, sold his soul to the devil in exchange for knowledge.) To strike a Faustian bargain, in the case of nuclear power, is to be willing to sacrifice anything to satisfy a need for knowledge or power, in this case, using a technology that is too unpredictable and uncertain — one that will fail and harm the nation's population and economy. Further, they would argue that the logical plan is to invest in low-energy-using technologies, promote public education about conservation, and make more efficient use of fossil fuels, wind, solar power, and other technologies. True leaders, they would argue, look before they leap and should pull back from a nuclear power gamble, investing instead in less complex and smaller-scale technologies. If the government invests in nuclear power, it should do so only with a limited subsidy and maximum oversight and supervision.

For further reading about nuclear power, I strongly suggest the MIT report titled *The Future of Nuclear Power* (2003) and Gertner's (2006) *New York Times* overview article. To keep track of the latest information, see the Web listings of the Uranium Information Centre (http://www.uic.com), the nonproliferation project Web site (http://www.carnegieendowment.org), the IAEA Web site (http://www.iaea.org), and the Bulletin of the Atomic Scientists.

The technological and political challenges of nuclear power are so complex and uncertain that they defy simple arguments and reasoning. Many people, perhaps the vast majority, view nuclear power through their worldview of technology, which I discuss in the next section.

Theory: Technological Exuberance or Precaution

Should we or shouldn't we? I pose that question about nuclear power in this chapter. The same question has been asked many times before and will surely be asked many times more. For example, less than a century ago, Americans had serious concerns about streetcars, trains, and automobiles. In this century, we hope for drugs, treatments, and procedures that will cure cancer, lower cholesterol, and, in general, increase the length and quality of our lives. Yet there is always the fear and sometimes the reality that new pharmaceuticals, new surgeries, and new technologies will fail, that people will die or be injured, and that unanticipated problems will arise.

The debate about the benefits and costs of new technologies has gone on for centuries. It heated up during the past 20 years because of the exponential increase in scientific exploration and the technologies derived from it. In this section, I summarize the opposite poles of the argument.

I do so with several caveats. First, these viewpoints are stereotypes. Not every person I call "exuberant" or "precautionary" would agree with the judgments that I have attributed to him or her. In my experience, exuberants disproportionately have been trained in economics or business, whereas precautionaries have biology and other physical science or non-economics social science backgrounds. However, there are exceptions.

Second, I believe that our reliance on the exuberance or precautionary positions is due to our inability to follow the impact of our decisions. With regard to time, the most sophisticated economic models depend on current and historical relationships (see chapter 7). Also, while models allow us to project two or three decades into the future, reliability decreases with each year. While there is a rich literature on the public perception of risk, there is little written about risk perception in the future. That small literature shows that younger people tend to be the most optimistic (Gidley, 1998; Hicks, 1996; Ono, 2003), but, more important, that the future starts to go dark after 15 to 20 years. People cannot think clearly beyond a generation.

Even when impacts are short term, tracing risk-related effects is a daunting challenge. Hofstetter et al. (2002) described the complexity of such efforts. For example, assume that there is a choice between building a nuclear power plant or a coal-fired power plant. First, there are direct risks related to these choices (e.g., worker exposures while building the facilities and mining the fuels). Second are the so-called upstream effects, impacts due to steps not taken because of the decision, such as research not undertaken and innovations never realized (e.g., no major new development of nuclear reactor technology in the United States for decades).

Third, once a decision is made, impacts, so-called downstream effects set in motion by the decision (e.g., the generation of more spent nuclear fuel), will occur. After the facility is constructed, the ripple creates two new issues (monitoring plant workers for exposure to radiation and managing spent nuclear fuels). Transportation of fuel, other materials, and waste products and employee commuting can all potentially affect off-site areas.

The fourth set of ripples follows economic resources spent on the project. Architects, designers, construction and plant workers, company executives, financiers, and stockholders are all affected. For example, areas with major nuclear waste facilities have hired thousands of highly paid technical experts to design and operate them (see chapter 4). While the surrounding areas may not be wealthy, a cadre of well-paid people work at the site. Also, when major facilities are constructed in areas that had previously been rural, then roads, schools, water and sewerage systems, and many other forms of infrastructure have to be added. And the facilities themselves, as well as the development due to the projects, may impinge on natural areas and cultural artifacts that had been important to the local population. All of these issues should be addressed in environmental impact statements (see chapter 7), but there are always gaps in the analyses and there is always second-guessing after the fact.

Finally, I personally believe H. L. Mencken's view of simple solutions. Mencken, a writer and critic and the editor of the *Baltimore Evening Herald* from 1906 until his death in 1956, observed that "for every complex problem there is an answer that is clear, simple, and wrong" (*Columbia Encyclopedia*, 2001). Without an understanding of the impact of decisions about technological innovations, we resort to simple worldviews to help us decide about future technology.

With these caveats noted, one of the two opposite camps is occupied by those I call exuberants — they are more typically called technological optimists or cornucopians after the idea that cornucopia is a horn of plenty. True exuberants view the world as a place of unlimited resources. Their far more cautious counterparts, whom I label precautionaries, are sometimes called technological pessimists or at other times neo-Malthusians — they preach limits to growth.

With regard to science, exuberants believe that human ingenuity can improve public health and the environment, increase wealth and distribute it across the globe, and help solve the world's political problems. While not discounting human creativity, their precautionary counterparts note that some of our creative efforts have led to tragedies and that unbridled technologically based growth is too risky. Whereas the first group wants to increase the pace of research, the second prefers a different speed — slow, slower, and, sometimes, reverse.

These different worldviews lead to sharply contrasting opinions about the future. With regard to resource depletion, exuberants do not believe that we will run out of scarce resources. In fact, they argue that scarcity leads to price increases, which in turn stimulate research, to more efficient use of resources, and to resource substitution. For instance, as oil and gas prices increase, we will rely more on nuclear power, as well as make more efficient use of fossil fuels. Precautionaries argue that petroleum, wood, water, arable land, and many other resources are being depleted at accelerated rates. Scientists and the technologies they produce, the precautionaries assert, will not be able to keep up indefinitely. Further, there will be unintended and unseen negative and potentially catastrophic consequences. For example, switching to nuclear power implies the need to manage nuclear waste in perpetuity and invites nuclear proliferation. It follows that we should not blindly march down the path of nuclear dependence.

Exuberants contend that we worry too much about pollution control, which leads to regulations that hurt the competitiveness of our businesses and hence reduces the amount of resources that protect our jobs, health, and environment. Rather than spending so much money on pollution control devices, we should instead create profits and use some of them to invest in technologies that will make more efficient use of our resources or find substitutes. Profit and reinvestment, exuberants argue, have made our environment cleaner than at any other point in history. By contrast, precautionaries argue that pollution kills and injures people and ecosystems and that problems like global warming may be irreversible. They call for strong pollution controls, recycling, and substantial investment to prevent emissions.

Exuberants tend to believe in mega-projects that concentrate people and capital to produce massive centralized facilities, such as large clusters of nuclear power plants or gigantic tankers and cargo ships that can transport products across the globe and then offload them in large ports from which they are dispersed on large rail and road networks. Precautionaries think on a smaller scale. They believe that a larger number of decentralized facilities are safer, more controllable, and less wasteful of resources. They want us to produce more food and energy locally, if possible, from renewable sources. Precautionaries want technologies that are simple to build, operate, repair, upgrade, replace, and reuse.

Finally, exuberants do not worry much about population growth because they see people as the key to economic, environmental, and political health. They observe that economic development typically leads to lower birth rates and a stabilized population. In other words, economic development equals a decrease in population growth and less poverty. In addition, they assert that birth control violates some people's religious beliefs. Once again, by contrast, the precautionaries see a need for providing people with birth control information and technology. Without it, there are more people to feed, more resources are used, and more people will die and suffer illnesses and other poverty-related consequences.

Large nuclear power plants, clearly, are among the most complex and mega-scale of projects, and most precautionaries, as noted earlier, are against them. Exuberants would tend to favor them, at least as an interim measure, to get us to the next technological solution. As the Bisconti surveys (2005) show, public opinion has become more favorable. Government's role is critical. The major democracies and their centralized government counterparts can use their powers to make it unprofitable and/or even illegal to use, devise, or test technologies that have a high probability of causing damage in the short or long term, or they can encourage such technologies.

Kemp (1990) offered an interpretation of NIMBYism that is consistent with the exuberant versus precautionary worldviews. Using the United Kingdom's efforts to site a radioactive waste disposal facility, he asserts that proponents of technological solutions invoke the NIMBY response as a way to discredit public concerns — to blame the public for not knowing more about the science and technology. Opponents of the facilities, he asserts, distrust the nuclear industry because of its problematic track record and because of legitimate concerns about local economic impacts and health and environmental effects. He added that some of these concerns could have been overcome if the developers had been more forthcoming and open. In other words, the NIMBY reaction, he believes, should be dismissed as distorting public experience and unhelpful in making policy. Kemp's (1990) observations are entirely consistent with my own experiences at public meetings at which technical experts discount a NIMBY reaction as based on ignorance rather than on their failure to reach out to the public.

The literature about these theories is substantial and remarkably heterogeneous with regard to methods of analysis and discourse. I recommend Simon and Kahn's (1984) and Simon's (1990) books as representative of exuberance and those by Commoner (1971), Meadows et al. (1972), and Ayres (1998) as illustrations of precautionary thinking. Equally interesting and notably different worldviews on technology and innovation are presented in books by Maddox (1972), Gilpin, (2000), Meyers and Raffensberger (2006), and de Bruijn and Norberg-Bohm (2005).

Tales

This chapter illustrates policies that could have such serious long-term ramifications that we should take extra time to consider options, including the implications of postponing our decisions. That is, what will happen if we do not decide immediately, for the next five years, or for the next decade, etc.? Will our economy be seriously damaged? Will technology dramatically improve and add options? Will there be much less environmental damage? Although nuclear power is the example, I could just as easily have used genetically modified organisms (chapter 5), placing dams on rivers and flooding their upstream areas, or other technology-based decisions.

While we grapple with such profound choices, incremental decisions slowly but surely either narrow our choices or allow us more time and flexibility. To illustrate the relationship between short- and long-term policies, I interviewed Connie O. Hughes, who is one of five Commissioners on the New Jersey Board of Public Utilities (BPU). This board was created by former Governor (and later President) Woodrow Wilson in 1911 to regulate railroads and is charged with ensuring adequate and safe utility services at a reasonable cost. The BPU regulates electricity, natural gas, telecommunications, water and wastewater, and cable television.

Commissioner Hughes characterized the BPU as an "economic regulatory agency" that sets utility rates, rules on consumer complaints, gathers information about best industry practices, and acts as a catalyst to improve New Jersey's capacity to deliver infrastructure. The five commissioners have both judicial and legislative roles. The judicial role is to adjudicate complaints; for example, if I complained that I was overcharged by my water utility, the BPU could hear that complaint. Hughes explained that this role has expanded as a result of the deregulation of the electrical power industry in New Jersey in 1999. With regard to its legislative role, the BPU sets rules. For example, it rules on the appearance of the utility bill. This is not a trivial issue because people become extremely frustrated when they cannot understand their bill.

Our conversation focused on the BPU roles that intersect long-term energy policy, more specifically, New Jersey's efforts to reduce energy demand and dependence on fossil fuels. According to Hughes,

> The state deregulated the electrical power industry in 1999 as part of the Electric Discount and Energy Compensation Act (EDECA). As part of that sweeping change, Governor Whitman and the legislature set a goal that we must shift to renewable fuels [in other words, reduce dependence on fossil fuels]. An interim goal for 2012 was set, and that was increased to 20 percent from renewable sources by the year 2020. We also set a goal to reduce the demand for electricity by 20 percent [20 percent below estimates for the year 2020]. If we can meet these objectives, then there will be less need for new power plants, including nuclear power plants, and massive transmission lines. Along with California, New York, Florida, and a few other states, New Jersey is trying to set policies that will relieve the pressure to make decisions that could backfire in the long run.

Hughes's statements are supported by data. New Jersey depends on fossil fuels for about 80 percent of its energy (petroleum, 49 percent; natural gas, 25 percent; and coal 4 percent). Nuclear power produces 13 percent. In 2003, the state provided incentives to residential and commercial customers and to schools to persuade them to install renewable, energy-efficient technologies. The BPU program offered discounts of up to 80 percent of the retail cost of energy-efficient appliances and technologies such as photovoltaics (solar electricity), wind, and biomass. New Jersey's Clean Energy Program received the Excellence in Energy Efficiency and Environmental Education Award (out of 3,000 applicants) from the U.S. Environmental Protection Agency and DOE and is held up as a model.

The program has diffused across the state. For example, Highland Park, my hometown, won the Clean Energy Municipality of the Year Award for 2006 by retrofitting the police and fire departments, the city hall, the library, and other city buildings and by planting trees throughout the borough. Similar awards have been given out to businesses, inventors, and universities, and the state is considered a national leader in diffusing solar energy, wind power, and other renewable forms of energy.

With regard to nuclear power, specifically, Hughes observed that the BPU does not have a regulatory role with regard to siting power plants. That role belongs to the New Jersey Department of Environmental Protection. She said, "If the board felt strongly about it, we could take a position. Personally, I am open to it. Nuclear power seems cost efficient and environmentally sound compared to other options. Each of the five commissioners is independent, so we would have to work together. The president of the board is a cabinet member, which means that he or she has direct access to the governor. Yet the president cannot speak for everyone else unless we concur. I can tell you that we do not want to be put in a position where we have to rely on dirty coal."

Hughes smiled when I brought up the question of politicizing groups like the BPU and replied:

Commissioners are appointed by the governor in New Jersey for a six-year term. They are confirmed by the state legislature, and the term is renewable. In other states, they are elected or chosen by the state legislature. Of course, there is always the possibility of partisan and ideologically driven decisions. But in our state, there is widespread support for policy that will ensure our energy supply while protecting the environment. Our clean energy program will help stabilize electricity costs, preserve natural resources, [and] reduce pollution and our dependence on fossil fuels. We have a master planning process, and I expect elected officials from both parties to support it.

I asked Hughes about her background — that is, preparation for serving as a BPU commissioner. She responded:

My training was in mathematics and then urban planning. I started in state government in 1977 in the New Jersey Department of Labor. I saw the interconnection between job training and unemployment and the need to develop data, analyze issues, and provide training to the workforce. I became deputy commissioner of the Department of Labor. Then I became chief of management and policy for Governor Donald DiFrancesco. In each of those jobs, I began to see more and more of the web of connections between different government agencies. Governor DiFrancesco wanted me to go to the BPU because he saw me as someone without an ideological agenda, someone who would try to build connections between BPU and agencies, including our federal counterparts.

We closed our conversation with another illustration of how short-term decisions can have long-term consequences. Hughes was BPU president on September 11, 2001. She noted:

I realized that our infrastructure was vulnerable and that we needed to take immediate action. I directed staff to ask utilities to prepare reports about the security of their infrastructure. We formed the first task forces in the nation to protect our huge investment in infrastructure. The information was considered confidential. The task force was charged with determining the best practices. Within three months, we had reports about water, telephone, cable, gas, and other utilities. I was named chair of a national committee aimed at protecting our infrastructure. Millions of dollars in grants have been provided to utilities to protect our critical infrastructure. The utilities did the work; BPU facilitated it.

The key message from my conversation with Commissioner Hughes is that prudent policy decisions made now can serve as a bridge to the future: They can buy time to find flexible solutions. Frankly, however, no one should expect to find someone of Hughes's caliber in policy-making positions in every state government agency. In my experience, people selected for leadership positions too often seem overqualified with regard to political lineage and underqualified with regard to capacity to contribute to the solution of complicated problems.

Tools and Tasks

Policy analyses of nuclear power and nuclear waste management rely on environmental impact analysis (see chapter 7). An environmental impact statement typically would include all or almost all of the tools described in chapter 7. Risk assessment methods are used to analyze potential health and ecological impacts, while economic tools are used to assess cost and regional economic impacts. Increasingly, surveys are conducted to determine public perceptions, and mass media coverage is examined as another way of understanding public reaction. In other words, the task of evaluating complex technologies affecting people and the environment for many decades is so challenging that we must use multiple tools to develop credible information for decision makers.

With regard to student tasks, one is to have the class select a controversial project, such as a nuclear waste management facility, a new highway, a coal-fueled power plant, a bridge, or some other major infrastructure expansion that requires a federal environmental impact statement. Students can divide themselves into groups based on their interests, such as health impacts, ecosystem effects, social and economic implications, and so on. The overall assignment is to discuss the choice advocated by the federal agency and to compare that choice with the alternatives presented in the environmental impact statement. Each subgroup within the class prepares a written report and makes an oral presentation. After these are debated, the class tries to arrive at a consensus. Even if it cannot, productive discussions would still ensue.

Two cautions should be observed with this assignment: First, some parts of environmental impact statements require technical knowledge beyond the capacity of many students and, second, environmental impact statements for large facilities can be thousands of pages long. Consequently, the instructor needs to screen the information so that the class is not overwhelmed. If the class is held in a location that requires a state or local environmental impact statement, it may be feasible to focus on a local project, such as a road extension, new housing development, or school construction.

A second assignment is to use some form of content analysis to review mass media coverage of the Three Mile Island and Chernobyl nuclear reactor accidents (see chapter 7). The major goals of the assignment would be to assess what the tone of the coverage was (frightening or reassuring) and how the media turned these accidents into dramatic, newsworthy stories (see chapter 2 for a discussion of newsworthiness). Time permitting, the class can view videotapes of the coverage, which are very graphic. Students would also benefit from comparing the tone of the media coverage with official NRC reports of the same events. The focus of this exercise should be what the differences were and why they existed.

The mass media task need not be confined to the most dramatic and traumatic events. If there is or was a controversial regional infrastructure project, a mass media versus official government document assessment could focus on that case.

An entirely different task is to help the class determine people's ability to understand the future. One approach is to ask people how they expect life to change during the next 20 or 30 years. Will it be better than it is today, about the same, or worse? Then, students should determine what explains the answers. I expect the class to find that for 5 to 10 years, people can describe specific health, environmental, job, and other personal expectations, as well as their forecasts about their neighborhood, region, and even the nation. However, beyond 10 years, I expect that most people will find it increasingly difficulty to be specific, and they will revert to their worldview, which includes their sense of technological optimism or pessimism, and their sense of personal efficacy.

A third potential task is a class visit to an advanced technology facility. Years ago, I was able to take a class to visit a nuclear power plant, a steel mill, a coal mine, and various other facilities. To a large extent, it is no longer possible to do this because of national security and liability concerns. Nevertheless, there may be regional exceptions. A less satisfactory but feasible alternative is to invite the director of one of these facilities to speak to the class. Typically, these directors are extremely energetic and enthusiastic about their technology. Before such a presentation, it is imperative that students understand the technology so they can ask tough, intelligent questions. Following the expert's presentation, the group can engage in an interesting discussion of what they heard.

PART II

Policy Analysis Tools

7

Policy Measurement and Assessment Tools

Introduction

This chapter focuses on eight process and analytical tools that are used to measure and assess the environmental impact of policies, their economic impact, and human reactions to them. Each of these tools is normally taught in a separate university course, sometimes multiple courses, and refresher courses are typical. I make no pretense of providing a comprehensive discussion, nor do I expect a reader who has finished the chapter to be able to critically evaluate a study that uses any of these tools. The goal is rather to recognize how these tools fit into environmental policy analysis and practice.

Environmental Impact Tools

Environmental impact tools include dozens of techniques and instruments developed by scientists, statisticians, and social scientists and applied to the task of assessing what happens when people are about to disturb the environment.

Environmental Impact Assessment (EIA)

The EIA is a mechanism to ensure that major projects or programs undergo a comprehensive review before construction or implementation. The review entails a multidisciplinary, multi-agency, public assessment of the environmental, economic, health, and social impacts of individual projects or program proposals, as well as the consideration of alternatives.

CONTEXT. The preparation of an environmental impact statement (EIS) was initially mandated at the federal level under P.L. 91-190, the National Environmental Policy Act (NEPA), which took effect on January 1, 1970. Broadly defined, the goal of this legislation was to "create and maintain conditions under which man and nature can exist in productive harmony and fulfill the social, economic, and other requirements of present and future generations of Americans" (P.L. 91-190, Chapter 55, 4331[9]).

The EIS has been described as an action-forcing mechanism that orders federal agencies to act in accordance with the goals of NEPA (Anderson, 1973). Title I, Section 102(2)(c) of NEPA requires all federal agencies to prepare an EIS on any "proposals for legislation and other major Federal actions significantly affecting the quality of the human environment" (42 U.S.C. 4332).

NEPA, specifically Section 102(c), requires that each EIS contain a detailed statement describing the following five factors:

1. The environmental impact of the proposed action
2. Any adverse environmental effects that cannot be avoided if the proposed action is implemented
3. Alternatives to the proposed action
4. The relationship between local short-term uses of the human environment and the maintenance and enhancement of long-term productivity
5. Any irreversible and irretrievable commitments of resources that would be involved if the proposed action is implemented

Consideration of these five factors should enlighten those who review them as to whether a proposal adequately falls within environmental standards and is socially beneficial or whether one or more aspects are in potential violation of environmental standards and constitute grounds for halting or modifying development or implementation.

NEPA was set up to be administered by the Council on Environmental Quality, which was established under Title II, Section 201, and then issued guidelines setting forth the rules and procedures agencies must follow to prepare an EIS. These guidelines, with the aid of over 30 years of legal interpretation, have defined the scope of the EIS document and the review responsibilities of the agencies. The requirement to prepare an EIS applies to a wide variety of actions by federal agencies. The following list points out some of the major actions that may require one (Bregman, 1999; Kreske, 1996):

1. Legislative proposals
2. Planned federal projects
3. Projects developed through federal grants
4. Changes in agency policies and operating procedures
5. Actions requiring federal licenses, permits, and other approvals
6. Actions with possibly controversial impacts

In the original act, states and municipalities "owe no duties under NEPA, but may be subject to alternative environmental legislation fashioned after NEPA." In fact, many states and local governments have NEPA progeny. State and local government EIA requirements vary. In general, some major differences involve less detailed content requirements, applicability to public or private actions, different administrative or overseeing agencies, preemption with regard to NEPA (federal law will normally take precedence), and a different role for public participation.

Most local EIS requirements are primarily directed at private development. The overseeing agencies are usually planning or zoning commissions or in some cases an environmental commission. The reader should note that environmental commissions may be purely advisory, whereas an environmental review component integrated into a planning and zoning commission may have legal authority to approve, deny, or request the alteration of a development proposal.

CONTENTS, STRENGTHS, AND WEAKNESSES. The EIA review process varies by level of government. I will limit my comments to NEPA, Section 102(2)(c). Although the wording varies by agency, the following six topics encompass the essence of EIS requirements:

1. Description of the existing environment
2. Description of alternatives
3. Probable impacts of each alternative
4. Identification of the alternative chosen and the evaluation that led to this choice
5. Detailed analysis of the probable impacts of the proposal
6. Description of the techniques intended to minimize any adverse impacts

Proponents of a project cannot afford to leave out any information because the courts have rejected EISs that were deemed not to be comprehensive. Hence, ideally, a multidisciplinary team should plan and do an EIS. To put it another way, a multidisciplinary team will greatly reduce the possibility of overlooking an important part. EISs have also been rejected because credible alternatives were not developed. One option that must always be considered is to not undertake any project at all at a particular time (the no-action alternative). The beneficial or adverse impacts of each alternative can be determined by comparing the expected future conditions with existing conditions and that no-action alternative.

NEPA and its state and local progeny are controversial. This section briefly summarizes the major strengths and weaknesses of the EIS process. One of the most important accomplishments of this process on the federal, state, and local levels has been its widespread use, at least prescriptively, as a technique for managing growth. Using the EIS is an explicit acknowledgment that development requires early planning to avoid degrading the quality of the environment.

The EIS has been viewed as a consciousness-raising endeavor and even among its critics has gained deserved praise. It is seen as a serious rejection of the idea of unchecked economic growth (see the environmental ethics discussion in chapter 5). In addition to generating important environmental impact data, the process has often spawned a more comprehensive, interdisciplinary analysis, including estimates of the secondary or indirect effects of a proposed action, and has stimulated an appreciation of interrelationships.

Aside from these broad strengths, the EIS process has some very specific strong points. Since NEPA forces federal agencies to prepare impact statements, the review procedure creates a system of checks and balances between federal, state, and local governments. Although an agency can legally ignore strong opposition to a proposal by states or localities, this is not likely to happen. The opportunity for public participation in federal decision-making processes is also enhanced because the EIS is legally determined to be a full-disclosure document that ideally must incorporate the opinions of willing commentators. Finally, the interdisciplinary team approach to the EIS should lead to better science. To summarize, the EIS process should lead to better planning, raise people's consciousness, result in better communication between scientists, and create a series of checks and balances, especially under good leadership (Keysar and Steinemann, 2002).

From an operational perspective, the accomplishments of the EIS process can be viewed purely from its past applications. NEPA has been instrumental in the cancellation or postponement of highways, dams, airports, nuclear waste disposal programs, outer continental shelf leases, and other proposals. More frequently, the process has resulted in shifts in location, design modifications, and other changes to mitigate undesirable environmental effects, including strengthened regulations.

At a vastly different geographic scale, regional, state, and local EIS officers have cited numerous cases of the preservation of unique local environments because of the EIS. They vary from large amounts of parkland to isolated dunes and a few small cedar trees. Each by itself is probably not very important. Cumulatively, they lead some people to conclude that the EIS process has been successful.

Although the EIS represents a prescriptive approach to protecting the environment, some critics have charged that it has been ineffective. One problem with the process derives from a fundamental contradiction in NEPA and many of the state and local statutes. On the one hand, the law creates the conditions for integrating environmental considerations into agency actions to protect the quality of the environment as a procedural duty. On the other hand, a fundamentally procedural requirement such as Section 102(2)(c) avoids making demands on an agency's substantive activity. An apparently defective substantive decision by an agency may be exempt from legal imposition as long as procedural requirements were followed.

A second important deficiency of NEPA and many of the state laws is that they exempt private-sector development from the EIS process. This shortcoming deserves special attention because such projects account for the vast majority of development on the local scale. NEPA and its progeny have been administratively extended to private actions by using federal, state, and other permit processes.

Despite these clever extensions, many of the potentially harmful environmental effects resulting from human activity are not addressed by an EIS or its equivalent.

One of the greatest drawbacks of the EIS process relates to administrative discretion. It has been contended that many actions with environmentally significant impacts are not accompanied by an EIS because agencies decide that the actions are not "major" or "significant" or do not constitute an agency "proposal" or "action." Agencies differ in their attitudes toward the EIS requirement. Those that feel constrained will try to circumvent the requirement in decision making or present a biased analysis. Therefore, one problem is that final EISs often become defensive documents packed with as much information as possible to protect the agency in case of a legal challenge. Although the information is interesting, it often amounts to a bundle of irrelevant material that avoids the significant environmental impacts of a proposal. This problem is especially evident in the often cursory and perfunctory discussion of alternatives.

Another of the most important categories of problems inherent in the EIS process involves the scientific evaluation of impacts. No matter how detailed or comprehensive the document may be, there appears to be no way of ensuring that all significant, scientifically ascertainable impacts will be included. At the outset, it is known that some scientific facts will be missing simply because information or data are lacking.

A closely related problem concerns the accurate measurement and weighting of impacts. Many have multiplicative rather than additive effects on the environment. Some pollutants have specific chemical reactions that may be impossible to measure accurately. The impact of some chemicals is not known. In addition, methods of weighting environmental impacts (reviewed in chapter 8) have limitations that are not always recognized or stated by their users. Overall, the limits inherent in estimating environmental impacts cast suspicion on the adequacy of many impact statements. And because EISs are viewed as advocacy documents, many people are suspicious and fear data manipulation.

The most widely publicized economic problems associated with the EIS process (in addition to the money government agencies spend on preparation) come from business. Developers argue that the EIS process is basically a no-growth or slow-growth policy that leads to economic recession. They cite the time lag inherent in preparing and reviewing EISs and the inflationary impact on building costs. This inflationary impact is further increased when delays result from NEPA litigation and potential injunctions.

Some, however, contend that the greatest economic problem is the grossly inadequate commitment of resources to the EIS process. They argue that these costs are justified by the need to protect and preserve the quality of the human environment. Rather than causing unemployment, the EIS process has created employment for environmental and social scientists, administrators, and lawyers and has created a need for materials from the commercial sector. More important, proponents contend that EIS-related costs may actually result in future benefits by avoiding adverse impacts that could have imposed greater costs if left unchecked.

Ultimately, the biggest weakness of the NEPA EIS and many of its state and local progeny is that it remains extremely difficult to modify an agency's or private developer's decisions, that is, to get all of the alternatives considered seriously (Steinemann, 2001). The formal EIS comes too late in the planning of most projects. If comprehensive planning has not been done before this stage, the best EIS may make no difference. The agency decision maker can build the project as long as the EIS describes the impacts. Discontent primarily with this last weakness of NEPA led Fairfax (1978) to argue that NEPA has wasted environmentalists' resources on paper shuffling when they could have been put to better use in reforming agency decision-making authority and mandates.

In my opinion, the severe critics and defenders of the NEPA EIS process have overstated their arguments. NEPA was the first comprehensive, politically acceptable step in an evolutionary process that should lead to refined impact assessments. In essence, NEPA says look before you leap, not that you cannot leap at all. In short, NEPA and its progeny are neither a panacea nor a failure.

LEARNING MORE ABOUT THE TOOL. There can be no single methodology or cookbook approach that is applicable to all EISs. This previous section presented the main topics to be included in an EIS and an order of presentation that will help identify alternatives, the significant impacts, and the trade-offs involved with any project.

A large literature on EIA is available. Books by Bregman (1999) and Kreske (1996) are the standards. There are some wonderful books and papers that provide a historical perspective on NEPA a few years after it became law (Anderson, 1973; Baker, Kaming, and Morrison, 1977; Burchell and Listokin, 1975; Canter, 1977; Cheremisinoff and Morresi, 1977; Greenberg et al., 1978; Jack McCormick & Associates, 1978; Jain, Urban, and Stacey, 1977; Liroff, 1976; Oregon State University, 1973; Ortolano, 1973; Warner, 1973). Taken together, these early reports present a picture of high hopes and some disappointments. I read the journal *Environmental Impact Assessment Review* to keep up with recent thinking. In addition, tens of thousands of EISs have been written, and all federal government documents are available. However, since they are sometimes thousands of pages long, I suggest reading the summary first. The U.S. Environmental Protection Agency (EPA) and other federal agencies provide Internet access to their documents and processes. The best way to determine the role played by a particular EIS is to examine the *Federal Register*, which publishes the records of decisions made by departments and agencies.

Risk Assessment

Mandated by the federal government and some state or other government bodies, including some international ones, risk assessment is a multistage process for determining the likelihood of adverse human and/or ecological effects of exposure to biological, chemical, and physical hazards. This section describes the risk assessment process, its strengths and weaknesses, and the way evidence is gathered and evaluated.

CONTEXT. Risk assessment was developed because of concern over the limitations of other methods used to manage risk. One method required using specific technologies or resources. For example, oil refineries were required either to build scrubbers that removed fumes before they dispersed or to switch to low-sulfur-bearing oil. According to some businesses, inflexible requirements stifle the creativity of private enterprise. A second option for managing risks is the outright banning of substances, such as asbestos, and carcinogens in food (see chapters 2, 3, and 5). However, if there are no obvious substitutes, banning can be economically painful. The third approach is to compare the benefits against the costs and then make a decision about the risk. Cost-benefit analyses are controversial (see chapter 8). In 1979, a U.S. interagency task force observed that assessing the risk of chemicals could be effective in determining which substances should be tightly controlled and banned to reduce cancer. The approach was to use the best available data (see Silbergeld, 1993) and to make conservative assumptions when data were not available.

CONTENT, STRENGTHS, AND WEAKNESSES. Risk depends on (1) the toxicity of the material, (2) its quantity, (3) the probability of release, (4) the dispersion of the hazard, (5) the population exposed, and (6) species uptake.

With regard to toxicity, substances are helpful in some forms and quantities and harmful in others. Asbestos is a wonderful fire retardant but a powerful carcinogen as well. Tetraethyl lead and methyl tertiary butyl ether (MTBE) (see chapter 3) are good antiknock compounds in the automobile engine, but both are also dangerous. DDT (dichlorodiphenyltrichloroethane) has the capacity to control malaria-carrying mosquitoes, yet it can wreck havoc on the environment (see chapter 5). Uranium products are used in medicine and in generating electricity (see chapter 6), but they can kill people and leave a massive legacy of nuclear waste (see chapters 4 and 6).

Epidemiologists and toxicologists identify the most dangerous hazards. Epidemiologists typically use human data. For example, researchers found that areas with shipyards had elevated rates of lung cancer (Blot et al., 1977). The high cancer rates were traced to shipyard employees who worked with and near asbestos insulation. Doctors noticed workers with a rare form of liver cancer that was traced to exposure to vinyl chloride gas. These are two simple examples of retrospective studies; that is, researchers notice patterns in the data after the exposure has occurred. The vast majority of epidemiological studies are retrospective and look back to link hazards and outcomes.

Retrospective epidemiological studies have problems, typically with unreliable information about previous exposures. Hence, there is a preference for prospective studies, such as the large one begun in 1948 in Framingham (Massachusetts); these follow a group of people over time to determine factors that affect their health. The Framingham database consisted of 5,127 men and women who were aged 30 to 62 years and did not have cardiovascular disease during the study period (1948 to 1952). The hazards were alcohol, smoking, obesity, high blood pressure, high cholesterol levels, and low levels of physical activity. Researchers followed people by examining them every two years and by monitoring local hospital records. Results indicated that those who had elevated cholesterol, who smoked tobacco, who consumed a good deal of alcohol, and who were obese were at relatively high risk of coronary heart disease and that exercise reduced risk. All of these findings are now accepted as the conventional wisdom.

The Framingham study used questionnaires, clinical examinations, and testing to obtain and verify results. The major advantage of the prospective design is that researchers do not have to rely on historical records and flawed memories and records. One disadvantage is that not every person can be followed for the full length of the study. Second, prospective studies tend to be expensive, requiring large sample sizes and long follow-up periods. The so-called nurses and doctors studies are two other multiyear large-sample prospective studies that have produced interesting findings about hazards. These three major prospective studies have given rise to hundreds of publications, which can be found by typing "Framingham study," "nurses' study," or "doctors' study" into an Internet search engine.

Epidemiological studies take a long time, typically a decade or more, before hazards can be identified. Therefore, the bulk of risk assessments rely on the testing of animals by toxicologists. Mice and other species are used as sentinels of human effects. The studies are designed so that useful results are achieved with as few animals as possible and as quickly as possible. This requires delivering much higher doses than humans would receive. The potency of the substance is enhanced by solvents, and the dose is placed in sensitive locations to enhance its toxicity. A substance that shows no risk at high and enhanced doses is assumed to be safe for humans. Tragically, there are exceptions, such as diethylstilbestrol (DES), which was harmful to the unborn children of pregnant women but not to laboratory animals.

Starting with epidemiological and toxicological data, scientists use mathematical models to estimate the excess risk associated with exposure to the substance in question. However, these models are controversial. One point at issue is the relationship between dose and response. Some models assume that human response increases directly with dose, that the relationship is linear. Another set of models—called threshold models—assumes that some substances are harmless unless a threshold dose is reached. There is a set of nonlinear-threshold and no-threshold models. Debates are common because the form of the model adopted by government regulators can markedly influence the results. The underlying scientific problem is that low-dose exposure and response data are scarce. Policy makers must decide which model assumption applies.

The quantity of hazardous material is the second element of risk assessment. Humans have produced massive amounts of hazardous materials, ranging from individual hazards such as cigarettes to weapons of mass destruction. The U.S. government's toxic release inventory (TRI) contains information about the accumulation and use of toxins by business, but not all hazard sources are included. We badly need the information. Without it, the results can be tragic. For example, thousands of unexploded land mines have been buried in Asia, Africa, and Europe, and every year thousands of people are killed or maimed. The day I began to write this chapter, a neighbor decided to pour some "stuff" down the drain. Within an hour, three birds were dead, the neighbor and his wife were taken to the hospital, and a worker who was fixing the porch of an adjacent house became ill. The substance was malathion, a pesticide that is no longer used in the United States (see chapter 5). So much dangerous material has been buried, neglected, and forgotten that we can expect to routinely hear about accidents caused by this legacy.

The probability that the hazard will be released is the third component of risk assessment. If we know the hazard posed by a substance and we know its location, then we should be able to contain it. But business and government resist spending money on containment if a problem is unlikely to occur; they do not want to put a second hull on an oil tanker or build more structures to protect nuclear wastes. Even when appropriate measures are taken to reduce the chances of breaching containment, the technologies may not work because they have become outdated. The World Trade Center was designed to withstand the impact of an aircraft, but not the large, new, almost fully fueled commercial airliners that hit on September 11, 2001. The Soviet reactors at Chernobyl are an example of a blatant case of lack of containment. With a design that included state-of-the-art containment, the meltdown would have been less of a disaster. A recent case was the failure of the levees after Hurricane Katrina in New Orleans. Flood waters were released with devastating consequences.

It is easy to say that these steps should have been taken. But with limited budgets, adding more protection at one location doubtless means reducing it at another. For example, if the New Orleans levees had been substantially increased and there was no hurricane, some critics would have second-guessed the federal government for building levees that were not needed. I am sure that some people would have called them political pork given to the state of Louisiana.

Dispersion of hazards is the fourth element of risk assessment. Contaminants can spread through direct contact, air, water, and land. Beginning in the mid-1970s, researchers developed mathematical and physical models to detect the spread of hazards. For example, air quality dispersion models are widely used in risk assessments and impact analyses of large sources of emissions, such as coal-fired electricity-generating stations and oil and chemical refineries.

By far the most interesting case I have encountered was at U.S. chemical warfare destruction sites. At one location, the army built a meteorological station so that it could follow the impact of potential releases of chemical agents into the atmosphere. Every day, when weapons were brought to the incinerator for destruction, the commander and staff decided on the worst-case accident. Their decision was fed into a computer model that figuratively dispersed the hazard into the atmosphere. The model could forecast how many people would be exposed and how many would likely die or be injured. That information was then sent to health officials in the surrounding area. Whenever a major change in daily operations was made, this exercise was repeated. This U.S. Department of Defense (DOD) program was an effort to link knowledge about toxins, air quality dispersion models, and local public health preparedness.

The population that is exposed is the fifth element of risk assessment. Cigarettes, alcohol, and some other hazards are ubiquitous. Fortunately, many facilities that produced very dangerous chemical, physical, and biological agents have been located in remote places far from population centers. But "far" is a relative term. For example, the U.S. Nuclear Regulatory Commission (NRC) requires an unoccupied buffer around all commercial nuclear power-generating facilities (see chapter 6). It also requires an assessment of population distribution out to a cumulative distance of 50 miles and a multidecade population forecast. While greater attention is focused on the number of people living within 5 miles, the electrical utility proposing the site has to be able to estimate a cumulative population distribution out to 50 miles so that exposures can be estimated and evacuation plans created.

Some nuclear plants have not been built or operated as a result of these estimates. I worked on one that was to be located 10 miles from the city of Philadelphia and 4.5 miles from Trenton, New Jersey. That location was looked at unfavorably by the NRC because of the potential population at risk and concerns about evacuation in the event of a problem. Another nuclear-powered electricity-generating facility constructed on Long Island, New York, was never opened because it was feared that the nearby population could not be evacuated in the event of an accident. A proposed facility across the river from the United Nations buildings in New York City was not constructed for the same reason. In these cases, the sites were located in more "remote" areas. However, some of these areas, such as Indian Point (at Buchanan in Westchester County, New York) are no longer remote. People and businesses have moved nearby. The electric power utility companies that own this and similar sites have been engaged in political and legal struggles to keep them open against strong opposition, now heightened by the fear of terrorist attacks.

The sixth component of risk assessment is uptake of the hazard and response to the dose. Some contaminants are bound up in soil or plants and in other ways that make them much less hazardous to humans. Others are in very dangerous forms. This concept of bioavailability is important. In Times Beach, Missouri, a small town near St. Louis, dioxin, a very hazardous chemical, was mixed with oil and spread on town roads. The material was in a form that could readily be absorbed by people. The town was evacuated. By contrast, dioxin-laden material in the Ironbound neighborhood of Newark, New Jersey, was bound up in the local soil and was not considered as dangerous.

Species vary in their sensitivity to exposure. Within the same species, sensitivity varies by age, sex, nutrition, size, route of exposure, and other factors. Science is only in the initial stages of trying to understand these complex relationships. Right now we operate with too many generalizations, such as assuming that the youngest and oldest populations are at the highest risk. A lot more needs to be learned.

A good deal of criticism has been aimed at risk assessment. One criticism is that the results are sometimes so uncertain. In some cases, the high estimate of risk is twice the low estimate. In other cases, the high estimate is 10 to 100 times greater than the low estimate. When the range is so great, the results are not very helpful.

Critics also assert that risk assessment is a way to hide ethical choices in details, that it implies a tolerance for risk, with the higher risk inevitably falling on people who are economically disadvantaged (see chapter 5). From the perspective of these critics, risk assessment is a mathematical shortcut for deciding how safe is safe enough in favor of the affluent and against the disadvantaged who do not have the funds to hire scientists and lawyers to gather data and to make their arguments to government officials and to judges and juries.

In 1993, Ellen Silbergeld, a senior environmental scientist and environmental advocate, observed that too much authority had been handed over to technological elites and that perhaps the public was better served by methods that were more easily understood and less easy to dazzle and obscure with numbers. Langdon Winner (1985), a political scientist and expert on the social impact of technology, remarked that the experience of environmentalists and consumer advocates who enter the risk debate will resemble that of a naïve soul who visits Las Vegas and joins a poker game in which the deck is stacked against him.

Peter Montague (1991), writing under the banner of the Environmental Research Foundation of Washington, D.C., concluded that risk assessment is fatally flawed. His detailed arguments are both technical and ethical. On the technical side, here are his conclusions:

1. Toxicological evidence based on laboratory studies is unacceptable because animals are exposed in controlled environments, whereas humans live in complex exposure environments.
2. Companies, claiming trade secrets, will try to avoid revealing all of their ingredients.

3. Humans vary a great deal in their response to contaminants, so what is "acceptable" for the average person is not acceptable for many people.
4. Risk assessments do not take into account substance interactions.
5. Studies ignore common impacts, such as headaches, fatigue, emotional distress, immune effects, and joint pain.

Supporters of risk assessment believe that a logical presentation of data, including full disclosure about uncertainties, can provide decision makers with more information than they would otherwise have and guide researchers to shortcomings that can be addressed. Further, they would assert that many of the criticisms, such as substance interaction, exclusion of ecological risk, and non-cancer endpoints, are being addressed, although they certainly are not being fully addressed.

In light of these criticisms, the federal government created a Commission on Risk Assessment and Risk Management (1997) to consider how risk assessment could be most effectively used in a regulatory framework. The commission (1997) published several volumes and seven appendices, all of which are available on the Internet, that explore the strengths and weaknesses of risk analysis. Dr. Bernard Goldstein (see chapter 3) served on that commission.

Melding risk assessment and the law is particularly difficult, more so for risk analysis than for EIA. The EIA process requires options and consideration and presentation of those options. But the bottom line is that the agency makes a choice: yes or no. The courts will not interfere unless it can be proven that the EIA process was not followed.

In my experience, the risk analysis process is much more difficult for the judges who are sometimes required to assess it. Scientific results are distributed along a continuum, that is, scientists typically find a most probable level of risk, but they realize that variations exist, and they try to estimate the probabilities of the estimates. Scientists do not relate to risks as "dangerous" or "not dangerous."

But judges do make decisions about danger. Although judges are tolerant of scientific methods, they struggle with how to use typical scientific results. The decision by the U.S. Supreme Court in *Daubert v. Merrell Dow Pharmaceuticals* (1135 Ct. 2786, 1993) (see chapter 3) demonstrates how the courts have tried to judge the quality of risk analysis data. Next, I will review how they have dealt with the conversion of continuous data into concepts that they can use, such as "safe," "significant," and "acceptable."

Benzene illustrates the difficulty of defining even these three common terms (Barnard, 1990). In the benzene case, the U.S. Supreme Court overturned a ruling by the U.S. Occupational Safety and Health Administration (OSHA), which had asserted that benzene, a ubiquitous substance that can cause leukemia, had no threshold below which there was no risk. The court rejected these arguments, asserting that OSHA had a responsibility to set a standard and that safe did not mean risk free. The court chose city air and driving a car as illustrations of activities that we would agree are "not unsafe." The court defined "significant risk" as a risk that was "not acceptable" to society in "ordinary life." Remarking that "significant risk" should not be defined as a "mathematical straitjacket," the Supreme Court pressed the agency to base a decision on the preponderance of evidence from risk assessments. In short, the courts have ordered agencies to use risk assessment and make judgments about a level of exposure at which workers, the public, and ecosystems will be safe. They want agency experts to set the standards. This case shows how difficult it is for the courts and science to meld. Scientists resist simple safe and unsafe levels, but attorneys require them. We can expect more of these difficult challenges, especially because scientific information is increasing rapidly.

LEARNING MORE ABOUT THE TOOL. The literature about risk analysis has virtually exploded during the past 15 years. EPA has published guidelines and workbooks, as have various other organizations. Because there is so much published material, it is easy to get lost in the details of doing specific kinds of risk assessments. Those interested in the process should refer to the reports produced by the Commission on Risk Assessment and Risk Management (1997). Also, the earlier National Research Council (1983, 1992) reports provide historical perspective, and excellent professional journals are available, including *Risk Analysis*, which is the flagship journal of the International Society for Risk Analysis.

I offer a final comment about EIA and risk analysis. Both methods offer challenging opportunities for young people educated in the social and physical sciences and the humanities. Those who have studied anthropology, geography, economics, sociology, history, physics, chemistry, biology, mathematics, computer science, planning, public policy, pharmacy, and engineering and who do not mind keeping a suitcase handy and working long hours on fascinating projects can find a job in the field. For example, one of my former graduate students worked on an EIA for a railroad that was going to be built to carry nuclear weapons on trains so that the Soviet Union could not destroy all U.S. nuclear weapons in a first strike. Another former student worked on a dioxin risk assessment of an abandoned pesticide factory in a dense urban setting.

Measuring Human Reactions

Policies depend upon public support, or at least tolerance. Elected officials, business leaders, citizen action groups, and every other person or group that wants to influence and understand people will try to take the pulse of public opinion.

Content Analysis

Elected officials, judges, advocacy groups, citizen advisory committees, diplomats, respondents to proposed public laws and actions, the media, and many others produce words and images. Their testimonies become data that can be

used to answer policy-related questions. Here is a partial list of the kinds of documents that comprise data: administrative records, agendas, announcements,
audiotapes of radio shows and interviews, budgets, charts, diaries, evaluations,
letters, memos, minutes, news clips, organizational archives, maps, proposals,
progress reports, and television videotapes.

CONTEXT. The most prevalent use of content analysis in environmental policy is
to study media reporting. Every one of the themes in the first six chapters has had
extensive media coverage. If I wanted to determine the message that television
was sending to the public about MTBE as a gasoline additive (see chapter 3), I
could obtain television coverage, then search for key words, such as "deadly,"
"high risk," or "water pollution," and examine the use of photos, graphs, and
other images used in stories about MTBE. I could assess sources (angry people,
government officials, business representatives), and I could check to see whether
evidence asserting risk is placed at the beginning of the story or at the end. To
illustrate, I will use the newspaper coverage of brownfields.

CONTENTS, STRENGTHS, AND WEAKNESSES. Content analysis is no different
from any other tool in that good research questions and a protocol for answering
them are required. For example, we conducted a content analysis of media coverage during the first years of the U.S. brownfields program (1993–1998) to answer
five questions (Greenberg and Lowrie, 1999):

1. What sources (e.g., government officials, business, environmental advocacy
   groups) are used in the stories?
2. Is the coverage of the program generally positive, neutral, or negative?
3. What benefits do the stories mention?
4. What barriers do they describe?
5. What do they say about community involvement?

With regard to data, in the late 1990s, when we first thought of the questions,
nearly all of the coverage was confined to newspapers, and nearly all of that was
in areas that had EPA brownfields pilot grants (see chapter 1). So one point of caution about content analysis is that the results are media specific. The results may
be different for television, radio, and magazines.

Searching for articles is critical. We searched for the words "brownfield,"
"brownfields," or "contaminated sites." Had we searched only for articles that
mentioned brownfield(s), we would have missed some coverage. Also, we
removed letters to the editor and articles that were not primarily about brownfields (articles that mentioned them only as part of a larger article about environmental issues or as a budget item or as part of a speech). We did include "hard
news" stories, which are usually about an event or activity that occurred within
the previous 48 hours. We included "feature" stories, which report on an issue,
set of events, or trend, and we included editorials as well.

While content analysis can be done without expert help, searches have become sufficiently complex that a major project requires such help. For example, if I were to search for legal documents, I would ask a law librarian to assist. Not to use an expert is asking for a data set that is not credible. The brownfields search produced 168 stories. The number rose from only 8 in the first year of the program to over 70 in 1998. Clearly, as the EPA's brownfields pilot innovation began to diffuse, the number of stories increased.

The analyst must create a protocol to answer the research questions. Words do not speak for themselves in a content analysis. The analyst has to identify the significance of the words and phrases in the context of policy questions. Whether the coding of the information is done by people or by computers, a good content analysis will have a protocol and a coding scheme. The protocol should have seven steps. First, what is to be coded? Is it every word? Phrase? Sentence? Paragraph? Some combination? I have tried all of them individually and in combination. If a computer package that scans the text and counts items is used, every word can be coded. In the case of brownfields, I could find out how many times the words "brownfields," "EPA," and "risk" were used in the story. Some of the new computer packages can provide word and phrase combinations. But, frankly, while these are utterly reliable compared with human counts, they have not helped me learn what the story is trying to say. Yet coding the entire story is too general. It is important to know where different supportive remarks and criticisms are found because people tend to read only the first part of a story.

Every data point choice has reliability concerns. By reliability, I mean whether someone reading the story more than once would make the same judgment or whether two people who read the same story would interpret it the same way.

Words are the safest choice for the unit of observation. Some words have different meanings, such as "lead" (metal or leader), "loaded" (rich or inebriated), or "bloody" (angry or covered with blood). Yet there are relatively few interpretation problems when words are the unit. Going to the phrase, sentence, or paragraph increases the reliability problem, that is, having different readers draw different conclusions from the same data. A paragraph can claim that risk is present with one source of information and deny it with another. Before the coding is done, the protocol has to state whether the same paragraph can be coded as asserting and denying risk or whether only the first statement will be counted.

Every protocol should have a coder training stage or, in the case of a computer analysis, a stage of assigning rules to the computer. Then the training should be checked with a pilot test to determine whether the results are reliable and whether they answer the questions. In this case, the two coders found an overall agreement of 93 percent on the five paragraph-level items and over 80 percent on every other item; this level of reliability is considered acceptable.

Content analysis produces counts for all of the information that is gathered. With regard to the brownfields study, the key finding was that the articles overwhelmingly cast brownfields in a positive light and used Superfund as a straw man to criticize (see chapter 1). The 168-story content study was updated by Ellerbusch in 2005. His goal was to determine how many brownfield stories mentioned any concern about health effects. He used LexisNexis Academic Universe, a searchable database, to study U.S. news. While this is a powerful search engine, Ellerbusch (2005) notes that some of the definitions in the database changed during the study period and so the time series is imperfect. His search terms were brownfield, brownfield + housing, brownfield + health, and brownfield + housing + health. Notably, had he used risk instead of health, he would found only a third of the articles. Also "housing" yielded far more articles than "residential." So each word in a search needs careful consideration.

A total of 15,402 articles were identified for the 1986–2003 period. The tendency, as in the earlier analysis, was for the stories to be reassuring about risk and yet for the risk-asserting paragraphs, if any, to go at the beginning of the story (see the discussion of newsworthiness in chapter 2). Overall, Ellerbusch's (2005) study suggests that the brownfields policy is still enjoying a honeymoon with the media.

From the tools perspective, these examples illustrate how rapidly the technology has changed the capacity to search the media. However, with a greater capacity comes the need to be extraordinarily careful about testing the choice of words. And the mere mention of a word implies neither a risk-asserting nor a risk-reassuring slant. The stories need to be read and interpreted.

LEARNING MORE ABOUT THE TOOL. The literature contains thousands of applications of content analysis. To learn more about the method, I suggest the following books, which represent a combination of the pre-computer and computer eras (Berelson, 1952; Krippendorff, 2004; Neuendorf, 2001; Pool, 1959; Riffe, Lacy, and Fico, 2005; Weber, 1985).

The field is trending toward the use of computer packages because they can produce near-perfect reliability and can be tied to an optical scanner. Another trend is to directly link the methods to massive databases and then to statistical packages for analysis. The most prominent example is the use of content analysis to assess computerized records from 42 federal government agencies as part of the Paperwork Reduction Act of 1995 (P.L. 104–13, 104th Congress, 1st session). These analyses include efforts to reduce paperwork, improve records management, and provide assistance to those who have legitimate reasons to access records (Moen, Stewart, and McClure, 1997).

Surveys

A survey is a method for collecting data about knowledge, beliefs, feelings, attitudes, and behaviors. Surveys are conducted of the public as a whole, of segments of it (e.g., elderly or teens), of occupational groups (e.g., physicians, professors, government employees), and of any group that is important to organizations.

CONTEXT. Surveys are a mainstay of policy analysis and practice. They take many forms, and each has strengths and weaknesses. This section will describe and illustrate the major forms.

CONTENTS, STRENGTHS, AND WEAKNESSES. Face-to-face interviews are one form of survey. For example, a focused interview is composed of a set of open-ended questions and typically lasts from 45 to 90 minutes. My greatest success with this form comes when I send the questions to the potential respondent one to three weeks in advance. Here are the first two questions that I sent to the three mayors who were interviewed about brownfields as part of chapter 1.

1. *Source of proposals:* When a site is contaminated, are ideas for redevelopment more likely to come from local government or from developers? Are developer-initiated proposals for brownfield sites better (more thorough, more thoughtful) than the proposals for uncontaminated sites or only slightly contaminated sites? Are they more complex or more expensive because of the cleanup cost and liability concerns? In other words, does the fact that there is contamination exclude many developers and/or bring in a special group of developers, architects, lawyers, and engineering firms? Does this limit the development potential of sites? What role does local business play compared with business that has no history in the city?

2. *Interactions with the state and federal government:* Is there more interaction with the Department of Environmental Protection, EPA, the Department of Transportation, and others? How do these interactions change the normal redevelopment process as compared to when the site is not contaminated or only minimally contaminated? Slow down? Cost more? Lead to bigger projects? Require you to modify your zoning or building requirements to accommodate the project? Use deed restrictions and other institutional devices more often? For example, is there more follow-up by nonlocal government agencies to make sure that there are no post-project development contamination problems?

Because the mayors knew the questions, they provided written reports and had senior staff on hand for meetings. I also asked for and got permission to tape the interviews. I followed up with other interviews. In short, the smart thing to do is to provide the questions ahead of time. It shows respect for the person being interviewed and leads to a more thoughtful and thorough response. Also, it is best to send the text of any direct quotes back to the respondent for review, especially if a prominent person is involved. The objective is to make sure that the respondent can articulate a point as clearly as possible.

Asking structured questions is a second type of survey approach. Normally, the questions are fully labeled, or at least the ends are labeled. A typical structured question makes a statement and then asks the extent to which the respondent agrees with it. For example, to open a conversation with individuals, I have made the following statement about a former nuclear weapons site: "I don't like the idea of transporting wastes from this site because I fear an accident or an attack." A scale of 1 to 5 was used to measure the extent of agreement, where 1 was "strongly agrees" with the statement and 5 was "strongly disagrees."

Both open and structured questions can be asked of groups. Focus groups consist of a set of people selected to represent a specific population. For example, one of my doctoral students wrote her thesis about the risks of leaving the hospital one day after breast cancer surgery. She interviewed people and also brought together two focus groups to discuss their experiences. The group setting stimulates interactions, leading to insights that individual interviews do not provide. Individual and group surveys can be tailored to specific people and conditions.

With regard to large public or group surveys, the audience is designed to represent the entire population or a major segment of it. Some are created to answer a specific policy question: Does the public want the federal government to support nuclear power? Others include pertinent questions that were part of a larger multipurpose survey. The distinction is important. The tailored survey takes a lot of time and money, but it can be focused on specific needs. When I have the time and the money, I prefer to create my own survey. However, sometimes I do not. The user of a multipurpose survey is at the mercy of the questions that have been asked. I have never found a secondary data set that had all the questions I wanted. Yet the multipurpose survey can be satisfactory for answering questions, and it is often free and available.

Another important distinction is between probability and nonprobability samples. A probability sample is one in which every member of the population (people, schools, cities, organizations) has a known and non-zero probability of being included in the sample. There are a variety of probability sample forms: simple random, stratified random, systematic, and clustered.

In a simple random sample, every subject has an equal probability of being selected. Once selected, the subject cannot be selected a second time. A typical simple random sample uses a table of random numbers or more likely a computerized list of random numbers applied to a list of potential respondents. The advantage of a truly random sample is that it represents the entire population. The disadvantage is that the person taking the survey may not be equally interested in everyone in the entire population and may not have a list of all the potentially eligible respondents.

In environmental research, key groups are often grouped into strata by age, race/ethnicity, location, income, education, and other factors. For example, we surveyed 793 people regarding their willingness to live in housing on remediated brownfield sites. The vast majority of these sites are found in a few cities. We know that people move only a short distance, so we concentrated half of the sample in the brownfield-rich cities and the other half in the rest of the state. This study illustrates stratified random sampling; the sample is random within the two strata.

Systematic sampling is a process of selecting every nth person or unit. If I had a list of 10,000 houses that I wanted to check for lead or asbestos levels but had the resources to take only 500 samples, I would take every 20th house (10,000/500 = 20). I would choose a random number from 1 to 20, say 18. I would then start on the 18th house and go to 38, 58, 78, 98, and so on until the 500 houses were done. It is important that the internal order not mean something important with regard to the outcomes. For example, if the houses happened to be arranged in blocks of 20 houses and all the corner houses (1, 21, 41, 61, etc.) faced a highway whereas the 18th house on every street was farther away, then these results probably would underestimate historical exposure to lead from autos.

The fourth probability-based sampling protocol is the cluster method. Instead of sampling directly from the target population, a preliminary step is to first sample from a unit such as a census tract within a city or a school. The reason for using the cluster sample approach is that no list of all the people or units is available. For example, we have a project that is examining pediatric asthma in a moderate-sized city. We cannot get a list of all the children with asthma, so we picked a few schools and then sought the cooperation of the school administration and school nurse. Once they supplied the list of students, we randomly selected children from within the eligible schools to test our protocol. The limitation of this cluster sample approach is that the schools we chose are in the poorest neighborhood of the city. We suspect that the asthma problem is notably greater in these schools than in other districts. The results, I believe, are biased toward a high prevalence of asthma.

Nonprobability samples do not require each member of the population to have an equal chance of being selected. Typically, these studies take advantage of location or an event to gain some preliminary data for a follow-up probability-based survey. Yet environmental researchers often find that the results of nonprobability samples are supported by probability samples (Englander et al., 1986; Goszczynska, Tyszka, and Slovic, 1991; Kleinhesselink and Rosa, 1991; Teigen, Brun, and Slovic, 1988).

Nonprobability samples are often used for studying hard-to-identify populations. Typical examples would be drug users and illegal immigrants. They are likely to be found at health care centers and religious institutions, for example: hence the label "convenience" sample. Another way of finding hard-to-locate people is called "snowballing." People are asked to identify other people who would likely respond to the survey. Then when those people are contacted, they are interviewed and, in turn, are asked for leads. So what starts out with two possible interviews leads to 6 more, and then to 15 more, and so on.

I recently used a nonprobability method for studying the risk management priorities of Asian Indian Americans, the most rapidly growing and most affluent Asian population in the United States. However, they constitute less than 2 percent of the national population. Even in places where the Asian Indian American population is larger, a standard probability sampling approach is not economically feasible. If we assume that this group accounts for 5 percent of the total population (1 out of 20), a normal sampling protocol would make 20 phone calls to find even one eligible person. The chance of that person's agreeing to participate is probably about 50/50, so getting one response would require 40 contacts. Each contact normally means 2 to 10 calls or mailed surveys. Only handsomely funded projects could afford such a design.

Another option to avoid nonprobability approaches would have been to purchase a list of persons with common Asian Indian American surnames. That list would be used as the random sample base. My experience with these lists is mixed. On one occasion, they were quite useful, but on two others, the sample proved to be distressingly unrepresentative of the hard-to-find population. One of the two cases was an Asian American population, which led me not to use a purchased list in the Asian Indian American study. I have heard similar stories from colleagues.

Faced with the lack of an economically feasible approach or the time and resources to draw a random sample, researchers turn to nonprobability-based convenience or snowball sampling approaches. One option is to place an advertisement in a newspaper, on a Web site, or in a written flyer that the entire community would read. That has worked well for us, but only when the newspaper or flyer had a large outreach. In the case of the Asian Indian American population, we went to religious institutions and asked for and received their cooperation to approach potential respondents.

Nonprobability samples are likely to produce results that are not representative of the population as whole. For example, the Asian Indian American respondents were disproportionately men. We corrected for that bias by weighting the results (weighting is explained later in the chapter). While not as useful as probability samples, nonprobability samples can provide good preliminary results, but they must be accompanied by a clear declaration of their limitations and how these might affect policy.

A good survey will have the following four attributes:

1. Clear questions to answer
2. An appropriate survey vehicle
3. Thoughts and expectations about sample size, sample methods, and non-response rates
4. Processes for guaranteeing confidentiality and dealing with other possible ethical concerns

With regard to questions, everyone who has ever conducted a written or face-to-face survey wants consistent and unambiguous answers. Writing good questions takes time and testing. Every survey I have ever written has undergone multiple evaluations. I work with experts who have written hundreds of surveys. They are always fine-tuning my questions, explaining to me why the question I wrote will not work in its current form. I also ask nonexperts to review the questions to be sure they make sense. I typically write too many questions, and so I also ask them to tell me which questions are redundant. In short, the key to a successful set of questions is patience and pilot-testing. It is important to plan far in advance and to have plenty of time to write the questions and have them reviewed and tested until they work. Even though I have many years of experience in writing survey questions, I take three to six months to move a survey into the field.

The method of delivering the survey depends on its objectives. Face-to-face surveys are wonderful for obtaining nuanced reactions from people. I have used them many times, often as a follow-up to a mail or phone survey. The disadvantage is that someone who truly understands the purpose and design of the study needs to be willing to talk with respondents. This takes time, money, and more experienced interviewers than are normally available. Conducting a focus group requires a room, transportation costs, refreshments, materials to guide the group through the discussion, and sometimes honorariums.

Most surveys rely on the mail or the telephone. Mail surveys start with a list of potential respondents. A good idea is to first mail a postcard to potential respondents telling them that the survey will arrive by mail in a week to 10 days. Then, the survey is mailed with a stamped envelope included for return. Potential respondents are usually sampled two or three times. It is important to keep track of all the surveys that are returned because of wrong addresses, people who have moved, or any other reasons for nonresponse. The advantage to mail surveys is that they can be done relatively inexpensively, especially if they are sent via bulk mail. The disadvantage is that each step (postcard, first mailing, second wave, and third wave) takes time. Mail surveys, in short, take patience.

Most analysts prefer telephone interviewing. One reason is that a sample can be gathered much faster than with a mail survey. Second, random-digit dialing techniques allow an analyst to access people with unlisted and new phone numbers. Another advantage is that telephone surveys are almost always done from a central location where people who speak Spanish, Chinese, or Korean can be available if needed. I relied on that capacity in my recent study of the environmental perceptions of 1,513 U.S. residents (Greenberg, 2005). Yet another advantage of telephone methods is that a supervisor can listen in on the conversations to make sure that the appropriate format is being used.

There are disadvantages as well. One is cost. The survey I mentioned that returned 1,513 samples for a 15-minute survey and required the services of persons who spoke Spanish, Cantonese, and Korean, as well as English, cost $117,000. That included conducting a pilot test, administering the questions, coding those data, and returning the results to me in a spreadsheet. It included no time for questionnaire development or analyzing and reporting the results. I did those parts of the survey myself. A growing problem with telephone surveys is the exclusive use of cell phones by some people, especially young people, and the use of automatic answering devices that do not allow access to eligible respondents.

I have said nothing about Internet surveys because I have not written any. But some colleagues who have report considerable bias in the returns. However, I expect that the number of these surveys will increase because of the wide use of computers. My concern about the computer as a delivery vehicle is sample bias.

Sample size and response rate are always issues. The more samples there are, the greater the likelihood that the sample is representative of the larger population. However, more samples cost more money. For simple random sampling, the number of responses needed is easy to estimate (see the examples later in the chapter). However, if stratification, cluster, or systematic random sampling forms are used, the calculations become more complex. For example, I could collect a simple random sample of 800 residents and ask them whether they would be willing to live in a condominium built on a remediated brownfield site. Perhaps half indicate that they would. The sampling error for this survey is ±3.5 percent at a 95 percent confidence interval. This means that I can be 95 percent confident that the actual proportion that would be willing to live on such a site is between 46.5 and 53.5 percent (50 ± 3.5). If I had had more money, I could have reduced the size of the sampling error by adding more surveys; for example, 1,000 surveys would have reduced the sampling error from ±3.5 to ±3.0 percent.

The response rate is the number of people who respond compared with the number of eligible respondents. Everyone wants a 100 percent response rate. It is possible to approach 100 percent by asking people to respond to questions about their self-interest, such as working conditions and salary increases. Asking for personal information that people consider private (e.g., deviant behaviors) may garner few responses. Also, if potential respondents do not understand the questions, there may be no responses. For instance, about six years ago, we conducted a comparative analysis of hazards in physically distressed neighborhoods of New Jersey and Accra, Ghana. When we piloted the study in Accra, people could not make sense out of the optimism-pessimism scale that we and others use in the United States and elsewhere, so we dropped the questions.

Response rates vary by the mode of delivery, the topic of the survey, and the cover letter or introduction over the phone. My experiences range from a less than 20 percent response to over 80 percent. The 20 percent return used a mailing to the general public living in an extremely distressed area; it had no mail follow-up; it asked questions about neighborhood conditions, criminal activity, and blight; and it contained just a cover letter from me. By contrast, the 80 percent return was a mail survey to tax assessors that began with a postcard and was followed by three rounds of mailings. That survey was accompanied by a letter that was signed by the governor's chief of staff and the state treasurer and asked the tax assessors for their cooperation.

Another reason for variation in response is how people count respondents and eligible respondents. For instance, if I receive 1,000 responses out of 2,000 eligible respondents, my response rate is 50 percent. But if 20 percent of the respondents did not answer important questions, my effective response rate would be 40 percent. With regard to the denominator, eligible people include completed interviews, refusals, and partial completions. The denominator also includes people who could not be reached because of their answering machines and call-waiting systems and people who needed a translation that could not be provided. Some studies report only completions, partial completions, and refusals as their denominators. This makes their response rates appear higher than they actually are. It is important that an observer see the components of the numerator and the denominator. In short, the response rate is not consistently defined in research and can lead to misleading statements about generalizability.

The utility of the results should not be judged merely on the basis of the response rate, however. Obtaining an almost 20 percent response rate in the distressed neighborhood study was disappointing, but it was more than people told me I would get. There were many abandoned houses, and people did not answer their mail. To provide some context, I should add that I was bitten by a dog while I was standing in the street talking to a resident about the neighborhood.

My point is that I wanted to learn about environmental hazards and the quality of these kinds of neighborhoods. My only realistic option was to not be disappointed by a low response rate, to follow up by talking with representative citizens and local officials, and to assemble news stories and other written accounts, all of which I did. The multidata source analysis helped me put together a composite, albeit imperfect, picture of what it was like to live in this tough neighborhood. In complex hazardous environments, a researcher needs to rely on multiple sources of information because every method will have limitations.

A final point about nonresponse and the representativeness of a survey involves the utility of weighting. Statistical methods can be used to adjust the sample so that it matches the population as a whole. For example, in the Asian Indian American survey I mentioned earlier, about half the potential respondents versus only about a third of the actual respondents were women. To make sure that my results would not be biased toward the views of men, I weighted the sample so that each male respondent counted for only 0.75 of a response $(0.5/0.667 = 0.75)$ and women accounted for 1.5 responses $(0.5/0.333 = 1.5)$. In other words, the sample is adjusted to match the population. Normally, the population and the sample do not match on multiple demographic characteristics such as age, race/ethnicity, income, and education. I have adjusted for up to three variables and computed a total weight. Then I compared the results with and without the weights. It may turn out that the weights do not change the results enough to change the conclusions. While weighting is a good idea, it does not eliminate differences between the population and the sample because not every relevant variable is measured in the census. For example, the U.S. census does not ask people about religion, yet religious preference and practice can influence results.

Confidentiality and ethical behavior are common elements of every survey. Major organizations such as universities, hospitals, governments, and businesses are committed to the protection of the people who act as research subjects. Hence, they have established Institutional Review Boards (IRBs) to protect subjects. Coming out of the Nazi experimentations with people and other blatant human rights violations, IRBs were primarily created to protect people from abusive treatment (Oakes, 2002; Penslar, 1993).

With regard to survey research, the most important issue is to protect confidentiality. Surveys are almost always anonymous, which means that no information that would disclose the name of the respondent is collected. The person in charge must prepare a cover letter or make a statement that explains the purpose of the study and tells people that their survey is anonymous and that they are not to indicate anything that will enable them to be identified. Further, they are not required to answer questions that make them uncomfortable (typically questions on income or religious affiliation). Finally, the street address, phone number, and e-mail address of the person administering the survey are provided (some IRBs require providing a contact for the board).

If people are to be identified by name or could be identified because of their position, then they must sign consent forms that indicate their approval. Finally, IRBs normally require a report of any complaints that the person taking the survey encountered.

LEARNING MORE ABOUT THE TOOL. Excellent reading and training about survey research are available. The reference list contains books published by Sage (Bourque and Fielder, 1995; Fink 1995a, 1995b, 1995c, 1995d, 1995e, 1995f; Frey and Oishi, 1995; Litwin, 1995; Stokes, 2003) as well as a few others (Campbell and Stanley, 1963; Dillman, 1978; Kish, 1965; Sudman, 1976). I also included some strong empirical studies by the Pew Research Center for the People and the Press that have good discussions of sampling in the context of large survey studies (1998, 1999).

Diffusion of Innovations

Every day we encounter advertisements touting commercial products that are supposed to make us smarter, richer, more attractive, and, in various other ways, happier. Because diffusion of commercial products is so tied to business, readers may wonder why tools to measure diffusion of innovations are in this book. The answer is that government policies are innovations that diffuse and affect our lives.

CONTEXT. One measure of a successful policy is that it is adopted and then diffuses. Every chapter in the first part of this book illustrates one or more government policies that stimulated innovative responses by business and the public or a business or public behavior that required a government policy response. The EPA brownfields program was a government innovation that stimulated cities and businesses to redevelop. Knocking in the automobile engine stimulated the application of leaded gas and then MTBE, both of which have led to environmental policy debates that have lasted for decades.

Monitoring diffusion has become increasingly feasible because of Internet databases. After data are secured, the innovation should be studied for an S-shaped diffusion curve. Specifically, when an idea is initiated, few embrace it. After it is judged to be successful, then there is rapid acceptance and diffusion. Eventually, the market becomes saturated, and the curve flattens at the top of the S. Finally, some innovations are replaced as new ones materialize (e.g., black-and-white televisions by color televisions; asbestos by other flame-retardant materials).

CONTENTS, STRENGTHS, AND WEAKNESSES. Studying innovations over time requires statistical and graphical tools. Innovations also spread across the landscape, so they can be studied with maps. The tools should help tell us where the innovation started and where it spread and could perhaps lead to insights into why it spread in some places and not in others.

Three elements of an innovation influence its diffusion and maintenance: the attributes of the innovation itself, its environmental context, and the characteristics of the innovators (Wejnert, 2002). With regard to the first of these, every new idea has attributes that make it easier or more difficult to diffuse and sustain. We know that nearly all of us prefer to adopt magic-bullet technical solutions rather than change our behavior. A pill or drug that promises to reduce weight and cholesterol in three weeks has much more appeal than a gradual change in diet and more exercise. In other words, users have to accept the innovation for it to last.

With regard to environmental context, innovations are successful in some places and times and not in others. We need to know more about the spatial and temporal diffusion of major environmental health-influencing innovations because that information will tell us how innovators deal with the diversity of norms, values, laws, religions, ideologies, and political issues that influence the adoption of and long-term prognosis for a public health-related innovation.

The biggest challenge in this era is the increasing marketing ability of innovators. Whether they work for government, business, or not-for-profits, their ability to sell an innovation is growing far more rapidly than our ability to assess and monitor its impact. The commercial marketing of alcohol, breakfast cereals, drugs, exercise equipment, food fads, various new forms of gambling, and other ideas is a daunting challenge to everyone who reads this book.

Without these three elements, an innovation will fail. Alcohol prohibition was a policy innovation that did not survive. Ultimately, this government policy lost political and public support in the changing social environment of the United States (Blocker, 2006).

Tobacco products are fashionable, they satisfy a craving, and they are addictive. Powerful business interests promote and defend these products. The environment for tobacco products has become more restrictive in the United States as a result of government policy and health education. Yet the industry itself is remarkably innovative. In the mid-20th century, tobacco companies hired physicians to market their products (Gardner and Brandt, 2006). In this century, they have developed flavored cigarettes (Lewis and Wackowski, 2006). Further, potentially enormous Asian markets suggest that this product will diffuse throughout the world despite some government efforts to restrict it in the United States.

Over 500,000 deaths out of 2.4 million a year are attributed to tobacco and alcohol (Mokdad et al., 2004). Hence, attempts to regulate tobacco products and alcohol arguably have been the most aggressive steps taken to protect public health in the United States. But there have been many other actions or products that directly or indirectly are supposed to protect and improve health, including air bags, air conditioning, car seats for children, computerized body scans, chemotherapeutic agents, cholesterol-reducing drugs, energy-efficient appliances, fluoride, magnetic resonance imagery, and many others.

LEARNING MORE ABOUT THE TOOL. To summarize, tables, charts, and maps can follow the diffusion of an innovation through time and space. Focus groups, large surveys, interviews, content analysis, and other methods discussed elsewhere in this chapter are needed to dig deeper in order to explain the process. Most of the tools are demonstrated in a series of books that focus on the spread of policies and technologies (Brown, 1981; Folmer 2001; Goldman and Eliason, 2003; Peterson and Mahajan, 1985; Resetar, 1999; Rogers, 1995).

Economic Impact Tools

Environmental policy decisions have economic consequences. For some people and organizations these can represent incredible opportunities. But others are devastated by environmental policy decisions. This section describes key methods we use to ascertain who are the economic winners and losers.

Life Cycle Cost

A life cycle cost analysis (LCCA) requires estimating the cost of a decision over its entire life span. Sometimes, LCCA is called "cradle-to-grave." Chapters 1 through 6 offer examples of how LCCA could be useful, such as in building and operating systems to manage nuclear waste, converting a brownfield site into a new housing development, controlling pests with chemical pesticides, and comparing the cost of energy produced by uranium versus other fuels. LCCA starts with the planning, research, and development of a new product and/or process. The second phase, usually the most expensive, includes estimating the cost of obtaining land, building facilities and processes, and then operating and maintaining them. Eventually, the facilities and processes become outdated and will need to be rebuilt or closed down and probably remediated. Some facilities will require long-term stewardship.

CONTEXT. Chapter 4, the economic costs and benefits criterion, illustrates LCCA with the management of nuclear waste. I believe that high-level nuclear waste is the most challenging use of LCCA because of the long half-life of some nuclear elements. Estimating the cost of maintaining facilities that may be needed for tens of thousands of years is beyond our current capacity. The best we can reasonably manage is several multigenerational increments.

But LCCA did not start with such complex projects. During the 1960s, the U.S. government determined that it was purchasing inexpensive products that did not perform up to expectations. LCCA was devised to help balance short- and long-term costs. It has spread from government to business.

CONTENTS, STRENGTHS, AND WEAKNESSES. I will use the construction of a hypothetical water treatment plant to illustrate LCCA. To begin with definitions, life cycle cost is the present-value dollar cost of that water treatment plant from its initial conceptualization to its closing, possible reuse, and stewardship, if required. Costs are incurred in three phases:

1. Initial costs to purchase the land and plan, design, build, and open the facility
2. Operating costs, in the form of fuel, chlorine and other chemical additives, and off-site shipping of residuals; maintenance/repair; and replacement
3. Modification and/or closure and stewardship

Water treatment plants receive untreated water from surface and groundwater sources. Determining the quantity that will be treated and the quality of the incoming supply is essential for designers during the initial phase. Once that information is known, then designers can consider alternative technologies, sites, and water distribution systems. When the number of options has been trimmed, more detailed designs would include land acquisition costs, legal fees, and construction costs. As the designers work on subelements of the project, they will begin to weigh the costs of construction equipment, worker salaries, and various other elements. If there is already a facility on the site, demolition and cleanup costs would have to be included.

The second phase of LCCA should include operation, maintenance, and repair costs, such as energy and other utilities, workers, and other operational costs. Maintenance and repair costs would be estimated, typically based on experience with similar facilities. In other words, the designers would build in routine maintenance and repair, such as changing light bulbs, fixing small leaks, painting, and other normal activities. A proper design will also include the replacement of large pieces of equipment that can be expected to be needed in the future—a generator, for example.

Many water treatment plants have been built in the United States, and even though each is unique in some respects, cost estimates should be reasonably accurate. But when a truly unique facility is being built, there will be a great deal of cost uncertainty, which will need to be incorporated into the LCCA. Designing a facility to destroy chemical weapons is fraught with uncertainty. Each of the eight facilities built in the continental United States for destroying these weapons was unique. Consequently, there were issues relating to the type of technology, its reliability, worker performance, and construction of the facilities (Greenberg, 2003). Before any chemical warfare agents were destroyed, the facilities were pilot-tested with very difficult performance requirements. Numerous public hearings were required, and many were well attended. There have been legal challenges as well. From a cost perspective, the destruction of the U.S. chemical warfare stockpile has had a very high life cycle cost.

Facilities age and innovation produces new technologies. During the third phase, LCCA should plan for making major modifications to the facility, if possible, and/or closing it down, cleaning it up, and, if feasible, reusing it.

In addition to the three phases of LCCA, analysts must consider financial issues. LCCA should take into account depreciation, the value of money, and discount rates. Depreciation measures the decrease in economic value over time because of obsolescence, physical deterioration, and losses in the utility of a facility during its productive life. With regard to the value of money, everyone has experienced the impact of inflation on dollar values, which we monitor by studying purchasing power. The discount rate is the interest rate charged for loans. For federal government projects, the Office of Management and Budget (OMB) provides guidelines on the value of money and the cost of borrowing it. Depreciation is often ignored for government-operated facilities like a municipal water treatment plant. A major cost occurs when components fail. By contrast, depreciation is normally part of the ongoing budget for privately owned facilities, which should have funds set aside.

LCCA has clear strengths and weaknesses. Users point to two advantages: The first and most important is that all costs become transparent. Decision makers can actually see an estimate of what they would be spending, not only in the short term, but in later years. Second, cost trade-offs become apparent. For example, a cheaper overall cost may depend on unrealistic estimates of the cost of a resource (e.g., water or a fossil fuel) or assume technological advancements that might never happen.

The longer the lifespan of the activity and facilities, the more uncertain the assumption that we can estimate costs. For example, the value of future dollars beyond the short to medium term is highly speculative. In chapter 4, for example, I noted that DOE must maintain, possibly replace, and eventually decontaminate and decommission large facilities that will be needed for many decades. In addition, some facilities must be designed, built, and maintained to contain extremely hazardous materials for hundreds to thousands of years. DOE's method

of developing life cycle cost estimates limits the annual rate of inflation incorporated into future worker wages and benefits, electricity and other utilities,
supplies, and all future construction costs at the same rate (2.7 percent in 1998)
used to discount these future costs back to their present value. Thus, unless some
degree of cost risk or uncertainty is factored into the base, all future cost
estimates are essentially grounded in what engineers and others believe such an
activity will cost to initiate and complete today.

DOE, following guidelines first established by OMB in 1992, applies a discount
rate that approximates the federal government's cost of long-term borrowing
to all future cost estimates as a means of comparing alternative solutions or proposals in terms of current dollars. This approach implicitly assumes two things:

1. That future long-term costs can be estimated with the same level of accuracy
   and certainty as an alternative project or proposal that could be started and
   completed in a relatively short (1- to 2-year) period
2. That the evaluation process should be based solely on the financial impact to
   current stakeholders and that preventing an event that might cost thousands
   of lives and/or hundreds of millions of dollars in damages and repairs 50 or
   more years from now does not carry the same weight or value

In short, it is difficult to estimate these financial costs many decades into the
future.

As a final note, it is important not to confuse LCCA with life cycle analysis,
which follows the environmental and health effects of decisions over their
lifespan (ISO, 1997; Weidema, 1998). The two tools can be linked, but they are
different.

LEARNING MORE ABOUT THE TOOL. Much of the literature is written for engineers and economists. For example, major reports and books have been written
about LCCA for bridges, roads and pavements, air traffic control, and other key
pieces of infrastructure (Hawk, 2003; Wang, 2002). The focus on infrastructure is
continued in journals such as the *Journal of Infrastructure Systems* and *Systems
Engineering and Analysis.* Fabrycky and Blanchard's (1991) *Life-Cycle Cost and
Economic Analysis* is a good starting text. My favorite is Mason and Tapinos's
(2000) treatment of economic transfers between generations, which includes
LCCA and other topics.

Regional Economic Impact

I became interested in this subject as a teen when the newspapers said that parts
of Brooklyn and northern Manhattan would be economically devastated if the
Brooklyn Dogers moved to Los Angeles and the New York Giants moved to San
Francisco. I remember being curious about how those spatial economic impacts
could be estimated. A decade later, I understood the tools.

CONTEXT. Usually, the first question an elected official asks about a policy is, How much will it cost? The second question is, How much benefit is there and who gets it? Understanding the economic benefits and costs of policies implies that we can estimate the impact on cities, towns, villages, and counties; states and multistate regions; the United States as a whole; and other countries. It means knowing what the immediate impacts are as well as being able to estimate the impacts in the future, sometimes decades into the future. Finally, we know that policies produced economic winners and losers; and analysts, if possible, try to estimate the impact of policies on different economic groups.

CONTENTS, STRENGTHS, AND WEAKNESSES. A set of economic analysis tools can help answer the economic impact policy question. Some of these tools have been widely used; others are less common, but are potentially important contributors to long-term regional modeling.

Input-output (I-O) models are built around large data tables that describe how the sectors of an economy interact with one another. For example, if I wanted to build a school for $50 million dollars, I would separate the costs of construction into cement, bricks, steel, nails, equipment, workers, and so on. The I-O model I use has 517 sectors, and it shows the "production recipe" for the goods and/or services that the construction industry sells, as well as the shares of its revenues that are consumed by other industries. It has separate categories for the bricks, glass, gypsum board, and many other items required to build a school.

I use detailed engineering and design plans to enter the expenditures into the appropriate business sectors of the I-O model, which then estimates all of the transactions that will occur within the economy to spend that $50 million. For example, a school requires a chemistry lab. Building it entails ordering wood, nails, paints, special desktops and hoods, and many other raw materials. Workers hired to build the room will spend some of their wages on food and clothing; some goes for insurance policies, and some may be saved. An I-O model follows these transactions through the economy. They produce business revenues; jobs; earnings; gross state product; and federal, state, and local taxes. Overall, I-O models have the capacity to draw intricate portraits of economic impacts.

While they sometimes seem to be crystal balls, I-O models have limitations. They assume that technology and productivity are fixed, that the patterns of future transactions are identical to today's. We have to assume fixed wages and prices in a standard I-O model, at least until the federal government updates the database, which occurs every five years. Several dynamic models have been proposed, but these are not yet in place. The clear limitation is the inability to estimate the effects of price changes, in particular, price rises that may result from commodity shortages.

There is a second broad category of widely used time-series simulation tools that can estimate economic impacts. The one I use for New Jersey, for example, is a system of nearly 300 equations, each of which is based on historical data for the state and the nation. Historical data used in building such models are typically available for 25 to 30 years. National forecasts of employment, wages, and prices drive the model's state forecasts, and the business-sector data are less detailed than in the typical I-O model.

The strength of econometric time-series models is their sensitivity to historical trends in the economy. Assuming that equations have been or can easily be developed, another major advantage of this kind of economic model is that the economy's temporal reaction from the time of an investment through its full yield of economic benefits can be estimated. This is done by comparing the model's baseline forecast with another forecast that accounts for the investment. The difference between the results for any one equation in the two modeling scenarios provides a measure of the economic impact.

The strength of the econometric time-series model — its entrenchment in historical trends — is also one of its weaknesses. That is, the model is constrained by the nature of past economic relationships, which cannot always inform us about the complete manner in which certain events or activities will unfold. Thus, unless severe shortages are part of a region's history, econometric time-series models may not respond appropriately to such impacts of catastrophic events without a lot of modifications. A second limitation is that full historical data by industrial sectors for employment and gross product are not available in as much detail as they are for I-O models.

Analysts have been developing modifications of these econometric models that allow them to be responsive to gradual changes in the economy. Nevertheless, no matter how sophisticated the model, we cannot account for major or sudden economic shifts that drastically change the pattern of historical business transactions. Predictions will be only as good as the data used in the models. We must have reasonable estimates of resiliency; that is, when there is a shock, how fast does the economy recover? How does economic restructuring take place? Is there overcapacity, and if so, where? Lack of capacity? Where are the key bottlenecks?

A good way of understanding the strengths and weaknesses of these tools is to demonstrate them with an example. My group used a multiregional econometric model to conduct an economic simulation of technological options for managing the salt wastes in the high-level waste tanks at the Savannah River nuclear weapons site in South Carolina (Greenberg, Lewis, and Frisch, 2002). The technology options included managing the waste in cement; separating the key elements and then managing them; and managing them together.

The goal was to determine the economic impact of the proposed new facility. The main region of analysis surrounds the Savannah River site, which is relatively poor in terms of income and job growth. The model also produced results for nine other metropolitan regions with major DOE facilities, in addition to an aggregate for the rest of the United States. One of the technologies required $1.4 billion (in constant 1999 dollars) for design, construction, and testing before treating radioactive waste during the 2001–2009 period. The second and third options cost much less. Though less expensive to build and operate, the second option was estimated to generate almost as many jobs and gross regional product in the local area as the more expensive technology. The reason was that nearly all of the engineering and design from prototyping through testing for the most expensive technology was to be performed outside the region. By comparison, the second technology was to be tested and built almost exclusively in the Savannah River area. The third technology (cement) also generated most of its economic benefits in the local region, but there were far fewer of them due to the smaller amount of mechanical equipment and engineering, thereby resulting in a much lower cost.

Apart from technology choice, the economic benefits to the region would be heavily influenced by how the project is financed. If the country as a whole pays for the facility, then the South Carolina region benefits substantially because it pays only a small portion of the cost. The regional economic benefits are reduced if DOE pays for this project from its existing national budget or from its environmental management budget, or especially by having the Savannah River site pay for it by delaying or eliminating other DOE projects in South Carolina. In terms of the local economic impacts in the region, the method of funding and where the design and testing take place matter as much as the selection of the remediation technology.

This analysis enabled DOE's chief financial officer to see where the economic benefits and costs were likely to fall. The major disadvantage is that two of the three waste management technologies had never been used at the scale proposed for these projects, and we had to assume that the engineering designs and associated costs were realistic. It was explained to the official that the estimates were based on multiple assumptions, some of which were questionable. Notably, one of these designs failed safety tests and was rejected. In other words, the results of elegant mathematical economic models must not be taken at face value.

LEARNING MORE ABOUT THE TOOLS. There is an enormous literature about these models, including some classic papers that are not highly mathematical (Leontief 1970, 1974) and that ultimately led to a Nobel prize in economics for Professor Leontief. The more mathematically inclined and those who are interested in more recent model developments can choose from many excellent papers and books (Conway, 2001; Guimaraes, Hefner, and Woodward, 1993; Lindall and Olson, 2003; Miller and Blair, 1985; Rose and Liao, 2005; Santos and Haimes, 2004; Treyz, 1993). With regard to environmental policy, the most interesting applications are aimed at the economic impact of natural disasters and those caused by people (Guimaraes, Hefner, and Woodward, 1993; Okuyama and Chang, 2004; Rose and Liao, 2005; Santos and Haimes, 2004). Finally, the *Journal of Regional Science* historically has published many of the new developments in the field of regional economic impacts.

Natural Resource Damage Assessment (NRDA)

Every time there is an oil or chemical spill or someone dumps hazardous material on the ground the environment is damaged. The Exxon Valdez oil spill is probably the most infamous example of this generation.

CONTEXT. We have all seen advertisements by personal injury lawyers inviting employees who have been injured on the job to call for a free consultation that could lead to a legal case against their employer. Forests, lakes, rivers, and other parts of the ecosystem cannot call an attorney, but the Comprehensive Environmental Response Compensation and Liability Act (CERCLA, 42 U.S.C., 9607) and the Oil Pollution Act of 1990 (OPA, 33 U.S.C., 2701) have made it possible for trustees to file lawsuits against business and government for damages that have occurred since 1980 to land, fish, wildlife, biota, groundwater, drinking water supplies, and other natural resources belonging to federal, state, or local governments; American Indian nations; and sometimes privately held property.

For purposes of assessing liability and the amount of damages, the injury can be directly caused by the event or indirectly precipitated by it. Damage can result from a single event or from chronic pollution. As was the case for the Exxon Valdez spill in Alaska, for example, the owners of an oil tanker can be held liable for a spill that kills birds, seals, and fish; for damages to beaches used for recreation; and for loss of business by a company that takes people on deep-sea fishing expeditions. The costs can be for cleanup, restoration, business losses, and government costs.

Responsible parties include current owners and operators as well as previous owners and operators at the time the damage occurred. For example, DOE is legally responsible for contaminating a water supply because of chronic small leaks into ground and surface waters. DOE may not have owned or operated the facilities that caused the leaks, but if the owners and operators were working for the department, then it can be held responsible.

In the case of CERCLA and OPA, the president is authorized to designate a government body (federal department, state, American Indian nation, etc.) to act as a trustee for the natural resources, and trustees are authorized to press for and collect economic damages. Many states have their own versions of the federal natural resource damage laws, and they can pursue damage recovery under federal laws or their own.

One of the fascinating legal realities of NRDA is that DOE and DOD are both trustees and defendants. While this seems like a potential conflict of interest, in reality it has caused these organizations to think about damages before they begin using or remediating a site. These two agencies cannot be sued by another federal agency, but can be and have been sued by state governments and American Indian nations (Fernald Citizens Advisory Board, 2004; State of Washington, Office of the Attorney General, 2004). Courts have upheld the concept of natural resource damages, including direct and indirect damages (with a few exceptions), and have held both the responsible parties and their insurance companies liable for damages.

Federal NRDAs occur only when a preassessment screening has shown that a discharge that can damage resources has occurred, that the resources have been damaged, that already available data that will reasonably assess the damages can be gathered, and that a response will not remedy the damage.

The amount of natural resource damage costs is not known, partly because the value of the settlement is frequently treated as confidential. The U.S. General Accounting Office (1996) estimated that DOE's potential natural resource damage costs could be from $2.3 billion to over $20 billion. We do know that settlement costs have increased substantially during the past decade. For example, the largest CERCLA-related settlement was approximately $130 million for damages related to mining/smelting in Montana (Smith, 2003). A decade ago, the Exxon Valdez oil spill cost the company $2 billion for cleanup and over $1 billion in damages (Renner, 1998).

A final point of legal context is that some legislation requires that damages be limited to restoration, rehabilitation, or acquisition of a replacement resource. However, some state offices have allowed more flexibility in how the money is used. For example, New Jersey's Office of Natural Resource Restoration has allowed some recovered funds to be applied to the study of methods of restoring habitats and species, controlling erosion, and other important scientific information. This is important because states conduct most of the NRDAs, although the most costly settlements involve federal agencies.

CONTEXT, STRENGTHS, AND WEAKNESSES. The value of a resource such as water is typically divided into human use and ecological services. For example, water is used in homes for bathing, cooking, drinking, and watering the lawn, as well as for sanitation; farmers use it to irrigate crops; and industries use it as an ingredient and require it for waste disposal. These uses are called consumptive, that is, the water is not available for the same purpose in the region after use. By contrast, nonconsumptive uses retain the quality and quantity of the water; for example, groundwater that is used to prevent the ground from settling is not pumped out. Ecological services include nourishing vegetation and wildlife and maintaining the flow and quality of water.

User values do not completely account for the value of water or any other natural resource. People greatly appreciate the less tangible qualities of the natural world, a truth that is translated into natural resource valuation techniques through a measure known as "existence value." This is made up of two underlying components: vicarious consumption and stewardship value. The first refers to the utility associated with knowing that others derive benefits from an environmental good, although the individual in question may not. Stewardship value describes the sense of obligation we feel to preserve the natural environment for future generations. Existence value is often much more difficult to quantify and therefore to accurately evaluate than user value.

Many methods have been used to value natural resources. I will touch briefly on the key tools. Market price methodology can be used if water is traded as a commodity. The value of water is the value of purchasing a replacement supply. Any increase in the market price for water as a result of contamination, or an associated lost service, can be used to calculate compensable damages.

Appraisers value a resource with and without diminution in quality and quantity. This technique is very similar to the previous one in that it does not capture the breadth of damages that would result from contamination of the aquifer.

Factor income methodology compares the pre- and postcontamination net profits associated with the goods or services under consideration, and value is assigned to the groundwater as a function of this difference. Any estimate using this technique would doubtless undervalue this resource, since it lacks the capacity to account for the many other uses made of this water and for its nonuse value.

The association between the quality of a natural resource and its recreational use value forms the basis for the travel cost methodology. As perceived environmental quality decreases in a location that is well suited to recreational and leisure activities, people are likely to visit it less often. There are discernible costs associated with traveling to and enjoying such recreation: Time, gasoline, and equipment are just a few. The denigration of a resource can thus be monetized through the use of an equation that relates the reduction in use to the costs of these inputs. Contamination of bodies of water that are used for recreation is frequently assessed in this way. One could potentially use this technique to measure the difference in order to assign a value to the water. Like many others, travel cost methodology also fails to capture all the uses and hence all the value.

Value can be estimated by examining the statistical relationship between the resource and other attributes of an area that is perceived as having higher environmental quality. This hedonic price method compares the selling prices of the homes and businesses there versus those of properties with equivalent amenities in the region of interest.

This method has a number of drawbacks. It operates on the assumption that a comparable region can be identified, and this is not always possible. Since the water has not been affected in a way that might be perceptible to the average homeowner, this criterion may not be satisfied. Finally, as with the other methodologies, hedonic pricing would be unlikely to capture the wide array of benefits that the aquifer provides to users.

The contingent valuation methodology (CVM) refers to a collection of techniques designed to establish a hypothetical market for a particular natural resource or resource service, and it can be used to determine the use values for nonmarket goods. It is also the only method capable of monetizing nonconsumptive uses and existence values, and it can be effective in solving the problem of nonrevelation of preferences for public goods. The ability of the method to capture use and nonuse values is due to the fact that respondents, in general, do not make a clear mental distinction between the two, and thus both are accounted for in their responses. The process is centered around the development of a survey to elicit responses related to willingness to pay for environmental quality. Through analysis of the data produced, it is possible to value the resource in question, usually through calculation of arithmetic-mean willingness to pay. In other words, the average number of dollars people are willing to pay is used to estimate the value. Much research has been dedicated to perfecting the CVM method so as to produce the most accurate and defensible results. Nevertheless, it depends on what people say they are willing to pay, which is not necessarily what they will pay.

I briefly summarized the limitations of each of the methods as I reviewed them. None is a perfect fit for every situation. The analyst must determine the method or combination of methods that can most effectively measure the damage. Ideally, the trustees and the agency have sufficient resources to use a hybrid of these approaches. However, in reality, they often do not have the resources to effectively use even one of these methods. Unless pollution has a striking impact, damage assessment is likely to consist of the cleanup and replacement costs.

Stepping back from the specific strengths and weaknesses of the individual tools, the NRDA process itself has some general strengths and weaknesses. Its major strength is that some compensation can be obtained for damage to valuable environmental resources. An indirect strength is that the threat of damage to natural resources has led government and private enterprise to think about how they can avoid it.

Overall, NRDA tools have four general limitations. The most obvious is that it is presumptuous to assume that humans can value complex environmental ecosystems, especially since our knowledge of how they function is so limited. At best, we are extracting obvious human economic values. Second, research shows that the data available to conduct NRDAs varies markedly by site. In some places and for some resources, we have credible data; in other locations and for other resources, our information is meager at best (Burger et al., 2004). Third, as noted earlier, the value of the settlements in many of the cases is not available for analysis. Fourth, the tools work best when there is measurable damage and we can determine the costs of damage, replacement, and restoration. Existence costs and future costs are much more difficult to estimate.

LEARNING MORE ABOUT THE TOOL. Some well-written books help explain the difficulties of valuing natural resources (Coker and Richards, 1992; Freeman, 2003; Kopp and Smith, 1993; National Research Council, 1997; Reisch, 2001). Because all of the federal agencies are involved, they have Web sites that explain their NRDA processes; for example, EPA, DOE, the National Oceanic and Atmospheric Administration, and the Department of Interior have such sites. Typing "natural resource damage assessments" into a search engine will lead to them. In addition, some excellent journals, such as *Land Economics,* the *Federal Facilities Environmental Journal, Environmental Management,* and *Environmental and Resource Economics,* have published reviews and case studies about NRDAs.

8

Decision-Making and Communication Tools

Introduction

Every environmental policy maker has his or her own decision-making style. Some want only a small amount of information from the six policy criteria; others require every bit of data and then come back for more. Some make irreversible decisions; others make tentative choices. Some announce policies personally; others try to avoid any publicity. This chapter summarizes the decision-making and communication tools available to policy makers.

Decision-Making Tools

People who believe that relying on nuclear power is an evil bargain with the technology devil, that dredging the local river is an immoral attack on aquatic ecosystems, and that creating genetically modified organisms is wrong make their decisions based on values. If, however, decisions are driven by information or at least can be influenced by scientific/technological information, then people will likely want to see checklists, weighted variables, and the results of optimization, cost-benefit or cost-effectiveness analyses, and simulations. This section reviews these tools.

Checklists

Checklists are compilations of decision-making factors, typically written as simple declarative statements or questions. I have prepared checklists ranging from 20 items to over 200. In the late 1970s, I prepared a checklist for use in mediating disputes about proposed industrial facilities. The goal was to focus the disputants on a range of issues that are normally associated with such facilities (Greenberg, 1979). This checklist had 22 preliminary questions and 40 follow-up ones. If the answer to the preliminary question was yes, then the second question needed to be answered.

The questions were divided into simple categories: air quality, solid waste management, water resources, and land quality. For example, one preliminary question focused on noise: Will construction of the facility, its operation, and/or attendant transportation activities produce a noise level above the ambient? If the answer was yes, then the two following questions would be answered: Will the sound level exceed 55 decibels outdoors or 45 decibels inside a residential development, school, hospital, library, or recreation area? Will this level exceed 70 decibels during the night and/or 80 decibels during the day? If the answer to either question was yes, then the proponent of the project could expect serious public protest and should figure out how to reduce the noise level.

In 2005, some colleagues and I prepared a checklist of 203 questions for the U.S. Department of Energy (DOE), which is charged with the long-term protection of major nuclear weapons sites (Greenberg et al., 2005). The 203 questions were divided into six major categories: (1) the toxicity and amount of the hazardous substance present; (2) containment of the substance; (3) potential dispersal, if containment is breached; (4) human and ecological populations exposed; (5) dose to and response of the public and ecosystems; and (6) authorities' response to the immediate event and the long-term threat.

Here are the first seven questions from the "Toxicity and Amount of Hazardous Substance Present" part of the checklist:

1.1. What information is available about known hazards, about multiple chemical hazards, and about potential exposure pathways (direct contact, soil, surface and groundwater, air) to on-site hazards? When were the data last updated? How is the information processed, stored, and made available? Is it in electronic forms? Is it on maps and/or in CSMs [conceptual site models, which are diagrams that show sources of contamination, paths over which contamination can spread, and barriers to the spread of contamination]? How often [are] the information and equipment updated?

1.2. Who is responsible for the data? Whom do they report to? What is their academic background? How much training to do they have and how often do they go for additional training?

1.3. What are the contaminants of greatest concern on the site? What kinds of human and/or ecological biomarkers are available for assessing and monitoring human and ecological exposure and risk associated with these contaminants? How does the site keep track of legal and administrative changes that affect the legal classification of these contaminants?

1.4. How does the site keep track of the amount of hazardous material that is added and lost because of chemical, physical and biological changes and destruction? How often is this done?

1.5. How does the site assess how changes in the amount and type of hazardous material affect the sustainability of the end state? How is new scientific information relative to the toxicity of site contaminants re-evaluated in light of existing exposure pathways and end state land uses? Is this done even if the legal rules for what is defined as a hazard do not change?

1.6.   What formal and informal processes are used to bring important information about toxicity and amount of hazardous materials to the attention of the site leadership and resolve issues? How much discretionary authority and budgetary resources does the site leadership have to resolve problems that are identified?

1.7.   What interactions occur between regulatory bodies responsible for environmental heath regulations and on-site management about these hazards? At what level in the organizations do these interactions occur?

If the first two of these questions cannot be satisfactorily answered, the implication is that DOE will have to do a lot of homework to develop a plan to protect the site in perpetuity. If the site has the answers, but the information is not frequently updated and/or site personnel are not trained or familiar with the latest information, then training will be essential. If the site cannot capture and transmit the information to key personnel, then another level of effort is required. The next set of questions examines a site's capacity to inspect and monitor changes and provide secondary prevention. The third set focuses on the site's ability to address issues identified during monitoring and surveillance. If problems are identified and cannot be quickly sent to managers and addressed, then the plan, no matter how well written, will not be sustainable.

This long checklist of over 200 questions was intended to challenge DOE site management and contractors. The larger context for this specific list of questions, and the general idea of checklists, is the reality that environmental management is a moving target. Etzioni (1968) proposed a process called "mixed scanning" to keep track of moving targets in a changing environment. He used military actions as an illustration, asserting that the military must first scan the entire field and then come back and focus on the most likely danger points. Troops re-scan the environment throughout the battle, reallocating resources as appropriate. In other words, Etzioni (1968) suggests checking the entire set of critical variables and focusing on those that appear to be potentially compromised. His point is that decision makers need to be flexible. Our 203 questions to DOE are intended to directly address the idea of mixed scanning by decision makers dealing with the monitoring and surveillance of hazardous materials in perpetuity.

Overall, checklists are a valuable tool because they should ensure that decision makers do not miss potentially important factors. They are the equivalent of the to-do lists we write to make sure we do not forget something. One limitation is that checklists imply nothing about the importance of any single item, and we know that some factors are more important than others.

Typically, checklists are welcomed by public/community groups that want to understand more about the impact of alternative policies. By contrast, agency staffs tend to be more narrowly focused around their organizations' mandate.

I have observed serious public disputes when agencies refused to deal with checklist items that were not part of their mandate. Both sides left meetings frustrated with each other.

Cost-Benefit and Effectiveness Tools

In contrast to conceptually simple checklists, cost-benefit analysis and its progeny try to aid decision makers by converting information into economic costs and benefits. In cost-benefit analysis, dollars become the bottom-line metric; the final evaluation of alternatives is the dollar cost versus the benefit of investing.

In a nation where money is the bottom line for so many decisions, it makes sense to balance the cost of an action against its benefits. Cost-benefit analysis formally began, as so many policy-related tools have, with a legal action by the federal government. In 1936, Congress promulgated the Flood Control Act (PL 74–738), which included the following wording: "The federal government should improve or participate in the improvement of navigable waters or their tributaries, including watersheds, . . . for flood-control purposes if the benefits to whomsoever they may accrue are in excess of the estimated cost."

The Flood Control Act stated the need to try to control the terrible effects of flooding along rivers, especially the Mississippi, and to facilitate transportation by water. The U.S. Army Corps of Engineers and later economists developed and refined cost-benefit analysis as a tool to aid decision makers.

Such analyses add the value of the benefits of actions and subtract the associated costs. The simplest form of cost-benefit analysis includes only direct financial benefits and financial costs, not environmental health and other important impacts. Using nuclear power or oil/gas to produce electricity (chapter 6) helps illustrate what the tool can and cannot do. Benefits include the value of the electricity created to the industry and its customers, and cost includes construction, operation, maintenance, and closure/monitoring after closure. The regional and national benefits can be estimated using some of the regional economic impact models described in chapter 7. Costs, however, are much more difficult to estimate. The cost of fuel, as we know from recent history, is highly uncertain. With regard to oil or natural gas, how much will those who control the supply increase the cost, and will they cut the supply? The economic and political threat to an energy-dependent country like United States is enormous and affects all of us. Nuclear power has equally complicated uncertainties, such as proliferation of nuclear weapons-grade materials, fear of accidents, and reliance on unproven generation and waste management technologies. Cost-benefit analyses include all of these factors as numbers, but some of them are so uncertain that the final cost and benefit estimates are problematic. To be fair, though, not every application of cost-benefit analysis is as complicated as nuclear power versus fossil fuel power and climate change.

Even when the policy choices seem less complicated than this one, the results can be extraordinarily controversial. For example, the U.S. Army Corps of

Engineers has built and operated dams across the country to reduce flooding and increase transportation, as required by the Flood Control Act. These efforts have been attacked as deliberately inflating the benefits and not including damage to the environment. The title of one of the strongest critiques—*The River Killers* (Heuvelmans, 1974)—captures the essence of the protest against trying to monetize complicated flood management projects: Critics assert that trying to measure everything in terms of dollars is destroying rivers.

The harshest attacks against cost-benefit analysis have come when estimating the value of human life is involved. Some people are angered by efforts to base decisions on dollars. Moore (1998) argues that one of the most positive environmental steps taken by the federal government was establishing air quality standards. Under the Clean Air Act of 1970 (PL 91–604), dollars were not to be taken into account in setting ambient air quality standards. Moore (1998) asserts that society has a responsibility to protect those who are particularly vulnerable to air pollution, such as elderly or infirm people and infants (a further discussion of ambient air quality standards appears later in the chapter).

Non-economics-based health and safety standards have been under attack by key business interests for over three decades. Efforts have repeatedly been made to change the Clean Air Act and other laws. Proponents of change assert that there are air quality levels below which there are no measurable effects and that the cost of meeting the standards is exorbitantly high and jeopardizes the economy (see chapters 3, 5, 6, and 7 for other examples). Opponents argue that health and environmental effects occur even if they cannot always be measured by excess death and morbidity, that the benefits of protecting the most vulnerable among us are worth the cost, and that using costs and benefits is against the core values of the United States and against common law. Moore (1998) summarizes cost-benefit analysis as an immoral effort by business to deflect business costs onto the public. Economists, especially those at Resources for the Future, have countered by asserting that costs and benefits must be part of the decision-making process because society cannot afford every environmental health and safety policy (Portney and Stavins 2000).

The cost of money in the future is another debatable issue in cost-benefit analysis. Government projects are required to use a fixed estimate of the future cost of money—that is, what government pays for the privilege of borrowing. While federal agencies use these numbers, there is no certainty that the estimated rate will reflect reality. In fact, a small change in the cost of borrowing can change a decision in cost-benefit analysis when the activity is expected to last 20 to 50 years (see chapter 4 for a discussion of DOE and chapter 7 for a brief explanation of discounting). For example, if I invest $1,000 in an account that pays a guaranteed percent compounded annually, invest no more money, and make no withdrawals, at the end of 30 years I will have accumulated $2,427. If I get only 2 percent interest, that $1,000 will be worth $1,811. If the interest rate is 4 percent, then my investment will be worth $3,243 at the end of 30 years.

In short, the value of money is extremely important and is another issue in cost-benefit analysis.

When I become involved with this sort of analysis, I ask the following five questions:

1. Options: What strategies and technologies are being compared, and how carefully is each one spelled out and justified?
2. Winners and losers: Who and what places benefit and lose?
3. Time: When will the benefits and costs occur?
4. Analytical assumptions: Are all the metrics explained and justified?
5. Sensitivity: Are the results tested by systematically changing the assumptions and tracing the implications of those changes?

Overall, cost-benefit analysis is by far the most controversial tool described in this book (although risk assessment is a close second; see chapter 7). By converting all of the benefits and costs of a proposed action into current dollars, cost-benefit analysis can be a powerful decision-assistance tool. Proponents laud its requirement that all considerations be included and measured as part of a single metric. Opponents argue that it inaccurately and immorally monetizes intangibles and distorts the values of benefits and costs to protect money instead of people. I am troubled by cost-benefit applications when there are high levels of scientific and other forms of uncertainty, particularly when the proposed project can affect large areas and the impacts persist for many decades.

Risk-benefit analysis is a related approach, but different at least philosophically because the costs of hazard reduction, and sometimes the benefits are acknowledged to be highly uncertain. Consequently, the results are expressed in terms of a probability distribution of possible benefits and costs. Cost-effectiveness analysis is another related tool but different from cost-benefit analysis in that the costs can be assessed in economic terms, but the benefits cannot. Hence, options can be compared only with one another (e.g., three different technological approaches for reducing air pollution).

All three of these economic-centered tools are criticized because they share two characteristics: (1) They choose actions in order of decreasing cost relative to a specified level of benefit, and (2) they systematically vary decision variables to assess the sensitivity of the outcome to key assumptions and data inputs. But dollars are still the driving force.

Optimization and Simulation Tools

Because checklists place equal value on every attribute of an environmental policy issue and cost-benefit analysis and its progeny focus on dollars, analysts have sought tools that will allow decision makers to consider multiple policy variables.

SIMPLE OPTIMIZATION AND SIMULATION MODELS. When environmental decisions can be narrowed down to critical questions that science can answer, then decision makers appreciate evaluations of plausible options that explicitly consider different impacts. For example, directors of state environmental protection agencies face multiple challenges, such as providing enough water during a drought; protecting water quality in rivers and underground aquifers; ruling on the location of proposed landfills, incinerators, waste transfer stations, and other facilities; protecting open space and cultural artifacts; and many others. These decisions have been addressed by using decision-making models.

One of the oldest forms is the linear or mixed linear/integer optimization model, which finds the best solution out of a multitude of possible options. Here is an example of optimization tools. In the preface, I described an actual case in which the commissioner of environmental protection was charged with finding a way to move water from places with a surplus to places with a deficit during a drought. This task implies satisfying three constraints. One requires that every town have enough potable water. If there are 100 towns, then there will be 100 equations, each of which requires that a sufficient amount of water go from the sources to the towns. But the amount of water taken from each supply is constrained by how much is available. Hence, equations are written to limit the amount of water that can be taken from each source. If there are 50 sources, there will be 50 equations, each indicating that the sources cannot be overdrawn. Another set of equations tracks the capacity of the pipes and pumps to move water from sources to locations where it is needed. With 50 sources of water and 100 places where it is needed, there are likely to be hundreds of transfer capacity constraints.

Once these equations have all been written down, if there is enough water, then it can be transferred through the network. However, there may be many paths through which it can go. To optimize over the network as a whole, an equation is written to direct the water through the system at the least cost to taxpayers.

Decision makers like this kind of model because it finds the least expensive solution, it finds other inexpensive options, and it identifies gaps in the network that the government can fix by adding pumps and pipes. This type of problem is usually not controversial because the model is pointed at a specific problem that everyone wants solved: People want communities to have enough water. However, as noted in the preface, when the model was applied to an actual crisis, there was opposition from some local governments that did not want to transfer their surplus water. The decision maker—in this case, the governor—ordered them to do so (see Greenberg, 1978, for this and similar examples).

There are dozens of examples of applying these tools to finding locations for badly needed facilities, regulating the flow of water over a dam, mixing fuels and other resources, and many others, as well as some excellent overviews of the subject (Greenberg, 1979; Nazareth, 2004; Ross, 1970).

MULTI-ATTRIBUTE DECISION-MAKING TOOLS. Multi-attribute methods try to simultaneously consider several objectives, such as quality of life and equity, in addition to costs and benefits. These models translate multiple objectives into specific outcomes. For example, if I wanted to choose among four locations for a new oil refining complex, a checklist would help me keep track of all of the issues to consider, and a cost-benefit analysis would help me understand the overall economic outcomes. A multi-attribute approach would start with stated objectives and metrics to measure them, such as the following:

1. Objective: Minimize the cost of construction, operation, maintenance, closure, and stewardship. Metric: Determine the total life-cycle cost of the facility.
2. Objective: Maximize worker safety. Metrics: Develop a worker health and safety surveillance program; introduce training; build passive physical engineering systems to protect workers; introduce operating rules.
3. Objective: Minimize the damage to the surrounding environment. Metrics: Build systems to control leaks from oil tanks and pipelines; change the rules for ships dumping waste into bodies of water.
4. Objective: Minimize the impact on surrounding tourist and fishing industries. Metrics: Institute rules that keep ships and waste discharges away from key areas; develop an emergency response plan.
5. Objective: Maximize the positive economic benefits in the surrounding area. Metrics: Hire local workers to build the facilities and work at the site; contribute to local government by building and maintaining roads and other essential infrastructure.
6. Objective: Minimize the disruption of the local community and social organizations. Metric: Contribute funds and other resources to help local community groups.

This list of objectives and partial list of metrics would be the input for the multi-attribute analysis illustrated in table 13. The metrics of each set are different. Some are measured by dollars, others by public involvement, others by public perception, and still others by environmental testing. However, for the tool to work, each must be measured on the same scale. In the example in table 13, each attribute is weighted between 0 (not at all a characteristic of the option/site) to 1 (entirely characteristic of the option/site). In the case of cost, for example, the first option/site has a cost attribute of 0.6, whereas the second has a cost attribute of 0.0—that is, the former is the best choice. However, option/site 2 is a better choice with regard to safety. Each of the four options/sites has relative strengths and weaknesses with regard to the six attributes.

The weight column introduces importance to the six attributes. I decided on a scale of 1 (least important) to 10 (most important) and then assigned 9 points to safety, 8 points to environment, and 8 points to cost. The other three attributes were assigned 3 or 4 points each. Multiplying the weight by the attributes of each option/site and then totaling those scores yields overall scores that range between 21.4 for option/site 3 to 13.2 for option/site 4. In other words, given the

TABLE 13

Simple multi-attribute example

Attribute	Weight (1–10)	Option/ Site 1 (0–1)	Option/ Site 2 (0–1)	Option/ Site 3 (0–1)	Option/ Site 4 (0–1)
Cost	8	0.6	0.0	0.3	0.4
Safety	9	0.4	1.0	1.0	0.3
Environment	8	0.3	0.8	0.8	0.5
Fishing/tourism	3	1.0	0.6	0.0	0.1
Economic benefit	4	0.3	0.4	0.9	0.6
Community disruption	3	0.2	0.4	0.0	0.2
Overall score		15.6	20.0	21.4	13.2
Rank		3	2	1	4

attributes and weights I assigned, option/site 3 is the best choice and option/site 2 is the next best. These scores and hence the ranking would change if the weights were changed.

This simple example also excludes so-called red flags, which are attributes that are simply unacceptable and make an option infeasible. For example, if a score of zero were considered unacceptable, then options/sites 2 and 3 would both be rejected. Option/site 2 has a score of 0.0 with respect to cost, and option/site 3 has a score of 0.0 with respect to fishing/tourism and community disruption.

The strength of this approach lies in its ability to assess multiple attributes and to do so in a transparent way. The limitations are quite obvious and include comparing attributes measured in dollars with attributes measured in perception and then assigning weights, which can easily be manipulated. The biggest limitation of multi-attribute models, however, is that, unlike my simple example, there could be as many attributes as there are items in a large checklist. This means that the transparency of having the information available for scrutiny is at least partly lost because there are too many details to track. Indeed, researchers have developed a variety of mathematical techniques for guiding us through all the data and presenting the results in a way that can be understood (Klir and Folger, 1988; Maclaren and Whitney, 1985; McAllister, 1980; Saaty, 1980; Zeleny, 1982; Zimmermann, 1987). However, these methods are themselves complicated, so relatively few people actually understand how to use them and tease out the subjective values and scientific judgments embedded in them.

Climate change, surely one of the most complex issues we face, has attracted a good deal of attention from those who favor multi-attribute models (Hobbs and Meier, 2000; Parson, 1997). Is climate change due to greenhouse gases, or is it a short-term phenomenon? Some of the variables to include are increasing temperature, rising sea level, damage to ecological systems, costs of preventing and adapting the economy, and related social impacts of climate change. This problem has spatial and temporal dimensions—the impact will vary by place and through time. Although checklists and cost-benefit tools can be applied, other approaches are perhaps more intellectually satisfying and more informative.

Having noted the complexity of the mathematical modeling of decisions, I would like to point out that environmental protection policy has also benefited from having decision makers and staff consult regarding their decisions and processes. The most notable illustration is *Unfinished Business* (U.S. Environmental Protection Agency [EPA], 1987), in which key members of the agency compared what funds were spent on with what they considered, on the basis of their scientific knowledge and experience, to be the greatest environmental risks. They concluded that there was a disconnect. That is, a good deal of money was being spent on projects (most notably hazardous waste management as part of the Superfund program) that they believed were less dangerous to the public than other programs that they felt created more risk (e.g., pesticides, indoor air quality). EPA's Science Advisory Board (1990, 1999) conducted similar studies, leading to a better understanding of the value of integrated decision making by experts from a wide range of disciplines and backgrounds.

Learning More about the Tools

During the past three decades, some excellent books have described these methods and their history (Dubois and Prade, 1988; Haddix, Teutsch, and Corso, 2003; Hammond and Coppock, 1990; Hobbs and Meier, 2000; Keeney and Raiffa, 1976; Klir and Folger, 1988; Kopp and Smith, 1993; Nas, 1996; National Research Council, 1997; Nazareth, 2004; Peskin and Seskin, 1975; Ross, 1970; Saaty, 1980; Zeleny, 1982; Zimmermann, 1987). Journals, including *Socioeconomic Planning Sciences*, *Environmental Management*, *Environmental Planning and Management*, *Environmental Modeling & Assessment*, and *Risk Analysis*, are the best place to find recent advances.

Communicating Policies

Policy decisions are made to change practice and often to send a message to a government agency, business, nongovernmental organization, or the public. The tools of the trade include laws and regulations, executive orders, court decisions, leadership changes, and budget messages. Laws and regulations are the most direct and obvious; budget messages are the most indirect and stealthy. This section summarizes these tools and presents suggestions for communicating with journalists and the public.

Laws and Regulations

At the federal level, members of Congress propose a policy as a bill. If a bill is approved, it becomes law. Both the House of Representatives and the Senate must agree on the language. Once they have, the proposed law goes to the president, who can approve it or veto it. Presidential vetoes can be overturned, but not often. Approved laws are called "acts." These are published in the United States Code (U.S.C.), which is the official record of all U.S. laws.

Laws spell out the broad objectives of policy decisions and the basic principles of implementation. Full implementation is delegated to government departments or agencies; for environmental laws, EPA is normally the lead agency. However, DOE and the Departments of Agriculture, Commerce, Housing and Urban Development, and Transportation, and the Department of Defense (DOD), among others, often play a role. Laws frequently delegate responsibilities to state and local governments. These, in turn, have their own set of laws/regulations, which are delegated to their departments and programs for implementation.

Departments and other responsible government agencies propose rules that regulate what is legal and what is not. Their proposed rules are published in the *Federal Register* or state equivalents so that interested parties can read them and respond. The responsible government agency is required to read and respond to every comment and hold public meetings. Sometimes, comments lead to modifications of proposed rules. The modifications are published, as is the final rule. Once a regulation is finalized in the *Federal Register*, it is incorporated into the Code of Federal Regulations (CFR), which has become readily accessible on the Internet. Nearly all the most important environmental laws/regulations are contained in CFR, Title 40.

The first seven chapters of this book discussed provisions of key laws and regulations, beginning with the Food, Drug, and Cosmetic Act of 1938 (see also chapter 5 for discussion of other pesticide/food-related laws). I have had reason to consult more than 50 federal laws that bear on environmental protection. This book is intended to be an analysis of policies and policy process, not an encyclopedic summary of all the laws. Accordingly, I have identified a dozen that I believe have had the biggest impact on the environment during the past half-century: They are as follows:

1. National Environmental Policy Act of 1970
2. Clean Air Act of 1970
3. Occupational Safety and Health Act of 1970
4. Federal Water Pollution Control Act Amendments of 1972
5. Endangered Species Act of 1973
6. Safe Drinking Water Act of 1974

7. Resource Conservation and Recovery Act of 1976
8. Toxic Substances Control Act of 1976
9. Comprehensive Environmental Response, Compensation, and Liability Act of 1980 (Superfund)
10. Nuclear Waste Policy Act of 1982
11. Asbestos School Hazard Abatement Act of 1984
12. Emergency Planning and Community Right-to-Know Act of 1986

The key laws cluster around 1970, beginning with the National Environmental Policy Act (see chapter 7). The first nine sent a clear message that the federal government intended to protect people, the air, the land, and water. These laws inaugurated a new era by telling business and government that they no longer could discard wastes, expose workers, and eliminate species without consequences. These laws have been branded as "command-and-control" regulations. I am not unsympathetic to the assertion that these laws commanded and controlled emissions to an extent never envisioned. Historical context is critical to understanding why these early laws were written with such strong rules. Specifically, with rare exceptions, U.S. businesses did not choose to curtail their environmentally abusive practices. Consequently, I believe that the initial rules had to be commanding and controlling.

The Clean Air Act of 1970 is illustrative. It regulates emissions from stationary locations (e.g., factories), and mobile sources (e.g., automobiles and trucks). The law charged EPA with establishing national ambient (outdoor) air quality standards to protect public health and the environment and "provide [an] ample margin of safety to protect public health" (Section 112 [b][1][B]). After considerable debate and later revisions, EPA created ambient air quality standards for the following six substances: (1) carbon monoxide, (2) oxides of nitrogen, (3) sulfur oxides, (4) particulates, (5) ozone, and (6) lead.

Primary standards were set to protect health, and secondary standards were set to protect welfare, although many of the secondary standards were set at the same level as the primary standards. Sulfur oxides, for example, have a more stringent secondary standard to protect crops, natural vegetation, structures, and water bodies from acid rain. The national ambient air quality standards were based on the science available in the 1950s and 1960s and included protective factors of 10 or more. In other words, if science pointed to a level of 5 parts per million as dangerous, the standard would be set at 0.5 parts per million, or even 0.05 parts per million, to protect the most vulnerable members of society.

This standard-setting approach was controversial and has been attacked as not justified. Opponents of the standards reviewed the underlying science and systematically criticized nearly every study. I believe that some of their arguments, such as the lack of validated studies, small sample sizes, and lack of confidence limits, were appropriate (see chapter 3 for a discussion of how scientists evaluate evidence). However, the advocacy intent of the criticisms was apparent; the strengths of the studies were not emphasized, and every conceivable limitation was used to assert that the evidence was too weak to support standards. The reality is that scientists and decision makers had only limited data at that time and to have waited for a high-quality data set and not to have built in a safety factor would have sent a message to the public and business that environmental protection was not a high priority. With minor modifications (for example, the particulate standard was revised to focus on fine particles), ambient air quality standards have remained unchanged for more than three decades.

In addition to the ambient air quality standards, states were required to develop state implementation plans that would improve air quality by restricting emissions. The federal government imposed automobile emission standards, and although these were not met immediately and were vigorously opposed by the automobile industry, such emissions eventually were dramatically reduced.

In later amendments, Congress focused on acid rain, ozone, and air toxics. All of these modifications involved major debates because they required manufacturers to install specific air quality improvement technologies and/or switch to less contaminating resources (see chapter 3, for example, on methyl tertiary butyl ether or MTBE).

Overall, compared with what we know today, the 1970 Clean Air Act was based on imperfect science, but markedly improved the quality of the air. Would it have been improved with a less aggressive approach? Perhaps, but history says no. Environmental policies before 1970 included more than half a century of ineffective local and state efforts (Stern, 1982). Air quality regulations began with efforts in cities like Chicago and Cincinnati to regulate smoke from furnaces and locomotives. Then some states passed regulations, but in my opinion these regulations and requirements were entirely inadequate. Starting in 1970, the federal government passed more than a dozen regulatory statutes, each mandating standards, technologies, permits, protocols, and other practices. As someone who was born in New York City and suffered from asthma as a child, I can vividly recall days when the sky near my father's place of business in Brooklyn was filthy. These aggressive federal government policies were essential. More than three decades later, we can ease back on the regulatory throttle for some programs (Higgs and Close, 2005), but not as much as some would like.

Executive Orders

The president, federal cabinet officers, other agency heads, chairs of congressional committees, and their equivalents at the state and local levels have the power to change policies without going through the tedious process of writing laws, regulations, and rules. The most important executive decision affecting the environment during the past three decades was the environmental justice executive order signed by President Clinton on February 11, 1994 (see chapter 5 for additional discussion). Executive Order 12898, "Federal Actions to Address

Environmental Justice in Minority Populations and Low-Income Populations" (Clinton, 1994), began with the following statement:

> By the authority vested in me as President by the Constitution and the laws of United States of America, it is hereby ordered as follows:

> Section 1–1. Implementation.

> 1–101. *Agency Responsibilities.* To the greatest extent practicable and permitted by law, and consistent with the principles set forth in the report on the National Performance Review, each Federal agency shall make achieving environmental justice part of its mission by identifying and addressing as appropriate, disproportionately high and adverse human health or environmental effects of its programs, policies, and activities on minority populations and low-income populations in the United States and its territories.

After stating the objective of his order, President Clinton created a working group, consisting of 11 department heads and several White House offices, to implement it. In other words, he made it clear who was to participate. He then set up reporting deadlines, data collection and analysis tasks, and other requirements. He noted that the working groups should hold public meetings, assigned responsibility for implementing the program, and added additional comments about costs and judicial review.

The intent of this executive order was to send a message and begin action on a topic that emanated from the civil rights movement of the 1960s. In 1990, after years of preliminary research, the Congressional Black Caucus met with EPA staff and argued convincingly that blacks, other minorities, and poor people were at higher risk of environmental exposure than their white and more affluent counterparts. The EPA administrator created a group called the Environmental Equity Workshop to report on the issue. In June 1992, the EPA report *Environmental Equity: Reducing Risk for All Communities* supported the environmental justice argument and offered 10 recommendations. One of these recommendations was to create the Office of Environmental Justice, which was done in 1994. With this debate and report as context, President Clinton issued his executive order (see also Woolley and Peters, 2006).

Executive Order 12898 was never intended to be the final word. The 11 responsible agencies were expected to use existing standards, permits, grant programs, licenses, regulations, and due process to reduce environmental injustice, but the order was intended to be a bridge to a law that would follow. That law did not pass. For example, on May 23, 2003, a decade after the executive order, Representative Mark Udall introduced the Environmental Justice Act, noting that although federal government officials had begun to implement Executive Order 12898, a national law was needed to "institutionalize" the effort so that it could not be abrogated by the stroke of a pen.

Representative Udall had good reason to be concerned. Article II of the Constitution grants the president executive power to facilitate the functions of the federal government. In 2006, the organization Conservative Action criticized President Clinton for abusing the executive order power, asserting that in 31 instances between 1993 and 2001, he wrote executive orders that violated states' rights, appropriated land, and gave federal agencies too much regulatory power. On this list of abuses were orders that protected migratory birds, sensitive lands, and cultural sites and rivers; advocated for waste prevention; protected children from environmental risks; and required the federal government to purchase vehicles that used alternative fuel. Notably, Executive Order 12898 was one of the 31 abusive executive orders the organization listed. Conservative Action hoped that President George W. Bush would revoke these orders. In fact, President Clinton had revoked executive orders that he considered anti-environmental when he took office. For example, on January 20, 1993, he eliminated the Council on Competitiveness, which some contended had been enacted by the Bush-Quayle administration to undermine environmental laws.

Despite the vulnerability of executive orders, as noted in chapter 5, President Clinton's Executive Order 12898 has had a profound impact on environmental policy. I believe that it is the most important environmental policy enacted during the 1990s. Environmental policy decisions can no longer blithely ignore environmental justice implications.

Court Decisions

Policy decisions produce winners and losers. Not surprisingly, every major environmental policy decision has been challenged in the courts. Some judicial challenges are blended into the chapters of this book, and they can be pursued further on the Internet. To illustrate the importance of legal challenges on environmental policy, I have picked two examples: the transportation of trash across state boundaries and the management of high-level nuclear waste.

Twice a week, I wheel my household trash to the curb in front of my house. Every two weeks, I separate and place glass bottles, aluminum cans, metal cans, newspapers, paper, and cardboard in separate containers and move them to the curb. The movement of trash seems like it should be an entirely local matter, but it is not. Americans generate two to three times as much trash per capita as the Japanese, the Canadians, and the residents of other urbanized and industrial nations. Picking up and disposing of trash in landfills or incinerators is expensive. We pay for it through our local taxes or contract individually with trash haulers.

We have also paid for trash management through pollution, especially the pollution of our water supplies and ecological systems. Anyone who believes that household trash does not contain hazardous constituents should think again. Not only are some of the constituents directly hazardous, but they can pollute water, cause fires and explosions, and lead to many other problems. In 1977, EPA reported damage caused by hazardous waste sites. The single largest category of sites consisted of landfills and dumps (24 percent). In 1981, before making money available through Superfund, EPA compiled a list of 20 sites considered so hazardous that it funded engineering studies before the law was passed. Eight of the 20 were landfills and dumps for municipal trash (Greenberg and Anderson, 1984).

With hindsight, we would never locate a disposal site near a wetland or on top of an underground aquifer, but that was common practice for many decades. Wetlands were cheap, undeveloped, and often accessible to urban areas looking for a cheap place to dump their trash. The Superfund legislation addressed abandoned landfills, and the Resource Conservation and Recovery Act (RCRA) of 1976 required major improvements in working trash management facilities. As a result of these laws, the number of landfills in the United States shrank from almost 10,000 in the late 1980s to less than 1,700 in 2005 (EPA, 2005). Small landfills and dumps closed and were replaced by incinerators, large regional landfills, and transfer stations required to move trash long distances.

The courts have been involved in trash collection and disposal for many years. Almost a century ago, the U.S. Supreme Court ruled that local governments can control garbage collection and disposal. More recently, the courts have become involved because trash management has changed from a local government responsibility to a big business. The solid waste industry employs more than 350,000 workers and is a $43 billion a year operation that depends on the free flow of trash across municipal, state, and international boundaries. On March 20, 2002, Bruce Parker, president and CEO of the National Solid Waste Management Association, testified against a proposed federal act that would have restricted the interstate flow of trash. He stated: "Restricted borders have no legitimate place in managing trash or any other problem in the economy."

Parker (2002) argued that the U.S. solid waste industry is the envy of other countries because of its ability to plan, build, and deploy resources where they are needed in a careful and orderly fashion. Approximately 11 percent of the trash that is generated crosses state boundaries for disposal (see also Congressional Research Service, 2001). The proportion has increased because of environmental regulations, principally the RCRA, that required major improvements and trash management. Thousands of small landfills closed and have been replaced by large landfills and incinerators, which also mean more interstate shipments and trash carried on roads and railroads (EPA, 2005).

Eastern and Midwestern states such as Connecticut, Illinois, Maryland, Michigan, Missouri, New Jersey, New York, Rhode Island, Vermont, and West Virginia send more than 15 percent of their municipal waste to other states. For example, New Jersey, where I live, exports waste to Pennsylvania, Virginia, and West Virginia and receives waste from New York. Every one of these shipments has been challenged in court by officials who emphasize environmental damage (water pollution at sites, air pollution from trash trucks) and social disruption caused by the movement of these trucks through the streets.

The counterargument is that trash is like any other product. Opponents of restricting shipments argue that so-called flow-control regulations support non-competitive monopolies against free competition. Article I, section 8, clause 3, of the U.S. Constitution (the Commerce Clause) empowers Congress "to regulate Commerce with foreign nations, and among several states, and with Indian Tribes."

Absent federal legislation, the courts have made a series of decisions, attempting to balance these competing interests. For example, on May 16, 1994, the U.S. Supreme Court ruled for private business in *C&A Carbone, Inc. v. the Town of Clarkston, New York.* The town's flow-control ordinance was declared unconstitutional because it "unreasonably" regulated interstate commerce. Previously, the Supreme Court had ruled that Michigan's solid waste management law violated the Commerce Clause because it "unambiguously" discriminated against international trade. Any laws, regulations, and economic incentives or disincentives that unfairly restricted or unduly burdened the movement of trash among the states and internationally were declared unconstitutional.

These legal decisions have clearly produced winners and losers. The winners include businesses that have invested in large solid waste management facilities that depend on the unrestricted movement of trash. The losers include some local and state governments that invested heavily in large incinerators and depended on surrounding jurisdictions to provide a constant flow of trash that would collect enough revenue to pay for these facilities. When flow control was declared illegal, some communities and private carting services obtained contracts with out-of-state waste management businesses that undercut local facilities. The most obvious evidence was that some local and county governments saw their bond ratings fall, and they were forced to reduce their workforce because their revenue stream was undermined (Gielecki, 1997; National Association of Counties, 1997; O'Leary, 1997).

The involvement of the federal courts in trash policy signals the failure of Congress and the Executive Branch to focus on finding practical solutions to environmental problems that are often quite important to local and state governments. The Supreme Court and the district courts will continue to play a key role in trash management and analogous issues unless or until Congress acts.

Sometimes, the courts become embroiled in policy decisions that involve sending a message to decision makers. In 2003, one such case sent a clear message to DOE, at least until the court's ruling was overturned. This case, which pitted the Natural Resources Defense Council (NRDC) against DOE, was decided by the U.S. District Court for Idaho. The court was asked to rule on DOE's Order 435.1, which was written in 1999 and defined some waste at Hanford (Washington), Idaho, and Savannah River (South Carolina) as "incidental," obviating the need to bury it in a geologic repository (see chapters 4 and 6 for a discussion of Yucca Mountain, Nevada). The NRDC challenged the department's order, claiming that it violated the Nuclear Waste Policy Act of 1982, which, according to the plaintiff, required that all of this waste be placed in a repository (see also chapter 6).

In the act, Congress defined high-level radioactive waste as follows: "(A) the highly radioactive material resulting from the reprocessing of spent nuclear fuel, including liquid wastes produced directly in reprocessing and any solid material derived from such liquid waste that contains fission products in sufficient concentrations; (B) other highly radioactive material that the Commission, consistent with existing law, determines by rule requires permanent isolation."

Judge B. Lynn Winmill (2003a, 2003b) disagreed with DOE's policy on a number of important points, including the standing of the NRDC to bring a suit and the appropriateness of a legal challenge based on the evidence at hand. Rather than focusing on all of the legal intricacies, I will concentrate on two points. First, Judge Winmill argued that DOE does not have the discretion to dispose of high-level waste generated from nuclear weapons production anywhere but in a repository. He focused on the word "shall" in the legislation, arguing that it means that there is no discretion in the final destination of the waste. He ruled that DOE does not have the authority "to adopt a policy that directly conflicts with its governing statute." By itself, the ruling represented at least a temporary setback to DOE. The judge, however, showed his frustration by sending a message about the wording in the DOE's order as follows: "The second is that HLW [high-level radioactive waste] incorporated into a solid form must either meet the concentration levels for Class C low-level waste or meet such alternative requirements for waste classification and the characterization as the DOE may authorize. These 'alternative requirements' are not defined, and those are subject to the whim of DOE." The judge's ruling was covered by major newspapers. The stories I read made a point of mentioning that DOE's ruling was in essence whimsical (see, for example, Wald, 2003). The judge's remarks hurt the credibility of the department, I believe, more than it changed DOE's practices.

DOE was sent a message, but like many other judicial rulings, the message was reversed. DOE appealed the judge's summary judgment for NRDC on November 5, 2004. Judge Fernandez reversed and remanded the summary judgment because the issue seemed unresolvable at this time. We need a "wait and see attitude rather than making assumptions" (U.S. Court of Appeals for the Ninth Circuit, 2004). Also, DOE was granted legislative relief in its appropriations bill, section 311, which included language that gave the secretary of energy authority to make decisions about spent nuclear fuel. In other words, DOE may yet prevail on this issue. The role of the courts, Congress, the Executive Branch, state and local governments, and nongovernmental organizations like the NRDC is always in play in these complicated environmental policy cases. I totally agree with Judge Fernandez's assessment that we need to wait and see about this particular issue; policy beliefs are far out ahead of science and technology on many issues.

Changes in Leadership and Resources

Laws, regulations, executive decisions, and judicial rulings are written policies. The message may sometimes be difficult to find and will need to be explained to the media and the public. However, attorneys, and others trained and experienced in decision making will understand or endeavor to understand the policy and any accompanying signals. Some policy decisions, most notably, changing leadership and resources, are less direct.

Indirect policy tools have a long political history. The literature distinguishes between public interest theory and capture theory. Public interest theory assumes that agencies focus on the public interest mandated by their mission (Levine, 1981; Mitnick, 1980). Capture theory (Peltzman, 1976; Stigler, 1971) asserts that businesses, workers, and other interest groups capture agencies and their missions.

Neither of these theories matches my experience with environmental policy. I have observed what the literature refers to as "external signals theory," which predicts that agency staffs respond to signals from the surrounding political environment (Magat, Krupnick, and Harrington, 1986; Noll, 1971). If Congress and the Office of Management and Budget (OMB) support budget requests, if the courts uphold agency rules, and if constituents and the media applaud the policies, then the agency is appropriately managing its mandate. If budget requests are challenged and constituents or the media are hostile or silent, then the agency must adjust to its environment (Cyert and March, 1963).

External signal theory implies that agencies should always be scanning the political environment for signals. Changes in leadership and budgets are not subtle messages. Moe (1982) showed how changes in Congress and the Executive Branch have changed policy. EPA is a case in point. Many friends and former students have worked for EPA or its state equivalents, and their performance, indeed, their continued employment, has been altered by new leaders and budget shifts.

CHANGING LEADERS. William Ruckelshaus, who served twice as EPA administrator (1970 to 1972 and 1983 to 1985) epitomizes a respected leader who supported staff and was perceived as supporting the agency's mission. Ruckelshaus was EPA's first administrator, and during his first term, he focused on the building of the organization, enforcement actions against major polluters, the creation of health-based air quality and emission standards (see the earlier discussion of the Clean Air Act), and the banning of the pesticide DDT (dichlorodiphenyl-trichloroethane) (EPA, 2006b; EPA Journal, 1983; Ruckelshaus, 1985).

After his first term ended, Ruckelshaus served as acting FBI director during the Nixon administration and then as deputy attorney general. He was called back to EPA by President Reagan for a second term in 1983 at a time when the agency was losing personnel and its reputation as a protector of the environment was in jeopardy. Ruckelshaus had some visible political warts; he had served in senior administrative positions for businesses, notably, Weyerhaeuser, Cummins Engineering (see the chapter 5 discussion with Charles Powers), and other large companies. Nevertheless, he was widely perceived as an administrator who could be trusted to support EPA's agenda and staff.

Nicknamed "Mr. Clean," Ruckelshaus earned praise during his brief stint in the Department of Justice. When President Nixon demanded that Ruckelshaus fire special Watergate Prosecutor Archibald Cox, Ruckelshaus resigned instead. His involvement in the so-called Saturday night massacre (October 20, 1973) left him with a reputation that enabled him to step into a difficult situation at EPA. He said:

> When I returned to EPA in the Spring of 1983, I was under no illusion that everything was just fine. I knew there would be some surprises. I was not disappointed. I was surprised at how emotional the issue of environment had become. Feeling strongly is one thing — giving reason a prominent holiday is something else. The relationship between the political appointees of the Reagan Administration and the press, the Congress, and the public was marked by deep distrust and fiery rhetoric. The environmental community was particularly outspoken in its opposition to anything the Administration proposed. (Ruckelshaus, 1985, see also EPA, 2006b)

Ruckelshaus replaced Anne Gorsuch (later Burford), EPA's first woman administrator. In my experience, she was the administrator perceived to be the least supportive of EPA's mission, programs, and staff. She stated: "The single greatest weakness within EPA — and from the very beginning, not just recently — is its lack of solid management skills, from top to bottom. . . . Traditionally, people come from the technical areas and are 'thrust up' to management posts. . . . If pressed to name the EPA's greatest strength, I would have to say that its real strength is the fact that the agency's mission enjoys enormous popular support among the people of America" (Gorsuch, 1985; see also EPA, 2006a).

Ruckelshaus quite deliberately praised EPA staff; Burford labeled them as dedicated workers who tended to promise too much. After arriving at EPA, she reduced the agency's budget and staff by more than 20 percent. Congress (members of both political parties) accused her of trying to dismantle the agency and particularly of trying to reduce enforcement against polluters. She and 20 employees were forced to resign after they were found in contempt of Congress for refusing to disclose documents related to a possible conflict of interest with the Superfund program. In 1986, Burford wrote a book (*Are You Tough Enough?*) in which she accused the Reagan administration of jettisoning her when she was doing what they had asked her to do (see also Sullivan, 2004).

No department or agency head, especially the head of EPA or its state equivalents, can escape controversy. Douglas Costle (EPA administrator from 1977 to 1981) told me that most of his decisions involved judgment calls because the scientific evidence was always ambiguous. The most demoralizing and serious problem occurs when staff members do not trust the director and feel that he or she is a Trojan horse planted to undermine them and the agency. The most poignant recently published example I found is in an essay by Eric Schaeffer (2002), who was formerly director of EPA's Office of Regulatory Enforcement. He said: "The Bush [George W. Bush] administration was able to undo the environmental progress we had worked years to secure. Millions of tons of unnecessary pollution continued to pour from these power plants each year. . . . Adding insult to injury, the White House sought to slash the EPA's enforcement budget."

Schaeffer accused the Bush administration of appointing Christine Whitman, former governor of New Jersey, to launch a stealth attack against EPA's enforcement programs. The administration's plan was to shrink the enforcement budget; divide the bureaucracy into dysfunctional and competitive groups; pack the courts with anti-environment judges; have members of Congress lobby against enforcement; return programs to states, some of which lacked the capacity to manage them; and repeatedly criticize enforcement for stifling innovation.

It is certainly not my intent to be critical of any administrator, especially since I worked on projects for Governor Whitman. However, it is my intent to underscore that perception often equals reality. A change in leadership is typically perceived, especially by staff and sometimes by interest groups and the general public, as a message that the agency or staff needs to be redirected to follow a different path. This can have a chilling effect on agency performance.

BUDGET CHANGES. Presidents, governors, and mayors do not always want to take the political risk of replacing a popular administrator. Instead, or in conjunction with a leadership change, they starve a program. George Carey, my doctoral advisor, told me to learn about people's priorities by checking their expenditures, not what they said was important to them. Following his advice will help us understand the importance attached to the environment, health, education, transportation, and other issues.

Some expenditures are mandated by law, while others are discretionary. Hence, overall budget statements can be misleading. With that caveat noted, I will use EPA's expenditures to illustrate budgets and expenditures as a tool of environmental policy. In 2005, the federal government spent $2.48 trillion (OMB, 2006). The Department of Health and Human Services and DOD dominated federal outlays, with budgets of $586 and $444 billion, respectively. By comparison, EPA's 2005 expenditures were $7.9 billion, almost a rounding error in the budgets of the two larger departments. By themselves, EPA's expenditure numbers do not mean that environmental protection is not important. For example, DOD and DOE have substantial environmental budgets, but environmental protection certainly has a lower priority than many other government programs.

More can be learned by looking at the changes in annual expenditures. Without correcting for a change in the value of the dollar, federal outlays in 1990 were $1.25 trillion, about half of the 2005 outlays. While overall outlays doubled, EPA's increased only 55 percent from $5.1 to $7.9 billion. At the top of the list of relative increases were the Departments of Homeland Security, Health and Human Services, Justice, and Education. Each had expenditures that were more than three times their 1990 outlays. At the bottom were the National Science Foundation, the National Aeronautics and Space Administration, the U.S. Army Corps of Engineers, DOD, and EPA, with increases of less than 60 percent between 1990 and 2005. Each of these programs invests heavily in science and engineering, which perhaps is the obvious message about the federal government's prioritization of science and technology.

The relatively small increase for DOD is misleading. In fact, the DOD budget has been on a roller coaster. Expenditures decreased from $290 billion in 1990 to $260 billion in 1995, a legacy of the end of the cold war and the now forgotten idea that it would produce a peacetime economic benefit that would be reinvested in the United States.

Compared with other agencies and departments, EPA's expenditure increase was relatively similar to that of its counterparts, from $5.1 billion to $7.2 billion between 1990 and 2000. But the budget has increased only another $700 million since then. It is easy to ascribe EPA's changing fortunes wholly to President George W. Bush's administration. However, such an explanation, while not without some merit, would miss other forces that have affected government expenditures, such as the election of more politically conservative states' rights members of Congress, greater conservatism expressed by the public, events such as the September 11, 2001, terrorist attacks, a major increase in automobile fuel prices, continued de-industrialization of the United States, and changes in international trade.

The public is less supportive of environmental protection than it was a decade ago. In January 2000, 70 percent of U.S. respondents to a Gallup poll chose the maintenance of environmental protection over economic growth. But in 2001, 2002, 2003, and 2004, the proportion that chose environment over economic growth dropped to 57, 54, 47, and 49 percent, respectively. Notably, this decrease from 70 percent in 2000 followed a decade-long increase from 58 percent in 1992 (Saad, 2004; Saad and Dunlap, 2000). I have argued that the decline is reversible and short-term, reflecting increasing public concern over the wars in Iraq and Afghanistan, terrorism, and concerns about the economy (Greenberg, 2005). The Bush administration and EPA budget cuts, at least to some extent, reflect the nation's priorities in the early 21st century.

Digging deeply into expenditures would lead to further insights about policy changes. For example, within EPA, the major loss in expenditures during the past two decades has been in the Superfund program, whereas other agency programs have experienced modest increases. To understand environmental policy, then, we must read the laws, regulations, rules, executive orders, and court decisions, or at least summaries of them, but we cannot assume that they equal reality. Rather, reality is created by those who implement a written policy with the resources they are given.

Explaining Environmental Policies

If decision makers want the public to understand their policies (and sometimes they may not), then they must communicate to the media, understanding the criteria for newsworthiness described in chapter 2. Also, they may choose to arrange public meetings.

Avoiding Pitfalls in Communication

This section describes what I have called the 10 commandments for communicating with journalists. The same points should be applied to public meetings, although much more emphasis must be placed on the first four and the last three points for a public presentation. I present these 10 suggestions two to four times a year to scientists, journalists, and students. My interest in communicating directly with journalists and the public began with several awful, embarrassing efforts, which led me to consult with journalism professors David Sachsman and Peter Sandman, former colleagues who made me realize that my media disasters were primarily my own fault and that they could be corrected. The 10 suggestions are offered in order of importance. The first seven are for individual speakers, and the last three are for groups of people and organizations.

1. *Individual: Assume Responsibility for What You Want Included.* Prepare a note no more than one page long that summarizes no more than three points that you feel are critical. Then make sure you focus on these points during your interview. If it is to be broadcast, prepare these points as 10- to 20-second bullets. It is important to avoid long lists of points. Too much information surrenders control of the story to the audience or the reporter, who will not know what you think is important. The reporter and public may not focus on your points entirely, but neither will they entirely neglect them, especially if you emphasize their importance.

2. *Individual: Do Not Assume that the Reporter/Public Knows Anything about the Policy or the Underlying Science.* Reporters are smart, but with rare exceptions they have not been well schooled in science or engineering. This means that you cannot afford to assume that they know the science underlying the policy. Nor will they necessarily have read the laws, executive orders, and judicial decisions before they call you.

    Science reporters for the *Washington Post*, the *New York Times*, the *Los Angeles Times*, the *Chicago Tribune* and other major metropolitan newspapers are likely to know a great deal. But assume nothing and be patient, offer to provide explanations and literature, and respond to phone calls before the reporter's deadline, which is probably inflexible.

3. *Individual: Be Prepared for Personal Questions.* Nearly all reporters and many members of the public initially look for unethical behavior, such as cover-ups, scandals, and purchased testimony. So be prepared for questions about your funding and ethics. Do not react angrily when asked if you have ever

received a grant from a business or were ever a consultant. If you have gotten a grant or been a consultant, explain what you did.

Reporters lose patience with experts who hide behind numbers and scientific theories. Be prepared for personal questions, such as, "Would you let your mother live near a hazardous waste site?" "Did you have your house tested for radon?" These probes are intended to get to your personal bottom line. If you allow your mother to live near a hazardous waste site, then you must not think it is very dangerous. If you have your house tested for radon, then you must be concerned about it.

Reporters recognize that readers are interested in people, not statistics. That is, to get the public to focus on the story, a reporter has to establish an emotional tie between the injured person/the person at risk and the audience. Psychologists have learned that as individuals, the public focuses more on one person with whom they may have formed a psychological link than on thousands of people they know nothing about. Psychologist Paul Slovic of the Society for Risk Analysis in Baltimore, Maryland (personal communication on December 3, 2006), told me that public indifference to risk increases as soon as more than one person is included in a story.

4. *Individual: Do Not Use Jargon, Comparisons, and Other Information That May Be Confusing.* Under pressure, experts too often resort to jargon, statistics, technical data, and risk comparisons. These assume knowledge and are likely to confuse reporters and the public. For example, telling a reporter that a hazard can cause an additional cancer risk of 4×10^{-6} after a lifetime exposure is an invitation to misunderstanding. What does that mean to someone who has not had math for years and does not know cancer death or mortality rates?

If you insist on using numbers, then you must explain them and place them in context. If you compare risks, you must make sure that you are comparing similar types of risk. Avoid comparing risks that are perceived to be different. For instance, do not compare the risk of living near an incinerator, highway, or electricity-generating plant with the risk of smoking or driving while intoxicated. The first three are considered "imposed" and "uncontrollable" risks; the last two are considered "voluntary" and "controllable." (See also chapter 3 for the discussion of factors affecting the public perception of risk.) If you insist on comparing different categories of risk, the audience will become angry and argue, or will not listen at all. You are much better off focusing on your three key points in a simple, comprehensible, and interesting way.

5. *Individual: Look for Confusion.* I monitor questions and body language. If the reporter or audience is asking questions that have nothing to do with my three key points and if people do not appear to be following what I am saying, I request a halt in the presentation and questioning so I can understand why I am confusing them. If possible, I try to direct the story back to my key

points. For example, if I am trying to explain that a brownfield redevelopment is a risky economic investment and the reporter continues to focus on cases where he or she thinks that investors have made excess profits (that discussion has occurred many times), then that disconnect needs to be addressed. Breaking in may seem inappropriate and rude, but it is much better than a misunderstanding that later on makes you feel foolish.

Also, monitor your own performance. If you make a mistake, correct it. If you do not know the answer to a question, say so and, if possible, refer the person to someone who can answer it.

6. *Individual: Describe the Limitations of the Research Supporting Policies.* Reporters and people look for irrefutable evidence, but we know that every environmental study has limitations. Explain the weaknesses, as well as the strengths, of your work. Do not exaggerate because reporters are likely to identify exaggeration by asking another expert. They will then ignore your work or undermine it by reporting the opposing viewpoint. In short, it is best to acknowledge that others may disagree with you and explain why.

7. *Individual: Suggest Other Sources and Perspectives.* Reporters are always looking for simple, workable policies, but most have learned that environmental and risk-related science and policy decisions are uncertain. Hence, it is best to acknowledge other policy options, explain them, and give the names of other sources who can articulate them. Never attack alternative policies as immoral or irrational because you may offend a reporter and/or members of the audience who may hold that position or be sympathetic toward it.

8. *Individual and Group: Organize the Communications Effort and Conduct a Lessons-Learned Follow-up.* Discuss what you plan to say (focus on your three key points) and who should be briefed, prepare a summary of your key points before the event, rehearse, and make sure you agree about who will respond to follow-up calls, e-mails, and letters. Before you speak for your organization, consider what you want reporters and audiences to remember and what you think the audience will want to know. Time permitting, consult media files and talk with others who are familiar with the journalists, audience, and topic. Think about things that can go wrong (not enough time, inclement weather, legal restrictions on what you can say) and be prepared with alternative plans. It is imperative that you consider the audience (general reporter, expert reporter, scientists/engineers, local environmental group, local residents). Scientific literacy, learning styles, and cultural attributes vary. Also, conduct a lessons-learned meeting with your colleagues afterward to discuss what you have learned and what can be improved. I cannot emphasize enough the potential benefits of lessons-learned follow-ups.

9. *Individual and Group: Coordinate with Other Speakers and Organizations.* Some policy issues attract multiple speakers. Be sure to determine who else may be having interviews with reporters or speaking to the public on the same issue.

If no one coordinates, reporters and the public are likely to get confusing messages. Obviously, people and organizations are entitled to have different opinions. However, you do not want to be blindsided by someone who asks you what you thought about remarks that were made yesterday on the same subject. So do some homework about other presentations.

10. *Individual and Group: Do Not Expect to Communicate Your Way out of Value Differences.* Discourse will not resolve issues based on fundamental differences that are immune to scientific and technical information. In my experience, reporters will not dwell on value-based issues, but public groups sometimes do, and if they dig in their heels, the possibility of clearing up misunderstandings based on misinformation may be lost, and the organization may end up worse off than before. I am not saying that we should avoid situations that can blow up in our faces. But I am saying that we should try to plan an event that that focuses on clearing up misunderstandings rather than degenerating into a dispute over who is more moral. We can acknowledge irreconcilable differences without focusing entirely on them.

Learning More about the Tools

There is an enormous literature about environmental laws, regulations, rules, executive orders, court decisions, leadership, and budgets. The laws, regulations, rules, executive decisions, and other official policies are reported in the *Federal Register*. State governments have their equivalents. People who are not lawyers or are not well trained in interpreting written and verbal statements may find many of these official documents to be formidable, if not impenetrable. However, typically the organization will quickly prepare a summary statement explaining the written policy. This will then be posted on the Internet. Major newspapers, such as the *New York Times*, the *Washington Post*, the *Wall Street Journal*, and others, will normally cover major legislative decisions.

For those who are thinking about pursuing environmental policy as a career, I would advise consulting some of the key academic environmental law journals, such as those published by Georgetown, Harvard, Stanford, and New York University (my favorite). The *Journal of Environmental Law* (published by Oxford University Press) is another high-quality source of interpretation and precedents.

Also, there are dozens of books on the market. Two I recommend are *Public Policies for Environmental Protection* (Portney and Stavins, 2000) and *Pluralism by Design: Environmental Policy and the American Regulatory State* (Hoberg, 1992), which is a historical review of U.S. environmental law through the Reagan administration. With regard to communications, there are many books; but, frankly, I do not like most of them because they focus too much on persuading people and not enough on listening. I recommend Hance, Chess, and Sandman (1988, 1990), National Research Council (1989), and Clark (1984) as well as the journal *Risk Analysis* as a way to keep in touch with the latest research.

REFERENCES

INTRODUCTION

Colten, C. (2005). *An unnatural metropolis: Wresting New Orleans from nature.* Baton Rouge: Louisiana State University Press.

Cumbler, J. (2005). *Northeast and Midwest United States: An environmental history.* Santa Barbara, CA: ABC-CLIO.

Hurley, A. (1995). *Environmental inequalities: Class, race, and industrial pollution in Gary, Indiana, 1945–1980.* Chapel Hill: University of North Carolina Press.

McShane, C. (1994). *Down the asphalt path: The automobile and the American city.* New York: Columbia University Press.

Melosi, M. (2001). *Effluent America: Cities, industry, energy, and the environment.* Pittsburgh: University of Pittsburgh Press.

Rome, A. (2001). *The bulldozer in the countryside: Suburban sprawl and the rise of American environmentalism.* New York: Cambridge University Press.

Stradling, D. (1999). *Smokestacks and progressives: Environmentalists, engineers, and air quality in America, 1881–1951.* Baltimore, MD: Johns Hopkins University Press.

Tarr, J. (Ed.). (2003). *Devastation and renewal: An environmental history of Pittsburgh and its region.* Pittsburgh, PA: University of Pittsburgh Press.

CHAPTER 1

Allen, S. (1996). Waste sites now paying dividends. *Boston Globe,* November 16, p. A1.

America needs a new system to achieve fast and effective cleanup of our environment. (1991, September 9). *Time,* pp. 52–53.

Bosselman, F., and Callies, D. (1972). *The quiet revolution in land use control.* Report prepared for the Council on Environmental Quality. Washington, DC: U.S. Government Printing Office.

Brachman, L. (1995, December 17). Toxic test case: In Georgia, a Superfund site that's actually getting recycled. *Washington Post,* p. C1.

Brenneman, R., and Bates, S. (Eds.). (1984). *Land-saving action.* Covelo, CA: Island Press.

Brown, M. (1979). *Laying waste.* New York: Washington Square Press.

Browner, C. (1993). Pollution prevention takes center stage at EPA. *EPA Journal, 19* (3), 7–8.

Burchell, R., Listokin, D., and Galley, C. (1999). *Smart growth: More than a ghost of urban policy past, less than a bold new horizon.* New Brunswick, NJ: Rutgers, the State University of New Jersey, Center for Urban Policy Research.

Burchell, R., Shad, N., Listokin, D., Phillips, H., Downs, A., Seskin, S., Davis, J., Moore, T., Helton, D., and Gale, M. (1998). *The costs of sprawl revisited.* Report 39. Washington, DC: National Academy Press.

Bush, G. (2001). Address of the President to the Joint Session of Congress, February 27, 2001. Available at: http://www.whitehouse.gov/news/releases/2001/02/20010228.html. Accessed August 28, 2003.

Castells, M. (1989). *The informational city: Information technology, economic restructuring, and the urban-regional process.* Oxford, England: Basil Blackwell.

Cervero, R. (1986). *Suburban gridlock.* New Brunswick, NJ: Rutgers, the State University of New Jersey, Center for Urban Policy Research.

Chertow, M., and Esty, D. (Eds.). (1997). *Thinking ecologically: The next generation of environmental policy.* New Haven, CT: Yale University Press.

Clark, T., and Goetz, E. (1994). The antigrowth machine: Can city governments control, limit, or manage growth? In T. N. Clark (Ed.), *Urban innovation: Creative strategies for turbulent times* (pp. 105–145). Thousand Oaks, CA: Sage Publications.

Clinton, W. (1998). Remarks by the president at the U.S. Conference of Mayors breakfast, January 30, 1998. Available at: http://clinton4.nara.gov/textonlyWH/New/html/19980130–25315.html. Accessed August 28, 2003.

Committee on Remedial Action Priorities for Hazardous Waste Sites. (1994). *Ranking hazardous waste sites for remedial action.* Washington, DC: National Academy Press.

Danielsen, K., Lang, R., and Fulton, W. (1999). What does smart growth mean for housing? *Housing Facts and Findings, 1* (3), 1, 12–15.

Davies, J. (2002). Urban regime theory: A normative-empirical critique. *Journal of Urban Affairs, 24* (1), 1–17.

Davies, J. (2003). The global spread and development of policies and political institutions. Available at: http://www.psa.ac.uk/sps/1997/davi.pdf. Accessed October 15, 2003.

Davis, T., and Margolis, K. (1997). *Brownfields development: A comprehensive guide to redeveloping contaminated property.* Chicago, IL: American Bar Association.

Delafons, J. (1969). *Land-use controls in the United States.* 2nd ed. Cambridge, MA: MIT Press.

Dennison, M. (1998). *Brownfields redevelopment.* Rockville, MD: Government Institutes.

DeSousa, C. (2004). The greening of brownfields in American cities. *Journal of Environmental Planning and Management, 47* (4), 579–600.

Dorfman, M., Muir, W., and Miller, C. (1992). *Environmental dividends: Cutting more chemical wastes.* New York: INFORM, Inc.

Doster, L. (1999, April 26). Stop growth initiatives called out of bounds. *Real Estate Finance Today,* 6–8.

Downs, A. (1994). *New visions for metropolitan America.* Washington, DC: Brookings Institution and Lincoln Institute for Land Policy.

English, M. (1999). A guide for smart growth. *Forum for Applied Research and Public Policy, 14,* 35–39.

English, M., Peretz, J., and Manderschied, M. (1999). *Smart growth for Tennessee towns and counties: A process guide.* Knoxville, TN: Energy, Environment, and Research Center and Waste Management Research and Education Center.

Environmental Task Force. (1983, Winter). Toxics ranked number 1 problem. *EcoAlert,* (1), 4.

Fainstein, S., and Fainstein, N. (1983). Economic change, national policy, and the system of cities. In S. Fainstein, N. Fainstein, R. C. Hill, D. Judd, and M. P. Smith (Eds.), *Restructuring the city: The political economy of urban redevelopment* (pp. 1–26). New York: Logman.

Freeman, H. (1990). *Hazardous waste minimization.* New York: McGraw-Hill.

Gibbons, J., Attoh-Okine, N., and Laha, S. (1998). Brownfields redevelopment issues revisited. *International Journal of Environment and Pollution, 10* (1), 151–162.

Gladstone, D., and Fainstein, S. (2001). Tourism in U.S. global cities: A comparison of New York and Los Angeles. *Journal of Urban Affairs, 23* (1), 23–40.

Greenberg, M., and Lewis, M. J. (2000). Brownfields redevelopment, preferences, and public involvement: A case study of an ethnically mixed neighborhood. *Urban Studies, 37,* 2501–2514.

Greenberg, M., Lowrie, K., Solitare, L., and Duncan, L. (2000). Brownfields, TOADS, and the struggle for neighborhood redevelopment: A case study of the state of New Jersey. *Urban Affairs Review, 35* (5), 717–733.

Harnik, P. (2000). *Inside city parks.* Washington, DC: Urban Land Institute and Trust for Public Land.

Harrison, N. (2000). *Constructing sustainable development.* Albany, NY: State University of New York Press.

Harvey, D. (2001). *Spaces of capital: Towards a critical geography.* New York: Routledge.

Hula, R. (2001). Changing priorities and programs in toxic waste policy: The emergence of economic development as a policy goal. *Economic Development Quarterly, 15* (2), 181–199.

Imbroscio, D. (1997). *Reconstructing city politics: Alternative economic development and urban regimes.* Thousand Oaks, CA: Sage Publications.

Imbroscio, D. (1998a). The necessity of urban regime change: A reply to Clarence N. Stone. *Journal of Urban Affairs, 20* (3), 261–268.

Imbroscio, D. (1998b). Reformulating urban regime theory: The division of labor between state and market reconsidered. *Journal of Urban Affairs, 20* (3), 233–248.

Janofsky, M. (1999, January 12). Gore offers plan to control suburban growth. *New York Times,* p. A16.

Jonas, A., and Wilson, D. (1999). *The urban growth machine: Critical perspectives two decades later.* Albany, NY: State University of New York Press.

Keating, W. D., and Krumholz, N. (Eds.). (1999). *Rebuilding urban neighborhoods: Achievements, opportunities, and limits.* Thousand Oaks, CA: Sage Publications.

Kelo et al. v. City of New London, Connecticut, et al. (2005). Docket for 04-108. Available at: www.supremecourtus.gov/docket/04-108.htm.

Kreitner, R. (1998). *Maryland smart growth program.* Baltimore: Maryland Office of Planning.

Landy, M., Roberts, M., and Thomas, S. (1990). *The Environmental Protection Agency: Asking the wrong questions.* New York: Oxford University Press.

Lane, A. (2003, May 4). Districts pick polluted sites for schools. *Star Ledger* (Newark), pp. 1, 14.

Lauria, M. (1997). *Reconstructing urban regime theory: Regulating urban politics in a global economy.* Thousand Oaks, CA: Sage Publications.

Leitich, S. (1998, July 19). Town will pay $85,000 as part of dump cleanup. *Home News Tribune* (Elizabeth), p. B2.

Leo, C. (1998). Regional growth management regime: The case of Portland, Oregon. *Journal of Urban Affairs, 20* (4), 363–394.

Loftis, R. L. (1995, March 13). EPA targets toxic sites in nation's urban areas. *Dallas Morning News,* p. A1.

Logan, J., and Molotch, H. (1996). The city as a growth machine. In S. Fainstein and S. Campbell (Eds.), *Readings in urban theory.* Malden, MA: Blackwell Publishers.

Meyer, P., and Lyons, T. (2000). Lessons from private sector brownfield redevelopers. *Journal of the American Planning Association, 66* (1), 46–57.

Meyer, P., and VanLandingham, H. (2000). *Reclamation and economic regeneration of brownfields.* Louisville, KY: EDA [Economic Development Administration].

Morgan, L. (2000, October 12). Scenes from a mall: Where once we worked, now we shop! Presentation at the Brownfields 2000 Conference, Atlantic City, NJ.

Mossberger, K., and Stoker, G. (2001). The evolution of urban regime theory: The challenge of conceptualization. *Urban Affairs Review, 36* (6), 810–835.

National Governors Association. (2000). *Where do we go from here? New mission for brownfields: Attack sprawl by revitalizing older communities*. Washington, DC: National Governors Association.

National Resources Defense Council and Surface Transportation Policy Project. (1997). *The toolkit for smart growth*. Washington, DC. Available at: http://www.tea21.org/smartgrowth/default.htm.

New Jersey Office of State Planning. (1999). *Communities of place: The New Jersey State Development and Redevelopment Plan*. Trenton, NJ: Office of State Planning.

Pelosi, N. (2005). Fighting GOP efforts to abandon the "polluter pays" principle for toxic waste cleanup. Available at: http://www.democraticleader.house.gov/issues/the_environment/ earth_day_2005/toxins.cfm. Accessed July 10, 2006.

Portney, K. (2003). *Taking sustainable cities seriously*. Cambridge, MA: MIT Press.

Portz, J., Stein, L., and Jones, R. (2000). *City schools and politics*. Lawrence: University of Kansas Press.

Powers, C., Hoffman, F., Brown, D., and Conner, C. (2000). *Experiment: Brownfields pilots catalyze revitalization*. New Brunswick, NJ: Institute for Responsible Management.

President's Council on Sustainable America. (1996). *Sustainable America: A new consensus*. Washington, DC: U.S. Government Printing Office.

Rusk, D. (1999). *Inside game/outside game: Winning strategies for saving urban America*. Washington, DC: Brookings Institution Press.

Savitch, H., and Kantor, P. (2002). *Cities in the international marketplace: The political economy of urban development in North America and Western Europe*. Princeton, NJ: Princeton University Press.

Schneider, K. (1991, July 18). Industries and towns clash over who pays to tackle toxic waste. *New York Times*, p. A14.

Sierra Club. (2005). Superfund's 25th anniversary: Hundreds of toxic waste sites continue to threaten health and water supplies. Available at: http://www.sierraclub.org/toxics/superfund. Accessed July 10, 2006.

Simons, R. (1998). *Turning brownfields into greenbacks: Developing and financing environmentally contaminated real estate*. Washington, DC: Urban Land Institute.

Simons, R. (1999). How many brownfields are out there? An economic base contraction analysis of 31 U.S. cities. *Public Works Management and Policy, 2* (3), 267–273.

Sinderman, M. (1999). Jersey Gardens, retail's urban oasis. Available at: http://retailtrafficmag.com/ar/retail_jersey_gardensretails_urban. Accessed January 13, 2004.

Smith, N. (1991). *Uneven development: Nature, capital, and the production of space*. Cambridge, MA: Blackwell Publications.

Solitare, L., and Greenberg, M. (2002). Is the U.S. Environmental Protection Agency brownfield assessment pilot program environmentally just? *Environmental Health Perspectives, 110* (suppl. 2), 249–257.

Stoker, G. (1995). Regime theory and urban politics. In D. Judge, G. Stoker, and H. Wolman (Eds.), *Theories of Urban Politics* (54–71). Thousand Oaks, CA: Sage Publications.

Stoker, G., and Mossberger, K. (1994). Urban regime theory in comparative perspective. *Environment and Planning C: Government and Policy, 12,* 195–212.

Stone, C. (1989). *Regime politics: Governing Atlanta, 1946–1988*. Lawrence: University of Kansas Press.

Stone, C. (1993). Urban regime and the capacity to govern: A political economy approach. *Journal of Urban Affairs, 15* (1), 1–28.

Stroup, R. L. (1997). Superfund: The shortcut that failed. In T. L. Anderson (Ed.), *Breaking the environmental policy gridlock* (pp. 115–139). Stanford, CA: Hoover Institution Press.

Superfund Fact Sheet. (1981). *EPA Journal, 7* (6), 13.

Tomsho, R. (1991, April 2). Pollution ploy: Big corporations hit by Superfund cases find way to share bills. *Wall Street Journal,* pp. A13–A14.

Towers, G. (1995). *Building democracy: Community architecture in the inner cities.* London, England: UCL Press.

Urban Land Institute. (1998). *Smart growth: Economy, community, environment.* Washington, DC: Urban Land Institute.

U.S. Bureau of the Census. (1996). *Statistical abstract of the United States.* 116th ed. Washington, DC: U.S. Government Printing Office.

U.S. Conference of Mayors. (2000). *Recycling America's land.* Washington, DC. Available at: http://www.usmayors.org. Accessed July 1, 2001.

U.S. Conference of Mayors. (2003). *Recycling America's land, A national report on brownfields redevelopment,* vol. 4. Washington, DC. Available at: http://www.usmayors.org. Accessed July 9, 2005.

U.S. Environmental Protection Agency. (1995). *EPA pollution prevention accomplishments: 1994.* EPA-100-R-95–001. Washington, DC: U.S. EPA.

U.S. Environmental Protection Agency. (2003). Brownfields glossary of terms. Available at: http://www.epa.gov/brownfields/glossary.htm. Accessed August 28, 2003.

U.S. General Accounting Office. (1999). *Superfund: Information on the program's funding and status.* RCED-00–25. Washington, DC: USGAO.

Van Horn, C., Dixon, K., Lawler, G., and Segal, D. (1999). *Turning brownfields into jobfields.* New Brunswick, NJ: John J. Heldrich Center for Workforce Development.

Vogel, M. (1998, May 7). $200,000 awarded for "brownfields" conversion. *Buffalo News,* p. D1.

Zremski, J. (1995, July 11). Congress weighs salvaging industrial cleanup sites: Development may be spurred by easing laws on hazardous waste cleanup. *Buffalo News,* p. B7.

CHAPTER 2

Aldrich, T., and Sinks, T. (2002). Things to know and do about cancer clusters. *Cancer Investigation, 20* (5&6), 810–816.

American Cancer Society. (2004). ACS history. Available at: http://www.cancer.og/docroot/AA/content. Accessed January 19, 2006.

American Cancer Society. (2005). Costs of cancer. Available at: http://www.cancer.org/docroot/MIT/content/MIt_3_2x_costs_of_cancer.asp. Accessed January 19, 2006.

Atkin, C., and Wallack, L. (Eds.). (1990). *Mass communication and public health.* Newbury Park, CA: Sage Publications.

Bailar, J., and Gornik, H. (1997). Cancer undefeated. *New England Journal of Medicine, 336* (22), 1569–1574.

Bailer, J., King, H., and Mason, M. (1964). *Cancer rates and risks.* DHEW Pub. No. 1148. Washington, DC: U.S. Government Printing Office.

Berridge, V., and Loughlin, K. (2005). *Medicine, the market and the mass media: Producing health in the twentieth century.* New York: Routledge.

Brown, M. (1979). *Laying waste.* New York: Washington Square Press.

Burke, T., Gary, S., Krawiec, C., Katz, R., Preuss, P., and Paulson, G. (1980). An environmental investigation of clusters of leukemia and Hodgkin's disease in Rutherford, New Jersey. *Journal of the Medical Society of New Jersey, 77* (4), 260–264.

California Department of Health Services, Environmental Epidemiology Project. (1994). *Investigating non-infectious disease clusters.* Sacramento, CA.

Centers for Disease Control and Prevention. (1990). Guidelines for investigating disease clusters of health events. *Morbidity and Mortality Weekly Report, 39* (RR-11), 23 pp.

Centers for Disease Control and Prevention, National Center for Health Statistics. (2003). U.S. Mortality Public Use Tape, 2001.

Clustering of health events [editorial]. (1990). *American Journal of Epidemiology, 132* (suppl.), S1–S2.

Colditz, G., Samplin-Salgado, M., Ryan, C., Dart, H., Fisher, H., Tokuda, A., and Rockhill, B. (2002). Fulfilling the potential for cancer prevention: Policy approaches. *Cancer Causes and Control, 13* (3), 199–212.

Dean, G. (1961). Lung cancer among white South Africans. *British Medical Journal, 2,* 852, 1599.

Dennis, E. (1990). *Covering the environment.* New York: Gannett Center.

DeRouen, T., and Diem, J. (1975). The New Orleans drinking water controversy: A statistical perspective. *American Journal of Public Health, 65,* 1060–1062.

DeRouen, T., and Diem, J. (1977). Relationship between cancer mortality in Louisiana drinking water sources and other possible causative agents. In H. Hiatt, J. Watson, and J. Winsten (Eds.), *Proceedings of the Cold Spring Harbor Conferences on Cell Proliferation, Origins of Human Cancer* (pp. 21–32). Cold Spring Harbor, NY: Cold Spring Harbor Laboratory.

Doll, R., and Peto, R. (1981). *The causes of cancer.* New York: Oxford University Press.

Epstein, S. (2003). *Stop cancer before it starts: How to win the war against cancer.* Chicago, IL: The Cancer Prevention Coalition.

Epstein, S. (2005a). The American Cancer Society is threatening the National Cancer Program [press release]. Cancer Prevention Coalition. Available at: http://www.preventcancer.com/press/release/june12. Accessed January 19, 2006.

Epstein, S. (2005b). *Cancer-gate: How to win the losing cancer war.* Chicago, IL: Baywood Publishing.

Epstein, S. (2006). American Cancer Society: The world's largest "nonprofit" institution. Cancer Prevention Coalition. Available at: http://www.preventcancer.com/losing/acs/wealthiest-links.htm. Accessed January 19, 2006.

Flatow, I. (2005, July 20). Investigating cancer clusters. National Public Radio, Talk of the Nation/Science. Available at: http://www.mindfully.org/Health/Cancer-Clusters-NPR.htm. Accessed January 25, 2006.

Fortunato, J. (2005). *Making media: The influence of constituency groups on mass media content.* Mahwah, NJ: Lawrence Erlbaum Associates.

Graber, D. (2006). *Mass media and American politics.* 7th ed. Washington, DC: CQ Press.

Greenberg, M. (1983). *Urbanization and cancer mortality.* New York: Oxford University Press.

Greenberg, M., and Chess, C. (1992, Fall). Communicating environmental risk through the mass media. *Public Manager,* 45–48.

Greenberg, M., and Page, G., Jr. (1981). Planning with great uncertainty: A review and case study of the safe drinking water controversy. *Socio-Economic Planning Sciences, 15,* 65–74.

Greenberg, M., and Schneider, D. (1996). *Environmentally devastated neighborhoods: Perceptions, policies, and realities.* New Brunswick, NJ: Rutgers University Press.

Greenberg, M., and Wartenberg, D. (1990). Understanding mass media coverage of disease clusters. *American Journal of Epidemiology, 132* (suppl.), S192–S195.

Greenberg, M., and Wartenberg, D. (1991). Communicating to an alarmed community about cancer clusters: A fifty state survey. *Journal of Community Health, 16* (2), 71–82.

Haenszel, W., Loveland, D., and Sirken, M. (1962). Lung cancer mortality as related to residence and smoking histories: I. White males. *Journal of the National Cancer Institute, 28,* 947–1001.

Haenszel, W., and Taeuber, K. (1964). Lung cancer mortality as related to residence and smoking histories: II. White females. *Journal of the National Cancer Institute, 32,* 803–838.

Halperin, W., Altman, R., Stemhagen, A., Iaci, A., Caldwell, G., Mason, T., Bill, J., Abe, T., and Clark, J. (1980). Epidemiologic investigation of clusters of leukemia and Hodgkin's disease in Rutherford, New Jersey. *Journal of the Medical Society of New Jersey, 77* (4), 267–273.

Hammond, E., and Horn, D. (1958). Smoking and death rates. *Journal of the American Medical Association, 166,* 1294–1308.

Hance, B., Chess, C., and Sandman, P. (1990). *Industry risk communication manual.* Boca Raton, FL: Lewis Publishers.

Harr, J. (1995). *A civil action.* New York: Random House.

Harris, R. (1974). *Implications of cancer-causing substances in Mississippi River water.* Washington, DC: Environmental Defense Fund.

Higginson, J., and Muir, C. (1979). Environmental carcinogenesis: Misconceptions and limitations to cancer control. *Journal of the National Cancer Institute, 63,* 1291–1298.

Hileman, B. (1982). The chlorination question. *Environmental Science and Technology, 16,* 15A–18A.

Hueper, W. (1966). *Occupational and environmental cancers of the respiratory system.* New York: Springer-Verlag.

International Agency for Research on Cancer. (2004). IARC's mission: Cancer research for cancer control. Available at: http://www.iarc.fr/ENG. Accessed January 19, 2006.

Kaiser, J. (2002). Texas surgeon vows to take next step in beating cancer. *Science, 296* (5572), 1394–1395.

Kasperson, R., Renn, O., Slovic, P., Brown, H., Emel, J., Goble, R., Kasperson, J., and Ratick, S. (1988). The social amplification of risk: A conceptual framework. *Risk Analysis, 8* (2), 177–187.

Levin, D. (1974). *Cancer rates and risks.* DHEW Pub. No. (NIH) 75–691. Washington, DC: DHEW.

Levin, M. (1960). Cancer incidence in urban and rural areas of New York State. *Journal of the National Cancer Institute, 24,* 1243–1257.

Manos, N., and Fisher, G. (1959). An index of air pollution and its relation to health. *Journal of the Air Pollution Control Association, 9,* 5–11.

Mason, T., and McKay, F. (1974). *U.S. cancer mortality by county: 1950–1969.* DHEW Pub. No. (NIH) 74–615. Washington, DC: DHEW.

Mazur, A. (2004). *True warnings and false alarms: Evaluating fears about the health risks of technology, 1948–1971,* Washington, DC: Resources for the Future.

McComas, K. (2003). Public meetings and risk amplification: A longitudinal study. *Risk Analysis, 23* (6), 1257–1270.

McCombs, M. (2004). *Setting the agenda: The mass media and public opinion.* Malden, MA: Blackwell.

National Academy of Sciences. (1973). Conference on Health Effects of Air Pollution, October 3–5, 1973. *Summary of proceedings.* Prepared for the U.S. Senate Committee on Public Works. Washington, DC.

National Cancer Institute. (2006). Cancer facts and the war on cancer. Available at: http://training.seer.cancer.gov/module_cancer_disease/unit5_war_on_cancer.html. Accessed January 19, 2006.

National Research Council. (1978). *Epidemiological studies of cancer frequency and certain organic constituents of drinking water: A review of recent literature published and unpublished.* Springfield, VA: National Technical Information Service.

National Research Council, Committee on Risk Perception and Communication. (1989). *Improving risk communication.* Washington, DC: National Academy Press.

Organic Consumers Association. (2005). Is the American Cancer Society more interested in cancer profit than cancer prevention? Available at: http://www.organicconsumers.org/Politics/cancer. Accessed January 19, 2006.

Page, T., Harris, R., and Epstein, S. (1976). Drinking water and cancer mortality in Louisiana. *Science, 193,* 55–57.

Powell, D., and Leiss, W. (1997). *Mad cows and mother's milk: The perils of poor risk communication.* Montreal, Canada: McGill-Queens University Press.

President's Science Advisory Committee Panel on Chemicals. (1973). *Chemicals and health.* Washington, DC: U.S. Government Printing Office.

Prindle, R. (1959). Some considerations in the interpretation of air pollution health effect data. *Journal of the Air Pollution Control Association, 9,* 12–19.

Proctor, R. (1995) *Cancer wars: How politics shapes what we know and don't know about cancer.* New York: Basic Books.

Protess, D. (Ed.). (1991). *Agenda setting: Readings on media, public opinion, and policymaking.* Hillsdale, NJ: Lawrence Erlbaum Associates.

Rogers, G. (1997). The dynamics of risk perception: How does perceived risk respond to risk events? *Risk Analysis, 17* (6), 745–757.

Rogers, P. (1978). Address. In C. Russell (Ed.), *Safe drinking water: Current and future problems* (pp. 4–10). Washington, DC: Resources for the Future.

Rothman, K. (1990). A sobering start for the cluster busters' conference. *American Journal of Epidemiology, 132* (suppl.), S6–S13.

Rothman, K., and Greenland, S. (2005). Causation in and causal inference and epidemiology. *American Journal of Public Health, 95* (suppl. 1), S144–S150.

Sachsman, D., Greenberg, M., and Sandman, P. (1988). *The environmental reporter's handbook.* Newark, NJ: Hazardous Substances Management Research Center.

Sandman, P., Sachsman, D., Greenberg, M., and Gochfeld, M. (1987). *Environmental risk and the press.* New Brunswick, NJ: Transaction Books.

Schiffman, R., and Landau, E. (1961). Use of indexes of air pollution potential in mortality studies. *Journal of the Air Pollution Control Association, 11,* 384–386.

Schneiderman, M. (1978). Water and epidemiology. In C. Russell (Ed.), *Safe drinking water: Current and future problems* (111–148). Washington, DC: Resources for the Future.

Shackelford, W., and Keith, L. (1977). *Frequency of organic compounds identified in water.* EPA-600/4-76-062. Washington, DC: U.S. Environmental Protection Agency.

Sixth Advisory Group. (2003). Report of an ad-hoc IARC Monographs Advisory Group on priorities for future evaluations. IARC Internal Report No. 03/001. Lyon, France.

Slovic, P. (1993). Perceived risk, trust, and democracy. *Risk Analysis, 13* (6), 675–682.

Starr, P. (1982). *The social transformation of American medicine.* New York: Basic Books.

Stocks, P., and Campbell, J. (1955). Lung cancer death rates among non-smokers and pipe and cigarette smokers. *British Medical Journal, 2,* 923–928.

Tarone, G., and Gart, J. (1975). *Review of the* Implications of cancer-causing substances in Mississippi River water *by R. Harris.* Bethesda, MD: National Cancer Institute.

Tobey, J. (1932). *Cancer: What everyone should know about it.* New York: Alfred Knopf.

Toxicology Excellence for Risk Assessment. (2004). Peer consultation of NIEHS's contribution to IARC monograph programme. Unpublished memo.

Transparency at IARC [editorial]. (2003), *Lancet, 361* (9353), 189.

U.S. Department of Health and Human Services. (2006). HHS budget. Available at: http://www.hhsgov/budgeet/06budget. Accessed January 19, 2006.

U.S. Department of Health and Human Services. (1996). *Healthy people 2000.* Washington, D.C.: U.S. Department of Health and Human Services.

U.S. Department of Health, Education, and Welfare, Public Health Service. (1974). *Facts of life and death.* Washington, DC: U.S. Government Printing Office.

Wargo, J. (1996). *Our children's toxic legacy: How science and law fail to protect us from pesticides.* New Haven, CT: Yale University Press.

Warner, S., and Aldrich, T. (1988). The status of cancer cluster investigations undertaken by state health departments. *American Journal of Public Health, 78* (3), 306–307.

Weitz, R. (2001). *The sociology of health, illness, and health care.* Belmont, CA: Wadsworth Press.

Wilkins, J., III, Reaches, N., and Kruse, C. (1979). Organic chemical contaminants in drinking water and cancer. *American Journal of Epidemiology, 110,* 420–448.

Wynder, E., and Gori, G. (1977). Contribution of the environment to cancer incidence: An epidemiologic exercise. *Journal of the National Cancer Institute, 58,* 825–832.

Wynder, E., and Hammond, E. (1962). A study of air pollution carcinogenesis. II. Analysis of epidemiological evidence. *Cancer, 15,* 79–92.

CHAPTER 3

American Public Health Association. (2005). In defense of science. *American Journal of Public Health* (special issue), *95* (suppl. 1), S1–S150.

Bohm, M., and Hirschhorn, J. (1999, November). *The national debate about the gasoline additive MTBE.* Issue Brief 12. Washington, DC: National Governors Association.

Brinkley, D. (2003). *Wheels for the world: Henry Ford, his company, and a century of progress.* New York: Penguin.

Brown, L., Renner, M., and Halweil, B. (2000). *Vital signs 2000:* The environmental trends that are shaping our future. New York: Norton.

Brownson, R., Boehmer, T., and Luke, D. (2005). Declining rates of physical activity in the United States: What are the contributors? *Annual Review of Public Health, 26,* 421–443.

Coburn, J. (2004). Confronting the challenges in reconnecting urban planning and public health. *American Journal of Public Health, 94* (4), 541–546.

Committee on Technical Bases for Yucca Mountain Standards. (1995). *Technical bases for Yucca Mountain standards.* Washington, DC: National Academy Press.

Committee on the Future of Personal Transport Vehicles in China. (2003). *Personal cars and China.* Washington, DC: National Academy Press.

Demographia, Inc. (2006). United States: Urbanized areas & core cities: 1950 to 2000. Available at: http://www.demographia.com/db-uza-us1950.htm. Accessed May 10, 2006.

Fiedler, N., Kelly-McNeil, K., Mohr, S., and Lehr, P. (2000). Controlled human exposure to methyl tertiary butyl ether in gasoline: Symptoms, psychophysiologic and neurobehavioral responses of self-reported sensitive persons. *Environmental Health Perspectives, 108* (8), 753–763.

Frank, L., Engelke, P., and Schmid, T. (2003). *Health and community design: the impact of the built environment.* Washington, DC: Island Press.

Fri, R. (1995, Summer). Using science soundly: The Yucca Mountain standard. *Resources,* 15–18.

Frumkin, H., Frank, L., and Jackson, R. (2004). *Urban sprawl and public health: Designing, planning, and building for healthy communities.* Washington, DC: Island Press.

Gettinger, S., and Hosansky, D. (1994). Oil state senator tosses match into gasoline additive debate. *Congressional Quarterly Weekly Report, 52* (28), 1940.

Giles-Corti, B., and Donovan, R. (2002). The relative influence of individual, social, and physical environmental determinants of physical activity. *Social Science and Medicine, 54,* 1793–1812.

Goldstein, B. (2001). Precautionary principle and public health. *American Journal of Public Health, 91* (9), 1358–1361.

Government Accountability Office. (2005). *Gasoline markets: Special gasoline blends reduce emissions and improve air quality, but complicate supply and contribute to higher prices* [abstract]. Washington, DC: GAO.

Gray, G., Baskin, S., Charnley, G., Cohen, J., Gold, L., Kerkuliet, N., Koening, H., Lewis, S., McClain, R., Rhomberg, L., Snyder, J., and Weekley, B. (2001). The Annapolis accords on the use of toxicology in risk assessment and decision-making: An Annapolis Center workshop report. *Toxicology Methods, 11,* 225–231.

Gray, G., Cohen, J., Cunha, G., Hughes, C., McConnell, E., Rhomberg, L., Sipes, I., and Mattison, D. (2004). Weight of the evidence evaluation of low-dose reproductive and development effects of bisphenol A. *Human and Ecological Risk Assessment, 10* (5), 875–922.

Greenberg, M., Popper, F., West, B., and Krueckeberg, D. (1994). Linking city planning and public health in the United States. *Journal of Planning Literature, 8* (3), 235–239.

Harder, B. (2003). The next MTBE: Contamination from fuel additives could spread. *Science News, 164* (22), 342.

Is airborne manganese a hazard? (1998). *Environmental Health Perspectives, 106* (2), A57–A58.

Jaroff, L. (1991, August 26). Crisis in the labs. *Time,* 45–51.

Joselow, M., Tobias, E., Koehler, R., Coleman, S., Bogden, J., and Gause, D. (1978). Manganese pollution in the city environment and its relationship to traffic density. *American Journal of Public Health, 68* (6), 557–560.

Kaiser, J. (2003). Manganese: A high-octane dispute. *Science, 300,* 926–928.

Katz, J. (1994). Home state interests prevail as ethanol rule squeaks by. *Congressional Quarterly Report, 52* (31), 2259–2260.

Krimsky, S., and Plough, A. (1987). The emergence of risk communication studies: Social and political context. *Science, Technology, and Human Values, 12* (3/4), 4–10.

Landrigan, P. (2001). MMT, déjà vu, and national security. *American Journal of Industrial Medicine, 39,* 434–435.

Lavizzo-Mourey, R., and McGinnis, J. (2003). Making the case for active living communities. *American Journal of Public Health, 93* (9), 1386–1388.

Lowrance, W. (1976). *Of acceptable risk: Science and the determination of safety.* Los Altos, CA: Kaufmann.

Marshall, E. (1984). EPA to repair leaks in leaded gasoline rules. *Science, 225* (4662), 605.

Marshall, E. (1993). Reinventing the automobile — and government R&D. *Science, 262* (5131), 172.

McCarthy, J. (2004). Clean Air Act issues in the 108th Congress. Congressional Research Service Issue Brief for Congress IB1010713. Available at: http://www.earthscape.org/p1/ES15767. Accessed February 13, 2006.

McCarthy, J. (2005, April 22). Clean Air Act issues in the 109th Congress. Washington, DC: Congressional Research Service Issue Brief for Congress, pp. 1–12.

McCarthy, J., and Tiemann, M. (2005, August 17). MTBE in gasoline: Clean air and drinking water issues. Washington, DC: Congressional Research Service Report for Congress, pp. 1–24.

McShane, C. (1994). *Down the asphalt path: The automobile and the American city.* New York: Columbia University Press.

Medlin, J. (2000). MTBE's effects: A sensitive issue. *Environmental Health Perspectives, 108* (8), A371.

Menkes, D., and Fawcett, J. (1997). Too easily lead? Health effects of gasoline additives. *Environmental Health Perspectives, 105* (3), 270–273.

Moffat, A. (1991). Methanol-powered cars get ready to hit the road, *Science, 251* (4993), 514–515.

MTBE: "Stealth" lobby stokes fuel additive debate. (1997, June 16). National Journal, Inc. News Features. Available at: http://nationaljournal.com/members/news/june/0616gw.htm. Accessed May 17, 2006.

Muller, P. (1981). *Contemporary suburban America.* Englewood Cliffs, NJ: Prentice-Hall.

Nadim, F., Zack, P., Hoag, G., and Liu, S. (2000, July). United States experience with gasoline additives. *Energy Policy, 29,* 1–5.

Ozonoff, D. (1985). "One man's meat, another man's poison": Two chapters in the history of public health. *American Journal of Public Health, 75* (4), 338–340.

Patton, D., and Olin, S. (2006). Scientific peer review to inform regulatory decision making: Leadership responsibilities and cautions. *Risk Analysis, 26* (1), 5–19.

Puplava, J. (2005). There is no plan "B." *Financial Sense Online.* Available at: http://www. financialsense.com/stormwatch/2005/1014.html. Accessed May 10, 2006.

Pytte, A. (1990). A decade's acrimony lifted in the glow of clean air. *Congressional Quarterly Weekly Report, 48* (43), 3587–3592.

Rosner, D., and Markowitz, G. (1985). A "gift of God"? The public health controversy over leaded gasoline during the 1920s. *American Journal of Public Health, 75* (4), 344–352.

Russell, A., St. Pierre, D., and Milford, J. (1990). Ozone control and methanol fuel use. *Science, 247* (4939), 201–205.

Sandman, P. (1989, November). Risky business. *Natural Resources and Environmental Administration,* 6–7.

Sandman, P. (1993). *Responding to community outrage: Strategies for effective risk communication.* Fairfax, VA: AIHA Press.

Schlesinger, J. (2005, November 16). Statement before the Committee on Foreign Relations, United States Senate. Washington, DC.

Schuck, P. (1986). *Agent orange on trial: Mass toxic disasters in the courts.* Cambridge, MA: Harvard University Press.

Scientists find MTBE degrades naturally. (1999). *Environmental Health Perspectives, 107* (11), A551–A552.

Service, R. (2002). Science invades the Magic Kingdom. *Science, 296,* 462–463.

Silbergeld, E. (1995). Annotation: Protection of the public interest, allegations of scientific misconduct, and the Needleman case. *American Journal of Public Health, 85* (2), 165–166.

Sun, M. (1985). EPA accelerates ban on leaded gas. *Science, 227* (4693), 1448.

Tenenbaum, D. (2000). Moving beyond MTBE. *Environmental Health Perspectives, 108* (8), 351.

U.S. Bureau of the Census. (2006). *Statistical abstract of the United States: 2006.* Washington, DC: U.S. Government Printing Office.

U.S. Environmental Protection Agency. (1995). Origin of the Reformulated Gasoline Program. Available at: http://www.epa.gov/otaq/rfgorig.htm. Accessed May 22, 2006.

U.S. Environmental Protection Agency. (2004). Methyl tertiary butyl ether (MTBE). Available at: http://www.epa.gov/mtbe. Accessed May 22, 2006.

Weinstein, J. (1995). *Individual justice in mass tort litigation: The effect of class actions, consolidations, and other multiparty devices.* Evanston, IL: Northwestern University Press.

Wheals, A., Basso, L., Alves, D., and Amorim, H. (1999). Fuel ethanol after 25 years. *Trends in Biotechnology, 17,* 482–487.

Yacobucci, B. (2004, December 17). "Boutique fuels" and reformulated gasoline: Harmonization of fuel standards. Washington, D.C.: Congressional Research Service Report for Congress, pp. 1–13.

Yacobucci, B., and Womach, J. (2002, February 21). Fuel ethanol: Background and public policy issues. Washington, DC: Congressional Research Service Report for Congress, pp. 1–19.

CHAPTER 4

Alexander, T. (1994). Stewardship and enterprise: The LDS Church and the Wasatch oasis environment, 1847–1930. *Western Historical Quarterly, 25* (3), 340–364.

American Association of Petroleum Geologists. (2001). Policy statement: Federal land withdrawals. Available at: http://dpa.aapg.org/gac/papers/fed_land_wdrawals.cfm. Accessed June 26, 2006.

Baker, B. (1999). U.S. Forest Service program builds bridges between government and public. *Bioscience, 49* (1), 18–19.

Barrett, C., and Grizzle, R. (1999). A holistic approach to sustainability based on pluralism stewardship. *Environmental Ethics, 21* (1), 23–42.

Bengston, D., and Fan, D. (1999). An innovative method for evaluating strategic goals in a public agency. *Evaluation Review, 23* (1), 77–100.

Brauer, J. (1995). U.S. military nuclear production sites: Do they attract or reject jobs? *Medicine and Global Survival, 2,* 35–44.

Brown, K. (1998). The great DOE land rush? *Science, 282,* 616–617.

Burger, J., Greenberg, M., Powers, C., and Gochfeld, M. (2004). Reducing the footprint of contaminated lands: U.S. Department of Energy sites as a case study. *Risk Management: An International Journal, 64* (4), 41–63.

Burger, J., Leschine, T., Greenberg, M., Karr, J., Gochfeld, M., and Powers, C. (2003). Shifting priorities at the Department of Energy's bomb factories: Protecting human and ecological health. *Environmental Management, 31* (2), 157–167.

Bush, G. (2004). Federal real property asset management. Available at: http://nodis3.gsfc.nasa.gov/displayEO.cfm?id=EO_13327. Accessed January 5, 2007.

Bzdok, C. (2007, January 12). Petition to intervene in administrative proceeding. State of Michigan, Department of Environmental Quality, Remediation and Redevelopment Division. RDD Order No. III-**-02. Copy of petition.

Constance, D., and Bonanno, A. (1999). Contested terrain of the global fisheries: "Dolphin-safe" tuna, the Panama Declaration, and the Marine Stewardship Council. *Rural Sociology, 64* (4), 597–623.

Dembeck, C. (2002. October 21). Army leaders look to private sector to revitalize underused depots. *Federal Times,* p. 1.

DeSouza, N. (1985). The social understanding of stewardship and mission. In N. Murphy (Ed.), *Teaching and preaching stewardship: An anthology* (158–168). New York: National Council of Churches.

Ecology Center. (2002, December 2). Citizens demand right to be heard in proposed "sweetheart deal" for DOE. *Ecology Center News.* Press release. Available at: http://www.ecocenter.org/releases/20021202dow.html. Accessed January 15, 2007.

Erikson, K. (1994). *A new species of trouble: Explorations in disaster, trauma, and community.* New York: Norton.

Fagan, B. (1995). Enlightened stewardship. *Archaeology, 48,* 12–14.

Fahrenthold, D. (2004, July 8). Chesapeake Lighthouses will undergo restoration. *Washington Post,* p. PG07.

Gaspar, C., and Van Burik, D. (1998). *Local government use of institutional controls at contaminated sites.* Washington, DC: International City/County Management Association.

General Accounting Office. (2002). *Military base closures: Progress in completing actions from prior realignments and closures.* GAO-02-433. Washington, DC: GAO.

Gill, B. (1996). *Stewardship: The biblical basis for living.* Arlington, TX: Summit.

Gorte, R., and Baldwin, P. (1999). RL30126: Federal land ownership: Constitutional authority; the history of acquisition, disposal, and retention; and current acquisition and disposal authorities. Available at: http://digital.library.unt.edu/govdocs/crs//data/1999/upl-meta-crs-1009/RL30126_1999. Accessed January 5, 2007.

Graf, W. (1990). *Wilderness preservation and the Sagebrush Rebellions.* Savage, MD, Rowman and Littlefield.

Greenberg, M., Lewis, D., Frisch, M., Lowrie, K., and Mayer, H. (2002). The U.S. Department of Energy's regional economic legacy: Spatial dimensions of a half-century of dependency. *Socio-Economic Planning Sciences, 36,* 109–125.

Greenberg, M., Lowrie, K., Burger, J., Powers, C., Gochfeld, M., and Mayer, H. (2007a). Nuclear waste and public worries: Public perceptions of the United States major nuclear weapons legacy sites. *Human Ecology Review, 14* (1), 1–12.

Greenberg, M., Lowrie, K., Burger, J., Powers, C., Gochfeld, M., and Mayer, H. (2007b). Preferences for alternative risk management policies at the United States major nuclear weapons legacy sites. *Journal of Environmental Planning and Management, 50* (2), 187–209.

Greenberg, M., Lowrie, K., Krueckeberg, D., Mayer, H., and Simon, D. (1997). Bombs and butterflies: A case study of the challenges of post–cold war environmental planning and management for the U.S. nuclear weapons sites. *Environmental Planning and Management, 40* (6), 739–750.

Greenberg, M., Mayer, M., and Lewis, D. (2004, Spring). Life-cycle cost in a highly uncertain economic environment: The case of managing the U.S. Department of Energy's nuclear waste legacy. *Federal Facilities Environmental Journal,* 67–82.

Greenberg, M., Miller, K., Frisch, M., and Lewis, D. (2003). Facing an uncertain economic future: Environmental management spending and rural regions surrounding the U.S. DOE's nuclear weapons facilities. *Defence and Peace Economics, 14* (1), 85–97.

Hall, D. (1990). *The steward: A biblical symbol come of age.* New York: Friendship.

Hanford cleanup to take four years longer than planned. (2005, December 1). *Greenwire.* Available at: http://www.eenews.net. Accessed January 5, 2007.

Hansen, K. (2004). *The greening of Pentagon brownfields: Using N-terminal discourse to redevelop former military bases.* Lanham, MD: Lexington.

Hogan, M. (1987). *The Marshall Plan: America, Britain, and the reconstruction of Western Europe, 1947–1952.* New York: Cambridge University Press.

Huntoon, C. (2000, March 21). Statement before the Subcommittee on Energy and Water Development, Committee on Appropriations, U.S. House of Representatives. Unpublished talk, Washington, DC.

Ireland, D. (1992). *Stewardship and the Kingdom of God: An historical, exegetical, and contextual study of the parable of the unjust steward in Luke 16: 1–13.* New York: Brill.

Janofsky, M. (2003, May 23). U.S.-Utah land accord incites unlikely critics. *New York Times.* Available at: http://query.nytimes.com/gst/fullpage.html. Accessed January 5, 2007.

Kamps, L. (2001, February 15). Environmental racism, tribal sovereignty, and nuclear waste. Nuclear Information and Resource Service. Available at: http://www.nirs.org/factshetts/pfsejfactsheet. Accessed January 15, 2005.

Killian, L. (1998). *The freshmen: What happened to the Republican revolution?* Boulder, CO: Westview.

Launius, R. (1995). A Western Mormon in Washington, DC: James C. Fletcher, NASA, and the final frontier. *Pacific Historical Review, 64,* 217–241.

Lawrence, G., Vanclay, F., and Furze, B. (Eds.). (1992). *Agriculture, environment, and society.* Melbourne, Australia: Macmillan.

Lewis, D., Frisch, M., and Greenberg, M. (2004). Downsizing and worker separations: Modeling the regional economic impacts of alternative Department of Energy workforce adjustment policies. *Regional Studies, 38* (1), 67–83.

Loomis, J. (2002). *Integrated public lands management.* 2nd ed. New York: Columbia University Press.

Lowrie, K., and Greenberg, M. (2001). Can David and Goliath get along? Federal land in local places. *Environmental Management, 28* (6), 703–711.

Marshall, S. (1996). Chemical weapons disposal and environmental justice. Chemical Weapons Working Group. Available at: http://www.cwwg.org/EJ.html. Accessed January 21, 2005.

Mitchell, R., Payne, B., and Dunlap, R. (1989). *Stigma and radioactive waste: Theory, assessment, and some empirical findings from Hanford, Washington.* Report No. 78. Worcester, MA: CENTED (Center for Technology, Environment, and Development).

Mollison, R., and Eddy, R. (1982, Winter). The Sagebrush Rebellion: A simple response to the complex problems of federal land management. *Harvard Journal on Legislation, 19,* 121–126.

Montgomery, S. (2003). Data file. *CQ Weekly, 61* (6), 1.

National Governors Association. (1996). NR-17. Land management and land use policy. Available at:http://www.nga.org/portal/site/nga/menuitem.8358ec82fb198d18a27 811050101oa0. Accessed June 26, 2006.

Nelson, R. (2001). *From waste to wilderness: Maintaining biodiversity on nuclear-bomb-building sites.* Washington, DC: Competitive Enterprise Institute.

Probst, K., and Lowe, A. (2000). *Cleaning up the nuclear weapons complex: Does anybody care?* Washington, DC: Resources for the Future.

Public Land Law Review Commission. (1970). *One third of the nation's land: A report to the president and to the Congress.* Washington, DC: U.S. Government Printing Office.

Purcell, R. (1998). Values for value: Integrity and stewardship. *Vital Speeches of the Day, 64* (24), 763–766.

Reagan, R. (1982, March 1). Federal real property. *Federal Register, 47,* 8547. Executive Order 12348, signed February 25, 1982.

Reisch, M. (1999). Chemical companies embrace environmental stewardship. *Chemical and Engineering News, 77* (49), 55–63.

Rescher, N. (2000). *Realistic pragmatism.* Albany: State University of New York Press.

Reumann, J. (1992). *Stewardship and the economy of God.* Grand Rapids, MI: Eerdmans.

Russell, L. (1985). Partnership in stewardship: Creation and redemption. In N. Murphy (Ed.), *Teaching and preaching stewardship: An anthology* (2–8). New York: National Council of Churches.

Russell, M. (1998). Toward a productive divorce: Separating DOE cleanups from transition assistance. *Annual Review of Energy and the Environment, 23,* 439–463.

Russell, M. (2000). *Reducing the nuclear legacy burden: DOE environmental management strategy and implementation.* Knoxville, TN: Joint Institute for Energy and Environment.

Science and Technology: From poachers to gamekeepers. (1998). *Economist, 348* (8082), 64.

Seastone, D. (1970). Regional dependency effect of federal land ownership. *Land Economics, 46* (4), 394–403.

Seelye, K. (2003, August 12). Bush nominates Utah governor to lead environmental agency. *New York Times,* p. A1.

Slovic, P. (2000). *The perception of risk.* London, England: Earthscan.

Smelcer, J. (1996). Two conservation myths from Alaska Native oral tradition. *Literary Review, 39* (4), 478–480.

Smith, A., Sciortino, S., Goeden, H., and Wright, C. (1996). Consideration of background exposures in the management of hazardous waste sites: A new approach to risk assessment. *Risk Analysis, 16* (5), 619–625.

Sorenson, D. (1998). *Shutting down the cold war: The politics of military base closure.* New York: St. Martin's Press.

State of Michigan, Department of Environmental Quality. (2006). What you need to know if you own or purchase property with environmental contamination. Available at: http://www.michigan.gov/deq. Accessed January 7, 2007.

Summary of Public Land Law Review Commission's recommendations. (1970). *Journal of Forestry, 68* (1), 468–474.

Sussex, A. (1997). Hanford: America's cold war legacy. Available at: http://www.mmmfiles.com/archive/hanford.htm. Accessed May 17, 2005.

Thompson, P., Matthews, R., and Van Ravenswaay, E. (1994). *Ethics, public policy, and agriculture.* New York: Macmillan.

Top-to-Bottom Review Team. (2002). *A review of the Environmental Management Program: United States Department of Energy.* Washington, DC: U.S. Department of Energy.

Udall, M. (1979, October). The "Sagebrush" Rebellion. *Congressman's Report, 17* (4). Available at: http://www.library.arizona.edu/exhibits/Udal/congrept/96th/7910.html. Accessed January 18, 2007.

U.S. Department of Energy. (1994). *Stewards of a national resource.* FM-0002. Washington, DC: DOE.

U.S. Department of Energy. (1997). *Accelerated cleanup: Focused on 2006.* Discussion draft. Washington, DC: DOE, OEM.

U.S. Department of Energy, Grand Junction Office. (1999a). *Long-term surveillance and monitoring program, 1998 report.* Grand Junction, CO: DOE, Grand Junction Office.

U.S. Department of Energy, Grand Junction Office. (1999b). *Long-term surveillance and monitoring program, fact sheet.* Grand Junction, CO: DOE, Grand Junction Office.

U.S. Department of Energy, Office of Environmental Management. (1995a). *Baseline environmental management report.* Washington, DC: U.S. Government Printing Office.

U.S. Department of Energy, Office of Environmental Management. (1995b). *Closing the circle on splitting the atom.* Washington, DC: DOE/EM.

U.S. Department of Energy, Office of Environmental Management. (2001). *Developing the report to Congress on long-term stewardship.* Washington, DC: U.S. Government Printing Office.

U.S. Department of Energy, Savannah River Operations Office. (2000). *Savannah River site strategic plan: 21st-century stewards for the nation.* Aiken, SC: DOE, Savannah River.

U.S. Environmental Protection Agency, Office of Solid Waste and Emergency Response, Federal Facilities Restoration and Reuse Office, Federal Facilities Environmental Restoration Dialogue Committee. (1996). *Final report: Consensus principles and recommendations for improving federal facilities cleanup.* Washington, DC: EPA.

U.S. House of Representatives, Committee on Commerce. (2000). *Incinerating cash: The Department of Energy's failure to develop and utilize innovative technologies to clean up the nuclear weapons legacy.* Washington, DC. Available at: http://www.mindfully.org/NVCS/DOE_incinerating_cash.htm.

Van Seters, A. (1985). The eye of the needle: Stewardship faithfulness today. In N. Murphy (Ed.), *Teaching and preaching stewardship: An anthology* (126–157). New York: National Council of Churches.

Walker, B. (2004, April 20). Bush administration again seeks exemptions for cleanup of toxic rocket fuel. Available at: http://www.ewg.org/issues/perchlorate. Accessed January 21, 2005.

Wilkinson, L. (Ed.). (1991). *Earthkeeping in the 90s: Stewardship of creation.* Grand Rapids, MI.: Eerdmans.

Winn, A. (1985). Holding the Earth in trust. In N. Murphy (Ed.), *Teaching and preaching stewardship: An anthology* (210–216). New York: National Council of Churches.

Woolford, J. (1999, October 26). EPA's national perspective on long-term stewardship. Paper presented at the SSAB (Site Specific Advisory Board) Workshop on Stewardship. Oak Ridge, TN.

CHAPTER 5

Africa Fighting Malaria. (2006). Available at: http://www.fightingmalaria.org/research.php?Category=Malaria%20Vector%20Control. Accessed June 7, 2006.

Agriculture could feed 40 billion. (1988, November 19). *Washington Post,* p. C15.

Alford, W. (2000, August). The more law, the more . . . ? Measuring legal reform in the People's Republic of China. Center for Research on Economic Development and Policy Reform. Working Paper no. 59. Stanford University. http://credpr.stanford.edu/publications/abstracts.html#58. Accessed May 23, 2006.

Anderton, D., Anderson, A., Oakes, J., and Fraser, M. (1994). Environmental equity: The demographics of dumping. *Demography, 31,* 229–248.

Ayres, R. (1998). *The turning point: The end of the growth paradigm*. London, England: Earthscan.

Barrett, J. (2006). The science of soy: What do we really know? *Environmental Health Perspectives, 114* (6), A353–A358.

Bate, R. (2003). POPs convention. Competitive Enterprise Institute: International Policy. Available at: http://www.cei.org/pdf/2318.pdf. Accessed June 7, 2006.

Becker, W. (2000). Neighbors in time: Development and use of some values for intergenerational justice from Jewish and Christian religious traditions. *Risk Analysis, 20* (6), 801–820.

Bernauer, T. (Ed.). (2003). *Genes, trade, and regulation: The seeds of conflict in food biotechnology*. Princeton, NJ: Princeton University Press.

Blackstone, W. (Ed.). (1972). *Philosophy and environmental crisis*. Athens: University of Georgia Press.

Bouman, H., Becker, P., Coopan, R. and Reinecke, A. (1992). Transfer of DDT used in malaria control to infants via breast milk. *Bulletin of the World Health Organization, 70*, 241–250.

Bryant, B., and Mohai, P. (1992). *Race and the incidence of environmental hazards: A time for discourse*. Boulder, CO: Westview.

Bullard, R., and Chavis, B. (Eds.). (1993). *Confronting environmental racism: Voices from the grassroots*. Boston, MA: South End.

Burros, M. (1993, June 27). U.S. will focus on reducing pesticides in food production. *New York Times*. Available at: query.nytimes.com/gst/fullapge.html. Accessed May 23, 2006.

Carson, R. (1962). *Silent spring*. Boston, MA: Houghton Mifflin Company.

Commission for Racial Justice. (1987). *Toxic wastes and race in the United States: A national report on the racial and socioeconomic characteristics of communities with hazards*. New York: United Church of Christ.

Commoner, B. (1971). *Closing the circle*. New York: Knopf.

Conway, G. (1997). *The doubly green revolution*. New York: Penguin Books.

Crocker, D. (2004). Cross-cultural criticism and development ethics. *Philosophy & Public Policy Quarterly, 24* (3), 2–8.

Daily, G., Ehrlich, A., and Ehrlich, P. (1994). Optimum population size. Available at: http://dieoff.org/page99.htm. Accessed May 23, 2006.

DaMotta, R. (Ed.). (2001). *Environmental economics and policy making in developing countries*. Cheltenham, England: Edward Elgar.

Dooge, J., Goodman, G., Rivière, J., Marton-Lefèvre, J., O'Riordan, T., and Praderie, F. (Eds.). (1992). *An agenda for science for environment and development into the 21st century*. New York: Cambridge University Press.

Ehrlich, P. (1968). *The population bomb*. New York: Ballantine.

Ehrlich, P., and Ehrlich, A. (1991). *Healing the planet*. New York: Addison Wesley.

Food and Agriculture Organization of the United Nations. (2000). Towards 2015/30. Technical interim report. Available at: http://www.ucsusa.org/food_and_environment/genetic_engineering/world-food-supply.html. Accessed May 23, 2006.

Food and Agriculture Organization of the United Nations. (2006a). New code of conduct on pesticides adopted. Available at: http://www.fao.org/english/newsroom/news/2002/10525-en.html. Accessed June 6, 2006.

Food and Agriculture Organization of the United Nations. (2006b). Unused pesticides in developing countries: 100,000 tonnes threaten health and environment. *FAO News and Highlights*. Available at: http://www.fao.org/news/1996/960607-E.HTM. Accessed June 6, 2006.

Foundation for Advancements in Science and Education. (1998). Exporting risk: Pesticide exports from U.S. ports, 1995–1996. Research report. Available at: http://www.fasenet.org/pesticide_report95–96.pdf. Accessed June 6, 2006.

Gaskell, G., Allum, N., Wagner, W., Kronberger, N., Torgersen, H., Hampel, J., and Bardes, J. (2004). GM foods and the misperception of risk perception. *Risk Analysis, 24* (1), 185–194.

Greenberg, M. (1993). Proving environmental equity in siting locally unwanted land uses. *Risk Issues in Health and Safety, 4,* 235–252.

Hall, D., and Moffitt, L. (Eds.). (2002). *Economics of pesticides, sustainable food production, and organic food markets.* St. Louis, MO: Elsevier.

Hardin, G. (1974). Lifeboat ethics: The case against helping the poor. *Psychology Today, 8* (4), 38–43.

Hugo, A. (Ed.). (1971). *Justice and equality.* Englewood Cliffs, NJ: Prentice Hall.

Kiely, T., Donaldson, D., and Grube, A. (2004). *Pesticide industry sales and usage: 2000 and 2001 market estimates.* Washington, DC: U.S. Environmental Protection Agency.

Leopold, L. (1949). *A Sand County almanac.* New York: Oxford University Press.

Livi-Bacci, M. (1997). *A concise history of world population.* 2nd ed. Cambridge, MA: Blackwell.

Lupien, J. (1999). Food perspectives and food demand beyond 2000. Available at: http://www.worldfoodscience.org/cms. Accessed June 6, 2006.

Malthus, T. (1798). An essay on the principles of population. Available at: http://www.ac.wwu.edu/stephan/malthus/malthus.0.html. Accessed June 6, 2006.

McConnell, R., and Hruska, A. (1993). An epidemic of pesticide poisoning in Nicaragua: Implications for prevention in developing countries. *American Journal of Public Health, 83* (11), 1559–1562.

McKibben, W. (1989). *The end of nature.* New York: Random House.

Meadows, D., Meadows, D., Randers, J., and Behrens, W. (1972). *Limits to growth.* Universe, NY: Club of Rome.

Nash, R. (1989). *The rights of nature: A history of environmental ethics.* Madison: University of Wisconsin Press.

Nash-Zurich, J. (2000, July 31). Grains of hope. *Time.* Available at: jcgi.pathfinder.com/time/archive.html. Accessed June 6, 2006.

National Research Council, Committee on Scientific and Regulatory Issues Underlying Pesticide Use, Patterns, and Agricultural Innovation. (1987). *Regulating pesticides in food: The Delaney paradox.* Washington, DC: National Academy Press.

Nelson, G., and Chassy, B. (2000). Meeting the demand for food/feeding the hungry: Are GMOs the answer? Available at: web.aces.uiuc.edu/wf/tutorials/gmo. Accessed May 23, 2006.

Oleskey, C., Fleischman, A., Goldman, L., Hirschhorn, K., Landrigan, P., Lappe, M., Marshall, M., Needleman, H., Rhodes, R., and McCally, M. (2004). Pesticide testing in humans: Ethics and public policy. *Environmental Health Perspectives, 112* (8), 914–919.

Paarlberg, R. (2000). The global food fight. *Foreign Affairs, 79* (3), 24–38.

Pardo, R., Midden, C., and Miller, J. (2002). Attitudes toward biotechnology in the European Union. *Journal of Biotechnology, 98,* 9–24.

Partridge, E. (Ed.). (1981). *Responsibilities to future generations: Environmental ethics.* New York: Prometheus.

Pearson, C. (Ed.). (1987). *Multinational corporations, environment, and the Third World.* Durham, NC: Duke University Press.

Pesticide Action Network UK. (1998a). *Desert locust control in Africa.* Pest Management Notes No. 4. London, U.K. Available at: www.pan_UK.org.

Pesticide Action Network UK. (1998b). *Prior informed consent.* Pest Management Notes No. 5. London, U.K. Available at: www.pan_UK.org.

Pesticide Action Network UK. (2005a). The list of lists. Briefing paper. Available at: http://www.pan-uk.org/briefing/list%20of%20lists%202005.pdf. Accessed June 7, 2006.

Pesticide Action Network UK. (2005b). Pesticides: More sales, more trade — and more hazards? Available at: http://www.pan-uk.org/pestnews/Pn32/pn32p16a.htm. Accessed June 7, 2006.

Pidgeon, N., Poortinga, W., Rowe, G., Horlick-Jones, T., Walls, J., and O'Riordan, T. (2005). Using surveys in public participation processes for risk-decision-making: The case of the 2003 GM nation? *Risk Analysis, 25* (20), 467–479.

Rawls, J. (1971). *A theory of justice.* Cambridge, MA: Harvard University Press.

Recena, M., Pires, D., and Caldras, E. (2006). Acute poisoning with pesticides in the state of Mato Grosso do Sul, Brazil. *Science of the Total Environment, 357,* 88–95.

Rosenberg, T. (2004, April 11). What the world needs now is DDT. *New York Times,* p. 38.

Runge, C., and Senauer, B. (2000). A removable feast. *Foreign Affairs, 79* (3), 39–51.

Schmidt, C. (1998). Natural-born killers. *Environmental Health Perspectives, 106* (9), A432–A437.

Setchell, K. (2006). Assessing risks and benefits of genistein and soy. *Environmental Health Perspectives, 114* (6), A332–A333.

Shrader-Frechette, K. (1981). *Environmental ethics, human health, and sustainable development.* Pacific Grove, CA: Boxwood.

Shrader-Frechette, K. (1991). *Risk and rationality.* Berkeley, CA: University of California Press.

Simon, J. (1990). *People, resources, environment, and immigration.* New Brunswick, NJ: Transaction.

Simon, J., Powers, C., and Gunnemann, J. (1972). *The ethical investor.* New Haven, CT: Yale University Press.

Singer, P. (1972). Famine, affluence, and morality. *Philosophy & Public Affairs, 1* (1), 229–243.

Stark, L. (Ed.). (2001). *State of the world 2001: A Worldwatch Institute report on progress toward a sustainable society.* New York: Norton.

Stemp-Morlock, G. (2006). Plant vs. pathogen: Enlisting tobacco in the fight against tobacco. *Environmental Health Perspectives, 114* (6), A365–A367.

Stewart, R. (2001). A new generation of environmental regulation? *Capital University Law Review, 29,* 21–141.

Stewart, R. (2002). Environmental regulatory decision making under uncertainty. *Research in Law and Economics, 20,* 71–126.

Toxic Trail. (2006). Available at: http://www.communityipm.org/ToxicTrail.htm. Accessed June 6, 2006.

Union of Concerned Scientists. (2006). Biotechnology and the world food supply. Available at: http://www.ucsusa.org/food/food_and_environment/genetic_engineering. Accessed May 23, 2006.

United Nations. (2005). World population prospects, the 2004 revision. Available at: http://www.un.org/News/Press/docs/2005/pop918.doc.htm. Accessed June 6, 2006.

University of Michigan. (2006). Human appropriation of the world's food supply. Current Lectures. Available at: http://www.globalchange.umich.edu/globalchange2/current/lectures/food_supply/food.htm. Accessed May 23, 2006.

U.S. Bureau of the Census. (1999). World population profile: 1998. Available at: http://www.census.gov/ipc/wws/wp98001.html. Accessed May 23, 2006.

U.S. Code: Title 7,136. (2007). Definitions, Chapter 6: Insecticides and Environmental Pest Control, II.

U.S. Environmental Protection Agency. (1972, December 31). DDT ban takes effect [press release]. Washington, DC.

U.S. Environmental Protection Agency. (2006a). EPA pesticide laws. Available at: http://www.epa.gov/pesticides/regulating/laws.htm. Accessed June 6, 2006.

U.S. Environmental Protection Agency. (2006b). EPA pesticide information sharing and technical assistance. Available at: http://www.epa.gov/pesticides/regulating/registering/data_sources.htm. Accessed June 6, 2006.

U.S. Environmental Protection Agency. (2006c). EPA pesticide international issues. Available at: http://www.epa.gov/oppfead1/international. Accessed June 6, 2006.

U.S. Environmental Protection Agency. (2006d). EPA pesticide registration program. Available at: http://www.epa.gov/pesticides/regulating/registering/index.htm. Accessed June 6, 2006.

Uva, M., and Bloom, J. (1989). Exporting pollution: The international waste trade. *Environment, 31,* 4–5.

Wargo, J. (1996). *Our children's toxic legacy: How science and law fail to protect us from pesticides.* New Haven, CT: Yale University Press.

World Health Organization, Roll Back Malaria (RBM) Partnership. (2006). Available at: http://www.rbm.who.int/cgi-bin/rbm/rbmportal/custom/rbm/home.do?tabId= 0&BV_SessionID=@@@@1048799268.1144534811@@@@&BV_EngineID=ccccaddhfhfeeifc fjmcghgdfghdfgo.0. Accessed June 6, 2006.

CHAPTER 6

Ayres, R. (1998). *The turning point: The end of the growth paradigm.* London, England: Earthscan.

Bella, D., Mosher, C., and Calvo, S. (1988). Technocracy and trust: Nuclear waste controversy. *Professional Issues in Engineering, 114,* 27–39.

Bernstein, J. (2004). *Oppenheimer: Portrait of an enigma.* Chicago, IL: Dee.

Bisconti Research, Inc. (2005, May 5–9). U.S. public opinion about nuclear energy 2005. Report for the Nuclear Energy Institute, Washington, DC: Bisconti Research, Inc.

Boholm, A. (2005). *Facility siting: Risk, power, and identity in land use planning.* Sterling, VA: Earthscan.

Carter, L. (1987). *Nuclear imperatives and public trust: Dealing with radioactive waste.* Washington, DC: Resources for the Future.

Cassidy, D. (2005). *J. Robert Oppenheimer and the American century.* New York: Pi Press.

Clary, B., and Kraft, M. (1988). Environmental assessment and policy failure: The Nuclear Waste Policy Act of 1982. *Policy Studies Review, 8,* 105–115.

Columbia Encyclopedia. (2001). Mencken, H. L. Available at: http://www.bartleby> com/65/me/Mencken.html. Accessed October 25, 2006.

Commoner, B. (1971). *Closing the circle.* New York: Knopf.

de Bruijn, T., and Norberg-Bohm, V. (2005). *Industrial transformation: Environmental policy innovation in the United States and Europe.* Cambridge, MA: MIT Press.

Energy Information Administration. (2006). U.S. nuclear reactors. Available at: http://www. eia.doe.gov/cneaf/nuclear/page/nuc_reactors/reactsom.html. Accessed November 1, 2006.

The future of nuclear power. (2003). Cambridge, MA: MIT. Available at: http://web.mit.edu/ nuclearpower. Accessed October 30, 2006.

Gazit, C. (1999). *Meltdown at Three Mile Island* [video recording]. A Steward/Gazit Productions, Inc., film for the American Experience (WGBH Boston). Written and produced by Chana Gazit, coproduced by David Steward. Alexandria, VA: PBS Home Video.

Gertner, J. (2006, July 16). Atomic balm? *New York Times,* section 6, pp. 36–47, 56, 62, 64.

Gidley, J. (1998). Prospective youth visions through imaginative education. *Futures, 30* (5), 395–408.

Gilpin, A. (2000). *Environmental economics.* New York: Wiley.

Hess, K. (1998). *Environmental site assessment. Phase I: A basic guide.* 2nd ed. Boca Raton, FL: CRC.

Hewlett, R., and Holl, J. (1980). *Atoms for peace and war, 1953–1961: Eisenhower and the Atomic Energy Commission.* Berkeley, CA: University of California Press.

Hicks, D. (1996). A lesson for the future: Young people's hopes and fears for tomorrow. *Futures, 28* (1), 1–13.

Hofstetter, P., Bare, J., Hammitt, J., Murphy, P., and Rice, G. (2002). Tools for comparative analysis of alternatives: Competing or complementary perspectives. *Risk Analysis, 22* (5), 833–851.

Houts, P., Cleary, P., and Hu, T.-W. (1988). *The Three Mile Island crisis: Psychological, social, and economic impacts on the surrounding population.* University Park: Pennsylvania State University Press.

International Physicians for the Prevention of Nuclear War. (2006). Nuclear reactors. Available at: http://www.ippnw.org. Accessed October 30, 2006.

Kemp, R. (1990). Why not in my backyard? A radical interpretation of public opposition to the deep disposal of radioactive waste in the United Kingdom. *Environment and Planning A, 22,* 1239–1258.

Kunreuther, H., Easterling D., Desvousges, W., and Slovic, P. (1990). Public attitudes toward siting a high-level nuclear waste repository in Nevada. *Risk Analysis, 10* (4), 469–484.

Lake, R. (Ed.). (1987). *Resolving locational conflict.* New Brunswick, NJ: Center for Urban Policy Research.

Lemons, J., and Malone, C. (1989). Siting America's geological repository for high-level nuclear waste: Implications for environmental policy. *Environmental Management, 13,* 435–441.

Macfarlane, M., and Ewing, R. (Eds.). (2006). *Uncertainty underground: Yucca Mountain and the nation's high-level nuclear waste.* Cambridge, MA: MIT Press.

Maddox, J. (1972). *The doomsday syndrome.* New York: McGraw-Hill.

Meadows, D., Meadows, D., Renderers, J., and Behrens, W. (1972) *Limits to growth.* New York: Club of Rome.

Medvedev, G. (1993). *No breathing room.* New York: Basic Books.

Meyers, N., and Raffensberger, C. (2006). *Precautionary tools for reshaping environmental policy.* Cambridge, MA: MIT Press.

Neal, A. (1998). *National trauma and collective memory: Major events in the American century.* Armonk, NY: Sharpe.

Norris, R., and Kristensen, H. (2006). Global nuclear stockpiles, 1945–2006. *Bulletin of the Atomic Scientists, 62* (4), 64–66.

O'Driscoll, M. (2006, July 17). Nuclear power: US, Russia formally endorse nuclear power agreement talks. *Greenwire.* Available at www.eenews.net/. Accessed July 17, 2006.

O'Hare, M., Bacow, L., and Sanderson, D. (1983). *Facility siting and public opposition.* New York: Van Nostrand and Reinhold.

Ono, R. (2003). Learning from young people's image of the future: A case study in Taiwan and the United States. *Futures, 35* (7), 737–758.

Paine, J. (1996). Will nuclear power pay for itself? *Social Science Journal, 33* (4), 459–473.

Popper, F. (1985). The environmentalist and the LULU. *Environment, 27* (2), 6–11, 37–40.

Portney, K. (1991). *Siting hazardous waste treatment facilities: The NIMBY syndrome.* New York: Auburn House.

Rosa, E., and Dunlap, R. (1994). Poll trends: Nuclear power — three decades of public opinion. *Public Opinion Quarterly, 58,* 295–324.

Simon, J. (1990). *People, resources, environment, and immigration.* New Brunswick, NJ: Transaction.

Simon, J., and Kahn, H. (Eds.). (1984). *The resourceful Earth: A response to Global 2000.* New York: Blackwell.

Spurgeon, D. (2006, September 6–8). Building nuclear power partnerships: Prospects for U.S. and global nuclear developments. Remarks at the World Nuclear Association Symposium, London, England.

Uranium Institute. (1999). Nuclear power in the world energy outlook. Available at: http://www.world-nuclear.org/sym/1999/birol.htm. Accessed October 31, 2006.

U.S. Department of Energy. (2006). *Report to Congress: Spent Nuclear Fuel Recycling Program plan.* Washington, DC. Available at: http://www.gnep.energy.gov/pdfs/snfRecycling ProgramPlanMay2006.pdf.

U.S. Nuclear Regulatory Commission. (2006). Nuclear reactors. Available at: http://www.nrc. gov/reactors/operating/list-power-reactor-units.html. Accessed October 30, 2006.

Walker, J. (2004). *Three Mile Island: A nuclear crisis in historical perspective.* Berkeley, CA, and Washington, DC: University of California Press and the Nuclear Regulatory Commission.

Walsh, E. (1988). *Democracy in the shadows: Citizen mobilization in the wake of the accident at Three Mile Island.* New York: Greenwood.

Weart, S. (1992). Fears, fantasies, and fallout. *New Scientist, 136,* 34–37.

World Nuclear Association. (2006). Nuclear electricity. Available at: http://www.world-nuclear.org/education/ne/ne6.htm. Accessed October 31, 2006.

WTRG Economics. (2006). Oil price history and analysis. Available at: http://www.wtrg.com/ prices.htm. Accessed September 26, 2006.

CHAPTER 7

Anderson, F. (1973). *NEPA in the courts: A legal analysis of the National Policy Act.* Baltimore, MD: Johns Hopkins University Press.

Baker, M., Kaming, J., and Morrison, R. (1977). *Environmental impact statements: A guide to preparation and review.* New York: Practicing Law Institute.

Barnard, R. (1990). Some regulatory definitions of risk: Interaction of scientific and legal principles. *Regulatory Toxicology and Pharmacology, 11,* 2001–2011.

Berelson, B. (1952). *Content analysis in communication research.* New York: Free Press.

Blocker, J. (2006). Did prohibition really work? Alcohol prohibition as a public health innovation. *American Journal of Public Health, 96* (2), 233–243.

Blot, W., Mason, T., Hoover, R., and Fraumeni, J. (1977). Cancer by county: Etiologic implications. In H. Hiatt, J. Watson, and J. Winston (Eds.), *Proceedings of the Cold Spring Harbor Conferences on Cell Proliferation: Origins of human cancer* (21–32). New York. Cold Spring Harbor Laboratory.

Bourque, L., and Fielder, E. (1995). *How to conduct self-administered and mail surveys.* Vol. 3. Thousand Oaks, CA: Sage.

Bregman, J. (1999). *Environmental impact statements.* 2nd ed. Boca Raton, FL: Lewis.

Brown, L. (1981). *Innovation diffusion: A new perspective.* New York: Methuen.

Burchell, R., and Listokin, D. (1975). *The environmental impact handbook.* New Brunswick, NJ: Rutgers University, Center for Urban Policy Research.

Burger, J., Carletta, M., Lowrie, K., Miller, K., and Greenberg, M. (2004). Assessing ecological resources for remediation and future land uses on contaminated lands. *Environmental Management, 34* (1), 1–10.

Campbell, D., and Stanley, J. (1963). *Experimental and quasi-experimental design for research.* Chicago, IL: Rand McNally.

Canter, L. (1977). *Environmental impact assessment.* New York: McGraw-Hill.

Cheremisinoff, P., and Morresi, A. (1977). *Environmental assessment and impact statement handbook.* Ann Arbor, MI: Ann Arbor Science Publishers.

Coker, A., and Richards, C. (Eds.). (1992). *Valuing the environment: Economic approaches to environmental evaluation.* London, England: Belhaven.

Commission on Risk Assessment and Risk Management. (1997). *Report on the accomplishments of the Commission on Risk Assessment and Risk Management.* Available at: http://www.riskworld.com/riskcommission/default.htlm. Accessed August 10, 2006.

Conway, R. (2001). The Puget Sound forecasting model: A structural time-series analysis of Ron Miller's hometown. In M. Lahr and E. Dietzenbacher (Eds.), *Input-output analysis: Frontiers and extensions* (431–450). New York: Palgrave.

Dillman, D. (1978). *Mail and telephone surveys: The total design method.* New York: Wiley.

Ellerbusch, F. (2005). *Residential redevelopment of brownfields.* New Brunswick, NJ: University of Medicine and Dentistry of New Jersey School of Public Health.

Englander, T., Farago, K., Slovic, P., and Fischoff, B. (1986). A comparative analysis of risk perception in Hungary and the United States. *Social Behaviour, 1,* 55–66.

Fabrycky, W., and Blanchard, B. (1991). *Life-cycle cost and economic analysis.* Englewood Cliffs, NJ: Prentice Hall.

Fairfax, S. (1978). A disaster in the environmental movement. *Science, 199,* 743–748.

Fernald Citizens Advisory Board. (2004). *Current issues: Natural resource damages settlement.* Cincinnati, OH. Available at: http://www.fernaldcab.org/index.htm. Accessed August 10, 2006.

Fink, A. (1995a). *How to analyze survey data.* Vol. 8. Thousand Oaks, CA: Sage.

Fink, A. (1995b). *How to ask survey questions.* Vol. 2. Thousand Oaks, CA: Sage.

Fink, A. (1995c). *How to design surveys.* Vol. 5. Thousand Oaks, CA: Sage.

Fink, A. (1995d). *How to report on surveys.* Vol. 9. Thousand Oaks, CA: Sage.

Fink, A. (1995e). *How to sample in surveys.* Vol. 6. Thousand Oaks, CA: Sage.

Fink, A. (1995f). *The survey handbook.* Vol. 1. Thousand Oaks, CA: Sage.

Folmer, H. (Ed.). (2001). *Frontiers of environmental economics.* Northampton, MA: Edward Elgar.

Freeman, A., III. (2003). *The measurement of environmental and resources values: Theory and methods.* 2nd ed. Washington, DC: Resources for the Future.

Frey, J., and Oishi, S. (1995). *How to conduct interviews by telephone and in person.* Vol. 4. Thousand Oaks, CA: Sage.

Gardner, M., and Brandt, A. (2006). "The 'doctors' choice" is America's choice": The physician in U.S. cigarette advertisements. *American Journal of Public Health, 96* (2), 222–232.

Goldman, E., and Eliason, L. (Eds.). (2003). *The diffusion of military technology and ideas.* Stanford, CA: Stanford University Press.

Goszczynska, M., Tyszka, T., and Slovic, P. (1991). Risk perception in Poland: A comparison with three other countries. *Journal of Behavioral Decision Making, 4,* 179–193.

Greenberg, M. (2003). Public health, law, and local control: Destruction of the U.S. chemical weapons stockpile. *American Journal of Public Health, 93* (8), 1222–1225.

Greenberg, M. (2005). Concern about environmental pollution: How much difference do race and ethnicity make? A New Jersey case study. *Environmental Health Perspectives, 113* (4), 369–374.

Greenberg, M., Belnay, G., Cesanek, W., Neuman, N., and Shepherd, G. (1978). *A primer on industrial environmental impact.* New Brunswick, NJ: Rutgers University, Center for Urban Policy Research.

Greenberg, M., Lewis, D., and Frisch, M. (2002). Local and interregional economic analysis of large U.S. Department of Energy waste management projects. *Waste Management, 22* (2), 643–655.

Greenberg, M., and Lowrie, K. (1999). Brownfields and the mass media. *Urban Land, 58,* 10, 13.

Guimaraes, P., Hefner, F., and Woodward, D. (1993). Wealth and income effects of natural disasters: An econometric analysis of Hurricane Hugo. *Review of Regional Studies, 23,* 97–114.

Hawk, H. (2003). *Bridge life-cycle cost analysis.* Washington, DC: National Research Council, Transportation Research Board.

ISO (International Standards Organization). (1997). CAN/CSA-ISO (Canadian Standards Association) 14040–00. *Environmental Management — Life Cycle Assessment — Principles and Framework.* Mississauga, Ontario, Canada: American Society for Quality.

Jack McCormick & Associates, Inc. (1978). *Effects of the National Environmental Policy Act on corporate decision-making.* Washington, DC: U.S. Department of Commerce, Office of Environmental Affairs.

Jain, R., Urban, L., and Stacey, G. (1977). *Environmental impact analysis.* New York: Van Nostrand Reinhold.

Keysar, E., and Steinemann, A. (2002). Integrating environmental impact assessment with master planning: Lessons from the U.S. Army. *EIS Review, 22,* 583–609.

Kish, L. (1965). *Survey sampling.* New York: Wiley.

Kleinhesselink, R., and Rosa, E. (1991). Cognitive representation of risk perception: A comparison of Japan and the United States. *Journal of Cross-Cultural Psychology, 22,* 11–28.

Kopp, R., and Smith, V. (Eds.). (1993). *Valuing natural assets: The economics of natural damage assessment.* Washington, DC: Resources for the Future.

Kreske, D. (1996). *Environmental impact statements: A practical guide for agencies, citizens, and consultants.* New York: Wiley.

Krippendorff, K. (2004). *Content analysis: An introduction to its methodology.* 2nd ed. Beverly Hills, CA: Sage.

Leontief, W. (1970). The dynamic inverse. In A. Carter and A. Brody (Eds.), *Contributions to input-output analysis* (17–46). New York: North-Holland.

Leontief, W. (1974). Structure of the world economy: Outline of a simple input-output framework. *Swedish Journal of Economics, 76,* 387–401.

Lewis, M., and Wackowski, O. (2006). Dealing with an innovative industry: A look at flavored cigarettes promoted by the mainstream brands. *American Journal of Public Health, 96* (2), 244–251.

Lindall, S., and Olson, D. (2003). *The IMPLAN input-output system.* Stillwater, MN: MIG, Inc.

Liroff, R. (1976). *A national policy for the environment — NEPA and its aftermath.* Bloomington, IN: Indiana University Press.

Litwin, M. (1995). *How to measure survey reliability and validity.* Vol. 7. Thousand Oaks, CA: Sage.

Mason, A., and Tapinos, G. (Eds.). (2000). *Sharing the wealth: Demographic change and economic transfers between generations.* New York: Oxford University Press.

Miller, R., and Blair, P. (1985). *Input-output analysis: Foundations and extensions.* Englewood Cliffs, NJ: Prentice-Hall.

Moen, W., Stewart, E., and McClure, C. (1997). The role of content analysis in evaluating metadata for the U.S. Government Information Locator Service (GILS): Results from an exploratory study. Available at: http://www.unt.edu/wmoen/pubications/GILSMD ConentAnalussis.htm. Accessed December 16, 2005.

Mokdad, A., Marks, J., Stroup, D., and Gerberding, J. (2004). Actual causes of death in the United States, 2000. *Journal of the American Medical Association, 291* (10), 1238–1241.

Montague, P. (1991). *Questions to ask about risk assessment.* Washington, DC: Environmental Research Foundation.

National Research Council. (1983). *Risk assessment in the federal government: Managing the process.* Washington, DC: National Academy Press.

National Research Council. (1992). *Issues in risk assessment.* Washington, DC: National Academy Press.

National Research Council. (1997). *Valuing groundwater: Economic concepts and approaches.* Washington, DC: National Academy Press.

Neuendorf, K. (2001). *The content analysis guidebook online.* Thousand Oaks, CA: Sage. Available at: http://academic.csuohio.edu/kneuedorf/content. Accessed December 16, 2005.

Oakes, J. (2002). Risks and wrongs in social science research: An evaluator's guide to IRB evaluation. *Evaluation Review, 24,* 443–478.

Okuyama, Y., and Chang, S. (Eds.). (2004). *Modeling spatial and economic impacts of disasters.* New York: Springer.

Oregon State University. (1973). *How effective are environmental impact statements?* PB-230–702. Springfield, VA: National Technical Information System.

Ortolano, L. (Ed.). (1973). *Analyzing the environmental impacts of water projects.* Alexandria, VA: U.S. Army Corps of Engineers, Institute for Water Resources.

Penslar, R. (1993). *IRB guidebook and videotape.* Washington, DC: U.S. Department of Health and Human Services, Office of Human Research Protection.

Peterson, R., and Mahajan, V. (1985). *Models for innovation diffusion.* Beverly Hills, CA: Sage.

Pew Research Center for the People and the Press. (1998). *Deconstructing distrust: Americans view government.* Washington, DC: Pew Research Center for the People and the Press.

Pew Research Center for the People and the Press. (1999). *Trust and citizen engagement in metropolitan Philadelphia: A case study.* Washington, DC: Pew Research Center for the People and the Press.

Pool, I. (Ed.). (1959). *Trends in content analysis.* Urbana, IL: University of Illinois Press.

Reisch, M. (2001). *Superfund and natural resource damages.* Washington, DC: Library of Congress, Congressional Research Service.

Renner, R. (1998). Calculating the cost of natural resource damage. *Environmental Science & Technology, 32* (3), 86A–90A.

Resetar, A. (1999). *Technology forces at work: Profiles of environmental research and development at DuPont, Intel, Monsanto, and Xerox.* Santa Monica, CA: RAND.

Riffe, D., Lacy, S., and Fico, F. (2005). *Analyzing media messages: Using quantitative content analysis in research.* Mahwah, NJ: Erlbaum.

Rogers, E. (1995). *Diffusion of innovations.* 4th ed. New York: Free Press.

Rose, A., and Liao, S-Y. (2005). Modeling regional economic resilience to disasters: A computable general equilibrium analysis of water service disruptions. *Journal of Regional Science, 45* (1), 75–112.

Santos, J., and Haimes, Y. (2004). Modeling the demand reduction input-output (I-o) inoperability due to terrorism. *Risk Analysis, 24* (6), 1437–1451.

Silbergeld, E. (1993). Risk assessment: The perspective and experience of U.S. environmentalists. *Environmental Health Perspectives, 101,* 100–104.

Smith, D. (2003). Status and trends of CERCLA-related natural resource damage assessments. American Bar Association, *Superfund and Hazardous Waste Committee Newsletter, 4* (3). Available at: http://www.abanet.org. Accessed August 10, 2006.

State of Washington, Office of the Attorney General. (2004, July 8). Gregoire to sue DOE over natural resource damages at Hanford [press release]. Available at: http://www..atg.wa.gov/releases/rel_doe_070804.html. Accessed August 3, 2006.

Steinemann, A. (2001). Improving alternatives for environmental impact assessment. *Environmental Impact Assessment Review, 21,* 3–21.

Stokes, J. (2003). *How to do media and cultural studies.* Thousand Oaks, CA: Sage.

Sudman, S. (1976). *Applied sampling.* New York: Academic Press.

Teigen, K., Brun, W., and Slovic, P. (1988). Societal risks as seen by a Norwegian public. *Journal of Behavioral Decision Making, 1,* 111–130.

Treyz, G. (1993). *Regional economic modeling; A systematic approach to economic forecasting and policy analysis.* Boston, MA: Kluwer Academic Publishers.

U.S. General Accounting Office. (1996, August 16). Letter report to the Honorable Frank H. Murkowski, Chairman, Committee on Energy and Natural Resources, U.S. Senate; Honorable John H. Chaffee, Chairman, Committee on Environment and Public Works,

U.S. Senate; and Honorable Robert C. Smith, Chairman, Subcommittee on Superfund, Waste Control, and Risk Assessment, Committee on Environment and Public Works, U.S. Senate, from U.S. General Accounting Office, Resources, Community, and Economic Development Division, B-272, 411. Available at: www.archive.gao.gov/paprpdf1/157492.pdf. Accessed December 3, 2004.

Wang, J. (2002). *A life-cycle cost estimating methodology for NASA-developed Air Traffic Control decision support tools.* Springfield, VA: National Technical Information Service.

Warner, M. (1973). *Environmental impact analysis: An examination of three methodologies.* Springfield, VA: National Technical Information Service.

Weber, R. (1985). *Basic content analysis.* Beverly Hills, CA: Sage.

Weidema, B. (1998). Application typologies for life cycle assessment. *International Journal of Life Cycle Assessment, 3,* 237–240.

Wejnert, B. (2002). Integrating models of diffusion of innovations: A conceptual framework. *Annual Review of Sociology, 28,* 297–326.

Winner, L. (1985). On not hitting the tar-baby: Risk assessment and conservatism. In M. Gibson (Ed.), *To breathe freely* (269–284). Totowa, NJ: Roman and Allanheld.

CHAPTER 8

Burford, A., with Greenya, J. (1986). *Are you tough enough?* New York: McGraw-Hill.

Clark, R. (1984). *Persuasive messages.* New York: Harper & Row.

Clinton, W. (1994, February 16). Federal actions to address environmental justice in the minority population and low-income populations. *Federal Register, 59* (32), 5 pp.

Congressional Research Service. (2001, July 30). Interstate shipment of municipal solid waste: 2001 update. Available at: http://www.fas.org/sgp/crs/intel/ Accessed November 21, 2006.

Conservative Action. (2006). Environmental regulations. Available at: http://www. conservative action.org/resources.php3. Accessed November 21, 2006.

Cyert, R., and March, J. (1963). *Behavioral theory of the firm.* Englewood Cliffs, NJ: Prentice-Hall.

Dubois, D., and Prade, H. (1988). *Possibility theory, an approach to computerized processing of uncertainty.* New York: Plenum.

EPA Journal. (1983). The return of an extraordinary public servant. Available at: http://www.epa.gov/history/admin/agency/ruck2.htm. Accessed December 2, 2006.

Etzioni, A. (1968). *The active society: A theory of societal and political processes.* New York: Free Press.

Gielecki, M. (1997). 9. Flow control and the interstate movement of waste: Post-Carbone. http://www.eia.doe.gov/cneaf/solar.renewables/renvewable.energy.annual/chap09. html. Accessed March 1, 2007.

Gorsuch, A. (1985). Views from administrators. Available at: http://www.epa.gov/history/topics/epa/15e.htm. Accessed December 2, 2006.

Greenberg, M. (1978). *Applied linear programming for the socioeconomic and environmental sciences.* New York: Academic Press.

Greenberg, M. (1979). *A primer on industrial environmental impact.* New Brunswick, NJ: Rutgers University, Center for Urban Policy Research.

Greenberg, M. (2005). Environmental protection as a U.S. national government priority: Analysis of six annual public opinion surveys, 1999–2004. *Journal of Environmental Planning and Management, 48* (5), 733–746.

Greenberg, M., and Anderson, R. (1984). *Hazardous waste sites: The credibility gap.* New Brunswick, NJ: Rutgers University, Center for Urban Policy Research.

Greenberg, M., Burger, J., Gochfeld, M., Kosson, D., Lowrie, K., Mayer, H., Powers, C., Volz, C., and Vyas, V. (2005, Winter). End-state land uses, sustainably protective systems, and risk management: A challenge for remediation and multigenerational stewardship. *Remediation,* 91–105.

Haddix, A., Teutsch, S., and Corso, B. (2003). *Prevention effectiveness: A guide to decision analysis and economic evaluation.* New York: Oxford University Press.

Hammond, P., and Coppock, R. (Eds.). (1990). *Valuing health risks, costs, and benefits for environmental decision making.* Washington, DC: National Academy Press.

Hance, B., Chess, C., and Sandman, P. (1988). *Improving dialogue with communities: A risk communication manual for government.* Trenton, NJ: New Jersey Department of Environmental Protection, Division of Science and Research.

Hance, B., Chess, C., and Sandman, P. (1990). *Industry risk communication manual.* Boca Raton, FL: Lewis.

Heuvelmans, M. (1974). *The river killers.* Harrisburg, PA: Stackpole.

Higgs, R., and Close, C. (Eds.). (2005). *Re-thinking green: Alternatives to environmental bureaucracy.* Oakland, CA: Independent Institute.

Hobbs, B., and Meier, P. (2000). *Energy decisions and the environment: A guide to the use of multicriteria methods.* Boston, MA: Kluwer Academic Press.

Hoberg, G. (1992). *Pluralism by design: Environmental policy and the American regulatory state.* New York: Praeger.

Keeney, R., and Raiffa, H. (1976). *Decisions with multiple objectives: Preferences and value trade-offs.* New York: Wiley.

Klir, G., and Folger, T. (1988). *Fuzzy sets, uncertainty, and information.* Englewood Cliffs: NJ: Prentice-Hall.

Kopp, R., and Smith, V. (Eds.). (1993). *Valuing natural assets: The economics of natural damage assessment.* Washington, DC: Resources for the Future.

Levine, M. (1981). Revisionism revised? Airline deregulation and the public interest. *Law and Contemporary Problems, 44* (1), 179–195.

Maclaren, V., and Whitney, J. (Eds.). (1985). *New directions in environmental impact assessment.* Toronto, Ontario: Methuen.

Magat, W., Krupnick, A., and Harrington, W. (1986). *Rules in the making.* Washington, DC: Resources for the Future.

McAllister, D. (1980). *Evaluation and environmental planning: Assessing environmental, social, economic, and political trade-offs.* Cambridge, MA: MIT Press.

Mitnick, B. (1980). *The political economy of regulation.* New York: Columbia University Press.

Moe, T. (1982). Regulatory performance and presidential administration. *American Journal of Political Science, 26* (2), 197–224.

Moore, C. (1998). The impracticality and immorality of cost-benefit analysis in setting health-related standards. *Tulane Environmental Law Review, 11* (2), 187–216.

Nas, T. (1996). *Cost-benefit analysis: Theory and application.* Thousand Oaks, CA: Sage.

National Association of Counties. (1997). *Think the lack of flow control hasn't hurt anybody? Think again.* Washington, DC. Available at: http://www.eia.doe.gov/cneaf/solar.renewables/ renewable.energy.annual/chap09.html.

National Research Council. (1989). *Improving risk communication.* Washington, DC: National Academy Press.

National Research Council. (1997). *Valuing groundwater: Economic concepts and approaches.* Washington, DC: National Academy Press.

Nazareth, J. (2004). *An optimization primer.* New York: Springer.

Noll, R. (1971). *Reforming regulation: Studies in the regulation of economic activity.* Washington, DC: Brookings Institution.

Office of Management and Budget. (2006). Budget of the United States government, Historical tables. Annual. Available at: http://w3.access.gpo.gov/usbudget/fy2006/ pdf.hist.pdf. Accessed November 30, 2006.

O'Leary, R. (1997). Trash talk: The Supreme Court and the interstate transportation of waste. *Public Administration Review, 57* (4), 281–284.

Parker, B. (2002, March 20). Statement of Bruce Parker, President and CEO, National Solid Waste Management Association, before the U.S. Senate Environment and Public Works Committee. Available at: http://epw.senate.gov/107th/Parker_032002.htm. Accessed November 21, 2006.

Parson, E. (1997). Informing global environmental policy-making: A plea for new methods of assessment and synthesis. *Environmental Modeling & Assessment, 2,* 267–279.

Peltzman, S. (1976). Toward a more general theory of regulation. *Journal of Law and Economics, 19* (2), 211–240.

Peskin, H., and Seskin, E. (Eds.). (1975). *Cost-benefit analysis and water pollution policy.* Washington, DC: Urban Institute.

Portney, P., and Stavins, R. (Eds.). (2000). *Public policies for environmental protection.* Washington, DC: Resources for the Future.

Ross, S. (1970). *Applied probability models with optimization applications.* San Francisco: Holden-Day.

Ruckelshaus, W. (1985). Views from administrators. Available at: http://www.epa.gov/history/topics/epa/15e.htm. Accessed December 2, 2006.

Saad, L. (2004). Environment not a pressing concern. Available at: http://gallup.com/poll. Accessed April 19, 2004.

Saad, L., and Dunlap, R. (2000). Americans are environmentally friendly, but issue not seen as urgent problem. Available at: http://gallup.com/poll/releases/pr000417.asp. Accessed May 19, 2003.

Saaty, T. (1980). *The analytic hierarchy process.* New York: McGraw-Hill.

Schaeffer, E. (2002). Clearing the air — why I quit Bush's EPA. *Washington Monthly.* Available at: http://www.washingtonmonthly.com/features/2001/0207.Schaeffer.html. Accessed December 2, 2006.

Stern, A. (1982). History of air pollution legislation in the United States. *Journal of the Air Pollution Control Association, 32* (1), 44–61.

Stigler, G. (1971). The theory of economic regulation. *Journal of Economics, 2* (1), 3–21.

Sullivan, P. (2004, July 22). Anne Gorsuch Burford, 62, dies: Reagan EPA director. *Washington Post,* p. B6.

Udall, M. (2003). Speech: Introduction of the Environmental Justice Act. Available at: http://thomas.loc.gov/cgi-bin/query. Accessed November 21, 2006.

U.S. Court of Appeals for the Ninth Circuit. (2004). *NRDC v. Spencer Abraham,* 15703–1515. Available at: http://www.atg.wa.gov/Hanford/documents/nov2004/pdf. Accessed January 8, 2007.

U.S. Environmental Protection Agency. (1977). *Waste disposal practices and their effects on groundwater.* Report to Congress. Washington, DC: U.S. Government Printing Office.

U.S. Environmental Protection Agency. (1987). *Unfinished business.* Washington, DC: U.S. Government Printing Office.

U.S. Environmental Protection Agency. (1992). *Environmental equity: Reducing risk for all communities.* Washington, DC: U.S. Government Printing Office.

U.S. Environmental Protection Agency. (2005). MSW facts and figures. Available at: www.epa.gov/msw/msw99.htm. Accessed November 10, 2006.

U.S. Environmental Protection Agency. (2006a). Biography: Anne Gorsuch. Available at: http://www.epa.gov/adminweb/history/administators/gorsuch.htm. Accessed December 2, 2006.

U.S. Environmental Protection Agency. (2006b). Biography: William Ruckelshaus. Available at: http://www.epa.gov/adminweb/history/publications/ruck/u2.htm. Accessed December 2, 2006.

U.S. Environmental Protection Agency, Science Advisory Board. (1990). *Reducing risk: Setting priorities and strategies for environmental protection.* Washington, DC: U.S. Government Printing Office.

U.S. Environmental Protection Agency, Science Advisory Board. (1999). *Integrated environmental decision-making in the 21st century.* Washington, DC: U.S. Government Printing Office.

Wald, M. (2003, July 4). Judge voids cleanup plan for wastes at bomb plants. *New York Times.* Available at: www.nytimes.com.2003/07/04politics/04NUKE.html. Accessed July 6, 2003.

Winmill, B. (2003a). *National Resources Defense Council et al.* [plaintiffs] *v. Spencer Abraham, Secretary, Department of Energy, United States of America* [defendant]. Judgment, Civ. No. 01–0413-S.-BLW, July 2.

Winmill, B. (2003b). *National Resources Defense Council et al.* [plaintiffs] *v. Spencer Abraham, Secretary, Department of Energy, United States of America* [defendant]. Memorandum Decision, Civ. No. 01–0413-S.-BLW, July 2.

Woolley, J., and Peters, G. (2006). *The American presidency project* (online database). Santa Barbara, CA: Gerhard Peters. Available at: http://www.presidency.ucsb.edu.ws/ ?pid=49631. Accessed November 21, 2006.

Zeleny, M. (1982). *Multiple criteria decision making.* New York: McGraw-Hill.

Zimmermann, H. (1987). *Fuzzy sets, decision making, and expert systems.* Boston, MA: Kluwer Academic Publishers.

INDEX

Note: Page numbers followed by a "t" refer to tables

Abbott School Districts, 32–34
ABC television, 55–56, 61, 63
Accra (Ghana), 208
acetylcholine, 133
acid rain, 71, 90, 127, 236
ACS. *See* American Cancer Society
Action Now (California), 45
Advisory Group for Federal Facilities (EPA), 122
AEC. *See* Atomic Energy Commission
Afghanistan, 104, 245
Africa, 75; DDT use in, 135–136; hazardous
  waste disposal in, 151; land mines in, 195;
  population growth in, 131; starvation in,
  132. *See also specific countries*
Africa Fighting Malaria, 135
African Americans. *See* minority populations
Agent Orange, 90–91
agriculture: chemical industry's takeover of,
  134, 142; lack of education about, in
  developing countries, 134, 142, 154; pesticide
  use essential to U.S., 141; stewardship
  theories in, 121; as water dependent, 132,
  133. *See also* crops; pesticides
AIDS, 64, 131
air pollution, 56, 94; from automobiles and
  trucks, 70–71, 239; and cancer, 50; and
  ethical investing, 153; reducing emissions
  contributing to, 16–17, 78, 79, 80, 81, 83t,
  92, 161, 169, 195–196, 235, 236–237;
  standards for outdoor, 228, 235–236. *See
  also* greenhouse gases
Alamogordo (New Mexico), 159
alar, 71
Alaska: land policy in, 98, 99; and MTBE, 93;
  oil spill in, 219, 220
alcohol: banning, 211, 212; diseases associated
  with overuse of, 51, 67, 107, 108t, 109, 212;
  in gasoline, 75; studies on use of, 194
Aldicarb (Temik), 67–68
Aldrich, T., 55
aldrin (chemical), 139
Alexander, T., 120
Alford, W., 142
Allen, Scott, 19
American Anglican, 8, 125
American Arbitration Association, 91
American Association of Petroleum
  Geologists, 101

American Cancer Society (ACS), 45, 47–48, 49,
  57t, 66, 67
American Housing Survey, 42
American Journal of Epidemiology, 54–55
American Journal of Health Promotion, 73
American Journal of Public Health, 73, 76, 91
American Plastics Council, 88
American Public Health Association, 77
American Society for Control of Cancer
  (ASCC), 47. *See also* American Cancer
  Society
Anchorage (Alaska), 93
anecdotal information, 87, 135
animal testing, 85, 86–88, 89, 93; courts' view
  of, 90–91; in toxicology, 194, 197
anthrax, 151
apartheid, 152
Archaeological Conservancy, 122
Archer-Daniels-Midland Co., 79
Arco (Idaho), 156
Are You Tough Enough? (Burford), 243
Argonne (Chicago), 105
Arizona, 100
aromatic amines, 49
arsenic, 49
asbestos, 49, 53, 56, 71, 193, 235
Asbestos School Hazard Abatement Act of
  1984, 235
Asia: green revolution in, 132; land mines in,
  195; population growth in, 131; tobacco use
  in, 212. *See also specific countries*
Asian Indian Americans, 205–206, 209
asthma, xii
Atlantic Ocean, 166
atlases. *See* maps
Atomic Energy Acts of 1946 and 1954, 159, 163
Atomic Energy Commission (AEC), 159, 160,
  162, 164. *See also* U.S. Nuclear Regulatory
  Commission
"Atoms for Peace" speech, 159
Austria, 156
automobiles: catalytic converters for, 77;
  electric, 81; engine-knocking problems in,
  70, 75, 80, 193, 210–212; size of industry
  related to, 70. *See also* air pollution;
  gasoline additives; highway construction;
  suburbs; transportation
Ayres, R., 179

ABOUT THE AUTHOR

Michael R. Greenberg is professor and director of the National Center for Neighborhood and Brownfields Redevelopment of Rutgers University and associate dean of the faculty of the Edward J. Bloustein School of Planning and Public Policy. His books include *Urbanization and Cancer Mortality* (1983), *Hazardous Waste Sites: The Credibility Gap* (1984), *Public Health and the Environment* (1987), *Environmental Risk and the Press* (1987), *Environmentally Devastated Neighborhoods in the United States* (1996), *Restoring America's Neighborhoods: What Local People Can Do* (1999), and the *Reporter's Environmental Handbook* (2003). Dr. Greenberg has been a member of National Research Council committees that focus on waste management, such as the destruction of the U.S. chemical weapons stockpile and nuclear weapons. He has received awards for research from the U.S. Environmental Protection Agency, the Society for Professional Journalists, the Public Health Association, the Association of American Geographers, and the Society for Risk Analysis. He serves as associate editor for environmental health for the *American Journal of Public Health* and as social science area editor for *Risk Analysis.*

3